THE DEMISE OF THE SOVIET UNION

The Demise of the Soviet Union

Analysing the collapse of a state

JAN HALLENBERG
Swedish National Defence College

Ashgate

Published by
Ashgate Publishing Limited
Gower House
Croft Road
Aldershot
Hants GU11 3HR
England

Ashgate Publishing Company
131 Main Street
Burlington, VT 05401-5600 USA

Ashgate website: http://www.ashgate.com

British Library Cataloguing in Publication Data
Hallenberg, Jan
   The demise of the Soviet Union : analysing the collapse of
   a state
   1.International relations - Forecasting 2.Soviet Union -
   Foreign relations - 1985-1991 3.Soviet Union - Foreign
   public opinion
   I.Title
   327.4'7'009048

Library of Congress Control Number: 2001099953

ISBN 0 7546 1953 2

Printed and bound in Great Britain by Antony Rowe Ltd,
Chippenham, Wiltshire

Contents

List of Tables

Preface

It is a cliché to state that work on a book has been a long journey. Yet in this respect I feel that no other metaphor can convey the time and the geography and the very life traversed during my work on the volume that is now finally completed. The project of which this book is a part, *The Transformation of the European Security System*, started in 1990-91. In this project I had the good fortune to co-operate with my two colleagues, Professor Kjell Goldmann and Dr. Alexa Robertson. They have been a constant support throughout the years that it took to complete this book. I particularly thank them for the incisive criticism that they gave to a full draft of the manuscript in the autumn of 1997. At the same time, I thank The Bank of Sweden's Tercentenary Foundation, which supported our research for several years. It is to be hoped that they can regard this book, even if it arrives late, as at least some solid output from our project.

Professor Nelson Polsby and the Institute of Government at the University of California — Berkeley — provided a congenial atmosphere for my wife, Dr. Ulrika Mörth, and me during the autumn of 1992. I wish to thank Professor Polsby for his kindness and encouragement both for me in my research, and for my wife's work on her Ph.D. dissertation. I also thank Professor Olof Ruin, both for good co-operation in administrative matters at the Department of Political Science, Stockholm University, during several years, and for his critical role in helping my wife and I to come to Berkeley. This fulfilled an old dream of mine as a teenager to be at Berkeley during some time in my career.

During one year of my research I was a lecturer at the Department of Social Science, then amalgamated into the Department of Thematic Studies, at Linköping University. I thank my colleagues there, in particular Dr. Ronnie Hjorth, for indulging in some of my fairly strange habits so that I could find time for my research.

During my years at the Department of Political Science in Stockholm I was also lucky to find two very able research assistants, Ms. Anna-Karin Thorstensson and Ms. Dorota Poprzecki. I thank them both for their help.

From 1996 on, I have been employed in the Department of Strategic Studies at what is now the Swedish National Defence College in Stockholm. It has been an interesting task to try to contribute to the 'academization' of what used to be a non-academic education of senior military officers in

Sweden. I thank Professor Bo Huldt and Colonel Lennart Uller (now retired) for their consistent support during several years of my work on this book. Of my other colleagues at the Department of Strategic Studies, I thank Dr. Gunnar Åselius for his valuable criticism of one draft of my work. I also wish to thank my two Ph.D. students and assistants, Lars Maddox and Arita Eriksson, for their help in the completion of this book. The librarians at the National Defence College Library have also been very helpful during the last few years of my work on this book. I am very grateful to them for that.

Finally, I thank my wife Ulrika for her consistent support and love throughout these many years of toiling on this never-ending project. It is indeed a privilege to have a relationship that is built on love between woman and man, as well as on an academic-intellectual respect and mutual understanding.

Stockholm
August 2001
Jan Hallenberg

Acknowledgements

I wish to thank the following publishers who have generously given permission to use extended quotations from copyrighted works: From 'Les Atouts de Gorbatchev: Une Évaluation', *Après Gorbatchev*, Présenté par Jean-Marie Benoist et Patrick Wajsman, written by André Besançon. ©1990 by Editions de La Table Ronde Reprinted by permission of the publishers, Editions de La Table Ronde. Excerpt, pp. 95-96 from Pierre Hassner, 'Gorbachev and the West', *The Washington Quarterly*, 11: 4 (Autumn 1988), pp. 95-103. ©1988 by the Center for Strategic and International Studies (CSIS) and the Massachusetts Institute of Technology. Reprinted by permission of the publishers, MIT Press Journals. From 'Causes of the Collapse of the USSR', *Post-Soviet Affairs,* Vol. 8, 1992, by Alexander Dallin. Reprinted with permission from *Post-Soviet Affairs*, Vol. 8, No. 4, pp. 279-302. ©V. H. Winston & Son, Inc., 360 South Ocean Boulevard, Palm Beach, FL 33480. All rights reserved. From *The Baltic States and the End of the Soviet Empire*, by Kristian Gerner and Stefan Hedlund. ©1993 by Copyright Routledge Ltd. Reprinted by permission of the publishers, Routledge Ltd.

Chapter 1
Introduction

1.1 Introduction

On 11 March 1985, Mikhail Gorbachev was elected General Secretary of the Communist Party of the Soviet Union. On 25 December 1991, Mr Gorbachev resigned as President, and the country ceased to exist. There have been innumerable books and articles written about what happened during these six and a half years, both during the time it occurred and afterwards. Many, if not most, of these writings analyse the policy processes inside the Soviet Union. Others emphasize the possible consequences for other countries of these events. Here, the focus is different.[1] My analysis starts by acknowledging that we know after the fact that the radical changes of Soviet society undertaken by Gorbachev ultimately ended in the dissolution of the very state that the Soviet leader tried to reform. My main research question is, how were the changes in the Soviet Union perceived while they occurred? Were they regarded in the same way everywhere? Were there differences among countries[2] or among professions?

Those who had to undertake the analysis of Gorbachev and the possible consequences of his policies had three judgements to make:
1) Were the changes under way limited or fundamental? (diagnosis)
2) Why did the changes occur? (explanation)
3) How would the process of change ultimately end? (prognosis).

This book concerns, first, who made what assessment and when in these three respects, and, second, how similarities and differences in these

---

[1] Two books with fairly similar themes to this one are G. Rozman (1992): *Japan's Response to the Gorbachev Era, 1985-1991. A Rising Superpower Views a Declining One* (Princeton, NJ: Princeton University Press), and *Rethinking the Soviet Collapse: Sovietology, the Death of Communism and the New Russia* (1992), ed. M. Cox (London/New York: Pinter). Rozman focuses his analysis more on the internal politics of Japan than I do regarding my four countries, however, and he avoids the issues of "prediction" and "explanation", which are so important to this book. In the Cox volume, many issues are similar to the ones covered here. The volume is, however, restricted only to Sovietology, a Sovietology that is, in contrast to here, in practice defined as a nearly exclusively Anglo-Saxon field of study.

[2] As presented in chapter 1.5, the four countries analysed in this book are France, Great Britain, Sweden and the United States. See, further, chapter 2.2.

judgements can be explained. There is a need for more precision on judgements two and three. What are the reasons behind the process of change that Mr. Gorbachev initiated upon taking office in March 1985, or soon thereafter? The prognosis has two dimensions. The first is, what will be the fate of Mr. Gorbachev himself and of his policies? The second is, what will happen to the Soviet system itself? It is the latter prognosis that is both the crucial one and the most difficult one. We will see in this book that there were several Sovietologists, in particular, who issued warnings about Mr. Gorbachev's personal future, by implication or explicitly, and they were at the same time uncertain about the likely fate of his policies. There were, however, clearly fewer who were able or willing to venture forecasts about the likely future of the entire system.

The book explores the respective contributions of three broad categories of explanations for any differences that may have existed in the three respects just mentioned. The *first explanatory category* is inspired by the literature on the role of perceptions in international politics. In this respect, my approach focuses, first, on the tendency that commonly goes by the name of "the fundamental error of attribution".[3] This has to do with how an observer perceives and explains events within a country that is classified as hostile, or at least potentially threatening, as compared to how the same observer tends to explain events in her own country.

A related tendency identified in this literature is that of *cognitive consistency*. In this view, observers who follow events and processes in another country tend to develop strong beliefs in a particular model of that country, a model that then tends to remain stable despite the fact that there may exist indications that the model is no longer applicable.[4] In particular, this second category of perceptions will be applied to the study of the Sovietologists — the academic experts on the Soviet Union. To what extent, I ask myself, did these scholars subscribe to particular models

---

[3] Note that the use of the term "fundamental *error* of attribution" indicates that there is a reference point, a "truth" against which the error can be measured. It is not easy to find such points in this case. In section 1.6.2 I will, however, spell out what I consider to be the benchmarks against which I can assess whether or not the "fundamental error of attribution" was at work in the analysis of the Soviet Union.

[4] On the role of perceptions in international politics more generally, see R. Jervis (1976): *Perception and Misperception in International Politics* (Princeton, NJ: Princeton University Press), and Y. Y. I. Vertzberger (1990): *The World in Their Minds: Information Processing, Cognition, and Perception in Foreign Policy Decisionmaking* (Stanford, CA: Stanford University Press). Two studies within the same tradition that focus more specifically on the fundamental error of attribution are D. Heradstveit (1979): *The Arab-Israeli Conflict: Psychological Obstacles to Peace* (Oslo: Universitetsforlaget) and E. Beukel (1989): *American Perceptions of the Soviet Union as a Nuclear Adversary* (London and New York: Pinter).

of the Soviet system that they tended to cling to in the face of ever more discrepant information? Did the use of academic models of analysis prevent them from recognizing the extent of the changes in the Soviet Union and from drawing the consequences of this in terms of the future development of the system? In this sense, this book also aims to contribute to the assessment of Sovietology as an academic field of study that was thoroughly tested by the collapse of the Soviet system.[5] This category of explanations is further explored in sections 1.2 and 1.6.

The *second explanatory category* pertains to national attributes. To the extent that I detect differences among nations in their analysis of the three judgements mentioned above, can those differences be explained by different outlooks on the world, by what has, in other studies, been called *foreign policy orientation*?[6] This explanatory category is rooted in different branches of research on international politics. It receives a more in-depth presentation in section 1.4.

The *third explanatory category* can be named "differences related to professions". This book analyses politicians, editorialists and those academic experts on the Soviet Union that were called Sovietologists. It is reasonable to believe that there were differences in the way representatives of these three categories of professionals approached, or at least publicly reported on, their analyses of the Soviet Union. My assumption is that politicians tend to avoid hard and fast, clear-cut judgements. They tend to say what is regarded as absolutely necessary in a given situation, make few attempts to analyse the basic reasons behind the actions of a perceived adversary, and avoid making prognoses about the future. I assume the role of the editorialists in elite papers in democracies to be more open as to their inclination to speculate about both the causes of change and the likely future of those changes. The academics are, by definition, possessors of intimate knowledge of their objects of study. This should make it possible for them to undertake prognoses that

---

[5] Other assessments of a similar kind include the *National Interest*, Special Issue: "The Strange Death of Soviet Communism: An Autopsy", No. 31 (Spring 1993), pp. 3-144; Cox, ed. (1998): *Rethinking the Soviet Collapse,* and to some extent R. Strayer (1998): *Why Did the Soviet Union Collapse? Understanding Historical Change* (Armonk, NY/London: M. E. Sharpe). The latter volume is, however, more geared towards identifying the existing explanations in the historical and social scientific literature, and less focused on the role of individual researchers at the time of the Soviet changes.

[6] See A. Robertson: *National Prisms and Perceptions of Dissent* (1992), Ph.D. thesis (Stockholm: Department of Political Science, Stockholm University), pp. 22-23, 265-278 and

are based on well-founded reasoning, should they regard this as a legitimate exercise.

My initial hunch was that it was in this last category that I would find both those who first detected that what was going on was a process of fundamental change, and those who were able to foretell where the process of change was going to end up. The special character of Sovietology as an academic field of study is further explored in section 2.3.

If the theoretical context of this work is thus the role of perceptions in international politics, the broad empirical field that my book focuses upon is the vast process of change in the security structure of Europe, occurring from 1990 onward, caused to a large extent by the events starting with the accession to power of Mr. Gorbachev. My approach is located in that field of foreign policy research that concentrates upon the very first steps by which actors start to respond to events in another state. What primarily concerns me is, in other words, *the analysis of foreign policy*. In the study of international relations within my field of political science, the states are crucial to analysis, even if there are different views as to whether they are exclusively to be analysed or not. Within those states, several actors participate in the debate on how the events in the external environment should be studied. This book focuses its empirical analysis on three of these actors. In my conception, in other words, the state is not the monolith so often assumed by previous students of international politics.

It should be underlined at the outset that it is not the purpose of this book to try to find the "correct" answers to the overall questions surrounding the Gorbachev years, if such answers can ever be found. Instead, my main purpose is to compare how analysts in different countries attempted to explain these riddles and to investigate whether they did indeed try to foresee what was going to happen in the Soviet Union, and, if so, whether they were successful in that effort.[7]

To start with the question of actors, I have selected three types to characterize each studied country's public analysis of Moscow's foreign policy. The *first* type is *the politicians*, the officeholders that have constitutional responsibility for the conduct of their nation's foreign

---

K. Riegert: *'Nationalising' Foreign Conflict: Foreign Policy Orientation as a Factor in News Reporting* (1998), Ph.D. thesis (Stockholm: Department of Political Science, Stockholm). Robertson calls the concept "external orientation" but the basic idea is the same.

[7] There are only two specific cases in which I will need to characterize two assessments of Soviet policies as "correct". This is when I assess the prognoses made by Sovietologists, in particular, about how the Gorbachev reforms, and the Soviet Union itself, would come out of the process starting in 1985. See, further, section 1.3.2.

policy. In operational terms, this means that I have studied the speeches given by the President and/or Prime Minister and the Foreign Minister in each country selected. A few additional officials are included to the extent that their remarks were presented in ways that made it obvious that they represented their governments in this respect.[8]

Politicians, it is often said, are bland and imprecise in their statements in general and on international politics in particular. Is this general attitude also reflected in this material? Are there any differences between the way the politicians express themselves that can be attributed to their foreign policy orientations? This was, after all, a very special case of change in the international system that forced the politicians to reflect and to react. My analysis shows that, as a general proposition, the view that politicians — speaking on foreign policy — are bland proves correct. There are, however, important exceptions. In particular, there were examples in the material from the U.S. where the depth of analysis in the official statements was anything but shallow and bland. Also in the U.S. material was the only case (in my material) where a shift in power resulted in the changing of the official perception of the events in Moscow, from a situation where the Soviet reform process was characterized in very positive terms, to a new situation where there was, for a time, considerably more official scepticism regarding the depth and permanence of the changes. This occurred at a stage in the Soviet reform process where I regard the changes that had by then been undertaken as substantial, both domestically and in foreign policy.

The *second* type is the *editorialists in* two *elite newspapers* for each country selected. My material indicates that there were some differences in the analysis of the Gorbachev years, influenced by different foreign policy orientations. More important, however, there are also results that showed the influence of another factor, a factor that I had not initially expected to be so salient: the party-political ideology represented by the newspapers.

The *third* type is the *Sovietologists*, where I have selected four — in the case of the U.S. six[9] — academic experts on the Soviet Union from each of four countries and analysed their writings from the perspective of their analysis of Soviet foreign policy. Since the Sovietologists were academics in the social and human sciences, I made a more detailed analysis of what they wrote on these matters — with respect to both whether they attempted to predict what was going to happen in Moscow

---

[8] For operationalizations on this point see section 1.6.
[9] For a presentation of the reasons for the choice of Sovietologists see section 1.6.1.

and how they attacked the explanatory problem with which this book is concerned[10] — than I did for the other two categories analysed. The more precise aspects of this analysis are explained later in this chapter.

The study of the Sovietologists, not surprisingly, shows a very considerable amount of disagreement on fundamental points. Overall, I found no Sovietologist in my admittedly limited sample who gave any correct point predictions about the coming fall of the Soviet Union. In other words, no one foretold the collapse of the Soviet Union in precise terms, identifying both the fact and the rough time frame during which it was presumed this would happen. There were, however, several cases in which Sovietologists' analysis contained what in this book is called a "correct forecast", i.e., a less precise way of telling what is likely to happen in the future.

It should be remembered that there is considerable controversy among scholars in the social and human sciences, including among Sovietologists, as to whether it is indeed an appropriate task for researchers to attempt to issue predictions. The reactions of different scholars who have looked at this manuscript have been extremely varied on this point: to what extent is it an appropriate undertaking to assess the "failure" of Sovietologists to forecast the collapse of the very system that they devoted their academic lives to study?[11] My position is that the assessment can and should be made, but in so doing the assessor must always keep in mind that some of the scholars who are evaluated do not accept the very premise of the evaluation. The question of whether or not scholars erred in not being able to foretell the collapse of the Soviet Union seems destined to remain a controversial one among academics.

Another related question is whether the case of the analysis of the Soviet Union is so special in terms of the requirements for at least striving for value-free, dispassionate analysis that its academic status is diminished because the scholars are too influenced by their personal biases. This is stating the point very bluntly, and it can by no means be finally resolved here. It is necessary, however, in my view, to highlight **the importance** of assessing

[10] As presented in more detail later, the explanatory problem is: Why did Mr Gorbachev start the reform process in Moscow? Cf. section 1.3.2.
[11] The volume edited by Michael Cox, *Rethinking the Soviet Collapse* (1998), is a very clear example of this tendency to view the record of Sovietology in assessing the collapse of the Soviet Union in very different terms. The assessments made by ex-Sovietologists in this volume range from Urban and Fish: "Does Post-Sovietology have a Future?", who state: "For political scientists working in Sovietology, the collapse of the USSR represented a colossal failure", p. 165, to the assessment of Robert V. Daniels in "American Soviet Studies: a Study in Success?" that "Taken as a whole, the work of Western Slavists and Sovietologists in their various disciplines was remarkably accurate and insightful in defining the elements of the crisis that overtook the Soviet Union", pp. 124-125.

not only the contents of the scholars' analyses of Soviet affairs, but also of the fundamental preconceptions that each individual scholar has brought to this analysis. The study of the Soviet Union continues to be the subject of controversy; witness for instance the debate that raged inside and outside France after the publication of *Le livre noir du Communisme* in 1996. A book with a focus such as this one has cannot avoid at least touching upon these matters.

My main interest in this book is in the first, analytic, stage of foreign-policy making. This means that I concentrated on how the elites interpreted events of relevance for the foreign and security policies of their countries. The politicians who were in charge of foreign-policy making are the official representatives of their countries. As such, they set the tone for the debate within their nations on questions as important as the ones under study here. A second voice of interest in the debate on foreign policy in democratic nations, the category of states analysed here, is that of the elite newspapers. In particular, the editorial pages of these newspapers are a crucial gauge of the more sophisticated analysis on foreign policy carried out within each nation. The third type of actor of interest for me is the category of academics that specialized on the workings of the Soviet system — the Sovietologists. Central to their profession was the claim that their object of study was fundamentally different from virtually all other states on earth. It is thus of value in itself to assess their analyses and, more demandingly, their ability to anticipate what was going to happen to Gorbachev's experiment, chiefly, but not exclusively, as it pertained to foreign policy.

The analysis in this book raises another question which is implicit in the logic of this study. This is the question of the limitations on the ability to plan for the future. Foreign and security policy, as well as defence planning, in the countries that I investigate here are built on the assumption that it is possible to foretell what will happen in the future, at least to the extent that one can create "scenarios" sufficiently precise to serve as the foundation for planning future policies. The collapse of the Soviet Union was, to put it mildly, a change that had important consequences for the future of policies within the realms mentioned in all four countries. This process, consequently, raises the question: To what extent is it possible to make plans for security and defence policies based on "plausible" scenarios when even conditions universally assumed to be unalterable prove otherwise?

1.2 The Analysis of the Role of Perceptions in International Relations

In 1976, Robert Jervis published *Perception and Misperception in International Politics*. This marked the real beginning of a whole new subfield within the study of international relations. In a broad sense, the whole approach of this book is inspired by the thoughts in this formulation from Jervis:

> We can...compare different actors' perceptions of the same object, situation, or other actor. If we can find appropriate comparisons, we can try to locate systematic differences in perceptions traceable to differences in ways of processing incoming information, differences in pre-existing images of others or general views of the world, or differences in specific experiences (Jervis, 1976, p. 7).

The field of perceptions in international politics is a very large one some 25 years after Robert Jervis wrote these lines. There have been several studies, not least of the relationship between the Soviet Union and the United States, in this field.[12] As evidenced by the second comprehensive appraisal of the field, Yaacov Y. I. Vertzberger's *The World in Their Minds* (Vertzberger, 1990), much of the analysis of the role of perceptions still has a somewhat tentative quality. In other words, the basic idea that perceptions do matter is intuitively very acceptable. Going beyond that, however, and specifying how, and in what way, these processes of perception do matter has proved more difficult. It is significant in this respect that Vertzberger's book has basically the same character as the one Jervis published 14 years earlier: very suggestive, rich in empirical examples, and ultimately unsatisfying in providing solid evidence as to how, more precisely, the processes of perception matter for international politics.

The conclusion that I draw from this state of the field of international perceptions is that empirical studies are necessary to clarify how, and under what circumstances, information processing matters in international politics. This work aims to make a modest contribution to the field by analysing, first, whether or not *attribution theory* can help us explain differences in assessments of the Soviet Union. Attribution theory concerns "the individual's attempts to comprehend the causes of behaviour

---

[12] See, for example, D. Welch Larson (1985): *Origins of Containment: A Psychological Explanation* (Princeton, NJ: Princeton University Press); E. Beukel (1989): *American Perceptions of the Soviet Union* (London/New York: Pinter); K. L. Shimko (1991): *Images and Arms Control: Perceptions of the Soviet Union in the Reagan Administration* (Ann Arbor, MI: University of Michigan Press).

and ha[s] proceeded from the assumption that spontaneous thought follows a systematic course that is roughly congruent with scientific inquiry" (Jönsson, 1990, p. 23). Put another way, "[a]ttribution theory specifies the conditions under which behaviour is seen as caused by the person performing the action, or by environmental influences and constraints" (Heradstveit,1979, p. 23).

Second, this book also highlights whether a process of perception known as the striving for *cognitive consistency* may have contributed to the difficulties that many analysts had in comprehending the scale of the changes in the Soviet Union and in assessing the far-reaching nature of the political processes that these changes set in motion. There are two respects in which I believe that cognitive consistency may have influenced perceptions of the Soviet Union. The first is expressed in the following way by Robert Jervis: "...when a statesman has developed a certain image of another country he will maintain that view in the face of large amounts of discrepant information" (Jervis, 1976, p. 146). The second related aspect has to do with the fact that beliefs about the character of the Soviet Union were central to all three categories of analysts studied in this book. This leads to the following tendency: "...the centrality of a single belief, as measured by the dependence of other beliefs on it, influences the degree of resistance to change in the sense that change in the belief necessarily requires changes in some or all other beliefs belonging to that belief subset....The greater the centrality, the greater the rigidity" (Vertzberger, 1990, p. 118. Cf. Rutland, 1993, p. 33).

I assume that this tendency towards cognitive closure may have been strongest for the individuals analysed in this book who were most directly dependent on their views of the Soviet system: the Sovietologists (Rutland, 1993, p. 33). To what extent did the analytic models that form the basis for their analyses of the Soviet Union serve as straitjackets that prevented the scholar in question from seeing the extent of the changes in Moscow and from realizing the consequences that these changes might lead to?

Central to the first line of study is "the fundamental error of attribution". This hinges on the distinction, just introduced, between the two ways of explaining the reasons why an actor behaves as she does. The first alternative is that the action is explained by *dispositional attributions*: the actor acts the way she does because of her inherent character. The circumstances do not matter, it is the inherent goodness or evil of the actor in question that determines behaviour. The second alternative is *situational attributions*. This means that the outside pressures under which he/she has to act explain the actions of the actor under study. In other words, in this conception the actor is unable to act in any other way because outside pressures are overwhelming. Daniel Heradstveit defines the fundamental error of attribution: "in making our inferences about behaviour there is a *tendency* to over-emphasise situational variables (the circumstances in which it occurs) when explaining our own behaviour, while when observing the behaviour of others, there is a tendency to over-emphasise dispositional (internal characteristics of the actor) variables" (Heradstveit, 1979, p. 24. Emphasis supplied, note omitted). He further specifies a central aspect of this tendency:

> The tendency to infer dispositional causes is *enhanced when the observer dislikes the actor who performs the blameworthy act...* The degree of involvement in the observed action also influences the attribution process. The higher the degree of involvement the greater the chance of attributional bias (Ibid., p. 25. Emphasis supplied, note omitted).

The fundamental error of attribution has been studied in international relations. Daniel Heradstveit found, in his book on the Arab-Israeli conflict, that this error contributed to an explanation of why members of the respective parties analysed why the other party acted the way it did. There was thus a strong tendency for Arabs to analyse the actions of the P.L.O. or of Arab governments, when they could be perceived as hostile, as caused by the situation. When the same individuals analysed the Israelis, the tendency was very strong to attribute hostile actions to dispositional factors (Ibid.). The opposite was true in the case of an Israeli: when analysing the Israeli side, actions that could be perceived as hostile were explained by situational factors, whereas similar actions by Arab actors were explained largely by dispositional attributes.

In particular, Heradstveit found that:

> If I have a devil-image of the opponent and the opponent behaves in an *indisputably* friendly way, I can still maintain my beliefs about the opponent by explaining his friendly behaviour as caused by environmental influences and constraints. His disposition to act in an unfriendly way remains the same — certain characteristics of the situation forced him to *temporarily* behave in a friendly way (Ibid., p. 125).

Erik Beukel has investigated this aspect in his book on U.S. perceptions of the Soviet Union as a nuclear adversary. To quote Beukel, when the fundamental error of attribution has manifested itself there has been "a tendency for attributers to underestimate the impact of situational factors and overestimate the role of dispositional factors" (Beukel, 1989, p. 21).

Correspondingly, when the attributers have explained the actions of their own side, they have tended to emphasize situational factors when explaining actions that could be perceived as hostile by outside observers. Beukel, in his study of the Cold War period, notes that "salient characteristics of the domestic political process in the United States induce US governments to represent the Soviet Union as a nuclear adversary in dispositional terms, which means that the fundamental error of attribution can be confirmed as to the process of perception in this case" (Ibid., p. 266).

In this volume, I study whether or not the processes inherent in the fundamental error of attribution are manifest in any of the analyses of the Soviet Union. This aspect is particularly applicable in the present context in connection with the assessment of whether or not Mr. Gorbachev had really made any substantial changes in Soviet policy generally, and in particular in foreign policy. My assumption is that the fundamental error of attribution may manifest itself in the work of analysts who tended to underestimate the extent to which the Soviet leader really did change Soviet policies during the second half of the 1980s. In other words, I assume that the fundamental error of attribution may be one possible explanation for a tendency to delay the recognition that Soviet policies had indeed changed. In section 1.6.2, I present the benchmarks against which this tendency will be measured here.

It should be made clear that the fundamental error of attribution is not a tendency that can be measured in terms of black and white. Instead, the nuances between what might be a manifestation of this error and what is clearly not such a manifestation are fluid and unclear. The present attempt tries to make the underlying premises explicit and thus open to assessment by the interested reader. As will be made clear later on, the events in Moscow from 1985 through the end of 1991 provide us with a few clear benchmarks against which one may assess whether or not an analyst can be said to have manifested the fundamental error of attribution. The analyst looking for manifestations of the fundamental error of attribution can do no more than present the logic of his reasoning and the arguments for his choices and then let the reader decide whether or not this reasoning is acceptable.

I also study whether or not the analysts may have suffered from cognitive closure. In this case, this may have manifested itself in a tendency to cling to an image of the Soviet Union that was firmly formed in the mind of the analyst and that was highly resistant to change, despite the existence of discrepant information. It is possible to surmise that this tendency may have been most likely to manifest itself in the case of the Sovietologists, whose very livelihood may be said to have rested on the continued existence of the Soviet Union.[13]

A more systematic assessment of the extent to which any of these academics may have manifested cognitive closure in their analyses of Moscow during the Gorbachev years is aided by reference points against which the assessments of the analysts may be judged. This book employs the tools of political science by classifying the fundamental intellectual premises of the Sovietologists, and to some limited extent analysts in other categories as well, in terms of the most prevalent and basic models that existed in Sovietology during the period up to 1991. The results of this attempt to classify the main models used by Sovietologists during the Cold War is in table 1.1.

While no simplified table can do full justice to the depth and width of a wide-ranging field of study, this classification is intended to provide an overview of the most important models used by Sovietologists. I have elected here to focus on more general models of Soviet behaviour rather than on specific models of Soviet foreign policy, as it was these underlying world-views that, in my view, shaped the study of the Soviet political system, rather than any more elaborate models of Moscow's international policies.[14]

Two fundamental problems arise when a scholar assesses the analysis of the Soviet Union. First the logic of my presentation may make it seem that there is a single identifiable reason for the fundamental change in, and the subsequent collapse of, the Soviet State. This is of course not so; the process of change can be seen from several angles. The second problem is that it may seem in hindsight that the collapse of the Soviet State was inevitable and that this could have been foreseen several years beforehand. It must be remembered that this is a given as we contemplate these matters ten years after the fall of the Soviet Union.

For those who studied what they perceived to be a very mighty state, the thought of any possible collapse cannot have been the very first idea that entered their minds.

This writer has the benefit of knowing how it all ended. This was not the case for the people scrutinized here. I see no way of totally avoiding this

---

[13] Peter Rutland makes a related point when he states that "'disciplinary group think'…stifled creative thinking and controversial ideas — the most controversial, of course, being that the USSR may one day disappear entirely!" Rutland (1998): "Who Got It Right and Who Got It Wrong? And Why?", p. 41.

[14] An additional model that might have been included, the Bureaucratic model, has been excluded here since the implications of this model are unclear for the most fundamental dimension of my analysis: implications for change.

Table 1.1   Basic Academic Models of Soviet Politics

Name	Characteristics	Implications for Change
Totalitarianism	— Highly centralized structure to change — Total party control over civil society — Soviet Union (SU) a special case	Extremely hard to impossible
Institutional Pluralism	— More decentralized structure — Influence of competing interest groups — SU comparable to other states	Possible to change, perhaps even fundamentally
Elite models	— Continuous re-generation of political elites — SU special case	Stagnation, hard to change
Modernization theory	— Socio-economic modernization creating new, "Westernized" elites — SU comparable to other states	Significant chances for change as economy, society and bureaucracy modernize

Source: Derived from B. Nygren (1986): "Approaches to Soviet Foreign Policy in Sovietology", Group for Research on Peace and Security Policy, Report No. 3, Department of Political Science, University of Stockholm, pp. 7-15; T. McNeill (1998): "Soviet Studies and the Collapse of the USSR: in Defence of Realism", in *Rethinking the Soviet Collapse*, M. Cox, (ed.), pp. 51-72; V. Shlapentokh: "Soviet Society and American Sovietologists: a Study in Failure?" in ibid., pp. 95-114.

problem, other than to make the reader aware of the fact that this author is also cognisant of it. I also believe that, even granted these two aspects, it is still worth posing the questions concerning the analysis of the fate of the Soviet Union, both for the inherent interest in the case at hand, and for what this may teach us about the more general problem of understanding developments abroad.

1.3 Explanation and Prediction in International Relations

1.3.1 Introduction

One of the purposes of this book is to assess two of the great issues of the social sciences and the humanities. The first is, how can one explain complex political processes? The second is, to what extent is it possible, even meaningful, to attempt to predict what is going to happen to the issues which constitute the researcher's area of expertise? In this case, the area of expertise covers the basic development of the country in which these scholars specialized: the Soviet Union. The cases on which these two questions will be assessed are, of course, first the reform process in, and then the collapse of, the Soviet Union. The inclusion of these two fundamental aspects of social science and the humanities in this book makes it necessary both to discuss them more generally and to spell out my own position in these two regards.

Since the category of scholars that I evaluate here belonged to a field of scholarship that was (and remains) multidisciplinary, there is always the risk that an assessor, like me, may use the tools and criteria of one discipline to judge scholars who belong to another discipline and who thus wish to be judged by the tools and criteria of their own discipline. In the case of this book, the three disciplines where competing perspectives of this type are most apparent are political science, my own discipline; economics and history.[15] It is interesting to note that the question of competing disciplinary perspectives on the same types of issue has, in the aftermath of the end of the Cold War and the collapse of the Soviet Union, led to a renewed interest in precisely the question that I'm addressing here.[16] I can do no more than signal my awareness of this problem. It is also explicitly

---

[15] The interested reader may note that I leave out one academic discipline that could have been interesting to analyse: sociology. This is not through any design on my part, but is rather a result of the process by which I selected the Sovietologists for analysis. See chapter 1.6.1. For an assessment of some of the issues covered in this book from a sociological perspective see "Symposium on Predictions in the Social Sciences", *American Journal of Sociology*, Vol. 100 (May 1995), pp. 1520-1626. The explanandum for the macro-sociologists in this symposium is "revolution" – thus permitting comparisons in the vein of, for example, Skocpol's well-known book on revolution from 1979 – not "collapse". In general, however, I regard the logic of our explanatory problems as sufficiently similar to permit overarching comparisons.

[16] A sample of the recent literature includes the following: J. L. Gaddis (1992/93): "International Relations Theory and the End of the Cold War", *International Security*, Vol. 17, No. 3, pp. 5-58; C. W. Kegley, Jr (1994): "How Did the Cold War Die: Principles for an Autopsy", *Mershon International Studies Review*, Vol. 38, Supplement 1, pp.11-41; J. N.

acknowledged that the perspective applied here to both explanation and prediction of human events and political processes is that of the political scientist.

In *The Fontana Dictionary of Modern Thought* seven separate types of explanation are enumerated.[17] I will limit myself to a short digression on what I see as the three most fundamental ways of explaining available in the two fields of science covered in this book.[18] The first is the causal explanation: what are the previous factors or events that caused the event to be explained, the explanandum? The second is the functional explanation: "In general, functional explanations account for causes in terms of their effects. That is, 'the character of what is explained is determined by its effect on what explains it.'"[19] The third is the purposive explanation: a phenomenon is explained by its intended effects, by the purposes that actors had when they undertook their previous actions.

In these terms, what is meant by "explaining" something should be seen in terms of the first type of explanation. In other words, I agree with the following statement: "At its core, real explanation is always based on causal inferences" (King, Keohane and Verba, 1994, p. 75, note 1). I am deeply aware of the fact that there is a long and very fundamental debate in the social sciences and the humanities about what constitutes a causal explanation and whether it is ever possible to reach such a level of explanation in social affairs. It is not my purpose to contribute to this debate in any way, simply to clarify my fundamental position. Nor is it my purpose to say that causal inferences are the only valid inferences in the social or the human sciences, but merely that for a study such as this it is the causal explanation that is the most immediately relevant.

Rosenau (1995): "Signals, Signposts and Symptoms: Interpreting Change and Anomalies in World Politics", *European Journal of International Relations* Vol. 1, pp.113-122; "Symposium on Predictions in the Social Sciences", *American Journal of Sociology*, Vol. 100 (May 1995), pp. 1520-1626; I. S. Lustick (1996): "History, Historiography, and Political Science: Multiple Historical Records and the Problem of Selection Bias", *American Political Science Review* Vol. 90, pp. 605-618; the 7 articles in the Symposium on History and Theory in *International Security,* Vol. 22 (Summer 1997), pp. 5-85 and M. Cox (ed.): *Rethinking the Soviet Collapse.*

[17] *The Fontana Dictionary of Modern Thought* (1977), eds. A. Bullock and O. Stallybrass (London: Fontana/Collins), pp. 222-223.

[18] This section is inspired by N. Gilje and H. Grimen (1992): *Samhällsvetenskapernas förutsättningar (The Basic Assumptions of the Social Sciences)* (Gothenburg: Daidalos), pp. 131-158.

[19] R. Keohane (1984): *After Hegemony: Cooperation and Discord in the World Economy* (Princeton, NJ: Princeton University Press), p. 80. Keohane quotes G. A. Cohen (1978): *Karl Marx's Theory of History: A Defense* (Princeton, NJ: Princeton University Press), at p. 3.

1.3.2 Predictions in the Social Sciences and the Humanities

Given an epistemological view of the social sciences and the humanities which regards it as appropriate to try to find causal explanations for events and processes, it is not a large step to the next fundamental element of this section of my analysis: prediction. The idea that one aspect of the scientific study of international relations should involve the ability to predict future developments in international politics originates in some strands of theorizing that regard it is as desirable to be able to look into the future of the processes studied. The quest for a "theory of international relations" in general is the framework in which this aspect of the present work should be seen. Hans J. Morgenthau, with his seminal book *Politics Among Nations*, first published in 1948, established what he called "the science of international politics".[20] Even if Morgenthau himself was careful about not promising too much in terms of being able to forecast the future, there has been a current in international relations theory claiming that it was one purpose of research to try to forecast the future.[21] As discussed by the historian John Lewis Gaddis (1992/93) in an influential article titled "Theory and the End of the Cold War", these claims have been made by scholars working in peace research and on operational code, as well as by deterrence theorists. Nearly 10 years after the fall of the Soviet Union, Davis B. Bobrow still characterized the aspirations of one of the disciplines under evaluation here — international relations — in the following way:

> Given its genesis, the agenda of international relations scholarship has always, if sometimes implicitly, included the future. Analyses of the past and the present have been seen as ways to contribute to 'well-founded' expectations about what will happen, the crucial dynamics at work, and the consequences of alternative lines of policy and conduct. That is neither surprising nor likely to stop (Bobrow, 1999, p. 5).

There is thus ample support for my belief that prediction and forecasting have been an important strand, at the very least, in the study of

---

[20] In my version of Morgenthau's classic work: *Politics Among Nations: The Struggle for Power and Peace*, 5th ed. (1973) (New York: Knopf), chapter 2 is simply titled "The Science of International Politics". The concepts of "prediction" or "forecast" do not appear in the index, however.

[21] One guide to the diverse applications of forecasting and predictions in international relations is *Forecasting in International Relations: Theory, Methods, Problems, Prospects* (1978), eds. N. Choucri and T. W. Robinson (San Francisco, CA: W. H. Freeman).

international relations. This book will, consequently, evaluate the extent to which the Sovietologists analysed in this study were able to foretell what was going to happen to Mr. Gorbachev's great experiment.[22]

There are two additional considerations to be made when one undertakes a thorough study of the use of forecasts and predictions in the social and human sciences. The first is the extent to which other sciences aspire to make precise predictions. The reader may feel that my way of characterizing the striving for predictions in the disciplines covered here exaggerates the extent to which scholars believe in the feasibility of trying to look into the future. The second consideration is the character of the main case on which I test the use of predictions in the social and human sciences: the collapse of the Soviet Union. What kind of case of predictions is this?

It could legitimately be said that few scholars in the social or human sciences aspire to make precise, point predictions about what will occur in the future. That is not to say that such aspirations do not exist. For instance, in an overview of the use of predictions in macro-sociology, Alejandro Portes wrote: "[t]heoretical advancement in political sociology, the sociology of immigration, and the study of crime and delinquency make it possible to advance fairly accurate predictions about such events as community voting outcomes, the entrepreneurial success of particular immigrant groups, and the presence and growth of criminal gangs" (Portes, 1995, p. 1625). The extent to which scholars in the natural sciences strive for precise predictions is difficult for a social scientist to estimate.[23] As I understand it, there are,cases both of disciplines where foretelling the effects of various acts are possible, such as in medicine, and others where such precision is more

---

[22] There has been some controversy in the literature after 1991 on whether or not the aspiration to predict the collapse of the Soviet State is the most crucial assessment of the scholarship. For support of this author's position that this is indeed one crucial question, see P. P. Everts (1992): "The Events in Eastern Europe and the Crisis in the Discipline of International Relations", K. Goldmann: "Bargaining, Power, Domestic Politics and Security Dilemmas" and P. Allan: "The End of the Cold War: The End of International Relations Theory", all in *The End of the Cold War: Evaluating Theories of International Relations,* eds. P. Allan and K. Goldmann (Dordrecht/Boston/London: Martinus Nijhoff Publishers); M. Cox (1998): "Whatever Happened to the USSR: Critical Reflections on Soviet Studies", in *Rethinking the Soviet Collapse,* ed. Cox, pp. 13-31. Cf. also R. Jervis (1991/92): "The Future of World Politics: Will It Resemble the Past?" *International Security,* vol. 16, pp. 39-46.

[23] For a discussion of the use of predictions in several natural and social sciences see also M. Hechter (1995): "Introduction: Reflections on Historical Prophecy in the Social Sciences" in "Symposium on Predictions in the Social Sciences", *American Journal of Sociology,* Vol. 100 (May 1995), pp. 1520-1527, especially at pp. 1521-1522. Hechter's general view is the same as mine: a sufficient number of scholars in the social sciences have attempted to use predictions in their scholarship for it to be a legitimate exercise to evaluate the success of their efforts.

difficult. Even in meteorology — a discipline in which striving for precision ought to be vital — there appears to be an acceptance that weather prognoses still are more forecasts in the sense presented here rather than point predictions despite technological developments in recent decades that have significantly increased the amount of data and the ability to analyse it.

The fact that there is this wide range of differences within disciplines outside the realm of the social and human sciences on the use of predictions does not exclude a thorough analysis of the problems and possibilities of such efforts in the latter sciences. While many scholars within these disciplines may deny that they strive to achieve any predictive ability, two conditions work to make the ability to forecast an important consideration for these disciplines. The first, as previously mentioned, is the fact that there are indeed scholars who do claim that it is a legitimate enterprise for academics to strive for the ability to predict. The second is that there is an expectation — on the part of both the politicians and the interested general public — that scholars with specialities that are perceived to be policy-relevant ought to have the ability to look into the crystal ball. One specific case where this tendency matters greatly relates to national security and defence policy planning — planning that is often based on a fairly crude way of looking into the future typically called making "scenarios". The relationship between academic scholarship and "scenario making" is thus one more argument for delving into the problems and possibilities of academic forecasting, in particular as it concerns topics of relevance for security policy.

The collapse of an established state, which is really the essence of what the analysts that I assess in this book are studying, is a rare but not totally unique occasion. The fact that the Soviet collapse happened to a state generally regarded to have been a superpower makes this case even more special. This second consideration, to my mind, has two consequences for the analysis in this book. One is that this was a very difficult case indeed to foretell.[24] The perception on the part of many if not most observers that the USSR was a very strong state meant that the thought that it might collapse was far from their minds. The test of the predictive ability of academics in particular is thus a very tough one. At the same time — and this is the second aspect of what type of predictive case the Soviet collapse represents — the very fact that the collapse was so unexpected and had such important and far-reaching consequences means that it is particularly important to study

---

[24] Cf., on this point, "Symposium on Predictions in the Social Sciences", *American Journal of Sociology*, Vol. 100 (May 1995), pp. 1520-1626.

and assess. What can we learn from the degree of success and failure in foretelling the Soviet collapse that can be applied to other important events and processes in international affairs? To what extent is it possible to look ahead in international relations? The case of the collapse of the Soviet Union raises precisely this type of question — and that is why it is so important to study.

My focus on "forecasting" and "predicting" events raises the question of what I mean by these terms. John Lewis Gaddis' treatment of this issue is illuminating. He distinguishes between "forecasts" and "predictions":

> a forecast is a statement about unknown phenomena based upon known or accepted generalizations and uncertain conditions ("partial unknowns"), whereas a prediction involves the linkage of known or accepted generalizations with certain conditions (knowns) to yield a statement about unknown phenomena.'...It follows from this that forecasts can be neither deterministic — "if A, then (inevitably) B" — nor conditional — "if A, then (under specified conditions) B". They are instead probabilistic statements: "if A, then (probably) B".[25]

Nazli Choucri further illuminates the differences between the two concepts:

> A prediction usually dispenses with probabilistic interpretations; a forecast is always conceived within a certain probability range. A prediction is generally made in terms of a point or event; a forecast is made in terms of alternatives. A prediction focuses upon one outcome; a forecast involves contingencies (Choucri, 1979, p. 4).

A third way to distinguish between these two types of attempting to foretell the future is suggested by Kjell Goldmann's concept of "sooner-or-later theories" (Goldmann, 1992, p. 88). "Sooner or later the Soviet empire will be no more", may be a relevant example of such a statement. One problem with such a way of foretelling the future, as Goldmann notes, is that it is possible to confirm but not to falsify. My purpose in this respect will thus be to determine whether the Sovietologists did try to foretell the future. If they did, how strict were they in the senses discussed here? Were any

---

[25] Gaddis, 1992/93, p. 6, note 2. Gaddis is quoting J. R. Freeman and B. L. Job (1979): "Scientific Forecasts in International Relations: Problems of Definition and Epistemology", *International Studies Quarterly*, Vol. 23, pp. 117-118, in his definition of "forecast" and "prediction".

predictions made of the strict type that goes further than what is indicated by
Goldmann's concept of "sooner-or-later theories"? Is it really possible in the
social sciences and the humanities to try to aim at predictions of the strict
type?

The only meaningful test of this aspect concerns the willingness, or
the ability, of the academics to try to foretell what was going to happen to
the very process of change itself. Would Mr Gorbachev be able to reform his
society, or was the Soviet Union going to collapse, and, if so, when?

My approach here may be taken as presupposing that all Sovietologists had the ambition of trying to predict what was going to happen in
Moscow. It is obvious that such a supposition would be incorrect. Several of
the Sovietologists analysed stated that they were dubious, if not downright
dismissive, about the possibilities, or even the meaningfulness, for academics
in the social or human sciences to try to predict events within their areas
of expertise. I do not regard it as in any sense less "scientific" not to try to
predict. I simply want to analyse first whether any of the Sovietologists tried
to foretell what was going to happen to Mr Gorbachev's reform processes,
and, second, if they did, were they correct?[26]

In chapter 5 I assess whether or not any one of 18 experts on the
Soviet Union was able to foretell what was going to happen to their object of
study in two respects. It is difficult to determine with any precision whether
attempts to predict the future have been successful or not.[27] Nevertheless, any
attempt to evaluate predictions in an academically satisfactory manner makes
it necessary to specify what indeed can be called a "correct" prediction.

Two dimensions are relevant when considering this question. The first
is that of precision. An illustration of this aspect is the difference between
a prediction along the lines: "the Soviet Union is in a state of decline..."
versus "the process of decline that the Soviet Union has entered will lead to

---

[26] Cf. J. L. Ray (1995): "Promise or Peril? Neorealism, Neoliberalism, and the Future of
International Politics", in *Controversies in International Relations Theory: Realism and the
Neoliberal Challenge*, ed. C. W. Kegley, Jr. (New York: St. Martin's Press). On pp. 349-350
Ray, in a response to John Lewis Gaddis' criticism of the international relationists' failure to
predict the end of the Cold War, discusses what expectations one may reasonably have on
the ability of such scholars, even under the best of circumstances, in predicting future events.
Ray's overall assessment can be summarized: "While it is not inconceivable that international
relations theorists might, on occasion, generate accurate forecasts of events like the end of
the Cold War, surely there will consistently be surprises of significant dimensions in world
politics...." Ibid. at p. 350.
[27] Cf. T. W. Milburn (1978): "Successful and unsuccessful forecasting in International Relations", in *Forecasting in International Relations*, eds. Choucri and Robinson, particularly pp.
87-91.

its dissolution...." The second is that of a time lag. Consider a hypothetical prediction, made on December 24, 1991: "tomorrow, the President of the Soviet Union, Mikhail S. Gorbachev, will resign and the Soviet Union will be formally dissolved." Since this occurred on the following day, December 25, 1991, the statement can't be regarded as a successful prediction in the sense specified here. If, however, an analyst is able to foretell in the fall of 1987 that "in four years time, Mikhail Gorbachev will resign and the Soviet Union will cease to exist," it is a very different matter.

To evaluate the ability of Sovietologists to foretell changes in Soviet foreign policy, there are two processes momentous enough to warrant inclusion. The first is the enormous change in Soviet foreign policy that gradually took place under Mr. Gorbachev's leadership. It is a matter of contention at what stage one can conclude that a fundamental change in this policy had really occurred. In this writer's opinion, such a change had taken place by February of 1988. The two pivotal points behind my reasoning are, one, the Soviet agreement to the destruction of intermediate-range nuclear missiles, resulting in the INF Treaty in December 1987, and, two, the agreement to withdraw forces from Afghanistan, which was publicly announced in February 1988. On the INF issue, the Soviet Union decisively broke, for the first time, with the previously sacrosanct principle that no arms control agreements could contain provisions that would make it mandatory to have large and intrusive inspections of military installations on Soviet soil.[28] Western suggestions for intrusive verification measures on Soviet soil as part of arms control agreements had previously been dismissed by Soviet leaders as suggestions that they would, if implemented, amount to "spying". The public commitment to withdraw from Afghanistan was a similarly fundamental break with previous practice in Soviet foreign policy. It was generally regarded as a central tenet of official Soviet Marxist thought that "socialism can only advance, never retreat". The retreat from Afghanistan was the first explicit break with this tenet.[29]

The second event that will be used to assess the Sovietologists' ability

---

[28] It could be argued that the confidence- and security-building measures (CSBMs) taken at the Conference on Security and Cooperation in Europe at a conference in Stockholm in 1986 contained such measures. My view is, however, that there was an immense difference in scale between the requirements in the two accords, with the INF Treaty requirements being infinitely more demanding. See R. L. Garthoff (1994): *The Great Transition: American-Soviet Relations and the End of the Cold War* (Washington, DC: Brookings), esp. pp. 590-593.

[29] Cf. Garthoff, 1994, pp. 733-748 for the "Gorbachev doctrine" on disentangling from interventions in the Third World.

to predict is the collapse of the Soviet State, ultimately consummated with the resignation of President Gorbachev on December 25, 1991. While this is not a case of foreign policy change in itself, it had profound consequences for this field of policy as well.

The dimension of precision means that I must be able to formulate a generalized type of prediction or forecast against which the efforts made by the Sovietologists, in particular, to foretell the future of the Soviet State can be assessed. This is more difficult in the first case, that concerning the change in Soviet foreign policy, than it is in the case of the dissolution of the very state itself. The change in foreign policy must always be regarded as a matter of degree, whereas the dissolution of the state is an either-or affair.

This leaves the issue of a reasonable time lag. It is impossible to state that there is a time lag that is both above criticism and applicable across many issues of human events. The social sciences and the humanities don't claim to be able to predict events in any precise fashion, at least not the vast majority of the scholars working within these two academic fields. My belief is that a reasonable time lag for predictions or forecasts on the first of these two issues is twelve to eighteen months. It is obvious that the time lag should not be too short, but it cannot be too long either, at least on the first of these two issues.

When it comes to foretelling that the changes in Soviet foreign policy would result in a fundamental alteration by February 1988, such an assessment would have to have been issued by February 1987 to be classfied as correct here. For the second predictive question it is possible to distinguish between a short time frame, one within which the analyst could foretell the results of the reform process in (foreign) policy undertaken by Gorbachev, on the one hand, and, on the other, a longer time frame within which the analyst could correctly forecast that the decline of the Soviet Union was indeed irreversible. The first time lag is here specified as having been stated no later than 18 months before December 1991, whereas the latter is regarded to be 10 years. In other words, to classify as correct, a forecast concerning the demise of the Soviet Union must have been issued no earlier than December of 1981 and no later than June of 1990.

One of the criteria that can be used to distinguish between prediction, in the sense in which this term is used here, and forecast as I define it, is the time frame. It seems reasonable to demand more of a prediction in this respect than of a forecast. To classify as a prediction an assessment has to contain a time period within which the predicted event is supposed to take place. It is also necessary for the prediction to be roughly correct in terms of the time within which it is foretold to occur. A forecast, by contrast, is by definition looser. Here, it is more a general sense, or perhaps an imprecise but highly suggestive formulation that provides the verification that a correct assessment has been made.

Based on the above-mentioned criteria, I have formulated four generic statements, each representing a prediction and a forecast, respectively, regarding the two issues specified above. The first generic prediction is "the Soviet Union will undertake a fundamental reorientation of its foreign policy under Gorbachev". If made within 12 months of February 1988 — in other words by February 1987 — this is regarded as a "correct prediction". The first generic forecast is: "one likely result of Mr. Gorbachev's new policies is fundamental changes in Soviet foreign policy".

The second generic prediction is "the end result of Mr. Gorbachev's new policies will be the dissolution of the Soviet state and/or the resignation of the Soviet leader". To qualify as a "correct" prediction this assessment will have to have been made by June 1990, at the latest. The second generic forecast is "the Soviet Union is in a process of decline that will likely result in the demise of the Soviet state itself". As the decline of a state is a very different type of process than the immediate results of a policy, it is reasonable to use a much longer time frame here. I have chosen to regard 10 years as the longest reasonable time span for this type of assessment. It is unavoidable that a choice of "acceptable time span" for predictions and forecasts involves a certain degree of arbitrariness. It is at least as difficult to specify the shortest acceptable time span between the making of the assessment at the very death of the Soviet State to be qualified as a correct forecast as it is to specify the longest acceptable time limit. A longer time should be used here than in the case of predictions as the precision of a forecast is much smaller. A forecast should thus have been made at any time between December 1981, at the earliest, and June 1990, at the latest, to be regarded as "correct" here.

1.3.3 Types of Explanation

A central concept in this book is "prediction". My way of conceiving prediction is very strongly linked to a particular view of what constitutes an "explanation". How can one meaningfully distinguish between different ways of explaining why Mr. Gorbachev and the Soviet leadership started the process of fundamental reform?

The explanation problem can be formulated as an explanation of (foreign) policy change. Why actors change their policies is a subject that has been well covered in the political science literature, not least in international relations. It is not possible to make a clear distinction in this respect between explanations purporting to account strictly for changes in foreign policy, on the one hand, and those aiming at a clarification of why Soviet policy changed in a broader sense, on the other. Any attempt to concentrate exclusively on explanations focusing only on foreign policy would reduce the number of cases of explanations to such an extent that any real comparison becomes meaningless.

My approach to classifying the explanations of Gorbachev's reforms is inspired by three different sources. One is "levels of analysis", which has been important in international relations for analysing and explaining.[30] In one of the first systematic applications of this idea to the problem of explanation in international relations, Kenneth Waltz asked, What causes war? The explanation, Waltz asserted, could be found at three levels of analysis. The first was identified in Waltz's expression: "The root of all evil is man, and thus he is himself the root of the specific evil, war" (Waltz, 1959, p. 3). Two more levels in Waltz's book complemented the individual level of explanation: the state level and the nature of the international system level. In addition to the three levels of analysis presented by Kenneth Waltz in 1954/1959, the individual, the state, and the international system, later writers added a fourth level: the bureaucratic level.[31] I concur with Steve Smith in that: "The level-of-analysis debate is a methodological not an ontological debate: it refers to how best to explain and not to how the world really is" (Hollis and Smith, 1990/91, p. 203). A second way of attempting to explain what happened to the Soviet Union is by analysing the concepts of Sovietology itself. Such an exercise, for example, is carried out to some extent in a special issue of *The National Interest* entitled "The Strange Death of Soviet Communism: An Autopsy".[32] The debate in this special issue is largely carried out based on some of the most important conceptions of the Soviet Union used by Sovietology throughout the last few decades of the existence of that country; these

---

[30] Cf. K. Waltz (1959): *Man, the State and War* (New York. Columbia University Press,); D. Singer (1961): "The Level-of-Analysis Problem in International Relations", in *The International System: Theoretical Essays*, eds. K. Knorr and S. Verba (Princeton, NJ: Princeton University Press), pp. 72-92 and B. Buzan (1995): "The Level-of-Analysis Problem in International Relations Reconsidered", in *International Relations Theory Today*, eds. K.Booth and S. Smith (Cambridge: Polity Press), pp. 198-216.

[31] For an analysis that distinguishes between the same levels of analysis, see M. Hollis and S. Smith (1990/91): *Explaining and Understanding International Relations* (Oxford: Clarendon Press), especially pp. 7-9 and 97-101.

[32] The National Interest: "The Strange Death of Soviet Communism", No. 31 (Spring 1993) pp. 3-144. ,

may be distinguished as "totalitarianism", "modernization theory" and "institutional pluralism". My analysis confirms that most Sovietologists used the "totalitarian model" to explain the collapse of the Soviet State.[33]

More directly applicable to the explanation problem at hand, however, are two other conceptions. One of these is the functioning and problems of the Soviet economy. It is obvious that this aspect has been crucial in the thinking of many specialists. This explanation is something more specific, as well as more profound, than simply stating that "the Soviet economy didn't work, which is why Mr Gorbachev undertook to start his reforms". Instead, it is, as used here, grounded in theorizing that regards market economies as vastly more efficient over the long term, as compared to socialist economies.[34] A second model that is derived fromSovietology (although it of course has other uses as well) concerns the role of the leader himself, as an individual. The prevalence of this type of explanation in Sovietology warrants its inclusion here. Mr Gorbachev and his actions are analysed in many different ways by the experts, and at least part of their explanations for why the policy changes took place often include him and his personality.

The third inspiration for the approach selected to classify the explanations of why policies changed in the USSR after 1985 is derived from an article by Isabelle Grunberg and Thomas Risse-Kappen.[35] The authors evaluate and assess the extent to which various theories of international politics can account for another explanatory problem: the end of the Cold War.

Grunberg and Risse-Kappen distinguish between three "theoretical traditions" in the study of international relations. The first is most commonly labelled realism. The second strand of theories concerns international co-operation and institutions. The third is what the authors call "unit-level approaches to world politics" (Grunberg and Risse-Kappen, 1992; Cf. also Deudney and Ikenberry, 1991). Explanations on this level thus focus on the state as well as on the individual.

---

[33] For one short article outlining the development of these models, with particular emphasis on "totalitarianism", see M. Malia (1993): "A Fatal Logic" in ibid. 80-90. See also P. Rutland (1993): "Sovietology: Notes for a Post-Mortem", ibid., pp. 109-122.

[34] Cf. D. Deudney and G. J. Ikenberry (1991): "Soviet Reform and the End of the Cold War: Explaining Large-Scale Historical Change", *Review of International Studies,* vol. 17, pp. 225-250 as reprinted in *Post-Communist Studies and Political Science: Methodology and Empirical Theory in Sovietology,* eds. F. J. Fleron Jr. and E. P. Hoffmann (Boulder/San Francisco/Oxford: Westview, 1993), pp. 205-237. The economic explation is particularly discussed at pp. 214-219.

[35] I. Grunberg & T. Risse-Kappen (1992): "A Time of Reckoning? Theories of International Relations and the End of the Cold War", in *The End of the Cold War*, eds. Goldmann and Allan, pp. 104-146. Cf. also Deudney and Ikenberry (1991).

In the first, realist, tradition, there are five fundamental building blocks. The first is that the nation-state is the unit of analysis. The nature of the system in which these units interact is anarchic; this forms the second building block — there is no government above that of the states themselves. This means, third, that the states are driven to protect their own fundamental interests as their most important behaviour. The effect of this is, fourth, that the system is characterized by arms races caused by the fact that states, to protect their basic interests, tend to accumulate weapons in a way that is described by the basic concept "the security dilemma" (Jervis, 1978). The fifth aspect is the centrality of the concept of "power". This is largely conceived by way of an emphasis on military strength.

Grunberg and Risse-Kappen label the second line of theoretical reasoning within international relations "theories of international co-operation and institutions". There are two variants of this theoretical strand. It is only the latter of these — "liberal institutionalism" — that is applicable here. There are similarities with realism in that anarchy is accepted as a general condition of international politics, but in this conception this is complemented by several issue areas in which international co-operation has developed to such an extent that international institutions, often called international regimes, create complex rules of behaviour for many actors in the world polity. In some cases, these institutions and regimes have the power to verify that the agreed rules are carried out. A central aspect of this way of reasoning is well captured by Grunberg and Risse-Kappen: "Generalized shared expectations of behavior and understandings are *constitutive* for successful interactions" (Grunberg and Risse-Kappen, 1991, p. 127, Emphasis supplied. Note omitted).

Grunberg and Risse-Kappen add a third and final conception where one might find explanations of change in international politics: unit-level approaches. Of these, there are three variants. The first of the variants — "republican and commercial liberalism" — is not applicable to my explanatory problem. The second version of the unit-level approaches — "domestic structures and coalition-building processes" — highlights the way changes in the international polity interact with the process of coalition-building that in principle occurs within all types of political systems. Changes in the international arena are believed to influence the domestic building of coalitions within elites. The third and final version of the unit-level approach concentrates on the individual (or group of individuals) who makes the decisions. There are several theories of cognition of interest on this level. These all concern how people filter and organize information to make sense of the complex world around them. One of them relates to cognitive consistency, which highlights how individuals strive for a conception of a problem area that is internally consistent. To the extent that they get information that is inconsistent with their basic mental construct, they tend either to disregard it or to try to fit it into their existing conceptual scheme. A second theory of cognition is attribution theory. In contrast to the theory of cognitive consistency, "attribution theory portrays the person as relatively open-minded in the search for truth, untrammelled by the need to maintain a favourable self-image or preserve a favoured belief" (Larson, 1985, p. 35).

One basic aspect of attribution theory is called the "fundamental error of attribution". This, as discussed above, means that an actor tends to explain his/her own action in terms of situational factors, whereas the action of potential adversaries tends to be ascribed to dispositional factors.[36] A third theory of cognition concerns learning. This way of theorizing is too complex to be adequately explained here. Suffice it to say that one way to explain Gorbachev's actions in the 1980s has been to ascribe it to learning on his part.[37]

My own classification of theories and models that may be used to explain change in international relations thus combines influences from all three of the above-mentioned ways of reasoning. The overarching device for classifying the theories will be the "levels-of-analysis" reasoning (see table 1.2). The categories in this table will be used in my assessment of how analysts explained the changes in Soviet policy, particularly foreign policy, undertaken by Mr Gorbachev and his colleagues.

---

[36] For a fascinating study applying attribution theory to the study of international conflict, see Heradstveit (1979).

[37] See Grunberg and Risse-Kappen, 1992, pp. 139-140 and the sources cited there.

Table 1.2   Types of Explanation of Soviet Change

Level-of-Analysis	Factors highlighted	Basic actors identified
Type of theory/model		
I. System level		
A. Realism	—The structure of the international system — anarchy — power	— The nation-state
B. International Co-operation and Institutions	— Increasing regulation by conventions, regimes, international organizations	— Nation-states and international institutions
II. State level		
A. Domestic structures and coalition-building processes	— The interaction between international factors and domestic politics	— Political elites
B. Socialist economy	— The inefficiency of socialist economy as compared to market economy	
III. Bureaucratic level	—The tendency of bureaucracy, at various levels, to intervene in policy making	— Bureaucrats at various levels
IV. Individual level		
A. Cognitive psychology and learning	— The complexity of information and decisions facing individuals in international politics	— Elite individuals
B. Individual explanation	— The personality of the leader	— Mr. Gorbachev

Source: Adapted from I. Grunberg and T. Risse-Kappen (1991): "A Time of Reckoning? Theories of International Relations and the End of the Cold War", in *The End of the Cold War,* eds. Goldmann and Allan, pp. 104-146; K. Waltz (1959): *Man, the State and War* (New York. Columbia University Press); D. Deudney and G. J. Ikenberry (1991): "Soviet Reform and the End of the Cold War: Explaining Large-Scale Historical Change", *Review of International Studies*, vol. 17, pp. 225-250.

Note: The table is not intended to present a stringent representation of all the logically available explanations of change in the Soviet Union. Instead, its purpose is to classify the main alternative explanations of the Soviet process of change that exist in the literature written by Sovietologists.

1.4 The Comparative Analysis of States: Five Hypotheses

If one is interested in comparing states as they react to what is happening outside their boundaries, then what dimensions are significant? What may explain differences in the ways individuals within them analyse and explain the outside world?

The first dimension is the size and power of the state. This notion has a solid foundation in the study of international politics: that strong and powerful nations have greater room for manoeuvre in the world than do small nations. Note that, in my conception, it is the traditional ways of "measuring" power that matter. Such aspects as the ones gauged by Kenneth Waltz are thus the ones that I have in mind: "size of population and territory, resource endowment, economic capability, military strength, political stability and competence" (Waltz, 1979, p. 131). The idea behind my conception is simply that when it comes to matters of security policy, it is possible to rank states roughly according to this conception. Thus my first hypothesis: the analysis of Soviet foreign policy is less inhibited in large, strong nations than is the case in weak nations, where there is more caution.

A second dimension has to do with ideology. This is a slippery notion in the study of politics, but I use it in a specific sense here. What is important is whether the country's fundamental political tradition is based on the idea of equality of opportunity — in other words, liberal democracy, with a market economy — or on a political ideology which advocates socialist policies, at least to some extent — in other words, social democracy. My second hypothesis is thus: analysts in a country whose main political ethos strongly supports the idea of liberal democracy, in which a market economy plays an essential part, are less likely to detect important changes in Soviet foreign policy than are analysts in countries where ideas of democratic socialism are prominent. On the other hand, when it comes to making the assessment that the Soviet Union is falling apart as a state, I anticipate that analysts in a country in which the political culture is very antithetical to the Soviet one will have a comparatively easier time in finding out that the downward spiral may indeed lead to the demise of the Soviet State. This may be compared to an analyst in a state where democratic socialist ideas are more prevalent, who would be expected to have a harder time in making the precise and accurate prediction that the Soviet system was in a terminal decline.

In other words, my third hypothesis is that in countries with a strong liberal-democratic political ideology, with a firm commitment to market economy, it is easier for analysts to detect that the Soviet system is moribund than it is for analysts in countries with a more positive attitude towards socialism in general.

Table 1.3   Comparing Analytic Responses to Foreign Events: Four Hypotheses on Causes for Differences

1: Power	Analysts in weak countries are expected to be more cautious in their analyses than are analysts in strong countries
2: Ideology I	Analysts in liberal states are expected to be less likely to detect changes in Soviet foreign policy than are analysts in countries with a tradition of democratic socialism
3: Ideology II	Analysts in liberal states are expected to detect earlier that the USSR is in "terminal decline" than are analysts in countries with a strong role for democratic socialism
4: Degree of control on debate on security policy	Analysts in countries with a tightly controlled decision-making process in security policy, and where academics are excluded from the policy-making process, are expected to be more cautious in their analyses than are analysts in countries with a more open security policy-making process, and where academics tend to become officials.

A third dimension concerns the way in which security issues are debated. It is here possible to identify a continuum ranging from countries where security issues and policies are very freely debated and in which political officials are only one voice in the debate, to countries where the debate on security policy is largely controlled by the politicians. One aspect of this is the participation of academics in decision making in foreign and security policy. In an open system, such participation is frequent, and in a closed one, such participation is rare.[38] Participation by academics is here seen both in the sense of activity in terms of writing articles, etc., and, particularly, in the sense of being officials in the political machinery. Thus the fourth hypothesis: in states where the debate on security policy is closed, controlled by the politicians, other actors tend tofollow their lead to a greater extent than in countries where security policy is more openly debated.

---

[38] I initially separated the dimensions of "openness in debate on foreign and security policy" from "degree of participation by academics". An anonymous reader pointed out, however, that essentially these two dimensions are one and the same and that the country that had an open debate also tended to have a high degree of participation by academics, and vice versa.

1.5 Choice of States to Analyse

The approach chosen here makes it necessary to consider several dimensions when choosing which states to analyse. Ideally, I should cover small and weak states as well as large and strong ones. Countries where there are values which are characteristic of liberal democracies should be studied as well as others where socialist ideologies have more influence. There should be at least one state where the debate about security policy is very restricted to official circles and where academic specialists are largely kept out of decision-making circles, and other states where debate is more open and where academics frequently move from their ivory towers to the seats of political power. It should be made explicit that it is impossible to select states representing each individual characteristic among the ones chosen here. The most that can be done is to choose countries for scrutiny that represent variations on at least some of the dimensions mentioned.

It would be hypocritical not to acknowledge that factors such as the researcher's own interests and abilities, for instance when it comes to language skills, also play a role in the selection of nations to study. These considerations have resulted in the selection of four states as objects of study. They are France, Great Britain, Sweden and the U.S. A brief outline of their characteristics in terms of my six dimensions is presented in table 1.4. Classifying countries in terms of so many dimensions as I have done above is bound to be controversial in some respects. However, most of these classifications ought to be easy to accept. The table also serves its fundamental purpose: to underline that the countries chosen represent different characteristics in terms of those four dimensions that I have selected for deeper analysis. I do not pretend to have conducted any analysis on my own of these dimensions, except in the case of the United States. My classifications are, instead, based on a reading of several sources for each country. The specific foundation for the classifications may be found in the literature cited in chapter 2. In my conception, the factors enumerated in table 1.4 are most applicable to the public analysis presented by the politicians. Research on the media also indicates that factors of this type do account for some of the variance between the coverage of international news in different countries (Riegert, 1998, and idem. 1991). The extent to which factors of this type may explain the ways in which Sovietologists approach the analysis of their subject matter is much less clear.

**Table 1.4   The Selected Countries Classified According to
the Hypotheses**

	Strength	Ideology	Openness of security debate
France	Strong	Mixed	Closed
Great Britain	Strong	Liberal/mixed	Medium/open
Sweden	Weak/medium	Social-democratic	Medium
U.S.	Superpower	Liberal	Open

Notes: 1) In terms of strength, countries can be classified as "weak", with "medium" strength, "strong", ending with "superpower";
2) The ideology dimension runs from "liberal", a state with strongly anti-socialist ideology, through "mixed", where values from both endpoints of the scale co-exist, through "socialist or social-democratic";
3) The security debate dimension goes from "closed" at one end, through "medium", ending in "open".
For arguments concerning the classification of each of the four countries on these three dimensions, see chapter 2.

As indicated by table 1.4 the four nations differ in many respects on the three dimensions, which makes it difficult to isolate the explanatory power of the respective factors. On the other hand, their differences also mean that the analysis can be more wide-ranging than would otherwise have been the case. The U.S. is classified as being on the extreme on all three dimensions, which makes this country in some sense a case apart from the three others. To a degree, I regard the U.S. as being in a category of its own, with the three European countries in many respects representing a distinctive second category.

1.6 Operational Choices

1.6.1 Choice of Actors to Analyse

This book explores the analysis of Gorbachev's foreign policy in four countries. In each country, three types of actor are scrutinized. The first group of actors comprises the officials constitutionally empowered to handle foreign policy. This means that the choice of actors, as well as the choice of sources, is relatively straightforward. France is the only country where there are three officials that fulfil my criterion of selection: the President, the Prime Minister and the Foreign Minister.[39] For Great Britain, it is the Prime Minister and the Foreign Secretary. In Sweden, it is similarly the Prime Minister and the Foreign Minister. In the U.S. I have analysed statements made by the President and the Secretary of State. In addition, I have analysed the Under Secretary of State for Foreign Affairs[40] in Sweden and the Under Secretary of State for Political Affairs in the U.S. The reason for their inclusion is the simple one that they have been prominently featured in the respective official publications in their countries where official foreign policy is presented. The period during which speeches and other messages have been studied is the same as that for the editorials in elite newspapers, from 1 March 1985 until 31 December 1991.

For the selection of elite newspapers, I have tried to choose one paper from the right of the ideological spectrum as well as one paper from the left. As will be elaborated in the cases of Sweden and the U.S., it was not possible to find newspapers that clearly belonged to each of these two ends of the political spectrum in each of the four countries. In the case of the United States, I have chosen to scrutinize editorials in *The New York Times* and *The Washington Post*. There are two reasons for this selection. The first is that these two newspapers are the foremost opinion papers in their nation. The second reason is that the political system in the U.S. does not really resemble that in Western Europe with a clear, ideological Left-Right divide. Therefore, the analysis of the U.S. need not necessarily match that for the West European systems in this respect.

In France, the choice was not difficult. I have taken *Le Figaro* to represent the French right, and *Le Monde* to exemplify the left. These two papers seem to me to be the traditional spokesmen for their respective parts of the French ideological spectrum. A relative newcomer such as *Liberation* does not really fulfil my criterion of being an elite paper, clearly etched out ideologically.

In Great Britain, the choice was somewhat more difficult. It is true that *The Times* has been the traditional elite voice of the right of the Britishpolitical spectrum. Changes in the ownership, and subsequently in the paper itself, during the last dozen years has, however, put that standing somewhat

---

[39] The question of sources for the statements examined is discussed in chapter 3, and in appendix 5 the politicians analysed are presented.
[40] Swedish title: "Kabinettssekreterare"

into question. Still, I settled for *The Times* after failing to be convinced that
any other paper had filled its role as a voice of the British traditional conservatives up until the time this study of newspaper editorials ends, in 1991.
Further to the left of the political spectrum, *The Guardian* seems to be the
natural choice for this study. *The Independent* has been an alternative, but the
paper was only established in 1986, so it cannot be seen as a traditional voice
of the moderate British left to the same extent as *The Guardian*.

In Sweden, there are only two quality morning papers with a nation-
wide circulation. The choice of *Svenska Dagbladet* (the Swedish Daily) to
represent the right and *Dagens Nyheter* (the Daily News) for the left was thus
an easy one. In Sweden, the distinction between a rightist and a leftist paper
is less clear-cut than is the case for the other two European countries. It is
especially the case that *Dagens Nyheter* is much harder to characterize as a
paper truly of the left on the Swedish political spectrum than is *The Guardian*
in the United Kingdom and *Le Monde* in France. In the Swedish case, the
contrast is, rather, between a paper clearly of the right, *Svenska Dagbladet,*
and a paper of the Swedish political centre, *Dagens Nyheter.*

The final category analysed in this book is the Sovietologists. One
issue here was how many Sovietologists should be chosen to represent
each nation. A second issue was the subsequent one of who those
individuals were to be. The first issue is complicated by the fact that the
number of Sovietologists is, of course, much smaller in a country like
Sweden than it is in the United States. Eventually, I decided to select four
Sovietologists from the three European nations represented in this study.
In the case of the United States, the selection, I felt, had to be larger for
two reasons. The first reason is that Sovietology as an academic discipline
was much larger in the U.S. in terms of the number of active scholars than
in any of the other three countries. The second reason is that it is in the
U.S. where the divide between an older generation of Sovietologists, the
"traditionalists", and a younger cohort of scholars, the "revisionists", is the
most pronounced.[41] I have thus taken care to select scholars belonging to
the older generation of U.S. Sovietologists as well as at least one scholar
belonging to the revisionists. After these initial considerations, I proceeded in
the following way to make the practical choice of individual Sovietologists.
First, I selected four Swedish Sovietologists. They are Anders Åslund,
Kristian Gerner, Stefan Hedlund, and Lena Jonsson.[42] These scholars

---

[41] On this point see S. F. Cohen (1985): *Rethinking the Soviet Experience: Politics and History
Since 1917* (New York/Oxford: Oxford University Press) chapter 1: "Scholarly Missions:
Sovietology as a Vocation", particularly at pp. 27-37.

receive a brief presentation in chapter 5. Second, I contacted each of them for suggestions of which Sovietologists to include in the other three countries. By way of this process, I eventually arrived at the list of Sovietologists presented in appendix 1.[43]

Since the Sovietologists are academics and thus presumably have a longer time perspective on their object of study, I decided to study their writings from early 1982 through 1992. After that date, I have been more selective and included only works that I regard as clearly relevant for my research questions. Where possible, all of their official publications have been perused for the main period of study. An emphasis has of course had to be made on material that can reasonably be believed, judging from the title, an abstract or other such information, to be relevant for the present project. Every effort has been made to find and examine at least all the major writings of each of 18 authors during this period. The arrival of the computer databases, as well as the Internet, has made this search much easier for three of the four countries: Great Britain, Sweden and the U.S. In the case of France, I have found it more difficult to first identify, and then find a copy of, each publication for the four Sovietologists selected. A special bibliography at the end of the volume (appendix 2a) identifies all the publications that have formed the basis for my analysis of the academic specialists on the Soviet Union.[44]

1.6.2 Analytical Issues

One aspect of this book is an inquiry into the importance of perceptions for the analysis of another country's (foreign) policy. As alluded to above, this is a wide field in which many suggestive statements but few solid results based on empirical analysis have been presented. My aim here is to focus on one limited aspect of this field of study. I investigate whether or not any of the analysts who followed events in Moscow exhibited any tendency to delay acknowledgement that the foreign policy of the Soviet Union had indeed changed, in a way that could be explained by the fundamental error of attribution.

---

[42] My friend and colleague Dr. Bertil Nygren was initially included in this group, and he contributed positively to my process of choice regarding Sovietologists in the other three countries. At a later stage I decided, however, to drop Dr. Nygren from my analysis, largely because he had too few publications on relevant topics during the time under study here.

[43] Along the way I also decided to limit the number of Sovietologists studied in the three European countries to four.

[44] The reference list for the 18 Sovietologists doesn't strive to contain all their publications produced over 10 years, a nearly impossible task; it includes only as many of their publications as possible that to some extent concern the matters under scrutiny in this book.

It should be noted in this first chapter that this is a tendency that analysts of international relations have borrowed from cognitive psychology. It is inherent in the character of factors of this type that they, at least at the current stage of research, do not lend themselves to clear-cut determination as to whether or not they have any explanatory value in a case like the present one. What they can do, however, is enrich the study of the factors that may influence how observers in one country perceive what is happening in another. We may, at the most, find support to confirm our belief that factors of this type affect how analysts characterize the events in another country. This may, in turn, contribute to the further enrichment of the study of perceptual variables in international politics. Gradually, our models and our analyses may become specific and precise enough to be able to reach further into the estimation of the role and influence of perceptions in international politics.

The assessment of whether or not the fundamental error of attribution exists, as well as my intention to test whether or not any correct predictions or forecasts were presented, makes it necessary to spell out what I characterize as the "objective reality" against which the analysis of Soviet politics will be evaluated. This exercise inevitably involves personal judgements of what really happened in the Soviet Union between 1985 and the end of 1991. The aspect of attribution theory that matters most for this book, the fundamental error of attribution, involves, among other things, the perceived tendency of some analysts to deny that the object of their study has indeed changed, particularly if they have a very negative view of their object of study in the first place. To reiterate what I stated in section 1.3.2, I assume that it is fair to say that the Soviet policies had changed, in a profound way, after some three years of Gorbachev's being in power, both in terms of foreign policy and domestic politics.[45] It is easiest to find two events that, to my mind, settle the issue in foreign policy. As mentioned previously, these two events are the signing of the treaty on intermediate-range nuclear forces (the INF Treaty), in December 1987, and the announcement that the Soviet Union had decided to pull back its troops from Afghanistan, which was made in February 1988.

Thus, this study assumes that by March 1988 the observer who regularly followed Soviet politics had clear signs that the foreign policy of that country had decisively changed. *An analyst who assessed Soviet foreign policy after March 1988 and expressly denied that this policy had indeed changed displayed the fundamental error of attribution.* In the domestic field,

---

[45] Cf. my brief account of the momentous events in and around the Soviet Union from 1985 through 1991 in section 2.4.

I believe that the same assessment should be made in the spring of 1989, at the latest. This is after the elections in March of 1989. These were the first elections in the history of the state that were less than completely controlled by the state. While the intentions of the Soviet leadership in holding these elections can be debated, it seems impossible to deny that the consequences of holding them were momentous in terms of Soviet domestic politics.[46] Thus, *an analyst who assessed Soviet domestic politics after April 1989 and denied that domestic policy had indeed changed displayed the fundamental error of attribution*. The first question to be asked here is whether any of the observers analysed here displayed this tendency. The second question concerns whether or not it is possible to find some explanation as to why an individual observer, country or newspaper might have this type of attitude towards the Soviet Union.

1.7 The Structure of the Book

The rest of the book is laid out in the following way. In chapter 2, there is a description of the role that relations with the Soviet Union played for each of the four countries during the post-war period. It is here, in other words, that I discuss the relevant aspects of what was earlier called foreign policy orientation. This chapter, with some exception for the United States, is not based on research carried out by myself, but is rather the result of a study of previous research. The focus is of course on aspects of particular interest for this book. This chapter also contains a section on the special character of Sovietology as an academic field. Finally, it contains a brief section on the sequence of events as they unfolded inside and outside the Soviet Union from early 1985 until the end of 1991. Chapter 3 consists of the analysis of the speeches made by the politicians in the four countries.

The editorials in elite newspapers are covered in chapter 4. In chapter 5 the writings of the Sovietologists are assessed. As stated above, the analysis in this chapter is more detailed when it comes to studying the extent to which the Sovietologists tried to make forecasts, or even predictions, about what was going to happen to the Soviet Union as a result of the new policies from 1985 on. In chapter 6 the analysis of Soviet politics is compared and assessed across actors within the respective countries, as well as across countries. It is here that I apply the hypotheses regarding possible

---

[46] For an analysis of the elections in 1989 from the perspective of the gradual democratization of the Soviet system, see J. F. Hough (1997) *Democratization and Revolution in the USSR 1985-1991* (Washington, DC: Brookings), pp. 140-174.

differences between countries in their analysis of Moscow. I also appraise what has been learned about the role of perceptions, as it concerns both attribution theory and cognitive consistency. I further discuss the attempts to make predictions about events and processes in the Soviet Union, as well as the difficulty of making predictions in social science more generally. The book concludes with suggestions for further research. These concern, first, the general difficulties of explaining and understanding international events and processes. Second, I discuss the question of whether the findings here indicate that the pursuit of predictions in the social sciences and the humanities is a worthwhile one, and, if so, how scholars should go about assessing their peers in this respect. Third, the relevance of the case of the collapse of the Soviet Union for what I have termed "scenario-making" in terms of planning for security and defence policy is assessed.

Chapter 2
The Setting:
Relations with the Soviet Union, Sovietology and an Historical Outline

2.1 Introduction

This book is a multidimensional study of how the political processes that occurred in the Soviet Union between 1985 and 1991 were perceived and analysed in four different countries. It involves a comparison between how the debate on Moscow was carried out in each of these countries. Second, it focuses on how 18 selected members of an academic specialty, Sovietology, approached their object of study. Third, the comparison, both across nations and across actors, with necessity involves an emphasis on the events in and around the Soviet Union during these momentous years. The purpose of this chapter is to present the setting in which this book should be seen, in each of the three respects mentioned.

2.2 Relations with the Soviet Union in Four Countries

2.2.1 Introduction

Relations with the Soviet Union were important for all of the four countries studied. This similarity hides important differences, not least when it comes to the interplay between each nation's political system and its pursuit of relations with Moscow. This book compares the way the processes of change and decay in the Soviet Union were perceived in four different countries. I have hypothesized that these perceptions may be influenced by various considerations, including some aspects of the domestic politics of the state in which the analysis was undertaken. This makes it is necessary to spell out my conception of the politics of relations with the Soviet Union in each of the studied countries. In addition, I make some observations on the scientific study of Moscow within each of these four nations. This entails both basic aspects of the development of Sovietology itself and of the interrelationship between the political power centre in each country and that country's Sovietologists.

2.2.2 The United States

The United States was the country of the four studied in this book in which relations with the socialist state loomed the largest in internal politics, with the case of Great Britain being the only possible contender. It must be remembered that, for Washington, only Moscow could pose a direct threat to the future survival of the U.S. as an independent nation in the 20th century. This sense of a unique peril emanating only from the Soviet Union is a crucial difference to the other three states, which have historical experiences of wars and threats emanating from several different sources. In response to a perceived global threat, the United States responded with a strategy that carries the name containment.[1]

The vital role of this strategy for U.S. foreign policy has been perhaps even more appreciated after having been successfully completed than was the case when it was being actively pursued. One only needs to look back at the foreign policy of Washington after the demise of the Soviet State to realize that a similarly fundamental strategic goal from which the rest of U.S. foreign policy flows is now lacking.

The basic foreign policy orientation of the United States is very different from that of any of the three other countries studied in this book. The most powerful state during this century, particularly during the last 60 years, would naturally develop a very distinctive global perspective. It is not possible here to do more than suggest briefly a few aspects of this perspective, especially as it pertained to the U.S. relationship with the Soviet Union during the period between about 1947 until 1991.

One such fundamental aspect was that two nations that had global interests and aspirations were bound to come into competition, if not outright conflict. This was irrespective of whether or not there were ideological differences between the two countries. The fact that such differences did indeed exist served to make the competition even more intense. The United States, built on the idea of a society of free citizens striving to make a good living in a market economy, contrasted very fundamentally with a Soviet society that was based on collectivism, a centralized state and a socialized

---

[1] There is an ocean of literature on U.S. foreign policy. Among the books that have formed the thinking of this author, S. Hoffmann (1968): *Gulliver's Troubles, Or The Setting of American Foreign Policy* (New York: McGraw-Hill) and J. L. Gaddis (1982): *Strategies of Containment* (New York/Oxford: Oxford University Press) have been among the most influential. The domestic context of the making of U.S. Soviet policy throughout most of the Cold War is analysed in *The Making of America's Soviet Policy* (1984), ed. J. S. Nye, Jr. (New Haven, CT: Yale University Press).

economy. The growth of the nuclear weapons arsenals of the two countrie-safter 1949 added yet another aspect to the rivalry. From the 1960s on, these two arsenals reached levels of power and destructibility so great that, if they were used indiscriminately, they could threaten the survival of most of the population on this earth.

These factors taken together served to make the U.S.-Soviet relationship a unique one in the history of the American republic. That the relationship was crucial for Washington's foreign and security policies goes without saying. Its special characteristics likewise served to make it essential for domestic politics as well. For many years the American polity was explicitly structured as a system that saw itself as the antithesis of the competitor centred in Moscow. This permeated many aspects of life in the United States (Nye (ed.), 1994).

One of several indications of the importance of the relationship with Moscow for U.S. domestic politics can be taken from opinion polls. During the Cold War, a sizeable proportion of U.S. respondents during presidential election years always identified "foreign policy" or "security policy" as the issue which came to mind when they were asked what is "the most important problem" facing the country.[2] During the presidential election years 1992 and 1996, "foreign affairs", "security" and/or "peace" never registered higher than 5% in any of several surveys examined.[3] It can safely be concluded that, for the U.S. public, foreign and security affairs have typically been considerably lower on the national agenda since the demise of the Soviet Union than was the case during the Cold War. The exception is, of course, in times of crisis, such as the one following the Iraqi invasion of Kuwait in August 1990.

[2] One exception to this was 1976, a year of détente with Moscow, where only 4% answered that "foreign policy" came to their mind when asked about the "most important issue" facing the country. For more on this, see J. Hallenberg (1991): *The Image of the Soviet Union in U.S. Presidential Elections 1968-1988*. Report No. 1991:3 (Stockholm: Department of Political Science, University of Stockholm) p. 65. Comparative figures from the presidential election years of 1968 through 1984 range from 31% in 1972, to 44% in 1968. The figure for 1988 was 10%.

[3] The Wirthlin Group conducted surveys in August, September, October and November 1992 in which the question: "What would you say is the most important problem facing the United States today, that is, the one that you, yourself, are most concerned about?" "Foreign Policy/ peace" scored from 3-5% in each survey. "Pocketbook/economy" scored consistently highest from 50-66%. In 1996 *The New York Times* and the Tarr group asked the question: "What do you think is the most important problem facing the country today?" in December and August/September respectively. "Foreign policy", "defense", and "war" scored no higher than 3%. The results are less clear than those in 1996 as to what was indeed perceived as "the most important problem". "Crime" and various "economy" subjects vied for first place, although never reaching higher than 16%. Source: File 468 Public Opinion Online (POLL) on the Dialog system.

The perceived importance of U.S. relations with Moscow gave aspiring politicians at the national level a foreign policy issue on which they could make themselves known and on which they could potentially gather votes. From the early 1970s until the late Reagan years in the 1980s, in particular, the President's powers to conduct policies towards the communist rival were somewhat curtailed by an interventionist Congress. Congressional conservatives were particularly active in questioning parts of the détente policies being conducted during the first half of this period (Destler, 1984). An important aspect of these internal disagreements over the making of policy towards the Soviet Union was the risk of conservative attack on policies that could be portrayed as "soft on communism", which meant that the decision makers had to be careful in their analyses of the policies carried out by Moscow lest they appear to be too trusting.

As an academic field of study, Sovietology in the United States was linked to events in international politics, and, in particular, to developments in the Soviet Union (see Dallin, 1982). Sovietology thus received its first strong impetus for expansion, after languishing for several decades, during the Second World War. A second period of expansion in the discipline followed the debate, often termed the "scare", in the United States after the Soviet launch of the Sputnik satellite in 1957, which preceded any U.S. launches of the same kind. There was also another aspect that made for more research in this field: an expansion of "area studies" in U.S. universities during the same period.

The relationship between political power in Washington and the Sovietologists was close. Several observations should be made about this connection. The first is that, with some simplification, one can distinguish between two types of Sovietologists in the United States. The first group can be labelled the "pure academics". These are scholars who saw it as their task to study their subject with the common methods of the social and human sciences. The debate between these scholars was conducted, in the main, the way all academic debates are, by way of scientific exchange of constructive, and sometimes not so constructive, criticism.

In a second group there were a number of scholars who regarded it as important not only, or perhaps in some cases not even mainly, to conduct scientific research on the Soviet Union. Instead, these scholars concentrated many of their efforts on taking part in the public debate on the Soviet Union and on how the United States ought to pursue its policies towards that country. It would be an exaggeration to say that the line between these two categories is razor-sharp and that the scholars in the second group were not academics. However, the distinction between the two groups contains important ingredients of both aspects (Cf Nygren, 1992, pp. 90-91 and Cohen, 1985, pp. 8-19).

Second, in the United States the older generation of Sovietologists contained a large and influential group with roots in the former Soviet Union and its neighbouring countries. How one judges the importance of this fact may vary, but it is beyond debate that this has influenced the way Sovietology was conducted in the United States throughout the post-Second World War years (Nygren, 1992, pp. 80-82).

Third, there are strong indications that Sovietology became politicized during the Cold War in the United States (Ibid., pp. 74-82 and Cohen, 1985, p. 8). The crucial question for this study is not whether or not there existed a link between politics and Sovietology, which is beyond doubt, but instead whether or not this link meant that Sovietology, and individual Sovietologists, were unduly influenced by politicization in the conduct of their research. There is no self-evident answer to this question. Indeed, it sometimes seems as if there are as many views on this issue as there are scholars who have commented upon it. Still, it should be remembered that Soviet studies in the U.S. were never as directly under political pressure as the study of China had been in the aftermath of the Maoist victory in 1949 (Daniels, 1998, pp. 117-118). The latter meant that several diplomatic as well as academic specialists on China lost their jobs in the 1950s and 1960s (Kahn, 1976). Nothing similar happened to the experts on politics in Moscow.

The question of politicization is linked to a fourth factor, the relatively open door between the government and the centres and universities at which the Sovietologists worked. It seems safe to say that the doors between academe and government were more open in the United States, certainly than in France or Sweden, with Great Britain being a case that is somewhat harder to judge (Nygren, 1992, pp. 96-127 and Cohen, 1985, p. 10). This can be linked to the fact that the U.S. polity is more open than the French one, in particular (Rosenau and Sapin, 1994, pp. 126-127).

Partly as a reaction, on the part of a younger class of scholars, to the perceived politicization of Soviet studies and of the dominance of the émigrés in the U.S., there developed in the 1970s an alternative school within Sovietology called revisionism. Scholars belonging to this school, such as Jerry Hough or Stephen F. Cohen, treated the Soviet Union not primarily as a unique case, but rather as a case that could and should be studied using methods common to social science, such as comparative methods.[4]

---

[4] See Cohen, 1985, pp. 27-37. I return to this issue in section 2.3.2.

Sovietology was much more developed in the United States than in either France or Sweden. In the case of Great Britain, the difference in comparison with conditions in the U.S. was more marginal since Sovietology was strong on the British Isles as well. In addition to the academic research, the Soviet Union was analysed in different U.S. government departments, including several intelligence agencies (Nygren, 1992, p. 15. Cf. Prados, 1982; Richelson, 1987 and idem., 1995; Freedman, 1986). The volume of analysis produced by these agencies was vast, and its results are gradually being made public as this book is completed some ten years after the collapse of the Soviet State.

In summary, relations with the Soviet Union were crucial to U.S. politics from around 1947 until the end of the Soviet State. This meant that relations with the other superpower to a significant extent impinged upon even domestic politics. Partly because of this, the study of the Soviet Union, Sovietology, developed with strong ties to the polity. This field of study, however, grew to encompass a very large number of scholars from different disciplines. Ties between government and Sovietology were also strong in that academic experts on the Soviet Union were fairly regularly recruited into the government in various capacities as experts. Together with other factors specific to Sovietology in the U.S., this meant that the discipline was relatively politicized. The question is whether or not this closeness to politics also meant that the study of politics in Moscow was politically biased. This remains a controversial issue ten years after the collapse of the Soviet Union. This book cannot conclusively answer this question, but it will attempt to address it.

2.2.3 Great Britain

One fundamental aspect of British relations with Moscow is the extent to which they must be seen in a bilateral and a multilateral context. London has pursued its policies towards this potential adversary both as a mostly faithful follower of the United States, on the one hand, and as a reliable partner of a multinational security alliance, NATO, on the other (Clarke, 1990, pp. 71-73. Cf. Light, 1990 and Clark and Wheeler, 1989, particularly pp. 5-8 and 230-242). It is difficult to overestimate the role of the Atlantic organization for British security and defence policy during the post-Second World War period (Richardson, 1993, p. 159).

The role of British nuclear weapons should be mentioned in this context as well. As Michael Clarke notes, there are several rationales behind the British nuclear forces. One of these has to do with their deterrent value in relation to a perceived risk of aggressive action by the Soviet Union during the Cold War. A second rationale has to do with the link that the British nuclear deterrent was perceived as forging between Britain and a "necessity" for the United States to become involved in a war in Europe if British nuclear forces were attacked.[5]

It thus seems only natural to point out the interlinkages between Washington and London, at the very least when it comes to the official policies towards Moscow during the period after 1945 until the fall of the Berlin Wall. It appears fair to say that Great Britain has been the least independent in its policies towards Moscow of the four countries studied in this book (Clarke, 1993, p. 73). A country that aimed to be loyal both to the United States and to the security organization that Washington dominates, that is NATO, simply did not allow itself the freedom of manoeuvre that other nations had in their security policy. For Washington, London's relationship with Moscow was often regarded as a litmus test of the loyalty of its allies. There was a more or less explicit demand from the U.S. that its allies respect its policies towards Moscow during the Cold War, and that the allies adjust aspects of their policies if Washington considered it necessary. In this sense, London was the most loyal ally that the U.S. had during the Cold War period (Keeble, 1990, p. 318).

This loyalty towards the United States does not mean, however, that Soviet affairs were not followed seriously in an independent way in the United Kingdom. One indication of this interest is that developments in the Soviet Union, and in Eastern Europe more broadly, were well covered in the British media in the 1980s, not least in editorials in elite newspapers (Clarke, 1993, p. 81). There is also a historical aspect of British hostility towards the Soviet State, a hostility that dates back to the very foundation of the communist regime in Moscow in 1917 (Ibid., p. 70). The dominant role of the Conservative (Tory) party, particularly during the period studied here, also meant that there was strong animosity between dominant British views of society and the Soviet model of collectivism. In this respect, the United Kingdom was similar to the United States. One difference between the two Anglo-Saxon nations from this perspective is the important role of the British Labour party, whereas a similar party representing democratic socialism is totally lacking in the United States.

---

[5] For a comparison between the British and French nuclear deterrents see M. Clarke (1993): "British and French Nuclear Forces after the Cold War", *Arms Control*, special issue: "Rethinking the Unthinkable: New Directions for Arms Control". The section referred concering British motives for possessing nuclear weapons is at pp. 119-120.

In British politics more broadly it has been the national defence role of nuclear weapons that has been a point of controversy between the two main parties, Tories and Labour, rather than any significant differences in their respective analyses of and policies towards the Soviet Union (Bullard, 1990, pp. 137-140). These diverging views on nuclear weapons were, however, connected to some differences in emphasis in the two parties' analyses of and proposed policies towards Moscow from 1979 until 1983/84. But as Mrs Thatcher showed an increasing interest in détente with the Soviet Union under Mr Gorbachev, and as Neil Kinnock started to move his Labour party back towards the mainstream of British politics on the nuclear issue, the two parties' differences in emphasis on these issues gradually lost importance.

Relations with the Soviet Union were, however, always controversial in Britain ever since the creation of the Soviet State. In 1924 a Labour government was brought down over a scandal relating to relations with Moscow (Andrew and Gordievskij, 1990, pp. 89-90) and during the 1980s there were several high-profile and controversial spy affairs. While Britain thus seems to have been the country in my sample in which relations with Moscow played the second most important role in terms of domestic politics, I would argue that in terms of the competition for political power at the highest level, these issues were still more important in the U.S. between 1947 and 1991.

When it comes to scholarly study of Russian affairs in the United Kingdom, there were, once again, important differences with the experience of the partner in what used to be known as the "special relationship". In contrast to the United States, it appears that there was a split between two main schools in British Sovietology from about 1945 until at least the 1970s. E. H. Carr, whose approach to the study of the Soviet Union after about 1945 can only be classified as sympathetic to the Soviet system, inspired one school. Carr was nevertheless, it must immediately be added, a very serious scholar. Clear anti-Sovietism, rather than a real scholarly approach, for a very long time dominated a second school of studies on the Soviet Union in Britain. Jonathan Haslam, in his essay on British Sovietology, captures some of the flavour of the basic disagreements: "In Oxford, the study of the Soviet Union never really existed to serious and sustained research until the early 1970s. It housed the counter-revolutionary culture of émigré George Katkov and former intelligence officer David Footman: non-Soviet Studies, one might say" (Haslam, 1996, p. 19).

These basic divisions, together with a general funding situation that was much worse than in the United States, combined to make Sovietology a less significant subject in Britain than it was in the United States (Morrison and Seton-Watson, 1982, pp. 32-49). This does not mean that there were not several excellent scholars in Great Britain after the Second World War who were specializing on the Soviet Union, simply that the number of such scholars was considerably larger in the U.S.

The linkages between the Soviet specialists and policy makers were less developed in Britain than in the U.S., with fewer academics moving into the corridors of power. There seem, however, to have been some fairly extensive informal links, with scholars being invited to brief the decision makers, and with foreign policy specialists who were serving in government following the scholarly debate fairly closely. One indication of this type of activity was the meetings and conferences that regularly took place at Chatham House, where the Royal Institute of International Affairs (RIIA) is located (Webb, 1994, pp. 84-85, 89-90). This indicates that the interaction between British Sovietologists and politicians was, in all likelihood, greater than was the case for either France or Sweden. Still, this type of informal contact is different from the "revolving door" practice in the United States, where scholars move from academe to government in numbers that are hardly equalled in any other Western democracy. To my mind it is clear that the role of U.S. Sovietologists during the period under study here was an obvious example of such practices.

In summary, in British domestic politics, relations with the Soviet Union were very important, but probably not quite as vital as they were in the United States. To an important extent, policies towards Moscow were conducted in the bilateral context of the "special relationship" with Washington, on the one hand, and in the context of the NATO alliance, on the other. In domestic politics, British relations with the second superpower were again important, but not salient to the degree that they were across the Atlantic Ocean. British Sovietology was initially much less significant than in the U.S. and was characterized by very serious disagreements. Only in the 1970s did serious scholarship on the Soviet Union, based in several academic centres, start. Gradually, this led to Britain's producing a number of important scholars in Sovietology. While their total number never approached that in the U.S., still, Britain produced a significant number of specialists on the Soviet Union. There was some interaction between the British Sovietologists and policy-making circles, even if this seems to have been on a smaller scale than was the case in Washington, particularly in terms of the scholars being invited to join the government. Overall, it is probably true to say that the British security debate was the second most open among the four countries studied here. In British media, Soviet and East European affairs were closely followed.

2.2.4 France

France has, ever since the presidency of Charles de Gaulle, carried out a security policy that has had very distinctive traits. The most important of these are well summarized by Philip H. Gordon: "...the absolute need for independence in decision making, a refusal to accept subordination to the United States, the search for grandeur and rang, the primacy of the nation-state, and the importance of national defense" (Gordon, 1993, p. 3).

Ever since President Charles de Gaulle in 1966 adopted an independent French policy towards Moscow, this bilateral relationship has been regarded as one of the prime examples of France's independent foreign policy. This independence has been tempered, to be sure, by France's membership in the Atlantic Alliance, but French statesmen and politicians have jealously protected its main aspects (see Hassner, 1988; Cf. idem., 1990, pp. 170-171). The French nuclear deterrent, permanently regarded by French politicians as independent of the U.S., in contrast to the case in Britain, has only contributed further to France's independent streak with respect to its foreign and security policy (Clarke, 1993, pp. 123-124).

The presence of a strong French Communist party with excellent relations with Moscow throughout most of the post-war period meant that French policy towards the Soviet Union was made in a very different domestic political context from that in the two Anglo-Saxon countries treated previously. During perhaps the first three decades after 1945, this factor, later combined with De Gaulle's foreign policies, made the Soviet Union more popular, or at least clearly less negatively perceived, in France than in the U.S. and Great Britain. This fairly positive view among the greater public changed substantially, however, in the 1970s. The reaction in France to what is called the "Solzhenitsyn factor" was much greater than in most other Western societies. The revelations about the Soviet Gulag served to change dramatically French perceptions of the Soviet Union for the worse. This was true for individuals of a leftist outlook as well as for more conservative people (Friend, 1989, pp. 74-80; cf. Hazareesingh, 1994, p. 33).

The French public can thus be characterized as being perhaps the most negative in the Western countries when it concerns their assessments of developments in the Soviet Union from about 1974 (Hassner, 1988, p. 43).

It is to be noted that this scepticism continued at least during the first two years of the Gorbachev regime (Ibid., p. 47). This fact is linked to aspects peculiar to the French political debate, not least the influence of philosophers and other intellectuals on the flavour of these debates (Hassner, 1988, pp. 26-27; cf. Hazareesingh, 1994, pp. 33-62).

The academic study of Soviet affairs had been less developed in France than in the United States and the United Kingdom. There are few, if any, examples of academic centres specializing on Soviet research in France, unlike in the other two countries just discussed. The Soviet specialists that existed in the social and human sciences were spread over a number of research establishments, particularly in the Paris area (Bonamour, 1982, pp. 50-59). I have found no scholarly treatment of the question of whether this, coupled with the strong centralization of both policy making and policy debate on security issues in France, meant that French Sovietologists played a very different role as compared to those of their colleagues in the two Anglo-Saxon countries. Evidence of a clear dividing line between, on the one hand, foreign policy practitioners within the government, and, on the other, specialists on international relations, indicates, however, that French academics in the international relations field only very rarely had official positions (Girard, 1994, p.55). The impression one gets as a scholar studying the role of French academics in foreign and security policymaking is that the scholars played a much smaller role than did the specialists at the French foreign ministry. My tentative assessment, from what little evidence the secondary literature gives, is that Sovietology was less important for the debate on relations with the Soviet Union in France certainly than in the U.S., but probably also than in Britain. It remains an empirical question for this book whether any such differences can be detected concerning the Gorbachev period.

In summary, relations with the Soviet Union were important in French domestic politics, but clearly less so than was the case in the U.S., and also less than in Britain. There is no evidence in the literature that the careers of leading politicians were made or broken based on public views of relations with Moscow in French politics, as was sometimes the case in the United States and, on occasion, even in Great Britain. The French public's views of the Soviet Union can be characterized as perhaps the most sceptical of the four countries analysed here, at least as seen from the mid-1970s until the late 1980s. French Sovietology seems to have been conducted by a fairly small number of individual specialists, not centred at any one specialized institution but spread throughout the French academic research system. With the clear dividing lines between the making of French security policy and academic analysis, it is fair to say that the border between politics and academia has been the most impenetrable in France of the countries that I have analysed in this book.

2.2.5 Sweden

During the period after the Second World War until it joined the European Union in 1995, Sweden opted for a foreign policy that combined internationalism, epitomized by a very strong commitment to the United Nations (UN) system, with a non-aligned strategy in security matters. This has meant that Sweden has regarded itself, and has sometimes acted as, a nation that somehow was situated between the two superpowers, that could even serve as a bridge between them. Symptomatic of this position was a domestic debate, particularly during the 1950s and early 1960s that took "the third point of view", a point of view that was equally close to — or distant from — Washington as it was to Moscow (Gerner, 1997, particularly pp. 148-149).

These factors have coincided with the fact that, for Sweden, first Russia, and then the Soviet Union since the early 18th century, always loomed as, first, the most dangerous enemy in war and, later, as the greatest potential risk to the country's independence and security. This meant that relations with Moscow consistently figured in Swedish domestic politics (Åselius, 1994). Partly because Sweden is a small country situated very close to the Soviet Union, there has only rarely been any great domestic controversy in Sweden over the relationship with its large neighbour to the East. There have been exceptions when the domestic politics of the relationship have been quite controversial, but it cannot be said that relations with the Soviet Union have influenced Swedish domestic politics to the extent that was the case in the United States, and probably not even to the same extent as in Britain.

After about 1980, however, relations with Moscow became more politicized. This was mostly a result of a wave of submarine incursions into Swedish territorial waters (Agrell, 1986). These incursions were extremely difficult to stop, and it was almost impossible for the Swedish Navy to identify who the perpetrators were. In September 1981, however, a Soviet submarine was stranded inside Swedish territorial waters, fairly close to one of the most important Swedish naval bases. A large debate ensued on how best to handle the submarine incursions, of which there were repeated reports throughout the 1980s and into the 1990s. Due to the difficulties in identifying who piloted those submarines, there was also a very large domestic discussion on whether one could indeed pin the blame on Moscow for all, or even most of, those incursions. However, the submarine crisis increased Swedish fears of Soviet military might. It also clearly increased the salience of Swedish-Soviet relations in domestic politics. The debate on the submarine incursions continued in Sweden until the end of the 1990s. This author is convinced that there were indeed a number of submarine incursions in Swedish territorial waters and that Soviet submarines carried these out.

Swedish public opinion can generally be characterized as having been wary towards the Soviet Union. The fear of a country that posed a possible threat to Swedish sovereignty can only be said to have increased during the 1980s with the submarine incursions, which were widely identified in the public debate as having been controlled by the Soviet Union.[6]

The Swedish analysis of the Soviet Union was carried out in many quarters in the country due to the importance of Moscow for Swedish security. There have been many such analysts inside the Swedish defence establishment, broadly seen. The academic study of the Soviet Union has also been fairly well developed, although, Sweden being a small country, the number of academic specialists was not very large. Those that did exist worked in different academic disciplines at various research institutions throughout the country (Tarschys, 1984, pp. 16-18).

Perhaps the most apt characterization of Sweden would be to place it somewhere between the United States, on the one hand, and France, on the other, when it comes to the importance of the relationship with Moscow for the domestic political context of foreign policy making. It has been important, but not vital. There are reasons to believe that the bilateral relationship between Stockholm and London, on the one hand, and Moscow, on the other, had a domestic salience, in terms of the struggle for power, that was roughly comparable.

One basis for this conclusion is the controversy that resulted from the series of submarine incursions, of which only two were officially certified as having come from the Soviet Union. As mentioned, this resulted in a very wide-ranging debate in Sweden which prominently included discussions on how one should regard the Soviet Union and what Sweden should, and could, do in response. No other series of events had similar ramifications for French relations with the Soviet Union during the period of Gorbachev's incumbency. The second basis for my conclusion that relations with

---

[6] See G. Stütz (1990): *Svenskar i den internationella förändringens tid (Swedes in the Time of International Change)*, Report No. 155, Styrelsen för Psykologiskt Försvar (National Board of Psychological Defence), April 1990, table 8, p. 54. A few examples from the data series where a representative sample of Swedes responded to the question "To what extent do you regard Sweden as being under threat from the Soviet Union?" illustrate opinions in Sweden during the 1980s. The submarine stranded outside the Swedish naval base at Karlskrona in the autumn of 1981 produced a jump from 14% who regarded the Soviet Union as a threat before the incursion, to 34% in the weeks following the event. During several subsequent surveys using the same question, the response rate hovered above 30% on every occasion until 1987, when it dropped to 19%. In 1990, it dropped still further, to 7%.

Moscow were more salient in Swedish domestic politics in the latter half of the 1980s than was the case in France is the fact that Russia has traditionally been the most important enemy of Sweden during the last 300 years. This image of Russia as an enemy was largely carried over to the Soviet Union when that country changed name and political structure following the Revolution in 1917. In this case as well, the image of Russia/the Soviet Union as *the* enemy/adversary was more strongly etched into the Swedish polity than has been the case for either France or Great Britain. The latter two countries have fought many more recent wars than Sweden and, consequently, the images prevalent in those two societies of who constitutes "the enemy" are much more diffuse.

2.3 Sovietology

2.3.1 Introduction: The Nature of Sovietology

One fundamental question that has to be addressed when one attempts to assess the record of Sovietology in studying the final years of the Soviet Union concerns the nature of the field of study itself. Was this a unique discipline, or was it "merely the specialized study of the Soviet Union from the standpoint of the familiar academic disciplines: history, economics, geography, occasionally sociology and anthropology, and above all political science" (Daniels, 1998, p. 115)? In one of the most thorough assessments made of Sovietology — Rethinking the Soviet Collapse — the authors differ in their conceptions. Some, like the editor Michael Cox, choose to call it a "discipline" while others choose the view that Sovietology was merely another case of the familiar "area studies" approach, and thus only one case among several. As a political scientist — who is not a Sovietologist — makes this assessment, it is undertaken in terms of the methods and principles of political science. I remain agnostic on the true nature of Sovietology, but I feel that it must be possible to assess it in the terms commonly used by political and to some extent other social scientists. This work thus does not aim to provide the final overall evaluation of Sovietology, but it does intend to evaluate the significant differences that existed among its practitioners concerning their analyses of Gorbachev's reforms and the Soviet collapse.

One of the peculiarities of the study of the Soviet Union can be presented by way of an analogy between the study of politics and life in 20th century Soviet society with that of the historical study of medieval times. In both cases, a crucial aspect that always needed the close attention of scholars was the scarcity of relevant and reliable empirical evidence. The art was, on the one hand, to hunt for as much empirical data as possible, and, on the other, to be critical constantly about the reliability and the validity of this data. From what scarce data then finally emerged, the scholar had to make empirical assessments and generalizations.[7]

A second characteristic peculiar to Sovietology was that many of the specialists on Soviet affairs, particularly during the first decades after the Second World War, were exiles from the East European states that had come under Soviet domination after 1945. This increased the risk of influences on academic research on the Soviet Union that had other origins than purely scholarly ones.

A third characteristic was the fact that the object of their study, the Soviet State, was typically very controversial and often regarded as menacing within the political realm of the countries in which the scholars worked. This meant that there was a constant risk that these scholars might take what could perhaps be called extra-academic aspects into consideration when publishing their analyses. A particularly severe problem was present when these three factors existed simultaneously, and thus served to reinforce each other.

These three factors, together with other relevant aspects, worked together to create a context that is well described by Robert Jervis: "[A]lthough mountains of governmental propaganda and scholarly books have been written about the Soviet Union, I suspect that few people have been convinced by anyone else's argument" (Jervis, 1981, pp. 56-59). Jervis' assessment focused on the situation in the United States, but the gist of his message can be applied to the other three countries analysed in this book as well.

2.3.2 The Problem of Evidence in Sovietology

The study of the Soviet Union was different from the study of most other countries in the 20th century. One fundamental reason for this was that a party that regarded itself as the central actor in Soviet society controlled the Soviet State, and believed that it was the task of this party to control information. In particular, the leadership regardedthis control as essential when it came to the processes by which political

---

[7] For a discussion of this problem, with special emphasis on the field of Soviet foreign policy, see J. Snyder (1984/85): "Richness, Rigor, and Relevance in the Study of Soviet Foreign Policy", *International Security*, vol. 9, especially pp. 95-99. Cf. Ron Hill (1998): "Social Science, 'Slavistics' and Post-Soviet Studies", p. 205.

decisions were made in the Soviet Union.

The basic consequence of this fact was that the study of Soviet politics and society was hampered by a lack of reliable empirical data. Specialists in the social sciences and the humanities were forced to resort to research practices that resembled those of archaeologists and historians of medieval times. In other words, based on what fragments were available on Soviet politics and the actors involved, the Sovietologists pieced together what information they had in chains of logical reasoning which aimed at reaching an overall understanding of the aspects of politics and society that were studied. This way of proceeding no doubt produced many penetrating academic studies of Soviet society, but such a situation, with a basic lack of data, also constantly meant that what little data existed was apt to be analysed very differently by different scholars. Basic disagreements about fundamental scientific approaches exist in other fields of the social sciences and the humanities as well, to be sure, but this tendency was probably stronger in Sovietology than in almost any other field of social or human science. How, indeed, can one expect there to be consensus, or even a few competing but parallel lines of reasoning, when the empirical data are not only scarce, but also subject to fundamentally different scientific analysis?[8]

2.3.3 The Émigrés and Sovietology

The second aspect of Sovietology relevant to this brief overview of the characteristics of a discipline concerns the personal origins of many of the leading scholars in the field. It is especially characteristic of the United States, first, and the United Kingdom, second, that an influential proportion of particularly the first generation of Soviet specialists after the Second World War were born either in what was Russia until 1917, or in states that were adjacent to what became the Soviet Union. It certainly cannot be claimed that such ancestry, by itself, invalidates the scholar as a serious academic student of Moscow and its politics. What is claimed, however, is that this fact, particularly if combined with the other two factors mentioned above, further served to distinguish the field of Sovietology from most other specialties in the social and human sciences in two respects. The first is that the East European ancestry of many early Sovietologists worked to make their basic attitudes towards the Soviet State both very negative and very

---

[8] Cf. R. Herrmann (1994): "Policy-Relevant Theory and the Challenge of Diagnosis: The End of the Cold War as a Case Study", *Political Psychology*, vol. 15, pp. 118-119. Herrmann concentrates on Sovietologists' attempts to analyse Soviet perceptions and motives, but his discussion is valid for the study of the Soviet Union more broadly as well.

hard indeed to change. The second is that these facts also tended to make such Sovietologists extremely dismissive of colleagues in the field, as well as of policy practitioners, who did not share their fundamentally negative and unchanging views of Soviet politics. These characteristics served to make several of the Sovietologists in this category active participants in the policy debate on the nature of the Soviet State and the implications that this nature ought to have for the policies their adopted country ought to pursue towards Moscow.[9]

It is clear that this tendency for the field to be dominated by a group of "émigrés" gradually became less characteristic for Sovietology, even in the U.S. and the U.K., as the 1960s turned into the 1970s. As previously mentioned, one factor contributing to the diminished influence of the émigrés was the fact that an alternative view of the Soviet Union emerged among scholars, particularly in the U.S., who were called the revisionists. Part of the motivation for the basic position of these academics was that they disagreed with several of the basic assumptions that characterized the established study of Soviet affairs in the United States, in particular (Cohen 1985, pp 27-37 and Nygren, 1992, pp.51-53). At the risk of oversimplification, one dividing line between the "traditionalists" and the revisionists was that the former regarded the Soviet Union as *sui generis* whereas the latter insisted that the same social scientific approaches that were used for the study of other countries could also be applied to Moscow.[10] It could be added that the clash between traditionalists and revisionists was probably strongest in the United States. This is one reason why one prominent revisionist — Jerry Hough — has been included among the U.S. scholars studied in this book. The trend of the decreasing influence of émigrés continued in the 1980s and the 1990s, when a new generation of scholars entered the academic scene.

2.3.4 Politics and Sovietology

A third aspect that was also very characteristic of the field was the close relationship between Sovietology as a subject and the policies towards Moscow pursued by the governments of the countries in which

---

[9] In the British case this tendency is discussed in J. Haslam (1986): "E.H. Carr and the Politics of Soviet Studies in Britain", especially at pp. 19-22. In the U.S. case the role and influence of the "émigrés" is treated in S. Cohen: "Scholarly Missions: Sovietology as a Vocation", in Cohen, 1985, pp. 1-12, 29; and in Nygren, 1992, pp. 80-82 in particular.
[10] This focus on social scientists – particularly political scientists – is due to this author's own belonging to this discipline. I believe, however, that the same general point applies to other academic disciplines as well.

the scholars worked. Given the important role of the Soviet Union in the foreign and security policies of all four nations scrutinized in this book, it was all but inevitable that the scholarship on the Soviet State would be used in some fashion in the political debate concerning the relationship between Moscow and the Sovietologist's home capital. When, as is the case for Sovietology, other characteristics of the discipline made it almost impossible to find anything approaching scholarly consensus even on basic parameters for study, the propensity to use Sovietology in the domestic political debate on the analysis of politics in the Soviet Union increased further. At the same time, these two characteristics taken together also increased the willingness of Sovietologists in many cases to take a step from the arena of academic analysis to the arena of policy debate. Indeed, the material surveyed for this book is replete with polemic articles written by many of the academic specialists, in which they brought their scholarly viewpoints to bear on the domestic policy debate, often in a fashion that contrasts their own "correct" perspectives on Soviet affairs with the "delusions" allegedly suffered by other scholars as well as by the official decision makers and their advisers.

This special characteristic of Sovietology makes it hard to differentiate between what should properly be regarded as scholarly analysis and what is better characterized as polemics related to policy. No such effort has been made in this book; the scholar has been considered as a scholar throughout his or her work, whether it is a 500-page volume on Soviet foreign policy or a short piece on the op-ed page of a newspaper. Indeed, I see no way of reliably making such a distinction between polemics and academic analysis in Sovietology. What I have attempted to do in this respect, particularly in my analysis of Sovietologists in chapter 5, is to give my personal assessment when the scholar has clearly moved from the scholarly over to the polemic.

The result of these conditions contributed to an analysis of the Soviet State that was marked by very fundamental differences among the scholars. Indeed, in reading the materials produced by the Sovietologists that I have surveyed during my work on this book, I have often reflected on the fact that it seems as if these renowned scholars cannot possibly be writing about the same country, so utterly contrary are their analyses.

2.4 A Chronology of Soviet Affairs 1985-1991

This book concentrates on how events in the Soviet Union between 1985 and 1991, in particular, were perceived and analysed in four countries. As this time becomes more distant, it seems necessary to provide a brief overview of the events that occurred during these momentous six and a half years of Soviet and Russian history. I make no claim to be a full-fledged Soviet specialist; I have simply tried to use the knowledge gathered during my readings for this book in spelling out what I believe to have been the most important events and processes.[11]

As mentioned before, the process analysed by the actors in this book ostensibly started on March 11, 1985, when the Politburo of the Soviet Communist party elected Mikhail Sergeyevich Gorbachev to succeed the deceased Konstantin Chernenko as party leader. It is less easy to identify the second notable step in the chain of events. However, 1985 also witnessed the first summit between a U.S. President and a Soviet General Secretary since 1979. Gorbachev and Ronald Reagan met in Vienna in November of that year. If nothing else, the fact that the general mood of the summit seemed fairly pleasant served to at least somewhat dampen the tensions that had previously characterized the relationship between the superpowers.

In early 1986, Gorbachev issued a comprehensive program for the elimination of nuclear weapons to be completed by the year 2000. Despite some elements of flexibility, the program was largely dismissed in the West as propaganda (Garthoff, 1994, pp. 252-253).

A second event of 1986 was the Twenty-Seventh Congress of the Soviet Communist party in February-March. The main report given by the party leader, Gorbachev, to the Congress was quite different in important respects to what had been the case for similar reports at earlier congresses. This was particularly true of the report's discussion of foreign policy and international affairs in general. This was one of the first occasions, if not the first, on which the Soviet leader used the new concepts of "global interdependence" and "mutual security" (Ibid., pp. 255-262).

The next event of political importance was the severe accident at the nuclear power plant in Chernobyl on April 26. The new leadership proved uncertain of how to handle the resulting international fallout, and lower-level bureaucrats did nothing to improve Soviet openness when it came to prompt and correct information to the outside world. Gorbachev, in a public

---

[11] This chronology will not be burdened with extensive notes. My sources, however, include R. L. Garthoff (1994): *The Great Transition: American-Soviet Relations and the End of the Cold War* (Washington, DC: Brookings); J. F. Hough (1997): *Democratization and Revolution in the USSR 1985-1991* (Washington, DC: Brookings); D. Oberdorfer (1991/92): *The Turn: From Cold War to a New Era* (New York: Touchstone) and, for the Bush years, M. R. Beschloss and S. Talbott (1994): *At the Highest Levels: The Inside Story of the End of the Cold War* (London: Warner Books).

speech given some three weeks after the accident, tried to put the matter into perspective. The speech included strong criticism of the West's presentation of the affair which, according to Gorbachev, amounted to "an unrestrained anti-Soviet campaign"(Ibid., p. 277). In all, the episode was a setback for Gorbachev's effort to open up the Soviet system. In retrospect, some analysts have identified Chernobyl as a crucial event in the downfall of the Soviet Union. It should be remembered that it was not commonly so perceived at the time.

During the summer of 1986 there occurred a few bizarre events involving spying. First, in August the FBI arrested Gennady Zacharov, who worked with the Soviet United Nations (UN) staff. Then, the Soviets arrested the American journalist Nicholas Daniloff. These events occurred against the backdrop of public discussions on whether or not there should be a second summit between Reagan and Gorbachev. After strong collaboration between Foreign Minister Shevardnadze and U.S. Secretary of State George Shultz, in particular, the matter was resolved and the two men were expelled from the respective countries in which they had been residing.

After the spy affair was resolved, there was another bizarre event: the summit that wasn't called a summit; the three-day meeting between the two superpower leaders and their most important advisers at Reykjavik, Iceland. In retrospect, this must truly be seen as one of the turning points in the Cold War. The discussions about nuclear arms were wide-ranging to a degree that had no real precedent in the period since the two countries had both acquired nuclear arms. It was very unclear afterwards precisely which proposals had really been discussed between Reagan and Gorbachev. The most radical proposal appeared to have been presented by Reagan to the effect that all nuclear arms ought to be abolished, but it was not clear whether this proposal had ever been officially introduced in the negotiations. What was clear, however, was that the two powers had come fairly close to very wide-ranging nuclear arms control agreements. In the end, the parties could not agree on one crucial point: the Soviet insistence that the U.S. agree to observe the Anti-Ballistic Missile (ABM) Treaty of 1972 in a way clearly limiting the ability of the U.S. to continue its research efforts into the possible establishment of a comprehensive Strategic Defense system (SDI). President Reagan refused to agree to any restrictions that would cripple his dream of establishing an SDI system.

After the perceived failure of the Reykjavik summit there were several months of fairly confused public discussion of the implications of the negotiations and their perceived failure, both in the two countries and more globally. One new sign that the Soviet leader was indeed different from his predecessors was that he released the Soviet dissident Andrei Sakharov and the latter's wife from several years of detention in Gorkij. This occurred in December 1986. The next month, dozens of other political dissidents were released from various forms of detention. That same month, January 1987, there was a Central Committee Plenum at which Gorbachev launched his drive for democratization inside the party. In February, the Soviet leader resumed the initiative on the negotiations into nuclear arms, which had come to focus on the issue of medium-range ballistic missiles in Europe (the acronym used was INF for Intermediate-range Nuclear Forces). The Soviet leader had previously proposed the elimination of these forces, but these proposals had always been tied to several forms of restrictions — on SDI, on British and French nuclear forces, etc. That same month Gorbachev for the first time proposed that the INF missiles should be abolished on both sides without any strings attached at all. In the middle of this year the first really important economic reform was also adopted, the Law on State Enterprise. This increased the flexibility of these enterprises, but it is also assessed as having contributed to the explosion in wages that happened later.

In the run-up to what became the very significant Washington summit of December 1987, diplomats from the two superpowers began to consult with a regularity that had few, if any, precedents in bilateral relations after the start of the Cold War around 1947. It is not possible, or relevant, here to cover all the details of the multifaceted negotiations carried out between the two parties during this time. Suffice it to say that there were many irritations, misunderstandings and setbacks. Most of these were, however, solved by the time Mikhail Gorbachev arrived in Washington on December 7, 1987. This summit meeting was very significant for at least two reasons. Substantively, it included the signing of the INF Treaty, which was the first time after the invention of nuclear weapons that the two superpowers decided to abolish a whole class of nuclear arms. Some critics pointed out that the total number of warheads taken out of active service only represented perhaps 3% of all the warheads held by the two countries. Still, the symbolic significance of the treaty was overwhelming. A second point that marks this summit as a crucial one in the process which gradually ended the Cold War was the behaviour of the Soviet leader and the reception he received from the U.S. media and the U.S. public.

Writing more than 10 years after the event it is hard to convey the novelty of these two aspects to readers who have little or no personal recollection of much of the Cold War period. Suffice it to say that previous Soviet leaders had been universally perceived outside their country as dour apparatchiks who understood nothing of Western society and who were only prepared to negotiate stiffly on points largely agreed to beforehand. In contrast, Mikhail Gorbachev was a new kind of Soviet leader. He could negotiate flexibly, and, most notable publicly, he knew how to charm a Western audience. When the Soviet leader got out of his limousine in Washington in December 1987 and started chatting with the public in the streets, this was something totally unprecedented in U.S.-Soviet relations. This incident, more than any other up to that point, brought home to large parts of the interested Western public that this was indeed a new kind of Soviet leader.

During 1988, there were new indications that Soviet policy was changing in a very profound way, both domestically and abroad. In foreign policy, the announcement first came that the Soviet troops intended to withdraw from Afghanistan, which had been invaded in late 1979. The formal UN agreement to this effect was signed in mid-April. The Soviet commitment to withdraw its forces by February 1989 was perceived as very significant by many observers at the time. This was because the Soviet withdrawal was seen as a break with the Brezhnev Doctrine, which had been the basis of Soviet behaviour in what it defined as socialist states for 20 years. Stated briefly, the Brezhnev Doctrine said that the sovereignty of socialist states was limited and that intervention was justified in such states if socialism was under threat. The exact significance of the Doctrine was unclear, but the Soviet withdrawal from Afghanistan was another unmistakable indication of a new and more flexible foreign policy.

Domestically, 1988 was also important for the Soviet Union. This was the year when many outside observers who followed Soviet affairs first became aware of the existence of an autonomous territory within Soviet Azerbaijan called Nagorno-Karabakh. Armenians overwhelmingly populated this piece of land. Starting in February 1988, there were disturbances and outright fighting between the Armenians of Nagorno-Karabakh and the Azeri authorities. The fighting gradually intensified into outright war between Armenia and Azerbaijan over control of the territory. This was not the first incident of nationalist violence under Gorbachev. A previous incident had occurred in December 1986 in Kazakhstan as a result of Gorbachev's decision to replace a Kazakh regional party chief with a Russian. Riots occurred as a result. Starting in the autumn of 1987, the dedicated observer could also note tendencies for the nationalist feelings in the Soviet Baltic republics of Estonia, Latvia and Lithuania to make themselves heard. Stalin had occupied these small, independent republics in 1940.

There were also the first real public indications in the spring of 1988 that Gorbachev's domestic position was less than totally secure. Most debated was the publication of an article in the Soviet newspaper *Sovjetskaja Rossiya* in March. This article was severely critical of Gorbachev's policies and it was published as the Soviet leader embarked upon a visit to Yugoslavia. After some three weeks, Gorbachev and his reform allies unleashed a media counteroffensive of their own, but the impression that there existed serious domestic opposition to the Soviet leader and his policies was a lasting one.

The relationship between Ronald Reagan and Mikhail Gorbachev probably culminated with the former's state visit to Moscow in May-June 1988. In retrospect, this summit is probably more important for the extensive media coverage it generated of the old "Cold Warrior" visiting the "enemy's" capital than for any substantive agreements signed. Still, the positive media atmosphere, as well as the obvious personal warmth between the two men, indicated a very different superpower relationship as compared to previous decades.

On the very day that President Reagan arrived in Moscow, May 28, a second law on economic reform was adopted. This was the Law on Economic Co-operatives. While the question of private ownership was still a controversial one at that stage, the new law on co-operatives can only be characterized as very liberal indeed. Together with the Law on State Enterprises from the previous year, it opened up the Soviet economic system to a significant degree. It should be underlined that these two laws were only the most important moves among several. Together, the economic reforms under Gorbachev were of importance not only in opening up the economy, but also in terms of their contribution to creating a more liberal climate in the political sphere.

As Reagan became more passive in the second half of 1988, in anticipation of his stepping down from power in January 1989, Soviet-American relations became less dynamic. This continued during the first few months in office of the new U.S. President, George H.W. Bush. Not until May of that year was George Bush prepared to move "beyond containment" as he put it.[12] This new commitment did not result in any immediate new agreements between the two countries, however. The dramatic events surrounding the new Soviet leader during the first half of 1989 were, instead, domestic. In March, elections, with some democratic aspects, were held to a Congress of People's Deputies. This was to consist of 2,250 members, of which a third were nominated by the Communist party and party-dominated

---

[12] Garthoff, 1994, p. 380. Bush used the phrase in a speech on 12 May 1989, in Texas.

organizations. Still, the elections meant a clear step towards Western-style democracy in the Soviet Union. Perhaps more important than the election itself was the fact that during the first month of its session, the proceedings of the Congress were televised. Here, for the very first time since 1917, Soviet citizens could see political issues openly debated in front of a national audience. The Soviet public was transfixed, and productivity was estimated by some as having declined by some 20 per cent during the month the transmissions lasted (Garthoff, 1994, p. 391). In retrospect, this seems to have been another crucial step in opening up the Soviet political system and, perhaps, in speeding the gradual decline of the communist system as Soviet citizens became aware that it was possible to discuss these issues without any real fear of reprisal.

The other crucial events in 1989 concerned Eastern Europe. Gorbachev had gradually relaxed direct Soviet control over the countries that were members of the Warsaw Pact, even if this was not publicly reported to any great degree. One more obvious indication of the new Soviet line in this respect was the tolerance accorded to the efforts of Polish leader Wojciech Jaruzelski to open up the Polish political system, by August to the point where he accepted a new government led by Solidarity, the worker's movement which had opposed the Communist party in Poland since 1980. Next in line was Hungary, where the leadership of what was in effect the Communist party decided in the summer both to change the name of the party to the Hungarian Socialist Party and to pursue policies more commensurate with the new name. In early autumn, Hungary opened its borders and let those who wanted to escape to the West do so. Throughout the spring and summer of 1989, Gorbachev continued with his speeches on a "common European home" and similar themes. He never once publicly threatened to act against the reform policies in either of the two countries mentioned.

Most important, however, were the changes in East Germany. Gorbachev visited the country in early October on the occasion of the German Democratic Republic's (G.D.R.) 40th anniversary. In one public speech while there, Gorbachev gave indications that the G.D.R. leaders then in office, notably the aging party leader Erich Honecker, had to adapt to the changes that were occurring throughout Europe. Around this time, demonstrations against the G.D.R. regime became a regular event in some cities. Honecker was soon replaced, but nothing could stop the disintegration of the state. On November 9, 1989, in a highly symbolic move, the East German leadership decided no longer to prevent G.D.R. citizens from crossing the border from East Berlin into West Berlin. The Berlin Wall, that despicable testament to the East-West conflict erected in 1961, was for all practical purposes destroyed. The solution to the "German question" and the subsequent reunification of Germany is worth its own treatment, but this is not the subject here. Suffice it to say that Germany continued to be an important issue even after the fall of the Berlin Wall. There were several negotiating rounds between various actors, particularly during the first half of 1990, involving then-Chancellor of West Germany Helmut Kohl and Gorbachev, as well as so-called four-power talks (the U.S., the U.S.S.R., France and Great Britain), referring to the four powers that occupied first Germany and then Berlin after the Second World War.

If 1989 was thus a year of enormous changes for the Soviet Union, both domestically and abroad, the focus shifted somewhat to internal events in 1990. The disturbances in various outlying republics had continued throughout 1989, with Nagorno-Karabakh only the worst of several trouble spots. In terms of the survival of the Soviet State as a unified entity, it was, however, perhaps not the shootings and massacres in several republics that were the most threatening, but rather the developments in the three small Baltic republics of Estonia, Latvia and Lithuania. There, a new generation of leaders was gradually coming to power. These represented overwhelming public sentiments, which initially supported greater autonomy within the Soviet Union but which gradually moved towards more radical steps ending with a clear strategy aiming towards full independence for each republic. Lithuania was first to go with a declaration of independence issued on March 11. Gorbachev, who obviously failed to understand the depth of nationalist feelings in the three republics, threatened intervention and suspended oil deliveries, but the Lithuanians refused to budge. The outside world was also keeping a close eye on these events. In late June, Moscow lifted its oil embargo, while the Lithuanian leadership agreed to suspend its declaration of independence temporarily. In May, Latvia also declared independence.

Meanwhile, in Russia itself domestic protest against the communist leadership increased. In February, perhaps a quarter of a million people demonstrated for democracy on the streets of Moscow. In March, Gorbachev and the communist leadership deleted Article 6 of the Soviet constitution, which had hitherto guaranteed the "leading role" of the Communist party (Garthoff, 1994, p. 420). At the same time as Gorbachev was working to diminish the so-far completely dominant role of the Communist party in the Soviet Union, he successfully created a stronger personal position for himself by creating a stronger Soviet Presidency. In 1990, there were also new elections, this time based in the respective republics. The most important of these were held in Russia, the heartland of the superpower. The fact that these elections were more or less free – at least in the Russian Republic – by democratic standards was of enormous significance, both in terms of opening up the domestic politics of the country and in terms of strengthening the platform of Boris Yeltsin as an alternative to Gorbachev (Hough, 1997, pp. 278-314). Yeltsin had been dropped from candidate membership in the Politburo of the Communist party and as mayor of Moscow in the winter of 1987-1988 after having been brought to the central Moscow leadership by Gorbachev. Yeltsin then made a political comeback in several stages. First, he won an impressive victory in the election to the Congress of People's Deputies in March 1989. Second, Yeltsin became what amounted to President of Russia in May 1990.

On May Day in Moscow, in another totally unprecedented event, Gorbachev and the rest of the leadership were booed off the stage at Red Square at the traditional demonstration. It was by now obvious to all interested observers that the domestic politics of the Soviet Union were changing at the very foundation. The fact that the Supreme Soviet of the Russian Republic declared sovereignty in June only made matters worse for Gorbachev.

In December 1989 at Malta, and in May-June 1990 in Washington, there were two summits between Gorbachev and the new U.S. President, George Bush. These resulted in several agreements, notably on the role and policies of the new Germany that was gradually taking shape. Ever since Gorbachev came to power, the two superpowers had also discussed further agreements on the control of strategic nuclear arms. These issues, however, proved more intractable than the ones surrounding the medium-range missiles in Europe. On conventional arms, a crucial treaty was signed at a large international conference in Paris in November 1990. This was the Conventional Forces in Europe (CFE) Treaty. It originated in the Helsinki process, which had started in the first half of the 1970s. The CFE Treaty meant limits on several kinds of conventional forces, including personnel and tanks. On October 3, Germany was formally unified.

In 1991, Gorbachev's domestic troubles continued. In the first few weeks of the year there were brutal military repressions in Lithuania and Latvia against the forces there working for independence. Gorbachev, who had received the Nobel Peace Prize in the autumn of 1990, was severely criticized both by democratic forces inside the Soviet Union and from abroad for, at the very least, failing to restrain the military forces, or, at worst, ordering the repressive action. Early 1991 also saw confirmation that Gorbachev had turned away from some of his more liberal policies, notably those concerning economic reform. The radical economic reform package that the Soviet leader had endorsed some months earlier was now in practice abandoned. Meanwhile, nationalist unrest continued in several republics. Gorbachev was working towards the goal of a new Union Treaty to replace the old one establishing the Soviet Union. He was joined by only 9 of the 15 Soviet republics.

As these events were going on, and as Gorbachev was having yet another summit with Bush in Moscow in late July, there was plotting under way in Moscow against the Soviet leader. On the afternoon of August 18, as Gorbachev was in his vacation dacha in Foros in the Crimea, an unexpected delegation arrived from Moscow. They informed Gorbachev that several of the leaders whom he had personally chosen had decided to declare a national emergency. Gorbachev was told to either sign a decree to this effect or to resign. The Soviet leader refused to do either. The ill-conceived coup collapsed in a couple of days. The leader who gained most from the aborted coup was Boris Yeltsin, who showed personal courage in standing up to the plotters in Moscow.

After Gorbachev returned to resume power some days later, nothing was ever the same in terms of his political power. Yeltsin quickly showed who now had the initiative in Soviet politics. Gorbachev gradually became convinced that he had to resign. The Soviet leader did so on December 25, 1991 and, at the same time, the Soviet flag was lowered for the last time from the Kremlin wall, and the Soviet Union ceased to exist.

Chapter 3
Official Analysis of the Soviet Union 1985-1991

3.1 Introduction

One characteristic of the early speeches given by the politicians after Gorbachev came to power is a clear caution regarding whether or not something important was going on in Moscow. Another shared feature is the general blandness of the statements analysed. To find penetrating analysis in any official speech made by a senior politician on important events in other countries seems to be a rare exception, if one is to judge from the material reviewed in this study. This does not mean that all the speeches forming the basis for the analysis in this chapter were uninteresting. On the contrary, they offered remarkably deep insights into the self-perception of the French officials and into the willingness of U.S. officials to discuss sensitive issues in the foreign and security policy spheres.

3.2 France

> D'abord il faut prendre en compte que la première visite faite en Occident par Monsieur Gorbatchev, c'est la France...Je vois là, d'abord, une marque de considération de la France. Sans doute cette marque de considération est-elle partagée par des autres.[1]
> First you have to note that the first visit made by Mr. Gorbachev to the West it is to France....To me that signifies a sign of esteem for France. This note of esteem is no doubt shared by others.[2]

Foreign Minister Roland Dumas marked one essential feature of French foreign policy: the perceived need for the country to play a special role.[3]

[1] Foreign Minister Roland Dumas, September 22 1985, *La Politique Etrangère de la France* [HEREAFTER: *Politique Etrangère*], September 1985, p. 29.
[2] All translations from the French are by the author.
[3] Among the large literature on French foreign and security policy, the contribution by P. H. Gordon (1993): *A Certain Idea of France: French Security Policy and the Gaullist Legacy*

This is one of the characteristics that recurred often in the French speeches on relations with Moscow. Throughout the early years, the French politicians often expressed reservations to the effect that it was the "style" rather than the substance of policy in Moscow that had changed after March 1985.

In 1986, events in Soviet foreign policy occurred blow by blow. In the French politicians' evaluations of these events, for example in the case of the Reykjavik meeting, they were more optimistic than officials from many other countries, insisting that the meeting was something other than a total failure, that it instead meant clear progress in U.S.-Soviet relations. At the same time, however, they also underlined France's special position in this process:

> Q. Depuis longtemps, les Européens se plaignent de ne pas être assez présents dans ce dialogue: est-que vous avez une idée pour faire avancer les choses?
> [François Mitterrand]: Non, moi je ne m'en plains pas du tout. Il y en a qui s'en plaignent, je les ai entendus. C'est une discussion entre Soviétiques et Américains, cela n'engage qu'eux...Mais nous n'avons pas, nous, à être engagés dans ce type de discussion tant que les deux superpuissances n'ont pas ramené à une niveau plus raisonnable, plus proche du nôtre, leur armement (François Mitterrand, *Politique Etrangère*, 28 October 1986, p. 141).
> Q. For a long time, Europeans have complained that they are not present in this dialogue: do you have any suggestion to remedy this situation?
> [Mitterrand]: No, I do not complain at all. There are those who complain, I have heard them. This is a discussion between Soviets and Americans, it only concerns them....But we do not have any place in these discussions as long as the two superpowers have not drawn down their levels of armaments to a level that is closer to ours.

For official France there was thus no problem with the fact that the two superpowers discussed their strategic armaments and other matters without France. France would only be ready to participate in such talks when the two superpowers had reached agreements that limited their nuclear armaments to levels approaching those that France possessed at that stage.

In a speech in Geneva in February of 1987, M. Jean-Bernard Raimond, the Foreign Minister, delved deeper in his analysis of the events in Moscow than most other politicians analysed in this book:

(Princeton: Princeton University Press) presents as good an overview as any of "the Gaullist legacy" in French foreign and security policy. See pp. 1-22 and 163-185 in particular. For a a list of the politicians holding the foreign policy positions in the four countries analysed during 1985 through 1991, see appendix 5.

Nous savons tous...que c'est une affaire extrèmement difficile que de toucher
à la nature du système. Ils auront un choix à faire, pourront-ils le faire?
Auront-ils la volonté nécessaire? Je ne le sais pas, je ne suis pas sûr qu'ils le
sachent eux-mêmes.
Sur le plan extérieure, ils ont beaucoup réfléchi, ils sont conscients du
monde extérieur, ils sont conscients de l'image de l'Union soviétique à
l'extérieur. A mon avis, ils savent parfaitement que l'affaire de l'Afghanistan
nuit terriblement à leur image.
Les nouveaux dirigeants soviétiques sont très soucieux de l'image de leur
pays et leur tâche est à cet egard difficile. Ainsi, ils se présentent toujours
comme des hommes de négociation, mais jusqu'à présent, on peut dire
que fondamentalement, ils n'ont pas changé les positions soviétiques sur la
substance (Jean-Bernard Raimond, Foreign Minister, *Politique Etrangère*, 19
February 1987, p. 121).
We all know...that it is an extremely difficult matter to touch the nature of a
system. They have a choice to make, can they make it? Do they have the will
necessary? I do not know, I am not sure that they know themselves.
On issues of foreign policy, they have done a lot of thinking, they are
conscious of the world outside, they are conscious of the image of the Soviet
Union abroad. In my view, they know perfectly well that the Afghan situation
has tarnished their image terribly.
The new Soviet leaders are very concerned with the image of their country
and their task is very difficult in this respect. They thus always present
themselves as men willing to negotiate, but up to now one can say that
fundamentally they have not changed Soviet positions.

This speech contained several elements characteristic of the French
analysis of Soviet politics in general, and foreign policy in particular,
throughout most of the Gorbachev years. The first characteristic was a
willingness to acknowledge that the first step towards fundamental changes
had been taken in the Soviet Union: the new leadership was clearly aware
of fundamental problems in the system, domestically as well as in foreign
policy. This awareness on the part of the Soviet leaders, in the French
estimation, went as far as an acknowledgement that changes to the basic
structure of the system were probably necessary. The second insight was that
even if there was an awareness in Moscow of the magnitude of the problems,
it was unclear, even to the new Soviet leaders themselves, whether they
had the willingness, and/or the ability, to really change the "nature of the
system" as deeply as was necessary in the view of French officials. The third
insight was that the Soviet leaders also realized that their global image was
bad, in particular referring to the contribution that the Afghan adventure had

made to the deterioration of this image. The link was made between the domestic problems, particularly in the economic sphere, and problems in foreign policy. The French politicians presented a view in which both the Soviet domestic policy sphere and the foreign policy sphere had their own independent needs for basic reform.

Towards the end of his brief period as Foreign Minister, which lasted only 27 months, Jean-Bernard Raimond returned to the subject of changes in the Soviet Union.[4] For the French Foreign Minister, speaking in the spring of 1988, the Soviet Union, like all other systems, was possible to change. It was not condemned, as so many analysts believed, to either stagnation or total collapse. Once a process of real change started, however, as it had started at the time the Foreign Minister spoke, there was a risk that it would lead to a development that could result in the destruction of the entire system. A second element in M. Raimond's analysis was that the Soviet leadership was also busy correcting what he termed two foreign policy "mistakes" of the previous regimes: the instalment of the intermediate-range nuclear missiles SS-20 in Europe, and the invasion of Afghanistan. In this sense, the French Foreign Minister identified two basic changes in Soviet foreign policy.

M. Raimond did not, however, detect any change in one of the fundamentals of post-Second World War Soviet foreign policy: "the extension of the Marxist-Leninist system to Eastern Europe". Even such a knowledgeable and insightful observer was thus unable to foretell what would happen to Soviet foreign policy, and to the status of the Central and East European countries, about 18 months later.

Even more notable is the fact that the French Foreign Minister failed to recognize the explosive potential of the nationalist issues in the Soviet empire as late as the spring of 1988. He even stated that there was a "consensus" on these issues in the Soviet Union, this despite the fact that there had already been fighting in and around Nagorno-Karabakh. His exact words on this topic are worth quoting:

> En Union soviétique il existe, qu'on le veuille ou non, un consensus fondé sur le nationalisme. Il peut y avoir des problèmes des nationalités, comme on le voit en Arménie ou dans les anciens êtats baltes, mais il n'en demeure pas moins que ce consensus existe.
> Or il en est bien différemment dans les pays d'Europe centrale. ...Précisément parce que ces pays ne connaissent pas le même consensus que l'Union soviétique et que, profitant de l'évolution de leur systême, ils

---

[4] See the long excerpts in appendix 3.

s'empresseraient d'échapper à la tutelle de leur protecteur (Jean-Bernard Raimond, *Politique Etrangère*, 20 April 1998, p. 66).
In the Soviet Union there exists, whether you want it or not, a consensus founded on nationalism. There may be problems with different nationalities, as we have seen in Armenia and in the former Baltic Republics, but still this consensus exists.
It is, however, very different in the countries of Central Europe....Just because these countries do not subscribe to the same consensus as the Soviet Union, and because of the evolution of their systems, these countries hasten to escape the tutelage of their protector.

It is notable that many of the politicians in the four countries analysed failed to understand, or at least to acknowledge publicly, the explosive potential of the nationalist issues for the future of the Soviet Union even fairly late, well into 1989.

During a visit to the United States, in connection with the annual General Assembly of the United Nations, M. Roland Dumas, the new French Foreign Minister after the victory of the socialists in parliamentary elections in 1988, gave his views on the reasons for why the great Soviet experiment had been undertaken in the first place (Roland Dumas, ibid., 27 September 1988, p. 46). M. Dumas noted that the Soviet system had deteriorated to a degree that was no longer tolerable, notably in the economic sphere. He also said that this had ramifications not just for the domestic situation inside the Soviet Union, but also for that country's continued status as a superpower.

M. Dumas went on to observe that the reforms under way could become difficult to carry out, as the logic of the internal reforms led towards decentralization, something very hard to implement in a system built on very strong centralization of power. The French Foreign Minister also noted that despite the difficulties for reform in the Soviet Union Mr. Gorbachev had, in working for fundamental reform: "...pour lui une grande force: la volonté réformiste de nombre de dirigeants, jointe à la formidable aspirations des nouvelles générations à plus de démocratie et de bien-être" (Ibid., p. 47) "...for him a great force: the reformist will of a number of leaders, tied to the great aspirations of the new generation for more democracy and well-being".

For official France, the explanation for the start of the reform process in the U.S.S.R. is thus to be found on what I call the state level of explanation, explanation II a, in table 1.2. In the French assessment, a new elite was being created, an elite that wished to change Soviet society profoundly.

During 1988, the French politicians more and more often tackled the question of where the process of change in the Soviet Union would end.

Foreign Minister Dumas responded in this way to a journalist's question in November 1988:

> A force de réformer le système, on finit par toucher sa nature. Voyez ce qui a été décidé pour l'agriculture. Il est évident qu'en ce domaine, les dirigeants soviétiques tournent le dos au système hérité de la Révolution de 1917. Les baux de très longue durée... ne remettront pas en question la propriété du sol, mais dans la pratique, cela y ressemble beaucoup. Jusqu'où ira cette évolution? Je ne pense pas qu'il soit dans l'esprit des dirigeants de l'URSS de revenir sur ce qui a constitué la base même du système économico-politique soviétique. Mais j'imagine assez bien que les améliorations et les transformations auxquelles ils procèdent, conduiront à terme à une modification du système. Je constate que certains dirigeants de l'Est ne sont pas scandalisés à l'idée de voir un jour le pluripartisme dans leur pays (Roland Dumas, Interview in *Quotidien de Paris, Politique Etrangère*, 16 November 1988, pp. 32-33).
>
> In the process of reforming a system you end up by touching its very nature. Look at what has been decided for agriculture. It is obvious that in this field the Soviet leaders have turned their back at the system they inherited from the Revolution of 1917. The long-term leasing system...does not raise the question of ownership of land, but in practice it resembles it a lot. Where exactly does this evolution lead? I do not think that the Soviet leaders have it in their minds to question the very foundations of the Soviet political-economic system. But I can well imagine that the improvements and the transformations that they are undertaking will in the end lead to a modification of the system. I note that some leaders in the East are not frightened by the idea of seeing a multi-party system in their countries one day.

M. Dumas was ready to anticipate that the end result of the reform process would be a "modification du système". The extent of this "modification" would, however, be limited in that the French Foreign Minister could not imagine any reforms that would touch upon the basic foundations of the system. There was, in other words, no anticipation here of the depth of the developments that were to follow, least of all any intimation of a coming collapse.

During November, 1988, M. Dumas was also ready to concede that what was happening in the Soviet Union might lead to a change in the fundamental security situation in Europe:

> Pour la première fois peut-être depuis l'immédiat après-guerre, une véritable diminution du niveau des forces sans affaiblissement de notre sécurité ne paraît pas hors de portée. Certes, au vue des équilibres existants, la

réalisation de cette espérance dépend plus de l'Union soviétique que des Occidentaux; mais pour la première fois, cette perspective n'est plus uniquement du domaine de discours, il n'est pas impossible qu'elle entre dans le champ de la réalité (Roland Dumas, *Politique Etrangère*, 18 November 1988, p. 42).

For the first time perhaps since the early period after the Second World War it seems as if a real lowering of our level of armaments seems possible without any weakening of our security. To be sure, when you take current imbalances into consideration the coming true of this hope depends more on the Soviet Union than on the West; but for the first time this prospect exists not only in the domain of speeches, it is not impossible that it may become reality.

For a Frenchman to state that the basic security of Europe, at least in the sense of levels of armaments, could really change indicates that the French political establishment realized that what Gorbachev was doing had potentially profound implications for the whole European security structure. Even if M. Dumas thus went far in his statement, we can still see that he was not yet convinced that the changes envisioned would be carried out; they were no longer impossible, but they were not yet finalised either.

In the late autumn of 1988 it is thus possible to conclude that the French officials were willing to concede publicly that the Soviet Union was in the process of fundamental change. In domestic politics this change was profound and irreversible, in the French estimation, whereas the changes in the foreign policy field were presented as potentially extremely important, but not yet irreversible.

One notable feature about the French reactions to what was happening in Moscow is that President Mitterrand was more cautious in his public speaking than were his ministers. This is illustrated in an interview with Soviet television made in November 1988:

Je suis très encouragé lorsque je voie cette direction prise qui est une direction courageuse, sans doute difficile. Difficile aussi à mettre en application parce qu'un immense pays comme celui là, avec des usages, des traditions, des structures, cela ne se modifie en un jour. Mais j'ai l'impression que c'est une bonne contribution à...rendre de plus en plus possibles l'établissement de relations normales et fraternelles entre les peuples et entre les Etats dès lors que la perestroïka, par example, serait arrivé à son terme. Je souhaite que cela réussisse (François Mitterrand, ibid., November 22, 1988, p. 50).

I am very encouraged when I see that the direction taken is a courageous one, no doubt a difficult one. Difficult also to put into practice because an immense country like that, with customs, traditions, structures, is not changed overnight. But I have the impression that it is a good contribution to...make more and more possible the establishment of normal and friendly relations between peoples and between States when perestroika, for example, has arrived at its goals. I wish that this may succeed.

M. Mitterrand was thus generally pleased with what was happening in Moscow. It was harder to find a clear assessment in his speeches that Soviet policies had indeed changed profoundly than it was in the case of his two Foreign Ministers.

In an interview with the regional press in France in February 1989, *le Président de la Republique* gave a fuller picture of his views of the Soviet leader, his problems and what the West could and should do to help him:

Une situation donnée, l'échec dramatique du régime soviétique et société, a produit un homme d'envergure capable d'exprimer les nouveaux besoins et d'en tirer les conséquences jusqu'à leur terme. Quelle que soit la suite des événements, Mikhail Gorbatchev aura modifié le cours de l'histoire.

Q. Quelles sont ses motivations?

R. Elles découlent de sa connaissance très aigüe de la réalité de son pays et du système dont il est aujourd'hui responsable. Devant le délabrement les institutions, l'étouffement des libertés et le désastre économique, je pense qu'il a longtemps réfléchi, là où il se trouvait, et qu'il se dit, approchant du pouvoir: 'le jour où je le pourrai, j'agirai.' Son action présente résulte de l'expérience vécue... (François Mitterrand, Newspaper interview, *Politique Etrangère*, 14 February 1990, p. 96).

In a given situation, the dramatic failure of the Soviet system and society have produced a man of stature able to express the new needs and to draw the consequences from that to their conclusion. Whatever may be the end of these developments, Michail Gorbachev will have modified the course of history.

Q. Which are his motivations?

A. They flow from his very acute knowledge of the reality in his country and its system of which he is today responsible. Facing the deterioration of institutions, the choking of liberties and the economic disaster, I think that he has contemplated for a long time in his position and told himself, as he approached power: 'the day I can act, I will act.' His current actions result from his experiences...

On the topic of what, if anything, the West might do to help the Soviet leader, the French President noted that little could be done in domestic politics, but "beaucoup" (ibid.) could be done to assist the Soviet Union in reforming its economy.

The French President chose to highlight the bad conditions in the Soviet Union as a cause of the reforms, as well as the personal recognition of this by Mr. Gorbachev, and the latter's extraordinary individual abilities. The analysis offered by the President in this quote approaches the specificity with which most Sovietologists approached the same topic. In the terms of table 1.2, the President offered explanations of the changes in Soviet policies that are suitably classified as level IV, the individual level. It is possible to detect both an aspect of cognitive factors, the realization on the part of Gorbachev that things were fundamentally wrong in some respects in his country in the mid-1980s, as well as some hints of the individual explanation, where the personal qualities of the Soviet leader were highlighted. The conditions of the Soviet State that Gorbachev encountered on taking power, that is, level II, the state level, in particular the economy, were also stressed.

When the confrontations started between the Baltic Republics and Moscow during the winter of 1990, the French government made a statement of support for the position of the Baltic Republics, a position to which it basically stuck throughout 1990 and 1991:

> ...la France n'a jamais admis l'annexion pure et simple en 1940 de la Lithuanie par l'URSS de Staline, c'est clair. Deuxièmement, le gouvernement de la France a salué comme il convenait la volonté clairement exprimée du peuple lithuanien de recouvrer son indépendance. Troisièmement et enfin, il a toujours été dit par le gouvernement qu'en raison de la complexité de la situation...il fallait rechercher les voies du dialogue et de la discussion. C'est la thèse que j'ai moi-même défendue et soutenue à l'occasion de chacune de mes rencontres avec les autorités soviétiques.
>
> Mais la situation se tend...Les dernières décisions du gouvernement de Moscou de réduire les relations économiques avec la Lithuanie peuvent être lourdes des conséquences (Roland Dumas, *Politique Etrangère*, 18 April 1990, p. 73).
>
> ...France has never accepted the annexation by Stalin's Soviet Union of Lithuania in 1940. Second, the government of France has appropriately saluted the clear willingness of the Lithuanian people to regain their independence. Third and finally, it has always been stated by the government that because of the complexity of the situation...the voices of dialogue and discussion had to be sought out. This is the thesis that I have myself defended and supported at all my meetings with Soviet authorities.
>
> But the situation is becoming more tense....The latest decisions by the Government in Moscow to reduce economic relations with Lithuania may have difficult consequences.

3.2.1 France: Conclusions

The magnitude of the changes carried out by Mr. Gorbachev met a sympathetic response in Paris. It is notable that these changes were more clearly discussed and evaluated in the speeches by the Foreign Ministers than in those by the President. It is possible to identify the late autumn of 1988 as the period when the French officials publicly conceded that the Soviet Union was in the process of undergoing fundamental changes. In the domestic sphere, these alterations were assessed as irreversible, whereas greater caution was displayed in the judgements on foreign policy. The statements in the latter policy sphere were still far-reaching if one considers the traditional French caution on basic security matters. The statement that the Soviet Union had indeed changed was never very clear-cut, but it was sufficiently explicit to warrant the conclusion that the autumn of 1988 was the turning point for official France in this respect.

The French explanation for why the reform process started in Moscow centred on the domestic situation, in particular the Soviet economy, which was noted as extremely inefficient and so weak that the existing system could no longer work to preserve a superpower status for the Soviet Union. M. Mitterrand also noted the special role played by the Soviet leader in changing his country decisively. In the terms of table 1.2 in this book, the French explanations of why the Soviet reform process started thus includes both explanation II b, state-level, mainly economic factors, as well as level IV, individual factors. In the latter respect, one finds elements of both a cognitive explanation — IV a, rethinking by a broader elite of which Mr. Gorbachev was simply the most important member, as well as of explanation IV b, the individual explanation. It was particularly M. Mitterrand himself who highlighted the latter perspective.

There were no clear-cut forecasts, much less any strict predictions, made by any of the French politicians. The non-socialist Foreign Minister Jean-Bernard Raimond, however, clearly discussed the future of the Soviet Union in at least one of his speeches. He was thus more willing to do so than was Roland Dumas, who both succeeded and preceded M. Raimond as Foreign Minister. Even though M. Raimond discussed the future in a way that generally strikes the reader who knows the outcome as foresighted, he made clear mistakes in his attempts to foretell the Soviet future. This is particularly true with respect to the nationalist issue, which in hindsight appears to be one of the most important explanations for the break-up of the Soviet empire. M. Raimond, as late as the spring of 1988, still maintained that there was a "consensus" on this issue in the Soviet Union in favour of maintaining the unified state.

A particular French foreign policy orientation manifested itself clearly in one respect in these allocutions. This was the tendency to note that France had a special role to play internationally, both generally and in its specific relations with the Soviet Union. It is hard to see how this tendency manifested itself in the specific analysis of Soviet affairs, however. In the case of the Baltic Republics and their striving first for autonomy and then independence, the French officials gave general support for the wishes of these Republics while urging that non-violent methods should always be used.

While the French speeches thus contained a sense of a particular French outlook on the world, it should be noted that this tendency rather had the character of a general foundation for the entire outlook on the world, as distinct from having any direct influence on the analysis of events in the Soviet Union.

3.3 Great Britain

In Great Britain Mrs. Thatcher made the now famous statement, "I like Mr. Gorbachev. We can do business together" (Shultz, 1993, p. 507) following a visit by Mr. Gorbachev to Great Britain in December 1984. This was four months before the Soviet leader became General Secretary of the Communist Party. The statement seems to imply a much greater willingness on the part of the British government to be flexible in its analysis of events in Moscow, and subsequently in its policy towards the Soviet Union, than really seems to have been the case, at least during the first three and half years of the new leadership in the U.S.S.R. Instead, the statements made by the London politicians subsequent to Mr. Gorbachev's accession to power were, in general, very careful.

A quote from Mrs. Thatcher herself, taken from a speech in Parliament in April 1987, captures the flavour of the language and the official analysis carried out by the British politicians throughout the first 3-4 years of Mr. Gorbachev's period in power.

> For the first time since the revolution 70 years ago, there is now an under-standing that the Soviet system, as it exists at present, is not working. It must become a more open society with a more incentive-based economy and more distribution of responsibility. We should welcome that change of

direction, and hope that increasing openness will lead to increasing discussion, and that that will lead to an increasing security with neighbours (*Hansard*, 2 April 1987, col. 1224).

Sir Geoffrey Howe, Foreign Secretary from 1985 through 1990, gave an assessment more directly pertaining to foreign policy in the same forum some two months later:

> It is indeed the impact of Mr. Gorbachev which enhances the prospect of change in the previously frozen immobility of East-West relations. I have no doubt that Mr. Gorbachev realises that he needs a stable international environment that will allow him to concentrate on his monumental task of domestic reform. There is some evidence that this realisation may be having some impact on his foreign policy decisions, but it remains far from clear that the full implications of this have been grasped by the Soviet leadership — far from clear that the destabilising ambitions and dogmas of past years have been abandoned (Ibid., 26 June 1987, col. 159)

In these early accounts of why the Soviet Union changed its policies under Mr. Gorbachev, the two British politicians thus explained the Soviet reform process by pointing to both the individual level of explanation, level IV, and to the state level, level II.

In a parliamentary debate on foreign affairs in November 1988, Secretary Howe offered a positive assessment of the process of change in Moscow, as well as some attempts to explain why that process started:

> It is refreshing to be able to explore, and often to diminish, our differences frankly and openly. Mr. Gorbachev has launched an historic process of political and economic reform in his country. His thinking has become more radical as he has come to realise the full extent of the overhaul that is needed. We welcome what Mr. Gorbachev is trying to do. If he succeeds, it will be an event of far-reaching importance for the Soviet Union and for the wider world. Surely we cannot be certain that he will succeed....The Soviet Union is not going to end up as a Western-style democracy. It is hard for Mr. Gorbachev to achieve democratic goals when the means at his disposal are essentially non-democratic. He wants to make the existing one-party system more efficient, not dismantle it (*Hansard*, 25 November 1988, col. 337).

The positive tone in the quote was somewhat counterbalanced by the fact that the Foreign Secretary continued by questioning why Moscow persevered in building such enormous amounts of new weapons every year, notably tanks. The main impression is still that the government in London by late 1988 looked quite favourably upon developments in the Soviet Union. The Foreign Secretary was, however, unsure about how far Mr. Gorbachev would reach in his efforts to reform the system. He also looked forward as far as stating that the end result would not be a democratic Soviet Union. The explanation for why the Soviet leader started this process of change, or at least the vague allusion in this respect, concerned the need for greater efficiency.

In an oral response to a question from a Member of Parliament a few months later, Geoffrey Howe linked the sorry state of the Soviet economy to the need for the authorities in Moscow to lower defence expenditures (Ibid., 11 January 1989, col. 837). This clearly indicates that, in the British perception, the need to reform the economy was one of the reasons behind the Soviet reform process. The Prime Minister, Margaret Thatcher, added another element to the explanation for why the Soviet reform process started when she noted in a parliamentary debate in November 1989 that "...these changes would not be happening were it not for President Gorbachev's courage and vision" (Ibid., 21 November 1989, col. 34).

Still another element in accounting for why the changes in the Soviet Union were undertaken, eventually resulting in such momentous events, was given by the new Foreign Secretary, Douglas Hurd, in January 1990: "The credit [for the changes in the East] does not go solely to Mr. Gorbachev; it must also go to the countries of the West, Europe and the United States, which stood firm at a time when the Communist dictatorships seemed impregnable" (Ibid., 10 January 1990, col. 939).

On the Baltic Republics' struggle for liberation, Prime Minister Thatcher, in a debate in the House of Commons in June 1990, supported the people of the Baltic States: "...we believed that the people of the Baltic states were entitled to the independence that they clearly wanted" (Ibid., 12 June 1990, cols. 137-138).

As the end of the Soviet Union drew near, Douglas Hurd still maintained that "It is not in the interest of the international community that the Soviet Union should entirely disintegrate, leaving no central authority to deal with those matters where central decisions are needed (United Nations General Assembly, 46th session, 27 September 1991, A/46/PV.8, p. 57).

In a debate in the House of Commons in early November 1991, Mr. Hurd took up the question of the Soviet disintegration:

...there is no doubt that the old system is smashed beyond recall. There is no doubt that its total failure has left the Soviet Union and the peoples of the republics in a disastrous state. The economy is disintegrating, the institutions are discredited, a very bad combination for any country or group of countries.

...So the centre will wither away, not as Engels imagined it would, but because of the fierce assertion of sovereignty in different forms by one republic after another (*Hansard*, 1 November 1991, col. 123).

3.3.1 Great Britain: Conclusions

The official British analysis of Soviet foreign affairs changed fairly remarkably by the autumn of 1988, after several years of scepticism concerning whether or not the Soviet process of change was really serious. By that time, however, Foreign Secretary Geoffrey Howe made the assessment that Moscow had indeed changed. He still hedged on his judgement, however, thus making a less clear-cut appraisal than his French colleague made at roughly the same time.

The British government gradually developed a fairly complex explanation of why, in its view, the great process of change in the Soviet Union started. This includes both the power perspective, explanation I a; the badly functioning socialist economy, explanation II b; as well as both individual-level explanations, the cognitive factors in explanation IV a, and the individual explanation, IV b. As in the French case, it is notable that it was the politicians at the pinnacle of power, M. Mitterrand and Mrs. Thatcher, who highlighted the "unique" and "courageous" qualities of their Soviet counterpart.

One feature that contrasts the British and French treatment of the Gorbachev years is that the British officials presented no really distinctive angle on the British-Soviet relationship. My assessment is that this supports my initial belief that the government in London would tend to hew closely to whatever was said and done in Washington when it came to relations with Moscow. One aspect that clearly shows this is that the Thatcher government highlighted the importance of successful policies on the part of the Western Allies as being one of the causes behind the changes undertaken by Mr. Gorbachev. There was no sense of this latter aspect in the official French material.

3.4 Sweden

In 1985 there were no official Swedish statements regarding the policies of the new Soviet leader. The meeting in Geneva between General Secretary Gorbachev and President Reagan was noted in a positive light. Concerning Swedish-Soviet relations, a quote from Foreign Minister Lennart Bodström shows the importance of the submarine crisis:

> The serious Soviet violations of Swedish territory have created problems in our relations with the Soviet Union.
> We have resolutely protested against these violations. We have also had a direct exchange of opinion with the Soviet Union. We have made it clear that we aim at good, correct and friendly relations. The basis must be respect for our national sovereignty and the inviolability of our borders (Foreign Minister Lennart Bodström: *Speeches and Statements in Swedish Foreign Policy 1985* (Stockholm: Foreign Ministry, 1986, November 26, 1985, p. 89. Cf. Prime Minister Olof Palme, ibid., December 12, 1985, pp. 94-95).

The very first specific Swedish reaction to General Secretary Gorbachev's new policies came in a speech by Prime Minister Olof Palme in February 1986 in a debate in the Swedish Parliament:

> The government has with interest noted General Secretary Gorbachev's proposal regarding the abolition of nuclear arms before the year 2000. We welcome the Soviet decision to prolong the moratorium on nuclear tests.[5]

The first time any more broadly based assessment of the new Soviet policies was made by a Swedish politician was when the new Swedish Prime Minister, Ingvar Carlsson,[6] gave a speech in February 1987:

> From the Soviet Union there are signals regarding the need for a renewal of Soviet society. New ways are being tried to get the Soviet economy moving again. The terms of the official discussion are being enlarged. The problems of now and of yesterday are discussed with more sincerity. Several important Soviet personalities — scientists, cultural personalities and others...have been allowed to leave their forced inner or external exile. We welcome all moves in this direction with satisfaction.

---

[5] Prime Minister Olof Palme: *Utrikesfrågor: Offentliga dokument m.m. rörande viktiga svenska utrikesfrågor 1986 (Foreign Policy Issues)* (Stockholm: Foreign Ministry, 1987), February 5, 1986, p. 37. All translations from Swedish are by the author.
[6] Prime Minister Palme was assassinated on February 28, 1986.

The ambitions of the new leadership to change and influence are obvious. How far it wants to go and can go down this road, and what repercussions its internal policies may have on other states, is something that we know less about. We are firmly convinced that a freer exchange of thought and people across the borders would benefit all the peoples of Europe. That we follow the developments in the Soviet Union, not least for this reason, is a matter of course (Prime Minister Ingvar Carlsson, *Utrikesfrågor*, February 6, 1987, p. 21).

In this speech, as in a speech by Foreign Minister Sten Andersson in Parliament one month later (Foreign Minister Sten Andersson, ibid., March 18, 1987, p. 5) the Swedish government acknowledged that things were indeed happening in Moscow. The processes that had been started were interesting for Sweden, both concerning the changes that they might lead to in domestic politics and for the consequences these could have for relations with other states. The tone of this assessment was more positive, particularly concerning the domestic reforms, than was the case in any of the other three countries at this point in time, early 1987. It should be added that the difference in this respect is not huge, particularly in relation to the British government. Still, the assessment about the positive intentions of the reformers in Moscow was clearly more pronounced in Stockholm than in London at this time. I regard this as support for my hypothesis that analysts in states where democratic socialism is strong – such as Sweden – were more apt to notice changes of a domestic nature in the Soviet Union early, as compared to analysts in countries where democratic socialism is less important.

During the second half of 1987, Under Secretary of State for Foreign Affairs Pierre Schori made an analysis of the Soviet situation that went a bit further than had been the case up to that point:

We have no illusions regarding this internal process in the Soviet Union. There has been no sudden change there concerning the virtues of political pluralism. But there is a growing realization that stagnation and decline will continue, with serious repercussions not just for the standard of living of the Soviet people, but also for the position of the Soviet Union globally, if economic policies are not corrected...
Which consequences the developments in the Soviet Union may have for other European governments remains to be seen. But one should be well mired in the ices of the Cold War, if one doesn't see glasnost and perestroika as something positive, not just for the Soviet Union, but for Europe as a whole (Under Secretary of State for Foreign Affairs Pierre Schori, *Utrikesfrågor,* October 1, 1987, p. 37).

The causes of the Soviet reform process were identified as being a fear of economic stagnation at home, with negative consequences for the country's position abroad. There was still caution, however, about the extent of the changes both domestically and in external policy. In no sense could one detect a clear statement that momentous and lasting changes had occurred in Soviet foreign policy – in the Swedish assessment – by the autumn of 1987. The first attempt at an explanation of the causes behind the Soviet reform process thus highlighted both cognitive factors, realization by the elite of the sorry state of affairs in the Soviet Union, and the bad conditions at the state level themselves. The explanation was thus focused on what I call level IV a, the individual level – cognitive factors, and also included level II, state-level aspects.

In a speech made in the spring of 1988, the Under Secretary of State for Foreign Affairs went one step further in his positive analysis of the Soviet reforms, this time with particular emphasis on foreign policy:

> After the coming to power of Gorbachev, the traditional Soviet rhetoric regarding disarmament has changed. It now expresses more concrete, pragmatic ideas. This new rhetoric and its ideas must be tested without any preconditions. We must take Gorbachev at his word, but at the same time check thoroughly what the declared Soviet willingness to disarm is worth in concrete negotiations...
>
> We don't know where the processes of change in the Soviet Union may lead. But Gorbachev's perestroika and glasnost mean that the old system is being questioned as never before. There is surely no intention to introduce democracy in the Soviet Union. But perestroika and glasnost are expressions of a longing to change the communist system in a fundamental way...
>
> By now 'new thinking' permeates foreign policy in Gorbachev's Moscow. In a joint declaration issued at Gorbachev's visit to Yugoslavia in March 1988, the parties affirmed that no one had a monopoly on how to interpret socialism. One can only hope that this is the first careful step by the Soviet leader away from the Brezhnev doctrine (Pierre Schori, ibid., April 21, 1988, pp. 40, 42-43, 44).

The Under Secretary of State for Foreign Affairs was now willing to discuss more fundamental aspects of Soviet international behaviour. He found reasons for hope that there had been lasting changes, or at least that such lasting changes were under way, in both disarmament policy and in the Soviet position regarding the Central and East European countries, hitherto epitomized by the Brezhnev doctrine. But, even in the spring of 1988, the official Swedish position, although positive, was still reserved; while acknowledging that there were hopeful signs of change in Moscow, both domestically and internationally, and that the West must try to respond, it was also alert to the possibility that these changes may not last.

In the Social Democratic government that was in power from Mr. Gorbachev's accession to power in 1985 until October 1991, the assessment of the changing global and regional situation, in foreign policy terms generally, and more specifically in terms of security policy, was to a large extent carried out by the Under Secretary of State for Foreign Affairs Pierre Schori. Prime Minister Ingvar Carlsson gave fairly few detailed speeches on foreign and security policy, and thus on developments in the Soviet Union. The more broadly based speeches on foreign policy during the time analysed here were mostly given by the Foreign Minister throughout most of that period: Sten Andersson. Mr. Andersson, however, gave much more emphasis in his speeches to developments in foreign regions such as Southern Africa and the Middle East than he did to what must be regarded as the most important process of change with strong and direct implications for Swedish foreign and security policy for four decades.

In November 1988, there was a debate in the Swedish Parliament on "Sweden's Relations with the Baltic Republics". It is remarkable that no member of the Swedish government took part in this debate (Riksdagsprotokollet (Proceedings of the Swedish Parliament) Prot. 1988/98: 30, 23 November 1988, pp. 36-57).

It is hard to avoid the conclusion that this caution about addressing a subject that was clearly sensitive to the authorities in Moscow supports my hypothesis to the effect that analysts, particularly officials, in weaker countries tend to be more careful regarding sensitive subjects than analysts in stronger nations. The Swedish government's treatment of the Baltic issues thus gives clear support for my first hypothesis in table 1.4. Sweden is a small country whose leaders believed that they had to be careful about assessing issues that were perceived as sensitive in a neighbouring state that these leaders also saw as a potential threat to Swedish security.

The first speech given by the Swedish Foreign Minister himself that featured any real assessment of what had been happening in the Soviet Union was given in December 1988:

> Perestroika and glasnost are directed towards greater openness. A development of society in a democratic direction has been started. The purpose of Gorbachev's reform process is to try to get a communist system to survive. The goal is to give the Soviet economy a vitality and strength that is great enough to make the country a superpower in other fields than just the military one.

We don't know where these reforms may lead. We don't know how far they can be taken.

But what is happening in the Soviet Union now is just what Europe's democracies have been hoping for decades. It is the beginning of a demolition of the Stalinist system...

We will not accept what is happening in the Soviet Union uncritically. We shall assess the developments there and the initiatives and proposals that come from Moscow carefully and realistically.

But we shall take Gorbachev seriously. That is in our own interest as well (Foreign Minister Sten Andersson, *Utrikesfrågor*, 3 December 1988, p. 75. Cf. Under Secretary of State for Foreign Affairs Pierre Schori, ibid., 29 January 1989, particularly at pp. 24-25).

By December 1988 a bridge seemed to have been crossed in the Soviet Union, in the assessment of the Swedish government. Whatever might happen to the reform process carried out by Gorbachev and his associates, there was no longer any going back to the old system. Indeed, the process would, in the Foreign Minister's phrase, lead to a "demolition" of the Stalinist system. At the same time, it is interesting to note that the Foreign Minister emphasized his belief that Mr. Gorbachev's goals were to preserve the communist system in the Soviet Union and to strengthen that country's position as a superpower.

The December 1988 speech quoted above was important in the Swedish government's continuing appraisal of Soviet events. Before this speech, what was said regarding the reform process in the Soviet Union, in particular as it concerned foreign and security policy matters, was often vague. After the speech, the new statements delved deeper, concerning both policy spheres. It is also noticeable that both the number of speeches and their specificity increased for both the Prime Minister and the Foreign Minister after December 1988.

In February 1989, the Swedish Prime Minister, Ingvar Carlsson, in addition to making an assessment about the positive developments in the Soviet Union, introduced a note of caution (Ingvar Carlsson, *Utrikesfrågor*, 3 February 1989, p. 37). He indicated that for all the talk of perestroika in Moscow, what mattered to the population in the end were the practical results that this process would bring. Without real progress in the living conditions of the population, he noted, there was a risk that the process of change could be turned against the Soviet leadership.

A sign of the magnitude of the changes in Soviet foreign policy, and of the resulting changes in Swedish policies, was the speech given by the

Prime Minister in June 1989, on the occasion of the Tenth Baltic Scientific Conference in Scandinavia. In this speech, the Prime Minister assessed developments in the Soviet Union. He also characterized the relationship between Sweden and the three Baltic Republics. According to the Prime Minister, it was not enough to characterize the Swedish attachment to the Baltic Republics as "sympathy" (Ingvar Carlsson, *Utrikesfrågor*, 7 June 1989, p. 86).

The concern of Swedes for the predicament of the Baltic Republics went further than that. The Prime Minister also gave several examples of how the Swedish government, in terms of practical action, had worked to support the Baltic Republics. The goal that Sweden pursued with these policies was, according to the Prime Minister, to "contribute to the success of restructuring, not just in the Baltic Republics but in the Union as a whole. We wish to fashion our relations with the Baltic Republics in a way that strengthens the policy of restructuring" (Ibid., p. 88). In other words, by June of 1989 the Swedish government made no views known on the issue of greatest interest to the Baltic Republics: did the outside world support their independence or not?

The issue of the possible independence of the three Baltic Republics heated up in the fall of 1989. The Swedish Foreign Minister visited the Soviet Union, including the three Baltic Republics, in November of that year. There he made a famous statement in which he said, in effect, "the Baltic Republics are not occupied".[7] A few weeks later, the Foreign Minister made a statement in Parliament about his trip and about Swedish-Soviet and Swedish-Baltic relations:

> During my talks in Moscow the Soviet Government informed me very clearly that it has a strong interest in Sweden's development of relations withthe Baltic Republics in several fields: economy, culture, trade and tourism. Political contacts are also welcome. I was also told that Moscow doesn't object to Baltic participation in the conference on the Baltic Sea that I envision will take place next year.[8]

---

[7] Swedish policies towards the Baltic Republics from 1989 through 1991 are covered in Dag Sebastian Ahlander (1992): *Spelet om Baltikum* (Stockholm: Norstedts). Foreign Minister Andersson's visit is covered in chapter 6, pp. 57-76. The circumstances surrounding the quote are on pp. 67-68. It should be noted that this statement is not included in the official publication forming the basis for most of my analysis of Swedish verbal foreign policy.

[8] Foreign Minister Sten Andersson, *Utrikesfrågor*, 16 November 1989, pp. 34-35. Sweden's relations to the Baltic Republics were further discussed in Parliament on 4 December 1989. See Sten Andersson's response to several parliamentary questions in ibid., pp. 22-27.

In the parliamentary debate following his speech, the Foreign Minister stated that "Perestroika has equally good chances to succeed as to fail" (*Utrikesfrågor,* 16 November 1989, p. 40).In the late autumn/early winter of 1989, the Swedish government thus was willing to acknowledge that the problems in the Soviet Union were very large indeed. In a speech in December, Prime Minister Ingvar Carlsson also warned that the reform process in the Soviet Union might "encounter reversals" (Ingvar Carlsson, ibid., 2 December 1989, p. 135). The Baltic issues heated up again in the beginning of 1990, particularly concerning Lithuania. The Swedish government was now clearly supportive of Lithuania's striving for independence:

> The Lithuanian people have in free elections clearly expressed their will to exercise their legitimate right to national independence by forming their own independent state. We have welcomed and supported this striving. The questions raised by the developments must be solved through political means, through negotiations and without improper pressures according to the letter and spirit of the Helsinki accords (Statement by Prime Minister Ingvar Carlsson, ibid., 28 March 1990, p. 41).

As the Soviet crisis deepened, the Swedish politicians duly noted this in their public speeches. The Foreign Minister made clear, however, that "We can't foretell where this development may lead" (Foreign Minister Sten Andersson, ibid., 10 October 1990, p. 88).

3.4.1 Sweden: Conclusions

In the official Swedish analysis, the point at which Soviet foreign and security policies were stated to have truly changed was by late 1988. There were allusions to Soviet change several times before that, but it was at this point that the Swedish politicians registered that the changes could no longer be regarded as reversible. It should be noted that this timing is similar to that of the other two European governments studied in this book. In the British instance, however, there were more reservations made by the officials responsible for foreign policy than was the case for the other two European countries.

The explanations for the Soviet reform process were tackled in several speeches. The most important explanatory level in the analytic terms of this book is level IV a, the cognitive level. The Soviet leadership — Mr. Gorbachev was not very much singled out as an individual — on this view realized that their country was facing difficult problems. This level of explanation was then linked to both level II b, a weakening of the socialist economy in the Soviet Union, and level I a, a fear that the Soviet Union might lose its international position.

The Swedish politicians made no forecasts, in the strict sense of the term. Starting in early 1989 several notes of caution were issued, however. These were to the effect that the Soviet reform process must lead from verbal openness to practical reforms to improve the population's living standard, lest the people should turn against the reformist leadership.

A Swedish foreign policy orientation can be detected in these official assessments, in two respects. The first is that the Swedish Social Democratic government was more clearly positive towards the Soviet reform experiment at an earlier stage, early 1987, than was the case for either France or' Great Britain. The differences on this point are a matter of nuance rather than a matter of substance. Still, the sense of understanding regarding the aspirations of the Soviet leadership that was so prominent in the Swedish Prime Minister's speech in February 1987 was not matched by any statements on the part of the leadership in either Britain or France around the same time. It is also to be noted that this difference pertains more to a general attitude towards change in the Soviet system than it does to the assessment of changes in Soviet foreign and security policies. The more positive nuances detected in the early Swedish assessments of the general process of change in Moscow are here regarded as supporting the hypothesis that a Social Democratic government would be likely to detect the Soviet reform process earlier than is a non-socialist government. This positive initial attitude, however, did not lead to the Swedish government's stating unequivocally that Soviet policies had irreversibly changed any earlier than was the case for Great Britain or France. Instead, such statements were made at roughly the same time as in the other two European countries. The best explanation I can find for this relative tardiness is the sensitivity of the Soviet Union for Swedish security, historically, geographically and in terms of power. This aspect supports, in other words, my first hypothesis to the effect that analysts in smaller nations are more careful in assessing events in countries that are powerful and potentially threatening than are analysts in stronger nations.

If the Swedish government was thus early in being positive towards the Soviet reforms, the second part of my hypothesis on the importance of ideology doesn't receive any support. This was the hypothesis that a Social Democratic government would be slower in detecting the downward spiral of the Socialist Soviet government than would a non-socialist government. Contrary to this expectation, the Swedish Social Democrats were early in pointing out the risks of a domestic backlash inside the Soviet Union. These warnings started to be issued in early 1989.

A second manifestation of the Swedish foreign policy orientation is the emphasis given to events in the Baltic Republics and to Swedish-Baltic relations. Here, the Swedish government was torn between sympathy for the Baltic aspirations — first for autonomy, and then for independence — and caution in dealing with the superpower neighbour. As mentioned, the attention to these issues was — in the main — very careful until 1990 when the Swedish government seems to have decided that it could no longer refrain, for reasons of domestic policy, from being more frank about the situation in which the three Baltic Republics found themselves.

3.5 The United States

In the first press conference that Secretary of State George Shultz held after the transfer of power in Moscow, he made a statement which epitomized the early U.S. response to the events in the other superpower: "I think that we have to remember that this relationship between the United States and the Soviet Union is a complicated, vitally important relationship; and while personalities matter... nevertheless, you have to look always at the interests and the values and the differences as well as the opportunities to resolve them...."[9] The statesman made clear that while personalities might be interesting, and change in them may drive the journalists into near-frenzy, the interests of states remained. This was particularly true with the superpower relationship.

In a way that is reminiscent of the treatment of the same issues over the course of several years in Sweden, it fell to Michael H. Armacost, Under-Secretary of State for Political Affairs,[10] to discuss developments in the Soviet Union in more detail during the early years of Gorbachev. The two top-level officials in Washington, President Reagan and Secretary Shultz, were content with discussing superpower relations in more general terms,

---

[9] Secretary of State George Shultz, *Department of State Bulletin* [Hereafter: *DSB*], 15 March 1985, pp. 32-33. Note that the speeches are here identified by the date they were delivered, plus the pages on which they are printed in the *DSB*. The date of the *DSB* will necessarily be later than that of the date of the speech's delivery.

[10] This position was, in the mid-1980s, at the third level in the organizational chart of the State Department, starting with the Secretary, followed by the Deputy Secretary, and then the four Under Secretaries of State. See C. W. Kegley, Jr. and E. R. Wittkopf (1987): *American Foreign Policy: Pattern and Process*, third ed. (New York: St. Martin's Press), p. 373.

prominently including very strong criticism against the Soviet Union's behaviour concerning its compliance with arms control agreements on strategic weapons (Statement by President Reagan to Congress 10 June 1985, *DSB*, p. 33).

Under Secretary Armacost was also the one who gave the most direct response to the Soviet move, in the summer of 1985, to suspend the testing of nuclear weapons. Not surprisingly, it was a negative response: "In coping with problems of arms control, propagandistic offers of moratoria are not the answer" (Under Secretary of State Michael H. Armacost, ibid., 9 September 1985, p. 58).

In a major address in San Francisco in October 1985, the Secretary of State talked about "Arms Control, Strategic Stability, and Global Security" (Secretary of State George Shultz, ibid., 14 October 1985, pp. 20-25). In the speech, he summed up the various Soviet proposals introduced since the shift in power by stating that they "could be a step forward",(Ibid., p. 24) while making clear that there was still a very long way to go before they would meet the basic U.S. demands for new arms control agreements.

Before the meeting between President Reagan and General Secretary Gorbachev in Geneva in November 1985, Secretary Shultz characterized what had been happening to the superpower relationship as "more of an atmosphere of exchanging views on these subjects back and forth than there has been in a while" (Secretary Shultz, ibid., 31 October 1985, p. 29). This somewhat positive assessment of Soviet behaviour was carried on in the various statements following the Geneva summit. The most solemn of these was the President's Address before a Joint Session of Congress on 21 November 1985, made upon his return from Geneva:

> We remain far apart on a number of issues, as had to be expected. However, we reached agreement on a number of matters, and...we agreed to continue meeting, and this is important and very good (President Reagan, *DSB*, 21 November 1985, p. 15).

The official U.S. assessment of Gorbachev's policies during the first nine months in office was thus that there were signs of an improved atmosphere, that there was a new dialogue, that the Soviet side was, after a long lull, again producing proposals and suggestions. The U.S. politicians were very explicit in their appraisals that this didn't necessarily lead to any progress on the issues of substance, but at least it meant a change of atmosphere. The assessments during the first year or so concentrated heavily on foreign policy matters, and the developments within the Soviet Union were hardly mentioned at all by the officials in my sample.

Thirteen months after Mr. Gorbachev came to power, the Reagan Administration presented its first overall estimation of events in Soviet foreign and domestic politics during this period. Again, it was Under Secretary of State Michael H. Armacost who delivered the message in a speech entitled "Dealing With Gorbachev's Soviet Union":

> In sum, developments on bilateral issues, human rights, arms control, and regional conflicts present a mixed picture. They suggest that, without sustained efforts on both sides, the competitive elements in our relationship will tend to overshadow the cooperative ones...
> The results of the Party Congress suggest the following conclusions...
> To date, these changes appear to be tactical rather than substantive. Mr. Gorbachev has injected new energy into the implementation of policies that are reasonably familiar. He has hinted at more far-reaching changes. But these hints have yet to be confirmed...
> Let me sum up. Soviet-American relations have not fulfilled the expectations generated by the Geneva summit. Yet, opportunities for progress exist, and we shall continue to work on a broad agenda involving arms control, bilateral issues, human rights, and the resolution of regional conflicts (Under Secretary Armacost, *DSB*, 8 April 1986, pp. 63-64, 66).

In the summer of 1986, the President reported on further positive developments, particularly in arms control. In remarks entitled "An Essay on Peace", Mr. Reagan emphasized his continued belief that the Soviet Union had an inherently expansionist character, and he also stressed that while Soviet arms control proposals were still not acceptable to the U.S., at the very least, "the Soviets have begun to make a serious effort" (President Reagan, ibid., 18 June 1986, pp. 21-22).

The next important event on the Soviet-American bilateral agenda was a summit that was not a summit, the fairly bizarre encounter in Reykjavik between the President and the General Secretary in October 1986. Many complicated issues were discussed at the meeting, and the fallout of the encounter included a very complex argument about what had really been discussed, and what had been agreed, or nearly agreed.[11] This is not the

---

[11] For an informed account about the Reykjavik meeting, set in the broader setting of the development of U.S.-Soviet relations, see R. L. Garthoff (1994): *The Great Transition: American-Soviet Relations and the End of the Cold War* (Washington, DC: Brookings), pp. 252-299. Cf. D. Oberdorfer (1992(1991)): *The Turn* (New York: Touchstone, pp. 155-209. Secretary Shultz (1993) gives his own account in chapter 36 of his memoirs *Turmoil and Triumph* (New York: Charles Scribner's Sons).

place to characterize these issues, since my focus is on the more long-term importance of the contribution that the Reykjavik meeting made to U.S. assessments of the Gorbachev phenomenon. One important example of such an assessment is an address by Secretary Shultz in San Francisco at the end of October 1986 entitled "Reykjavik: A Watershed in U.S.-Soviet Relations":

> My own judgment is that in a few years we will look back at the meeting at Hofdi House as something of a watershed, a potential turning point in our strategy for deterring war and encouraging peace....
> For the first time in the long history of arms control talks, a genuine possibility of substantial reductions in Soviet and American nuclear arms appeared....We have begun to discuss with the Soviets a safer form of deterrence, one based less on the threat of mutual annihilation....
> Whether we can achieve concrete results and early agreements now depends on the Soviets (Secretary Shultz, *DSB*, 31 October 1986, pp. 22, 25).

This is the most dramatic change in official attitudes towards the Soviet Union, in the material I reviewed at such an early stage in the Soviet reform process. A representative of the other superpower — locked in a global struggle for decades with Moscow — stated that a meeting in Iceland in the fall of 1986 was "something of a watershed". The superpower competition must be assumed to have been of such importance to the United States that any reference to a "watershed", even if only a potential one, by the official charged with foreign policy was a momentous occasion. To convey adequately the drama inherent in this new characterization of Soviet foreign policy, the reader must be reminded that the Reagan Administration had, up to that point, been regarded — both at home and abroad — as perhaps the most "anti-Soviet" of all administrations after the start of the Cold War.

What could be the reasons for the far-reaching assessment made by the Secretary of State in the San Francisco speech? My view is that it was a mixture of the reaction to the personal style of the new Soviet leader and to his willingness to discuss concretely potentially revolutionary change affecting the superpower relationship concerning nuclear weapons. The Soviet Union had made tremendous efforts for decades to keep up with Washington in the development and refinement of nuclear weapons, to the point where Moscow was, in the mid-1980s, regarded as being the equal of the United States in terms of strategic nuclear weapons strength; indeed some observers in the U.S. regarded the Soviet Union as being superior. For a Soviet leader to be willing to discuss seriously potentially fundamental changes to this situation must have struck the leading U.S. officials as, at the very least, a very strong indication that here was, at last, a Soviet leader who might be both willing and able to change the very essence of the power relationship between the two countries. My interpretation of this new attitude on the part of Secretary Shultz thus emphasizes the uniqueness of the superpower relationship as compared to the relationship between Moscow and the other three countries assessed in this book. It was between Washington and Moscow that the risk of a confrontation — a confrontation that might escalate to nuclear war — was most directly felt on both sides, and it was, consequently, in this bilateral relationship where the most dramatic bilateral negotiations happened. This relationship was therefore the one in which the Soviet leader was most directly tested in direct, bilateral encounters. What Secretary Shultz saw in this respect at Reykjavik must have made a deep impression on him. The openness with which the Secretary discussed the essence of the superpower relationship at such a comparatively early stage, to my mind, also supports my hypothesis that in countries with open security debates, sensitive issues tend to be addressed with fewer inhibitions than in other nations where security is held more tightly within the central decision-making circles. Since the United States is clearly the nation, of the four nations in my sample, where the policy debates are most open, Secretary Shultz's early assessment of the consequences of Reykjavik gave obvious support to my fourth hypothesis, in section 1.4 (cf. table 1.3).

In December 1987, during a summit meeting in Washington, President Reagan and General Secretary Gorbachev signed the INF Treaty, the first agreement between the two superpowers that meant the actual destruction of one class of nuclear weapons. The INF Treaty, together with a range of less important bilateral agreements and the very process of holding regular summits, indicated a new stage in relations between Moscow and Washington. The public assessments made in Washington of these developments can be seen in two steps.

The first is from a speech by President Reagan at the ending of the summit:

> Individual agreements will not, in and of themselves, result in sustained progress. We need a realistic understanding of each other's intentions and objectives, a process for dealing with differences in a practical and straightforward manner, and we need patience, creativity, and persistence in what we set out to do. As a result of this summit, the framework for building such a relationship has been strengthened (President Reagan, Departure Remarks, *DSB*, 10 December 1987, p. 17).

Secretary Shultz made a more wide-ranging assessment of relations with Moscow in an address in Seattle in February 1988:

> It is much in vogue now...to attribute to Gorbachev the credit for this progress. Clearly, the Soviet Union contributed, and we welcome that....
>
> Yet the truth is that the agreements that have been reached recently and the prospects for future progress are founded in American 'new thinking' and innovation, both in our broad strategy and in our solutions to specific problems...
>
> I find it difficult to believe that our relations with the Soviet Union will ever be "normal" in the sense that we have normal relations with most other countries. There are only two superpowers in the world. We are vastly different in the ways we view the role of the individual in our societies and in the ways we relate to other countries. The relationship between us will always be unique. It seems unlikely that the U.S.-Soviet relationship will ever lose what always has been and is today a strongly wary and at times adversarial element....
>
> But I believe...[t]he case can be made that we are near the threshold of a sustainable U.S.-Soviet relationship (Secretary Shultz, ibid., 5 February 1988, p. 41).

In foreign policy, the Soviet Union was, in early 1988, recognized as having carried out very important, if not quite fundamental, changes. This might, in the decision-makers' estimation, in time lead to the building of a "sustainable" relationship. It is to be noted, however, that any such new relationship between the U.S. and the Soviet Union as might be envisaged would, by its nature, be different from any other U.S. bilateral relationship. The Secretary of State was at the same time very careful when he assessed the domestic aspects of change in the Soviet Union. He noted various attempts and intentions, but his caution in characterizing the extent of the domestic changes was still very conspicuous. It is interesting to compare the tone of this speech to that in the speech the Secretary gave, reflecting on the Reykjavik meeting. In the latter, Secretary Shultz gave equal emphasis to the willingness for change on the part of the Soviet Union and to the correctness of the policies pursued by the Reagan Administration as explanations for why such momentous changes were conceivable in the superpower relationship. By early 1988, the emphasis was clearly on the "correctness" of the Reagan Administration strategy as the main cause behind the important turn for the better in this dyad.

In April 1988, President Reagan further reflected on U.S.-Soviet relations:

> The Soviets have rarely before, and not at all in more than three decades, left a country once occupied...Afghanistan was a critical, strategic prize for the Soviets...We believe that they still hope to prop up their discredited, doomed puppet regime, and they still seek to pose a threat to neighboring Pakistan...
> So we ask: Have the Soviets really given up these ambitions? We do not know. We cannot know until the drama is fully played...
> Some say the Soviet Union is reappraising its foreign policy these days to concentrate on internal reform. Clearly, there are signs of change. But if there is change, it is because the costs of aggression and the real moral difference between our systems were brought home to it. If we hope to see a more fundamental change, we must remain strong and firm (President Reagan, *DSB*, 21 April 1988, pp. 2-3).

In late May and early June of 1988, President Reagan visited Moscow. It is remarkable that this trip, as well as the remaining eight months of the Reagan Administration, produced so little in terms of any in-depth assessment of the developments in Soviet foreign policy, as well as in domestic affairs. The most remarkable utterance of the period, from the perspective of this book, was Mr. Reagan's reply, during his Moscow visit, when asked if he still believed that the Soviet Union was an "evil empire": "I was talking about another time, another era" (Garthoff, 1994, p. 352. See also Oberdorfer, 1992, p. 299. Cf. President Reagan, News Conference, Spaso House, Moscow, *DSB*, 1 June 1988, p. 33). It was as if the strength of the Reagan Administration had all gone by mid-1988, and the American polity was suspended as it awaited the next President.

The new President, George H.W. Bush, was notably cautious in his first important public speech given in February 1989:

> It's a time of great change in the world, and especially in the Soviet Union. Prudence and common sense dictate that we try to understand the full meaning of the change going on there, review our policies, and then proceed with caution. But I've personally assured General Secretary Gorbachev that at the conclusion of such a review, we will be ready to move forward. We will not miss any opportunity to work for peace. The fundamental facts remain that the Soviets retain a very powerful military machine in the service of objectives which are still too often in conflict with ours. So let us take the new openness seriously. But let us also be realistic. And let us always be strong (President George H.W. Bush, *DSB*, 9 February 1989, p. 3).

The difference in the analysis between what President Reagan and Secretary of State Shultz were saying in the first half of 1988 and what President Bush was saying in February 1989 is notable. There was a note of caution in President Bush's speech that was nearly absent in the previous year. This type of change in assessment of Soviet behaviour, occurring following a change in leadership, is unique in my material. The difference between the United States and the other countries in this respect is, of course, that it was only in the U.S. that a change in the leadership occurred at the time when changes in Soviet politics were most pronounced. The assassination of Prime Minister Palme in Sweden, and the subsequent change in leadership to Ingvar Carlsson, occurred in 1986, too early from this point of view. Likewise, when John Major replaced Margaret Thatcher in late 1990, the developments had already gone so far that the change made little or no difference in terms of the analysis of Soviet affairs. Nor did the French changes of government, first from socialist to non-socialist in March 1986, and then back again in May 1988, really make any mark on the analysis of Soviet affairs.

What were the reasons for the caution shown by President George H. W. Bush during his first months in office? I believe that it is due to at least two circumstances that make the U.S. act differently from the other three states assessed in this book with respect to its foreign policy. One cause of the circumspection shown by U.S. leaders from mid-1988 to mid-1989 in their assessments of the breadth and durability of the foreign policy changes carried out by Mr. Gorbachev is thus built into the U.S. political system, as it awaits the transfer from one administration to another. It is as if the superpower is no longer able to make bold moves — or at the very least, there is a strong tendency to avoid or postpone bold foreign policy moves until after the old administration winds down and the process of first determining who will lead the next one, and then letting the new leader personally assess the situation in office, is under way. While this tendency in all likelihood also exists in France, Great Britain and Sweden in similar situations of transfer of power, it is clearly more pronounced in the United States.

Another explanation could be found in the personality of the new President, as this played out in the domestic political context of the United States. In the terms introduced in chapter 1, President Bush can be surmised to have believed, or at the very least suspected, that Mr. Gorbachev was behaving in an acceptable way in foreign policy not because of any fundamental change in the nature of the Soviet Union, but rather because the Soviet State had no choice in view of the domestic and international situation. In other words, President Bush tended — early in his presidency — to make situational attributions when he explained the foreign policy behaviour of Moscow. Since he was not yet convinced that the character of the Soviet State had changed, he was not prepared to state that dispositional attributions were applicable when assessing Soviet behaviour towards other countries. It was only later into his presidency that Mr. Bush was indeed convinced that the very character of the Soviet State had changed as a result of Mr. Gorbachev's leadership. The tendency that the President displayed in this respect is intimately tied to the special political circumstances in the United States during the Cold War. While relations with the Soviet Union were important for all four countries, the sensitivity of the bilateral relationship in terms of the political position of the highest leader of the land was clearly higher for the President of the United States than was the case for either the President of France, the Prime Minister in Great Britain or the Prime Minister in Sweden.

After nearly four months in office, President Bush returned to the relationship with the Soviet Union:

> In sum, the United States now has as its goal much more than simply containing Soviet expansionism — we seek the integration of the Soviet Union into the community of nations. As the Soviet Union moves toward greater openness and democratization — as they meet the challenge of responsible international behavior — we will match their steps with steps of our own. Ultimately, our objective is to welcome the Soviet Union back into the world order. ...
>
> We hope perestroika is pointing the Soviet Union to a break with the cycles of the past — a definitive break. Who would have thought we would see the deliberations of the Central Committee on the front page of Pravda, or dissident Andrei Sakharov seated near the councils of power? Who would have imagined a Soviet leader who canvasses the sidewalks of Moscow and Washington, D.C.? These are hopeful, indeed remarkable — signs. Let no one doubt our sincere desire to see perestroika continue and succeed. But the national security of America and our allies is not predicated on hope. It must be based on deeds. We look for enduring, ingrained economic and political changes (President George H. W. Bush, *DSB*, 12 May 1989, p. 16).

For all that had happened in Soviet foreign and domestic politics by mid-1989, President Bush was — in his official speeches — still suspicious that all these things that looked good might in the end turn out to be just temporary alterations in policy, not the fundamental restructuring of Soviet foreign policy that the U.S. hoped for. Mr. Bush's way of expressing himself on this occasion gives further support to my belief that attribution theory provides at least part of the explanation for why he was so prudent in his assessments of the Soviet State during this early part of his presidency.

President Bush's Secretary of State, James Baker, spelled out the details of U.S. worries about the Soviet Union, and about what Washington expected from Moscow, in a speech also delivered in May 1989. To the Bush Administration, for all the positive things happening in Moscow, there were still worries of several kinds. The Soviet military was still intact and the country continued to dominate Eastern Europe.[12]

In a speech followed by a question-and-answer period in June 1989, Secretary Baker responded to the question of ethnic disturbances in the Soviet Union by characterizing them as "rather significant problems for the leadership" (Secretary of State James Baker, *DSB*, 9 June 1989, p. 58). He added that, in his estimation, reforms in Soviet domestic politics had advanced further than in the economic sphere.

In the material from the politicians, it was that from the United States that gave the most detailed and ambitious attempt to explain and analyse the Soviet reform effort. This occurred on three occasions in particular — two statements to congressional committees and one important speech — in the period from October 1989 to April 1990. The open hearings in the U.S. Congress thus served to produce what, among all the public speeches given in any of the four countries studied in this book, most resembles an academic analysis of the actor the United States was facing in the global arena. Only short quotes are included here. Longer excerpts are printed in appendix 3:

> I believe a combination of four factors convinced the Soviet leadership of the need for reform.
> The first was the overall decline in economic performance. ...
> A second factor promoting reform was the decline in the competitive position of the Soviet economy. The gap between the U.S.S.R. and the West was growing, not narrowing. Even more shocking, the Soviets could see the newly industrializing economies surging forward. ...
> The military implications of Soviet economic failure were a third reason for reform. The Reagan Administration's military buildup proved difficult to counter without drawing off an even greater share of civilian resources and increasing the already heavy defense burden. ...
> The fourth factor was the emergence of new leadership in the Soviet Union. This leadership represented a new generation. ...
> It would be a mistake, however, to conclude that the challenges are too

---

[12] Secretary of State James Baker, *DSB*, 4 May 1989, pp. 37-38. A long excerpt from this speech is printed in appendix 3.

daunting or that the impediments to success are too great. So far Gorbachev has secured greater power over the years, and he reveals every intention to "stay the course." The jury is still out on whether he will succeed or fail (Secretary of State James Baker, Statement to the Senate Finance Committee, *DSB*, 4 October 1989, pp. 20-26).

It is rare, at least in this author's experience, that decision makers present such detailed analysis of the foreign policy problems they face in the official arena. It is clear that the analysis presented by Secretary Baker was to some extent influenced by research going on during these extraordinary years by specialists in the field of Soviet domestic and foreign policy, in particular by those specializing in the Soviet economy. This statement contained an explanation of the reasons why the Soviet Union started its great experiment in the economic and political spheres. It contained a detailed analysis of the problems that the reform experiment was facing at the time when the speaker was giving his statement, that is, in the fall of 1989. Finally, it contained an attempt to foresee what would happen to the great Soviet experiment, or at least it tackled the question of the future as well.

Another notable aspect of the statement is that it was the economic sphere that the Secretary of State concentrated on when he gave his most elaborate statement,[13] indeed the most elaborate statement of any high-level U.S. official on the developments in the Soviet Union from 1985 to 1991. It is somewhat odd that the Secretary of State, responsible directly under the President for the carrying out of U.S. foreign policy, chose to concentrate so heavily on economic matters in this statement and largely neglected foreign policy issues. The most logical thing for a Secretary of State to do in such a situation, if he wanted to give a public exposé of issues facing his country in international affairs, would be to go before the two committees concentrating on foreign policy rather than the two most important economic committees.[14]

During October 1989, the Secretary of State also gave a speech to the Foreign Policy Association in New York, which was his most public presentation of U.S. views of superpower relations at that time.

---

[13] The statement of 4 October 1989, is largely repeated in a similar statement to the House Ways and Means Committee on 18 April 1990. See *Department of State Dispatch*, 18 April 1990, pp. 26-31. The only additions of importance concern the situation in Lithuania. It should be noted that the *Department of State Bulletin* ceased publication at the end of 1989 and was replaced by the *Department of State Dispatch*.
[14] Raymond Garthoff, 1994, pp. 385-389, discusses the making of U.S. Soviet policy at the end of 1989, including the role of the two speeches analysed here. Cf. also Beschloss and Talbott, 1994, particularly pp. 123-125.

This speech was the one that had the most important public impact at the time.[15] These statements indicated a rather complex explanation for why Mr. Gorbachev had elected to start the Soviet reform process. In this explanation, rethinking by the Soviet leadership, an explanation of type IV a in my explanatory framework, was prominent. The factors that, in the Secretary's analysis, fed into the cognitions of the Soviet leadership included the failings in the domestic sphere, in particular the economy — explanation II b in my framework. The Soviet leadership, in this view, also realized that domestic stagnation might have consequences for the international position of the Soviet Union, explanation I a. In other words, in the U.S. explanation of the causes behind the Soviet changes, all levels of analysis, save the bureaucratic one, were included.

3.5.1 The United States: Conclusions

Of the four countries studied in this book, it was in the United States where the most frequent and detailed assessments of Soviet affairs were made in the official material. There is no reason to disbelieve the common view that superpower relations were crucial to Washington for more than four decades after 1947. In addition, this voluminous public discussion of relations with the Soviet Union gives support to my hypothesis, offered in chapter 1, that the United States is the country of the four in which the debate on security policy was the most open. In none of the other three countries was there anything approaching the number and detail of the public assessments offered by the U.S. officials.

Yet another hypothesis received support from the analysis of the official material: that it was in the U.S. that academic participation in policy making was the most developed of the four countries. The clearest indication that this was so comes from the several speeches and statements given by Secretary of State James Baker, particularly from the autumn of 1989 until the early spring of 1990. In these speeches, the Secretary clearly brought in aspects from academic research on Soviet affairs, particularly in the economic field. Again, there was nothing even resembling this detailed input from academics in the material from any of the other three countries.

The detailed diagnosis offered by the U.S. politicians of events in the Soviet Union contained another element that singles out the United States among the four countries. This is the fact that it was only in the United States where one could note a shift in the analysis of Soviet events towards a more

---

[15] Cf. Garthoff, 1994, p. 386. Long excerpts from the speech are printed in appendix 3.

cautious general assessment as late as 1989. This was when Ronald Reagan was preparing to leave office and his former Vice President, George H.W. Bush, was first running to succeed him and then settling into the presidency. Particularly until mid-1988, President Reagan and other members of his administration were optimistic and far-reaching in their assessments of how far the Soviet reforms had led domestically and in foreign policy, and how far they might lead in the future. In this respect, the first few months of the Bush Administration marked a change towards greater caution, both regarding the extent of domestic policy change and, in particular, regarding how significant the changes had been in Soviet foreign policy.

In my analysis, there are two main explanations for the fact that there was this unique period of pronounced caution only in the United States during a period when important changes in Soviet foreign policy had clearly been perceived abroad. The first has to do with what may be called the structure of the U.S. political system. This is the fact that for an administration that cannot continue in office — after having served two terms — there is a tendency to be very careful about tying the successor's hands in important policy realms; at the very least this is true in foreign policy. This tendency for circumspection can be said to continue as the new President settles into office during the first six months or so.

The second explanation for the caution shown by the Bush Administration in assessing the changes in Soviet foreign policy during the President's first months in office can be found in the personality of the President. In the terms of attribution theory, the new President was careful to make an analysis of Soviet foreign policy, early in his presidency, that emphasized the situational factors propelling Moscow towards foreign policy change. He did not want to be too bold in stating that the very essence of the Soviet State had changed at that stage; in other words, he did not want to use dispositional attributions in his analysis of Soviet behaviour. It seems obvious that the President's behaviour on this point is connected to his perception of the domestic political context in which he perceived the relationship with Moscow. President Bush was thus clearly aware that this relationship was sensitive and might, if handled badly, affect his domestic political position, both more generally and in terms of his standing within the Republican party. One consequence of this was that it was only later in his presidency that the new President was prepared to move towards the latter type of analysis of Soviet foreign policy changes.

Broadly seen, the U.S. diagnosis of the extent of the Soviet reforms proceeded in clear steps. By the time of the Geneva summit in October

1985, the assessment was made that even if very important differences remained between the two powers, the very fact that they had agreed to have regular meetings constituted important progress. Thereafter, the assessment gradually grew more positive, with Secretary Shultz a few months after the Reykjavik summit ready to characterize this meeting as "something of a watershed". After the Washington summit of December 1987, the Secretary was prepared to go further in his positive assessments. While stressing his belief that relations between Washington and Moscow could never be normal in the way Washington's relations were with almost all other states, the Secretary still, in a crucial formulation, for the first time characterized the bilateral relationship as possibly "sustainable". A few months later, President Reagan went still further in assessing the extent of Soviet foreign policy changes, while still hedging on whether these were indeed irreversible or not.

In their explanations for why the changes in Soviet policy had occurred, the U.S. statesmen prominently included the disastrous Soviet economy in a way that resembled the public analysis in the other three countries. This factor was linked to the Soviet ability to remain a superpower in the international arena. One element in this explanation is, however, unique for the United States. This was the emphasis placed on the role of the outside world, in particular Washington itself, in pressuring the Soviets to undertake these changes. It is clear that the U.S. leadership perceived a relationship in which the actions and strategies of its own side weighed heavily in the analysis and the eventual policies on the Soviet side. It is possible here to identify the self-perception of the United States as a superpower, a power whose policies directly influenced Soviet behaviour. Even if the official French speeches also contained an element of recognizing the importance of their own nation in international politics, they never went so far as to assert a clear causal influence on what happened in Moscow, as the Americans did. I regard this element as support for my first hypothesis in table 1.3: analysts in strong nations have many fewer reasons for caution in their analyses of foreign events than do analysts in weak nations.

To reiterate, the case of public discussion in the United States on events in the Soviet Union following the accession to power of Mr. Gorbachev gives support to three of the hypotheses presented in chapter 1, table 1.3. First, the insistence that both the initiation of the Soviet experiment, and then the collapse of the state itself, could largely be attributed to U.S. pressure supports the hypothesis that the official U.S. analysis of developments in the Soviet Union was suffused by the realization that the U.S. is a superpower. Second, the very candid assessment of Soviet events indicates the greater openness of the U.S. debate on security policy compared to the case in the other three countries. Third, the elaborate statements made by Secretary of State James Baker in the autumn of 1989, in particular, gave support to my hypothesis that, in the U.S., academic participation in the official security debate is greater than in the other countries. There was no such example of direct academic influence on the public speeches on Soviet affairs in any of the other three countries.

3.6 Conclusion

The character of the official speeches covering Mr. Gorbachev's years in office was typically that of a bland allocution saying nothing in particular, thus confirming the notion that most analysts have of politicians' speeches. The politicians knew that they had to comment on what was going on in Moscow, but there was, in many cases, not much content in what they said. The material still contained answers to the three fundamental questions posed in beginning of this book, even if the diagnostic and the explanatory aspects were, as expected, much better covered than the predictive one.

On the issue of assessing the extent of Soviet changes, there were few variations of any significance in the material. Thus 1988 was the year when politicians in all four countries were ready to proclaim that what was happening in the Soviet Union was more than just superficial activity. It was easiest to pinpoint the time at which this official assessment was made in France, Great Britain and Sweden. In the case of these three countries, clear statements to this effect were made by the late autumn and early winter of 1988. For Sweden, the assessment, first officially made in December 1988, was in the form "Perestroika is for real," and the crucial speech concentrated on the domestic reform process, with foreign policy implicitly being a corollary of the domestic changes. In the French case, the Foreign Minister, at roughly the same time as in Sweden, discussed both domestic and foreign policy. He went further in his assessment of the extent of change up until that point in the domestic sphere, but his assessment of foreign policy changes was almost equally far-reaching. In the British case, the statement that changes had indeed occurred was unequivocal at the same point in time. The difference was that, for London, the continued military activities in the Soviet Union were still regarded as a warning sign that the changes in that country might not be as fundamental as one might otherwise believe.

The only exception to this pattern of making official acknowledgements, typically by the second half of 1988, that the Soviet Union had indeed changed both foreign and domestic policies to an important extent and then sticking to this view was in the United States. Secretary of State George Shultz made a statement to the effect that U.S.-Soviet relations were on the verge of a fundamental breakthrough as early as October 1986. Even if there was somewhat more caution in the statements by Shultz and the President for 18-20 months after that, still, there were elements in those speeches as well that identified important new elements in Soviet foreign policy. After the Moscow summit in May-June 1988, however, the penetrating assessments of Soviet foreign policy by the President and the Secretary of State ceased. As may be seen from the brief review in chapter 2.4, this was not due to the fact that the Soviet reform process stalled; the explanation must, rather, be sought on the U.S. side.

In my analysis there are two basic explanations for the anomaly, when seen in a comparative perspective, that the regularly given, thorough assessments made by officials at the highest political level ceased to be issued by mid-1988, and when they resumed after the new President, George H.W. Bush, took office in January of 1989, these statements were notably more cautious than had been the case twelve months earlier. The first explanation for this has to do with the structure of the political process in the U.S. The presidential election process had an obvious influence on the public assessment of Soviet affairs during the 12-month period in question. This is the tendency for a "lame-duck" administration — an administration where the President cannot be re-elected once he has served the two four-year periods that are the constitutional limit — to leave some leeway for a successor, and not to tie the latter's hands, a tendency that is probably most pronounced in the foreign and security policy spheres. This tendency for caution continues into the early period of the new presidency as well. This is obviously an explanation that is applicable in this case.

A second explanation can be found in the personality of the new President, George H. W. Bush. As a politician steeped in the rhetoric and practice of the Cold War, Bush was likely to be very careful indeed about not rushing too far too fast in embracing Mr. Gorbachev, and in not acting as if the Soviet Union had indeed fundamentally changed, whether in foreign or in domestic policy. In the terms of the attribution theories applied in this study, President Bush initially used a situationally based explanation for the actions of the Soviet Union in the foreign policy sphere. In other words, he acknowledged that Moscow under Mr. Gorbachev was acting in a way that was different from before. However, he attributed this to the situation in which the leadership of the Soviet Union found itself, with economic and other problems that had to be managed. He did not employ terms during the first six months or so of his presidency to the effect that the Soviet policy changes had been so far-reaching as to have altered the basic character of the Soviet State; in other words, he did not use dispositional attributions. If an individual over a long time uses situational attributions to characterize the actions of a former adversary when there is overwhelming evidence that this adversary indeed has changed his policies, then we can talk about the fundamental error of attribution. In this case, President Bush was, after some months, ready to concede that Soviet policies had indeed changed in important and lasting ways. His behaviour in this respect, in other words, cannot be characterized as a flagrant and lasting case of the fundamental error of attribution. I would, however, argue that he was indeed influenced by the factors identified in attribution theory in clinging overly long to caution in his assessments of the extent of change that had taken place in Soviet foreign policy by the first half of 1989.

A second basic question asked in this book is, How do the analysts explain why the reform process in the Soviet Union started? It was in the United States that the most elaborate explanation for events in Moscow was given. Secretary of State James Baker gave most of these in several statements starting in October 1989. Some of the earlier statements made by his predecessor, George Shultz, were also fairly detailed. According to these statements, a mixture between outside pressure from the United States and deficiencies in the Soviet system, notably in the economic sphere, caused the initiation of the reform process in Moscow. The latter in turn had ramifications for domestic policies, for the competitive position externally and for the continued military strength of the country. In addition, the Americans mentioned the importance of the new leadership without strongly focusing on Mr. Gorbachev as an individual. The official U.S. explanation for why the reform process started in Moscow thus included elements from levels-of-analyses I, the system level; level II, the state level; and from level V, the individual level.

The French and Swedish explanations for the initiation of Soviet reforms were not fundamentally different from the U.S. one, but they were clearly less developed. The French put greater emphasis on what I termed the cognitive explanation in table 1.2, explanation IV a. In other words, a crucial factor behind the initiation of the reforms was, in the French view, the fact that the new Soviet leadership had recognized the shortcomings of the system and, as a result of this assessment, took action to ameliorate these deficiencies. This cognitive emphasis is notable in the French material. An interesting difference between the President, M. Mitterrand, and his Foreign Ministers can be found in this respect. The former underlined the unique qualities of Mr. Gorbachev as an individual, whereas both of his Foreign Ministers made the point a general one covering the new Soviet leadership more broadly seen.

The Swedish explanations for the start of the reform process were less elaborate than was the case for France and, even more so, for the United States. Still, the ingredients were roughly the same as in the other two countries. The Swedes underlined the importance of the failures of the Soviet economy and the consequences this could have both for the living standards of the Soviet population and for the ability of that country to remain a superpower. The cognitive aspects highlighted by the French were also briefly mentioned in the Swedish material, but in a general way that did not single out Mr. Gorbachev.

For Britain, the same question was explained by both type I a, the continued strength of the West and type II b, the deficiencies of the socialist economic system in the Soviet Union, and by both of the explanations at the individual level — the cognitive aspects covered in type IV a and the individual explanation, IV b. Although the British officials never gave any speeches that resembled the most important ones given by Secretary Baker, still, the parallels were strong between the explanations offered by Washington and London. This serves to underline my assessment in section 2.2.3 that Great Britain's policies towards the Soviet Union were closely aligned to those pursued by Washington.

It is not surprising that the politicians did not really try to predict, or even forecast, the future of the Soviet experiments. In the case of the Swedish and the U.S. material one can, however, detect indications that the leading politicians were aware that the Soviet reforms might not necessarily end in success. Such warnings existed in the Swedish speeches from early 1989 on, and in the U.S. from the second half of 1989 on.

Another result of the analysis in this chapter has already been presented. This is the fact that there was one clear exception to the rule of bland statements in assessing foreign events, and that is the material from the United States. In the hypotheses presented in chapter 1, I wrote that in the U.S. the debate on security policy tends to be wide-ranging, and that there is an important element of academic participation both in government more strictly conceived and in the broader security policy debate. My analysis of the public speeches on Soviet affairs from March 1985 until the end of 1991 in four countries gave support to both of these hypotheses. In none of the other three countries was the public speechmaking as wide-ranging and as detailed, and in none of the other three countries was there any intimation at all of the politicians listening to scholars when they made their assessments. In addition, the power hypothesis, the fact that the United States was a super-power and that one could, consequently, expect less inhibition in terms of the analysis of the Soviet Union, was also supported. This was most clearly the case in the consistent emphasis upon the importance of U.S. policies, first in getting the Soviet reform process started, and then in contributing significantly to the system's ultimate demise.

The case of Sweden also gave some support to similar hypotheses concerning factors that might influence the public speeches by officials in a country with the political characteristics of Sweden. This is the fact that the Swedes very early on made very sympathetic assessments of, in particular, the domestic restructuring in the Soviet Union. This supports my hypothesis that analysts in a country where democratic socialism is influential would tend to show greater sympathy towards reforms in the socialist Soviet Union as compared to the tenor of the assessments in countries where the ideology, in the sense of dominant state ideology, was anti-socialist. It is to be noted that the difference between Sweden and Britain, in particular, is certainly not vast in this respect. Prime Minister Thatcher gave a sympathetic speech about changes in Moscow at roughly the same time as did her Swedish counterpart. In the Swedish allocution one can, however, detect an understanding of the Soviet situation and sympathy for the reform process that is lacking in the equivalent British statement.

It could further be argued, even if the evidence for this is less strong, that the public analysis in Sweden also gave support to one more hypothesis: that in a small country the assessment of the security policy implications of Soviet foreign policy changes are made in a very careful way. One can detect a sense in which the Swedes were quite sympathetic to the domestic policy changes in the Soviet Union, indeed that they made positive evaluations of these earlier than those in any other country. When it came to assessing the Soviet policy changes in the foreign and security policy spheres, however, the Swedes were notably more careful, as epitomized by their treatment of events in the Baltic Republics. The Swedish government was, in other words, quite circumspect about declaring that basic aspects of foreign policy had changed in a country that had traditionally been regarded as the greatest threat to Swedish security.

In the analyses I made of the public speeches given in Great Britain and France on the subject of Soviet affairs, there were no such clear indications that the hypotheses presented in table 1.3 in this book were supported. In a more general sense one could, however, detect how the foreign policy orientation of France was reflected in the public policy material. This was when the French politicians underlined the special role played by France in international affairs, most clearly shown by the reaction to the fact that Mr. Gorbachev's first visit to a non-Warsaw Pact country after taking office went to France.

Another significant aspect of the analyses presented by the two larger European states is that there are clear parallels in some respects in their assessments of what was happening in Moscow. One was that the two leaders, Mrs. Thatcher and M. Mitterrand, had a special inclination to focus on the personal role of Mr. Gorbachev as a leader in initiating the Soviet reform process. It is as if the heads of two large European powers had a special affinity for the plight of a fellow leader in Moscow, as well as for the positive aspects that they detected in his actions. Perhaps one can even sense a tendency on the part of Prime Minister Thatcher and President Mitterrand to focus on, perhaps even to overestimate, the role of the individual in controlling and changing complex policy processes.

There are also some results that gave support to my belief that the analysis of Soviet affairs would be similar in London to that presented in Washington. This was especially true in accounting for why the reform process started, where officials in both nations found reasons for this in power politics, explanation I a; in the disastrous workings of the socialist economic system, explanation II b; and at the individual level. On the latter score, however, the U.S. officials tended to emphasize the cognitive explanations more, IV a, whereas the British leadership also gave credit to the personal role of the Soviet leader, explanation IV b.

Two individuals, out of the 18 politicians whose speeches have formed the basis for the analysis in this book, can be singled out as presenting something considerably deeper than the banal generalities that so often seem to characterize foreign policy speeches. One of these is a very familiar figure to all readers of this book: James A. Baker III, the Secretary of State under President George Bush. Baker formed close personal relations with some individuals on the Soviet side, in particular with Soviet Foreign Minister Eduard Shevardnadze. In addition, he used public appearances, specifically when giving statements in front of congressional committees, to present what can only be characterized as penetrating analyses of what was going on in the other superpower.

The other individual who delved deep in his public analysis of Soviet foreign policy, and of Soviet developments more generally, was M. Jean-Bernard Raimond. He was French Foreign Minister under the "cohabitation" period of 1986 to 1988. This was one of the two periods where President François Mitterrand, a socialist, had to coexist with a non-socialist government, the first of which had Jacques Chirac as Prime Minister.[16] M. Raimond was willing to address the difficult questions concerning the Soviet process of change in his speeches, to an extent that is uncommon in my material. One notable aspect about his analysis was his failure, despite obvious expertise in Soviet affairs, to foresee the enormous destructive power for the Soviet state that lay in the nationalist issues.

It may very well be that the politicians in democratic nations test the limits of expertise in their internal deliberations on foreign policy, in particular when it comes to assessing what is happening to the world around them. It was only in the case of the U.S. that my material gave any indication that this might be the case, however.

---

[16] On the politics of French foreign policy under President Mitterrand see Pierre Hassner (1988): "France and the Soviet Union" in *Western Approaches to the Soviet Union*, ed. Michael Mandelbaum (New York: Council on Foreign Relations) and P. H. Gordon (1993): *A Certain Idea of France: French Security Policy and the Gaullist Legacy* (Princeton, NJ: Princeton University Press) pp. 144-160.

Chapter 4

The Analysis of Gorbachev's Foreign Policy in Eight Elite Newspapers[1]

4.1 Introduction

The story of events in the Soviet Union during the tumultuous years between 1985 and 1991 received intensive coverage in many newspapers throughout the world. The present chapter analyses this material in eight newspapers, two from each of the countries covered in this book. In keeping with the focus of this work, it is the editorials published in these papers that form the basis for the analysis.[2] Among these editorials, I have looked for all that have been focused on Soviet affairs. The number of editorials found that fulfilled this criterion is given for each newspaper and each year in appendix 2 b.

Six of the eight newspapers covered in this book had an editorial page that printed from two up to five or even six editorials per day during the period in question. The exceptions were the two French newspapers. *Le Monde* published only one daily editorial-type article on the front page that strongly resembled an editorial during the years studied here.[3] This article is here classified as an editorial. In the case of *Le Figaro* the situation is similar. The conservative French newspaper had no editorial page during the period under study. It did, however, in a fashion similar to that of *Le*

---

[1] The general criteria for choosing among editorials were as follows: all editorials containing assessments of Soviet foreign policy were included. The exception was editorials which simply mentioned Soviet foreign policy in a sentence or two, with the main focus being on other issues. In addition, all editorials covering assessments of Soviet internal politics have been perused. Of these, all editorials covering issues not distinctly peripheral in Soviet political developments have been studied more carefully. In appendix 2 b there is detailed information on how many editorials have been included from each paper for each year.

[2] To be precise, I must add that there are clear differences when one tries to identify editorials in newspapers in different countries which deal with Gorbachev and Soviet politics in general. This book has greatly benefited from the use of computerized searches of editorials in the following newspapers: *Dagens Nyheter, the Guardian* (from 1987 on), *The New York Times, Svenska Dagbladet, The Times* (from June 1, 1988), and *The Washington Post*. Only in the cases of *Le Figaro* and *Le Monde* have I been unable to use this method for identifying editorials, despite valiant efforts by my research assistant Ms. Anna-Karin Thorstensson to obtain help from *Le Figaro's* staff in particular.

[3] It could be added that *Le Monde* published only published six issues per week, which makes the total number of articles published on the Soviet Union (310) for the seven-yer period even more impressive. *The Times* and *The Guardian* were also only published six times per week.

Monde, publish a front-page, single-column article in bold type every day. This article is here classified as equivalent to an editorial.

4. 2 The French Newspapers

4.2.1 Le Figaro

In the French case, the two newspapers analysed were *Le Figaro*, which is to the right on the ideological spectrum, and *Le Monde*, which represents a more leftist outlook.

   Le Figaro, in its very first editorial on Gorbachev, made clear its belief in the stability of the Soviet system, and the resulting difficulty in changing it, by the following statement:

> Pendant quelques années en tout cas, M. Gromyko, qui s'est imposé de longue date comme le principal architecte de la politique étrangère soviétique, a toutes chances de rester, dans son domaine, le mentor dont les avis font loi ("Nouvelle donné", *Le Figaro*, 12 March 1985).
> Mr. Gromyko, who has for a long time been accepted as the main architect of Soviet foreign policy, has all chances to remain, at least for a few years, the mentor whose views carry the day in his field.[4]

   The paper continued to espouse this basic view in its assessment of the nuclear disaster at Chernobyl in April 1986: "Le drame de Tchernobyl démontre — à supposer que l'on a pu se faire quelques illusions — que sur l'essentiel rien n'a changé un U.R.S.S. depuis Staline" ("L'aveu forcé", ibid., 2 May 1986) "The drama in Chernobyl shows — if you make the assumption that you could have made yourself any illusions — that essentially nothing has changed in the Soviet Union since Stalin."

   There is thus no doubt whatever that, for the editorialists at *Le Figaro*, the Soviet Union was a totalitarian system. This negative attitude regarding both the intentions of the new Soviet leader, and his prospects for carrying out change should he really want to, continued into 1987. In February of that year, the conservative French paper published a more comprehensive assessment:

---

[4] All translations from the French are by the author.

En réalité, Gorbatchev mène une double offensive. A l'intérieur, son objectif, c'est de jeter bas l'appareil de Brejnev pour le remplacer par le sien. Son pouvoir ne sera assuré que le jour où il aura réussi. L'opposition aussitôt suscitée par les reformes, dont il vient de se faire l'avocat devant le plénum du comité central, n'a pu que le renforcer dans cette conviction. ...
Second objectif: l'extérieur. Il s'agit de séduire l'Occident. L'Union Soviétique ayant raté la troisième révolution industrielle — celle de l'informatique — Gorbatchev a besoin des techniques étrangères pour maintenir le statut de grand puissance de l'URSS. Les cent quarante détenus qui sont en train d'être liberé d'un goulag qui en contient quatre millions, c'est de la petite monnaie pour l'aide attendue de l'Ouest" ("Qui est Gorbatchev? Les deux objectifs", *Le Figaro*, 12 February 1987. Cf. "Offensive de charme", ibid., 24 October 1988).
In reality Gorbachev carries out a double offensive. Domestically, his goal is to discard Brezhnev's apparatus to replace it with his own. His power will not be assured until the day that he has accomplished this. The opposition immediately engendered by his reforms, reforms that he just advocated in front of the plenary of the Central Committee, has only made him more determined in this conviction. ...
Second goal: foreign policy. He intends to seduce the West. Since the Soviet Union has failed in the third industrial revolution — that of information technology — Gorbachev needs foreign technologies to maintain the U.S.S.R.'s position as a Great Power. The one hundred and forty detainees who are about to be released from a Goulag that contains four million, that is only small change for the aid attended from the West.

Le Figaro continued to show total mistrust for the Soviet leader's intentions. He might change here and there in foreign policy, and in domestic matters that Western powers linked to foreign policy, but he had no intention whatever, in the view of the paper, of changing anything fundamentally in the Soviet Union, whether in domestic affairs or in foreign policy.

Le Figaro did not even view the INF Treaty, regarded by many other analysts as a clear indication of important changes in Soviet foreign policy, in this light. The paper noted that if there was one loser in this deal, it was Europe. The Soviet Union, it asserted, had moved towards the attainment of several important goals by way of this Treaty. First, it wanted to reach its old goal of creating a rift between the U.S. and its allies in Western Europe ("Un accord dangereux", ibid., 19-20 September 1987). Second, the Soviet Union could, through the impact of the Treaty, influence and encourage that part of the European public, notably in West Germany, that wanted to see Europe denuclearised ("Un grand absente", *Le Figaro*, 7 December 1987). Third, the two earlier factors would lead to a process that could have only one end result — a Europe totally dominated by the Soviet Union ("Le risque du repli", ibid., 8 December 1987).

It's hard to imagine a clearer indication of the world-view that informed these writers. They were exponents of realism *par préférence*. In the terms of Sovietological models presented in table 1.1, the conservative French newspaper clearly subscribed to the totalitarian model. If anything, the paper regarded the INF Treaty as increasing the risk of Soviet domination in the whole of Europe.

Another fundamental question about the events in the Soviet Union concerned whether the system, domestically, really could be reformed. *Le Figaro*, as late as November 1987, was of the opinion that this was impossible, but that this very inability to reform condemned the system "à la décadance" ("L'onde de choc", ibid., 24 November 1987).

During the last months of 1988, there was a new tone in the assessments of the Soviet leader. The paper explicitly concluded that Mr. Gorbachev had indeed proved his intention to change fundamental aspects of Soviet policy, both foreign and domestic. According to the paper it was not possible to overlook the many instances through which Mr. Gorbachev had shown this intention. The examples given were both international and domestic ("L'attrait de la liberté", *Le Figaro*, 31 December 1988). In March 1989, the paper went even further in its general assessment of the importance of events in the Soviet Union. It classified this as constituting nothing less than "une révolution".

> Sans doute le plus étonnant et le plus lourde de conséquence de tous ceux que cet univers ait connues depuis la fin de la Seconde Guerre mondiale. On peut débattre à longeur de pages sur les succès ou l'insuccès probable de l'ouverture gorbatchévienne. Mais le fait est qu'elle se déroule sous nos yeux et que, quoi qu'il arrive, elle aura jété la Russie soviétique dans une ère radicalement nouvelle. ...
>
> Un cas de figure exceptionnel. Le vieux régime soviétique est entré pour toutes sortes des raisons — stagnation économique insupportable, dépenses militaires exorbitantes, désir d'une partie de la nomenclature de vivre comme les Occidentaux, difficultés de maintenir par la force la stabilité d'une empire trop grand, trop divers — dans une phase de mutation accélérée. Personne ne sait sur quelle forme d'État débouchera l'aventure actuelle. La Russie soviétique sort le gangue totalitaire. Elle n'est pas pour autant devenue une pays libre.

Néanmoins, on peut dès maintenant qualifier la cascade d'événements qui depuis quatre ans ébranlent le centre et le périphérie de l'immense Russie. C'est une révolution ("Le cours de l'histoire", ibid., 28 March 1989).

Without a doubt the most astonishing and most eventful of all those that that universe has known since the end of the Second World War. One may debate page after page the likely success or failure of Gorbachev's opening. But the fact is that it is happening before our very eyes and that, whatever happens, this will have thrown Soviet Russia into a radically new era. ...

An exceptional case in point. The old Soviet regime had for all sorts of different reasons — unbearable economic stagnation, exorbitant military expenditures, desire on the part of some in the nomenklatura to live like people in the West, difficulties to maintain stability by force in a too large, too diverse empire — entered into a phase of accelerated change. Nobody knows what type of state that evolves out of the current adventure. Soviet Russia is leaving the scourge of totalitarianism. She has still not become a free country.

Nevertheless, one may from now on qualify the cascade of events that since four years shaken the centre and the periphery of the immense Russia. It is a Revolution.

Le Figaro thus identified the turn of the year from 1988 to 1989 as the period when it was obvious that Mr. Gorbachev had altered Soviet policies in fundamental ways, domestically as well as in foreign policy. In contrast to most of the other newspapers, in the case of the French conservative paper it is possible to pinpoint the period when it acknowledged that alterations, important ones, had inceed occurred in Gorbachev's Soviet Union.

In addition to identifying an important turning point in Soviet politics, the editorial published on 28 March 1989, contained an explanation of why, in the paper's estimation, the Soviet reform process had started. There were two reasons given: the economic stagnation and the exorbitant military expenditures. In addition, the paper identified a bureaucratic explanation. *Le Figaro* believed that the fact that part of the Soviet nomenclature wanted to acquire a Western lifestyle contributed to the start of the reform process. Finally, the paper pointed to the difficulty of governing a vast state such as the Soviet Union. In other words, the paper highlighted explanations on level II, the state level, and level III, the bureaucratic level, in its accounting for the reasons why the Soviet Union undertook the grand reform experiment under Mr. Gorbachev. On the state level, the paper highlighted both the structure of the system and the inefficiency of the socialist economic system. It is notable that the paper chose to emphasize the structural reasons and not the individual factors.

While granting that Moscow had changed both its domestic and foreign policies, *Le Figaro* remained more sceptical concerning alterations in the latter policy sphere, even after March 1989. Regarding foreign policy, the Paris daily maintained a degree of scepticism for some time. It acknowledged that Soviet policies and tactics had changed, but it still believed that Moscow intended to pursue its old goals. Among these there were initiatives which were creating a rift between the U.S. and its allies in Europe, a striving for the denuclearization of (Western) Europe, all with the old end-goal in sight: Soviet domination of the whole of Europe. This assessment gradually changed, but there were still remnants of it as late as May 1990, when the Soviet Union was described as aiming for "l'equilibre que [Gorbatchev] rêve d'édifier, sur le ruines de l'empire de Staline, est germano-soviétique" ("Parler clair", *Le Figaro*, 31 May 1990) "the equilibrium that [Gorbachev] dreams to construct, on the ruins of Stalin's Empire, is German-Soviet".

In early 1990, the conservative French paper offered a broader assessment of where the entire process of change in the Soviet Union might end. It quoted with obvious support the famous book by the French Sovietologist Hélène Carrère d'Encausse, entitled *L'Empire Eclatée*. It noted that this book foresaw the start of nationalist sentiments in various parts of the Soviet empire. It ended its editorial: "Le réveil a sonné" ("L'empire éclaté", ibid., 15 January 1990).

The assessment that the end of the Soviet empire could be envisaged was repeated in a second context, that of a discussion regarding the Lithuanian striving for independence during that same winter and spring ("L'héritage en pièces", ibid., 12 March 1990).

A third step in this process was, for the French conservative paper, the demonstrations against Mr. Gorbachev on Red Square on 1 May 1990.[5]

The editorial on the declaration of independence by Lithuania, published on 12 March 1990, was clearest in terms of offering any attempt at forecasting:

> C'est vraiment la deuxième mort de Staline. Au cinquième anniversaire de l'arrivée au pouvoir de Mikhail Gorbatchev, l'indépendance, que la Lituanie est sur le point de proclamer, constitue un événement historique. La décision de Vilnius semble annoncer le début de la fin pour l'immense empire soviétique laissé en héritage par le "petit père des peuples" ("L'héritage en pièces", *Le Figaro*, 12 March 1990).

---

[5]"Ébranlement", ibid., 2 May 1990. Cf. "Le double jeu de Gorbatchev", ibid., 21 December 1990, where the paper comments on the resignation of Foreign Minister Eduard Shevardnadze and his speech upon resigning.

It is truly the second death of Stalin. By the fifth anniversary of the coming to power of Michail Gorbachev, the independence that Lithuania is on the verge of declaring constitutes an historical event. The decision taken by Vilnius seems to indicate the beginning of the end for the immense Soviet empire that "the little Father of the peoples'" had left as his legacy.

In the terms of this book, *Le Figaro* thus presented a forecast that the Soviet Union was in a process of terminal decline. This forecast was stated not just once, but at least three times in the first half of 1990. In other words, the conservative French paper presented a correct forecast of the end of the Soviet reform process more than 18 months before the event.

Le Figaro did not often deal with the aspirations of the Baltic republics for more independence ("L'héritage en pièces", ibid., 12 March 1990). This did not prevent the paper from being critical of President François Mitterrand and German Chancellor Helmut Kohl when the two, during the spring of 1990, issued a statement urging the authorities in Lithuania to suspend their unilateral declaration of independence and negotiate with Moscow (cf. Garthoff, 1994, p. 425, note 26 and Oberdorfer, 1992, pp. 399-404). The paper classified the statement as "choquant"("Choquant", *Le Figaro*, 28-29 April 1990) and noted that France had never formally approved the Soviet annexation of the Baltic states in 1940. At the very least, France should, in the paper's view, refrain from issuing public statements disapproving of a European people's striving for independence. It should be noted that this did not mean that *Le Figaro* explicitly supported the Lithuanian wish for independence, at least not up to the end of 1990.[6]

4.2.2 Le Monde

Le Monde noted "un accent krouchtchévien" ("Un geste peu crédible", *Le Monde*, 9 April 1985) in one of Gorbachev's very first speeches on foreign affairs as General Secretary in April 1985. The paper maintained a largely sceptical attitude towards the new Soviet leader for quite some time. In the autumn of 1985, it approvingly noted that the new leader used a quite different language than his predecessors, which it found refreshing, while still observing that words would have to be followed by deeds before any real changes in Soviet foreign policy could be seen ("Prendre date", ibid., 5

---

[6] The fact that it was impossible to find issues of *Le Figaro* from 1991 in Sweden made it impossible to analyse this paper's view of events in the Soviet Union that year. Attempts to contact the paper in France proved fruitless in terms of finding more editorials.

October 1985). The so-called Stockholm agreement on confidence-building measures and other security aspects was noted in September 1986. The Paris paper recorded that the Soviet Union had changed one crucial aspect of its security policy in relation to this agreement: it now showed an increasing willingness to accept verification on Soviet soil of arms control agreements. The paper did not believe, however, that this conclusively proved that the new Soviet leader had really changed this aspect of security policy for good ("Une percée", *Le Monde*, 23 September 1986).

The release of Andrei Sakharov in December 1986, as a climax to a year of important changes in Soviet policy both domestic and foreign, led the paper to the assessment that Mr. Gorbachev was now at "le Rubicon" ("M. Gorbatchev et le Rubicon", *Le Monde*, 28-29 December 1986). Whether the General Secretary was yet prepared to cross this river, or if indeed he would ever cross it, was still too early to tell, however. The paper noted that the central committee of the Communist Party had not met for many months, which indicated a power struggle.

It was only as a result of the Washington summit of December 1987, which included the accord on the abolition of Intermediate-range nuclear missiles (the INF Treaty), that *Le Monde* went so far as to state that something important had changed, at least in Soviet foreign policy. "Il se confirme que les relations entre Soviétiques et Américains sont passées, depuis le sommet de Washington en décembre dernier, de la détente à l'entente, en attendant que se développe plus leur coopération" ("De la détente à l'entente", ibid., 24 February 1988) "It is confirmed that the relations between the Soviets and the Americans have, since the summit in Washington last December, passed from détente to entente, while waiting for the further development of their co-operation." The paper noted that this development between the two superpowers had already gone further than the Nixon-Brezhnev détente some fifteen years earlier.

Even following the summit in Moscow in May-June 1988, *Le Monde*, while positively regarding many of the accords and the general tone of the summit, still noted that the changes in Soviet policy were not yet really institutionalized. It was clear that enormous changes had occurred in Soviet policies, domestic as well as external, by mid-1988. Even if this was so, these changes would not be irreversible until fundamental changes had also been undertaken in Soviet institutions. By mid-1988 this had not yet happened ("Adieu à 'l'empire du mal'", ibid., 3 June 1988).

This difficulty in pinpointing when *Le Monde* stated that Soviet policy had changed is indicative of the more general problem in the analysis of the newspaper editorials of identifying a specific time at which these articles unequivocally asserted, "Soviet (foreign) policy has changed". As shown in chapter 3, it was generally possible to identify such a moment for the politicians. They regarded it as part of their task in practising their country's foreign policy to make assessments of this type, to state to their domestic audiences as well as to their international interlocutors that a certain condition in their international environment had changed. In the case of the majority of the editorialists, by contrast, there was no such tendency. The inclination of the editorialists was, rather, to note, on the one hand, that changes had indeed occurred in Soviet policies, but that, on the other, these were to a large degree dependent on the position of Mr. Gorbachev as an individual, and were not solidly based in institutional changes.

The issue of nationalism, including the Baltic questions, began to be covered on page 1 of *Le Monde* in early 1988 ("'Glasnost' et nationalités", ibid., 25 February 1988 and "Identité balte", ibid., 18 June 1988). Throughout 1988 the paper gave more attention to the disturbances in the Caucasus than it did to stories about the Baltic republics.

The coverage of Mr. Gorbachev's years in power from about mid-1988 until the first half of 1990 in the editorials of *Le Monde* was, to a large extent, focused on two factors. One was *the leader himself*, and his leadership style, which were seen in a very positive light:

> L'opération, enfin, a été conduite dans un style à couper le souffle qui caractérise de plus en plus le numéro un du Kremlin, et dont son image, en URSS comme à l'extérieur, ne peut que profiter. On s'interrogeait il y a quelques jours sur le point de savoir s'il était sur le défensive ou s'il avait décidé de prendre l'initiative. La réponse est nette, et c'est à lui qu'est revenu le choix de dramatiser une situation dont il ne semble, à aucun moment, avoir perdu le contrôle ("Une offensive éclair", ibid., 2-3 October 1988).
>
> The operation was conducted in the breathtaking style that more and more characterises the number one in the Kremlin, and from which his image, within the U.S.S.R. as well as outside it, cannot but profit. One asked oneself a couple of days ago whether or not he was on the defensive or whether he had decided to take the initiative. The answer is clear and it has fallen to him to dramatise a situation that he does not seem to have lost control of for a single moment.

Le Monde thus gave a picture of a very determined and strong leader who was ready to act, in this case in the fall of 1988. It portrayed a leader, moreover, who was in total control of the political situation. At the same time, however, and this was the second factor, "La 'perestroïka' [est] en danger" ("La 'perestroïka' en danger", ibid., 27-28 November 1988). The danger to perestroika came from the outbreaks of *nationalist violence* in the outlying republics, in particular those in the Caucasus. This danger had increased still more, in the eyes of the paper, by the violent confrontation in Tbilisi, in Georgia, which occurred in April 1989. There it was for the first time the "forces de l'ordre" ("Bavure ou provocation?", ibid., 11 April 1989) who were the main culprits, and not the mobs and various irregular forces as had previously been the case, for example in Nagorno-Karabakh.

As 1989 progressed, the French paper became more nuanced in its treatment of the "active" Soviet leader. It noted that the fact that most of his main rivals had lost their positions in the main centres of Soviet power meant that Mr. Gorbachev could no longer blame anyone else if his reforms failed ("En première ligne", ibid., 27 April 1989).

Simultaneously, the nationalist issues continued to worsen from the Soviet leader's perspective. The fact that the Baltic Republics contested the very basis of their accession to the Soviet Union in 1940 was characterized in the following way in August, 1989: "De tous les problèmes que posent les relations entre les nationalités au sein de l'URSS, celui-ci menace donc directement l'existence même de la fédération dans ses frontières actuelles" ("La fédération menacée", *Le Monde*, 25 August 1989; cf. "Et maintenant la Lituanie?", ibid., 28 December 1989) "Of all the problems that relations between nationalities inside the U.S.S.R. poses, this one directly threatens the very existence of the federation within its current borders". More than two years before the eventual collapse of the Soviet State, *Le Monde* identified what many analysts in retrospect regard as one of the vital causes of its demise: the nationalist question. The political strength of the situation in the Baltic Republics in this regard was at the same time highlighted.

The seriousness of the situation in the Soviet Union, as illustrated by events in and around the Baltic republics, continued to worsen in the early months of 1990. Now, *Le Monde* saw no more of the extremely dynamic leader it so vividly characterized some 28 months earlier. What was characteristic of Mr. Gorbachev's handling of the crisis surrounding the declaration of independence by Lithuania in early 1990 was, rather, that "il est bien tard" ("Moi ou le chaos?", ibid., 13 January 1990) "it is very late".

It was during this period, in January 1990, that the French leftist paper, essentially for the first time, ventured to issue what was at least very close to a concrete prognosis:

C'est bien pourquoi le cycle infernal enclenché en Transcaucasie ramène en fin de compte au problème que posent, de manière infiniment plus policée, les Baltes: après la Lituanie, c'est L'Azerbaïdjan sûrement, la Géorgie sans doute, qui vont réclamer leur indépendance. Et il est difficile d'imaginer comment la "féderation rénovée" que M. Gorbatchev appelle de ses vœux pourra étre édifiée sur les ruines encore fumantes de son empire ("Un nouveau Liban?", *Le Monde*, 16 January 1990).

This is why the infernal cycle put in motion in Trancaucasia leads in the final analysis to the problem that is posed, in an infinitely more civilised way, by the Balts: after Lithuania, it is surely Azerbaijan, no doubt Georgia, who will demand their independence. And it is difficult to imagine how the "renewed federation" that Mr. Gorbachev wishes to reach could be built on the still smoldering ruins of his empire.

At the very least, *Le Monde* was very sceptical indeed concerning the chances for any remake of the Soviet "Union". The logical conclusion of the paper's views was rather that the Soviet Union, in its then-existing form, was doomed. In contrast to its French competitor, *Le Figaro*, however, *Le Monde* never explicitly made a forecast to this effect.

The changes in Soviet foreign policy were, however, much more positively assessed in *Le Monde* than in the other French paper. The new ways in which East-West relations were handled in 1990 were characterized in the following way: "...la souplesse de la diplomatie soviétique permet maintenant de faire en deux jours le travail qui prenait naguère des années" ("La souplesse du Kremlin", ibid., 15 February 1990) "...the flexibility of Soviet diplomacy now makes it possible to accomplish in two days the work that previously took years."

Le Monde never explicitly tried to explain the reasons behind the start of the Soviet reform process. This was despite the fact that events in the Soviet Union received immense attention in the paper during Mr. Gorbachev's years in power. Out of 310 issues at the most per year, with only one editorial-type article published each day, *Le Monde* published one such article on the Soviet Union more than one time out of ten in each of the years from 1986 through 1991.[7] This was a very heavy emphasis indeed on Soviet affairs, especially if one considers that this single article in each issue might cover not only foreign affairs, but also domestic, i.e., French, issues.

---

[7] Cf. appendix 2b.

4.2.3 Conclusion: The French Newspapers

The two French newspapers differed only marginally in their diagnosis of the domestic Soviet situation. *Le Figaro* was the clearer of the two in its assessment that the leadership in Moscow had indeed changed Soviet domestic policy permanently. In the conservative paper's eyes, the Soviet Union was undergoing enormous, even "revolutionary" change by the first few months of 1989. This was an important change from the previous years of Gorbachev's rule, which had invariably been characterized in negative terms. There were still caveats even in 1989, though. *Le Figaro* noted that this change had not resulted in full democracy by that time, nor in the Soviet Union's becoming a "free" country. Yet, the changes had been so many and so multifaceted that the country had — by early 1989 — changed forever. This change of mind is all the more remarkable considering the fact that *Le Figaro* gave perhaps the most negative assessments of all the papers covered here during the period from 1985 until the autumn of 1988.

Le Monde, which gave Soviet events extensive coverage in its only editorial-type article, discussed the basic structure of the new Soviet Union during 1988 and moved closer to a clear-cut assessment that the country had changed by March 1989. Still, in contrast to its French counterpart, one cannot find a specific point in time where *Le Monde* made the outright assessment that "the Soviet Union has changed for good". There were always reservations that characterized the political situation as being too complex for making such a clear statement.

With respect to foreign policy, the conservative French paper was again the most explicit. *Le Monde* tended to concentrate on domestic developments in the Soviet Union after mid-1988, whereas for *Le Figaro*, foreign policy was more in focus even after that time. By mid-1988 *Le Monde* classified the superpower relationship as being more positive than the détente of the early 1970s, while still warning that the changes seen to that point in Soviet policies were not irreversible.

Another difference between the two newspapers was that in *Le Figaro* there was a greater distinction between the analysis of domestic and foreign policy than there was in *Le Monde*. Even if the conservative paper clarified its view that the Soviet Union was indeed in a process of truly fundamental change by March 1989, these assessments focused on domestic matters. With respect to foreign policy, *Le Figaro* continued to note both positive and negative aspects well into 1990.

Only *Le Figaro* attempted to explain why the Soviet reform process started. The paper gave four reasons. These were focused on explanations at level II, the structure of the state. There were aspects concerning the totalitarian system as well as those that focused on the failings of the socialist economy. The conservative French paper also mentioned the wish of part of the Soviet leadership to live like those in the West. The latter is classified as belonging to explanatory level III, the bureaucracy.

The French newspapers, furthermore, touched upon the likely future of the Soviet experiment. *Le Figaro* was most specific in this respect as well. The Paris daily published three editorial articles in the first five months of 1990, the thrust of which was that the Soviet Union had entered a process that would lead to the end of the Soviet empire and/or the resignation of the Soviet leader. This is, in the terms specified in section 1.3, a correct forecast about what would happen in the Soviet Union issued more than 18 months before the Soviet State collapsed.

Le Monde likewise tried to look into the Soviet future. On at least two occasions in the first half of 1990 it discussed what was likely to happen to Gorbachev and his experiments. The paper did not go any further, however, than pointing out the risks of failure for the Soviet leader. There was no forecast issued.

In the chapter on the political analysis of Soviet affairs in the Gorbachev era, I found that the French material clearly reflected a French view of international affairs. This was the sense that there was something special about the relationship between the Soviet Union and France due to the special position of Paris in international politics. This tendency was not equally strong in the two French newspapers. There was, to be sure, a French angle on bilateral relations between Paris and Moscow here as well. When it comes to the overarching questions of greatest importance to this book, however, it was hard to find any real traces of a French foreign policy orientation in the analysis presented by the two Paris newspapers. The factor that rather seemed to influence the contents of the two French newspapers' analysis of Moscow from 1985 to 1991 strongly was the political ideology to which each newspaper subscribes.

4.3 The British Newspapers

4.3.1 The Times

The conservative British newspaper was, like its French counterpart, initially very negative towards the process of change in the Soviet Union. A quote from *The Times'* very first editorial on the new Soviet leader exemplifies this:

> The passing of the Chernenko era is unlikely to result in any immediate or dramatic change in the USSR or in its relations with the West. ...
> As a man long experienced in struggling with the endemic problems of the Soviet economy, Mr. Gorbachev might well promote energetically various new projects — already circulating in draft proposals — to make the system more efficient. He could prove to be a man with whom Western politicians feel more at home than with Lenin's heirs. Many certainly have pinned their hopes of improved relations on a pro-détente Gorbachev administration. But neither a natural desire for cheap credit and advanced technology to strengthen the Soviet economy nor an even more natural wish to avoid a nuclear holocaust makes Mr. Gorbachev a new star on the horizon. We have been here before ("Mr. Gorbachov's Hour", *The Times*, 12 March 1985).

This basic wariness towards the new Soviet leader was further illustrated by the paper's response to Mr. Gorbachev's announcement of a freeze in nuclear testing in early August 1985. This is characterized as "precisely the kind of empty propaganda gesture, which we have seen so often over the last few years" ("Mr. Shevardnadze's Smile", ibid., 2 August 1985).

The Times reacted fairly positively to the summit meeting between President Reagan and Mr. Gorbachev in November 1985, as well as to the fallout from the first few months afterwards (see "Hard Work Ahead", *The Times,* 22 November 1985 and "Home from the Summit", ibid., 25 November 1985). Still, even in the first half of 1986, Mr. Gorbachev's reformist intentions were negatively compared to those of one of his predecessors, Mr. Khrushchev ("Thirty Years on at the Kremlin", ibid., 14 February 1986).

During the second half of 1986, the tenor of the analysis of Soviet affairs gradually changed at *The Times*. The first indication was an article about the outcome of the Stockholm conference on confidence-and-security-building measures. In this context, some observers detected a greater willingness on the part of Moscow to accept verification of arms control measures on its own territory than had ever been the case up to that point ("Verifying Progress", ibid., 21 August 1986).

The coverage of the Reykjavik meeting of October 1986 also contained some positive coments about Soviet policies (see "Ripples from Reykjavik", *The Times*, 17 October 1986 and "Zeroing in on Europe", ibid., 24 October 1986). The gradually more positive tone in the conservative British paper's analysis of events in and around Moscow culminated in a fascinating editorial published just before the end of 1986:

> At the end of 1986, there are only faint intimations of change. If they become clearer in 1987, it may then become possible to talk of a second phase in the October Revolution. This would be a phase in which the sense of mission coupled with insecurity which has pervaded Soviet foreign policy is replaced by a Soviet readiness to take its place in the international arena as a normal state. It would be a phase in which criticism of the Communist Party was permitted, in which the remaining heirs of the Russian intelligentsia could play a role with pride. It would be a phase in which the invasion of Afghanistan, the detention of Andrei Sakharov and the death of Anatoly Marchenko could not happen.[8]

This is not a real prediction about what was likely to happen. Still, coming from a conservative newspaper that had, up to that point, generally shown an extreme scepticism about a Soviet foreign policy that it almost without exception characterized as "militaristic", "expansionist", and bent upon achieving the goal of nurturing a break between the U.S. and its West European allies, this language was remarkably different from before. It also contained a very imprecise prognosis that was generally correct in its foretelling of the developments that were to occur in the coming years.

During 1987 and 1988 there were many editorials on Soviet affairs in *The Times*.[9] The paper analysed Soviet developments with an eye for positive developments in both domestic and foreign affairs. It is hard, however, to identify a point at which the paper determined that the Soviet Union had permanently changed for the better. Instead, there was always a sense of "yes, but..." in these assessments, particularly on Moscow's foreign policy. "Yes, the Soviet Union has changed vastly, but there are still risks." A quote from an editorial published in late 1988 is indicative:

> The West needs to remember, though many like to forget, that it was the defence build-up of the Reagan administration which forced the Soviet Union to realise that its own economy could not for long afford the military superiority it had achieved. ...Because America now deals with Mr Gorbachev

---

[8] "If...", *The Times*, 30 December 1986. Anatoly Marchenko was a Soviet dissident who died in a labour camp in the late autumn of 1986. The treatment of dissidents was one of the issues on which the Western newspapers assessed the degree of change in Soviet policies.

[9] For precise data see appendix 2b.

from a position of strength, today's youngsters in the West can look to a safer, more peaceful world than their parents or grandparents ever could ("Peace through strength", *The Times*, 11 December 1988).

But Mr Gorbachev must be given his due too. He is rightly perceived as a socialist with a human face, a man whose underlying humanity is sensed not only by world leaders but also by hard-bitten crowds on the sidewalks of New York ("Peace through strength", ibid., 11 December 1988).

It would be difficult to find a more clear-cut example of "realism" as a world-view, a basic view of what ultimately determines the behaviour of nations in the international arena.[10] *The Times* was open to the changes that were occurring in the Soviet Union, but the paper's fundamental view of international affairs did not change during Mr. Gorbachev's years in power. Still, even if *The Times* was more sceptical than most of its newspaper counterparts, it must be concluded that by December 1988 the conservative British paper had also determined that the Soviet Union had by then changed its foreign policy very substantially. As discussed in connection with the analysis of *Le Monde*, however, *The Times* also exhibited a clear tendency to note changes as they occurred, but it reserved judgement concerning whether or not these changes would last.

Even if *The Times* thus acknowledged that the Soviet Union by December 1988 was very different from before, the paper's basic opinion of the Soviet system remained, even after four years of reforms under Mr. Gorbachev, that "Mr Gorbachev is attempting, and not all that successfully, to change a system that should be scrapped altogether" ("Evidence — not dogma: Gorbachev's visit to Britain", ibid., 9 April 1989). *The Times*, in other words, regarded the Soviet system as unreformable. The only way to change it permanently would be to abolish the system altogether. Since the system had not been successfully reformed in economic terms, there was no point in the West trying to give it massive economic aid.

The Times' diagnosis of developments in the Soviet Union under Mr. Gorbachev thus took a positive tone in many respects. Underlying this was, however, a fundamental scepticism about the possibility of ever carrying out really meaningful domestic reforms of the Soviet system, an outlook resembling that associatied with the totalitarian analytical model so prominent in Sovietology. Regarding foreign policy, the paper also acknowledged that the Soviet leader had undertaken many positive new

---

[10] Cf. chapter 1.3.3.

steps. It refused to believe, however, that these were made purely out of the goodness of Mr. Gorbachev's heart. Instead, it was to a significant extent the constant political and military pressure from the West, particularly the United States, which was finally bearing fruit. This analysis did not preclude an acknowledgement from the paper that the Soviet leader was a humanist. In the newspaper's view, such personal aspects were, however, in the end always secondary to the fundamental structural characteristics that ultimately determined the course of foreign and domestic politics, whether in the Soviet Union or in other countries.

In its explanation of why Mr. Gorbachev embarked upon his perestroika and other policies, *The Times* linked the sorry state of the Soviet economy with the Soviet Union's external power. Both were influenced by Mr. Reagan's policies of military build-up which, in the paper's view, forced the Soviet leadership to realize that it had to both reform its economy and scale down its external expenditures if the system were to remain at all viable ("Peace through strength", ibid., 11 December 1988).

In addition, the paper acknowledged that Mr. Gorbachev was aware of the problems that existed in Soviet society as he took power in 1985. It mentioned, in particular, economic "stagnation"("Momentum of Change: Soviet National Conference", ibid., 4 July 1988), the bureaucratization of the state, with, for instance, a "duplication of functions between the communist party and a government which has been elected only in the loosest of senses" (Ibid.). As a result of the economic downturn, the Soviet leader realized that the system was unable to provide a decent living standard for its population. Based upon this analysis, he then acted to try to change the system.

In other words, in its accounting for the reasons why the Soviet reform period started in 1985, *The Times* combined explanations from level I, a realist perspective on international politics; level II, the sorry state of the economy; and level IV, the individual level. For the conservative British paper, it was an article of faith that one crucial reason behind the Soviet changes was outside pressure, emanating mainly from the United States (see for example "A Summit of Significance: Moscow Summit", ibid., 5 June 1988).

Equally, however, *The Times* acknowledged that Mr. Gorbachev's personal qualities, particularly his ability to analyse the shortcomings of his state and to draw practical conclusions therefrom, were a crucial explanation for why Soviet policies changed to such a large extent from 1985 on.

The Times and France's *Le Figaro* are the only two papers of the eight surveyed here that successfully made a forecast concerning the dissolution of the Soviet Union. In the case of the British Conservative paper, its most precise prognosis was printed in the fall of 1989:

> The 1990s will be dominated by two events so enormous in their significance that they will change the shape of world politics as we have known it these past 40 years.
> The breakup of the Soviet Empire and the reunification of Germany will have consequences that most politicians have yet to grasp. ...
> Of the two great events that will dominate the next decade, the breakup of the Soviet empire is the more important, for without it there could be no reunion of Germany. But what is at stake for Moscow is more than just the loss of its European satellites like East Germany. The whole Soviet Union of more than 100 nationalities is about to burst asunder in much the same way that the British Empire fell apart only the day before yesterday. ...
> During the 1980s it has become clear that the Soviet Union is in even steeper economic decline, and this will encourage its subject peoples to dash for freedom, too.
> But the collapse of the world's last great imperial power is bound to be messy. There is a danger of enormous communal conflicts, with attendant ethnic unrest and race riots...There will be hardliners in the Kremlin who will want to send troops to quell the rebellious provinces..... These hawks will be supported by generals dismayed that the break-up of the Soviet Empire will mean the end of the Soviet Union as a superpower. ...
> We do not know how Mr Gorbachev will react to such forces, or if he will survive them. But it is clear that, as the Soviet Disunion gathers pace, the world could become, at least temporarily, a more dangerous place, especially if a reactionary Russian regime resorts to external military adventures as a diversion to keep its restless nationalities in line ("The Fourth German Reich", *The Times*, 12 November 1989).

In the terms introduced in chapter 1, I regard this as a correct forecast, made 25 months in advance, that the Soviet Union was going to disintegrate as a state. The time lag is imprecise. On the other hand, this forecast is the most detailed in the large amount of material that I have covered for this book. Most of these details had proven correct as 1989 turned into 1990, and then into 1991. The Times frequently returned to the topic of the chances for a continuation of the Soviet Union as a sovereign state, but the editorialists, on these occasions, were less precise about what would likely happen than they were in the editorial excerpted above.[11]

The struggle of the Baltic Republics to break free of the Soviet Union received much coverage. The first time the issue was mentioned was in late February 1988, if one excludes an editorial in the autumn of 1986 about a possible visit by the Pope to Lithuania. In December 1989, *The Times* placed the whole problem of the nationalities into a broader context regarding the Soviet empire. The Baltic aspirations were seen as just one instance of a much broader process, with potentially devastating consequences for the future of the Soviet State. One phrase from the editorial catches the crux of the argument: "Without a ruling Communist party apparatus, drawn from each national group in the empire owing allegiance to the centre, the nationalities will reassert themselves and demand independence" ("A brave, unsure new world", ibid., 31 December 1989). The Communist party could no longer fulfil this role, however, because its omnipotence was no longer deemed acceptable.

During the first half of 1990, there was a rapid development in Lithuania, culminating in a declaration of independence issued by the new leadership in the republic in March. *The Times* was strongly supportive of the policies of the new Lithuanian government. At the same time, it was critical towards the Western governments that, in the paper's view, were too understanding of Mr. Gorbachev's situation and less faithful to their democratic ideals than they ought to be. This editorial from late March 1990 gives the gist of the paper's views:

> The silence coming from the White House, Downing Street and most West European chancelleries as the Kremlin attempts to intimidate Lithuania into submission is deafening, and shaming. The reality is that, though no shots have been fired and no tanks have run over armed protesters, the Red Army has occupied Lithuania these past two weeks to dissuade it from self-determination. ...
>
> There could be no clearer example of the principle of self-determination in action, a principle which progressive folk used to get very exercised about; but now no longer, it seems, if it means upsetting Mr Gorbachev ("Still on guard", *The Times*, 28 March 1990).

[11] See, for example, "A Russian Commonwealth", *The Times*, June 14, 1990 and "Time running out in Moscow", ibid. 17 November 1990. In the latter editorial the Soviet Union is compared to previous empires which have declined and fallen, like the Ottoman and the British Empire. Perhaps, like for them, the decline may take "decades" writes the paper. As late as in March 1991, the paper is still off in its prognosis: "Will there still be a Soviet Union in a year's time? Probably yes, but it may well be smaller than at present." "No zeal for union", ibid., 19 March.

4.3.2 The Guardian

The Guardian was more positive towards the new Soviet leader and his policies than its British counterpart. It believed that the Soviet State could be reformed. A quote from *The Guardian's* very first editorial about Gorbachev in power captures the flavour of the basic argument:

> The new, permanent leader, like his two fleeting predecessors, can only rule by consent and agreement amongst the power barons who surround him. There will be no overnight upheavals. There will be merely gradual shifts of direction. Yet, even so, the swift emergence of Mr. Gorbachev is an event of signal and stretching importance. Whilst change comes slowly to the Soviet Union, change does come. ...
>
> It is, above all, the style of the man that is different. As his London hosts discovered, he smiles; he pumps hands and pummels shoulders in crowds (working them, for all the world, like a Western politician running for office); and he makes jokes. No Russian leader since Khrushchev has had such instant media appeal; and Gorbachev, unlike Khrushchev, is a smooth operator, not a flamboyant peasant ("This time there's a difference", *The Guardian*, 12 March 1985).

With the exception of a very negative assessment of Gorbachev's handling of the nuclear disaster at Chernobyl in April 1986 and its aftermath ("Safety must take over from silence", ibid., 1 May 1986) *The Guardian* continued to be well disposed towards the policies and proposals emanating from the Kremlin. By the time of the release of Andrei Sakharov in December 1986 the paper continued to be clearly more positive towards Mr. Gorbachev's new moves in foreign policy, and it was more inclined to believe that the Soviet leader's intentions concerning his domestic reforms were benevolent than was *The Times* ("Gorbachev's new broom keeps on sweeping", *The Guardian*, 20 December 1986).

In an editorial published in June 1988, *The Guardian* gave its views of the Soviet leader, as well as of how it saw the future of relations between that country and Western Europe after more than three years of the Soviet experiment:

> The wonders never cease. Mikhail Gorbachev does not pause for rest, allows no lull, gives events their own pell-mell momentum. He is, more clearly than ever, bent upon the radical restructuring of the Soviet Union; and it is a test, to glory or destruction, of his vision. ...

Once the USSR is locked more closely to the economic fortunes of the West, seeking loans and investment as a vast new market opens up, then the certainties we have known since 1945 will dwindle away. ... Economic interdependence makes its own friends, and enemies; incontrovertibly, though, it rewrites the bases of relationships. ... Too far along the road? Perhaps; but only a little too far. Mikhail Gorbachev, a driven man, moves as though there were no tomorrow ("No pause for rest along the road", *The Guardian,* 29 June 1988).

This quote effectively catches several elements characteristic of the liberal British newspaper's views of the Gorbachev experiment. There was the positive view of the Soviet leader's reforms, expressed in terms of clear admiration for him as a politician and a world leader. Indeed, *The Guardian* was the newspaper in the sample studied here that had the most sympathy for the policies and intentions of Mr. Gorbachev. There was also the belief that the Soviet Union would be tied into the Western economic system by way of economic interdependence. This is an indication of *The Guardian's* world-view, which was very close to what, in the study of international relations, is known as the interdependence school. This, once again, is in stark contrast to *The Times'* realist world-view.[12] It is also obvious that by June 1988 *The Guardian* had concluded that the Soviet Union had taken fundamental steps in foreign policy, steps that were of such magnitude that they deserved a response from the countries in the West.

There was yet another difference between the ways the two British newspapers analysed the Soviet phenomena. *The Times* took a more detached, inquisitive view, whereas *The Guardian* had a stronger tendency to take Mr. Gorbachev's words at face value and to base its assessments more or less directly on the Soviet leader's own perspective. The conservative paper's approach was partly based on its more negative appraisal of both the Soviet system more generally and of the new Soviet leader in particular, but there was also a probing element in the conservative paper's analysis that was mostly lacking in the liberal paper's editorials.

As the conditions in the Soviet Union worsened in 1988, *The Guardian* demonstrated its awareness that the gamble was such that the whole system might fall apart if Mr. Gorbachev lost control of the situation. The "violent

---

[12] One issue which clearly illustrates this difference in outlook is the U.S. Strategic Defense Initiative (SDI). *The Times* is strongly in favour, cf. for example: "Geneva Intermission", *The Times*, 23 April 1985, whereas *The Guardian* is against, see: "A case against Star Wars", *The Guardian*, 1 May 1985.

stirrings of nationalism" ("Nerve, and a helping hand for Mikhail", *The Guardian*, 24 October 1988) were identified as possibly contagious. In the view of the paper, the Western countries had an important role to play in the Soviet drama. Indeed, it appears as if *The Guardian* believed that aid from the West could be even more important than processes inside the Soviet Union in determining the Soviet future: "His survival — two or three years hence — will depend on Western assistance" (Ibid.). *The Times* was much more sceptical about aiding what it called "a basket-case economy"("Evidence — not dogma: Gorbachev's visit to Britain", *The Times*, 9 April 1989), at least before a wide-ranging economic reform had been carried out.

As the Soviet drama unfolded, *The Guardian* gave its overall view in an editorial in February 1990:

> There is a real sense now that the Soviet President is not the master but the driven, manipulating servant of events. ...
> The wonders of accelerated glasnost are extreme; the perils of collapsing perestroika dog them every step of the way. This is an end game without any predictable end in sight ("An end game with no end in sight", ibid., 8 February 1990).

The Guardian identified the extreme fluidity of the situation, but it never actually predicted that the Soviet system was going to collapse, as *The Times* did. By early 1990 the liberal paper had a very different view of the situation in Moscow, however, as compared to its views some 20 months earlier. The paper still admired Gorbachev, but there was a realization that developments were so complex that they were outside the control even of this "master politician" (Ibid.).

The issue of the independence struggle of the Baltic Republics received a sceptical treatment in *The Guardian*. The paper viewed the issue of when the Baltic States should receive their formal independence as distinctly secondary in importance for the West, as compared to its interest in the stability of the Soviet Union:

> Why are these few millions of frustrated Scandinavians insulting the man who has lifted the shadow of a third world war, and risking the new peace which has benefited all Europeans? They could push Mr Gorbachev into harsher sanctions, or even the use of force, resulting in an unavoidable deterioration in relations with the West at a time when matters of great

moment, notably the reunification of Germany, await settlement. Or, a Baltic debacle could provoke a coup by the army and the conservatives in the Party which would bring President Gorbachev down. These may still be remote possibilities, but they are real, and they are dire. ...
The West has treated Baltic demands for help with great caution, and has in practice backed Mr Gorbachev's sanctions on Lithuania. We have been right to do so. The stability of the Soviet Union as a whole is more important than the instant satisfaction of Baltic national aspirations. On the other hand, the stability of the Soviet Union, and Mr. Gorbachev's chances of continuing as its effective leader, would best be served by a far sighted decision to let these people go — on Soviet terms, on a Soviet time scale, with appropriate trade and transit treaties, and after making them jump through appropriate Soviet legal hoops: but let them go, nevertheless ("At sea in the Baltic", *The Guardian*, 3 May 1990).

The aspiration of the Baltic peoples for freedom, for being able to decide for themselves whether or not they wanted to belong to the Soviet Union, was thus for *The Guardian* a less important issue in the larger scheme of things. The paper still believed that the Balts should receive independence eventually, but it was very explicit in its demand that these small nations should take care that the procedures by which they approached their goals must follow proper Soviet rules.

The explanation for why the reforms were started under Mr. Gorbachev was not very developed in *The Guardian*. In fairly veiled allusions, the newspaper pointed to the failing of the socialist economy in the Soviet Union to provide the state with sufficient growth. This was an explanation of type II b, in the terms of my table 1.2.

4.3.3 Conclusion: The British Newspapers

The Times and *The Guardian* were quite different in their general diagnoses of Soviet developments. The conservative paper had a very negative view of the Soviet system, as well as of the prospects for change from the beginning of Mr. Gorbachev's tenure in office. This is contrasted with the liberal paper's much more optimistic initial opinion, both concerning the chances for changing the Soviet system and regarding the personal qualities of the new leader. *The Times*, while it very conscientiously noted all the positive changes in Soviet foreign and domestic policies, never wavered from its basic outlook that the Soviet system could not be reformed and ought to be abolished. One untypical editorial published in late 1986 was the only exception to this rule.

It is notable that despite these important differences in their basic views of the Soviet system, the two British newspapers were not very different in their diagnoses of the changes, in particular those concerning Soviet foreign policy. This happened in 1988. Both papers also still displayed the caution characteristic of most editorial pages surveyed here when it came to making a clear-cut assessment that Soviet policies had changed for good, issuing caveats at the same time as they noted important changes. *The Guardian*, true to its more positive assessment of the Soviet leader, came closer to actually stating that the changes by mid-1988 were indeed lasting, while *The Times* always issued more reservations. Indeed, it would be a contradiction for *The Times* to acknowledge that a system that the paper basically regarded as "unreformable" has indeed changed for good.

The Times presented a more multifaceted explanation of why the Soviet reform experiment started than did *The Guardian*. A prominent part of this explanation, on the part of the conservative paper, was pressure from the United States. This pressure, mainly the defence build-up under President Reagan, made the Soviet leadership realize that it could not maintain its military strength without reforming the Soviet economy. The inefficiencies of the Soviet economic system were also singled out, explanation II b. In addition, *The Times* gave a prominent place to the personal role of the Soviet leader in first recognizing the domestic problems his nation faced and then in doing something to try to correct those perceived shortcomings. The two explanatory factors were at level I a and IV b in the terms of the explanatory framework applied here. For *The Guardian*, it was in principle only the failings of the socialist economy in the Soviet Union, explanation II b, which were singled out.

The Times was, together with *Le Figaro*, the most explicit and successful of the eight newspapers scrutinized in this book in trying to foretell what would happen to the Soviet reform process. The Soviet disintegration was forecast in the late autumn of 1989. This was done is some detail, in a way that identified several things which would come to be realized during the final two years of the Soviet Union. *The Guardian*, while duly noting how the Soviet leader had lost control of his state by the first months of 1990, never issued any forecast of what the final outcome of the events in Russia might be.

It should be noted that the two British papers had distinct outlooks on international politics that clearly differed. *The Times*, which tellingly put the headline "Peace Through Strength" on one of its editorials, clearly distinguished itself as subscribing to realism. *The Guardian* was almost equally explicit in its beliefs in interdependence as the perspective to hold on international relations.

One of the general points of focus in this book concerns whether differences in analysis of Soviet events can be explained largely by the nationalist lenses through which analysts in different countries perceive what is happening, or whether differences of political ideology would be the more likely explanation. The analysis of the two British newspapers indicates that the ideological dimension was important for explaining why they differed in their investigation of events during Mr. Gorbachev's years in power. The most important point on which this can be detected concerns *The Times'* correct forecast, made in the autumn of 1989, to the effect that the Soviet Union would collapse in the 1990s, while *The Guardian* issued no such prognosis. It is at least arguable that the negative attitude that *The Times* brought to a political system that is classified as totalitarian made it more likely to detect the downward spiral of the system than was *The Guardian*, which held a less negative view of the system.

4.4 The Swedish Newspapers

4.4.1 Svenska Dagbladet[13]

The conservative Swedish daily initially manifested an attitude towards Mr. Gorbachev that strongly resembled that shown by its two conservative counterparts in France and Great Britain. An editorial from the beginning of April 1985 is illustrative:

> In an interview published in Pravda Mikhail Gorbachev stated that the Soviet Union from now on has put a moratorium on the deployment of new medium-range missiles in Europe. ...
> These words can be seen as lights in the darkness by anyone who so wishes, but on the whole the Pravda interview showed, as expected, that the change of leadership in Moscow hasn't changed the Soviet Union's security policy. Apparent concessions are offered to hide an unchangeable basic position.[14]

---

[13] Svenska Dagbladet = The Swedish Daily.
[14] "Gorbachev's Initiative", *Svenska Dagbladet*, 9 April 1985. Cf. "Gorbachev's Teeth of Steel", ibid. 28 September 1985. All translations from the Swedish are by the author.

In connection with the Soviet leader's visit to Paris in early October 1985, *Svenska Dagbladet* discussed Moscow's foreign and security policy. The paper highlighted his aims, which were stated to be a weakening of the Western alliance and the guarantee that the Soviet Union would be militarily superior. Mr. Gorbachev's new policy proposals were characterized as "propagandistic initiatives"("A Russian in Paris", ibid., 5 October 1985).

The conservative Swedish paper's views of the Soviet system and of international politics in general were thus very similar to those held by *The Times*. *Svenska Dagbladet* classified the Soviet system as totalitarian, and it had a realist view of international relations.

In October 1986, *Svenska Dagbladet* published an editorial that was clearly critical of both superpowers. This was in connection with the fallout from the complex and confused meeting between the two superpower leaders at Reykjavik (see in particular "The Superpower Game", ibid., 24 October 1986).

During 1987, the paper began to acknowledge that things were indeed happening in the Kremlin. It still cautioned against too far-reaching conclusions concerning the significance of this, however ("Behind the Kremlin's Walls", ibid., 2 November 1987).

In the second half of 1988, the Swedish newspaper acknowledged that the changes in Moscow had indeed been profound. This more welcoming attitude was always mixed with an uncertainty concerning whether Mr. Gorbachev was really firmly entrenched in the seat of power in Moscow, or whether he risked being overthrown:

> This totality of concrete actions creates confidence. Gorbachev is obviously serious with his outstretched hand, and he has already taken several steps himself to establish a new climate in international politics.
>
> A response from other actors is appropriate. ...Whether he succeeds in finding solutions to all political and economic difficulties is still very uncertain, and we know, furthermore, that it was not the weakness of the outside world that caused a change of course in Moscow ("Gorbachev's dramatic day", ibid., 9 December 1988. Cf. also "Peace and freedom", ibid., 3 June 1988).

The position of the paper was thus, starting from mid-1988, that yes, the new Soviet leader was indeed for real; he was attempting to change his political system in fundamental ways. What was not certain, however, was whether the system was willing to accept the type of wide-ranging change that the Soviet leader planned to accomplish. *Svenska Dagbladet* thus always remained reserved on the fundamental point of whether or not the Soviet system was indeed reformable.

During 1989 the newspaper took some further steps in the development of its views about the scope of the reforms undertaken by the Soviet leader. In May it stated that the Soviet Union was no longer "totalitarian" ("Soviet premiere", *Svenska Dagbladet*, 25 May 1989). The fall of the Communist regimes in Eastern Europe in November 1989 made the paper move even further in its acknowledgement of "the breadth of Gorbachev's perestroika"("East views West", ibid., 25 November 1989).

While the analysis of the Soviet system under Mr. Gorbachev thus moved gradually towards acceptance of the good intentions of the leader himself, the conservative Swedish newspaper continued to reserve judgement as to whether or not this meant that the Soviet system itself really had changed for good. *Svenska Dagbladet* did not really explain why Mr. Gorbachev started his reform experiment.

The paper never ventured any clear forecast concerning where the Soviet reform experiment might end up. The closest it came in this respect was in an editorial from early 1990:

> The moment of truth has arrived for Mikhail Gorbachev and his perestroika. As soon as two weeks into the new year the crisis that was to be expected has become acute. ...
>
> A revolutionary situation has developed [in and around Nagorno-Karabakh]. The people are arming themselves and are ready to settle their scores with their opponents, with guns in their hands.
>
> In Lithuania and the rest of the Baltic states we see a revolutionary development of a completely different kind. ...
>
> Will Gorbachev be forced to abandon his perestroika to preserve his own position or is the Russian central power in the multinational Soviet Union finally losing its grip on the last empire in Europe and the world? ("The Last Empire", *Svenska Dagbladet*, 16 January 1990).

Another characteristic aspect of *Svenska Dagbladet's* editorial coverage of Soviet affairs was its emphasis on the Baltic Republics. A first editorial on the aspirations of the Baltic peoples was published comparatively early, in August 1987. The Baltic issues thereafter received constant attention from the paper. Fourteen months after its first editorial on the issue, in October 1988, it was for the first time ready for a more wide-ranging assessment of what might be at stake:

The concessions that Gorbachev has already made to the Baltic strivings for sovereignty have been warmly welcomed in the three countries, but the euphoria may be temporary. The Balts must probably guard themselves against illusions and show great patience if they are to be able to look after their interests in the long run. The progress that has already occurred may, however, easily inspire new demands for full democracy or full national independence. In that case the limit of Moscow's tolerance will be passed and the reaction will be fast and ruthless ("Baltic balancing act", *Svenska Dagbladet*, 13 October 1988).

One more characteristic aspect of *Svenska Dagbladet's* coverage of the Gorbachev years was the considerable attention the paper devoted to bilateral issues between the two countries. There were two specific topics. The first, and more important, had to do with the intrusions by submarines into Swedish territorial waters that started around 1980. *Svenska Dagbladet* was absolutely clear in its judgement that these incursions were carried out by Soviet submarines. The second issue may be broadly termed espionage. There were many editorials in the paper highlighting various activities, deemed suspicious by the editorialists, by people from Eastern Europe in Sweden. These activities were not always directly linked to Soviet policy, but there is no doubt that the paper regarded these events as ultimately emanating from the Soviet Union.

4.4.2. Dagens Nyheter[15]

The other Swedish morning paper, *Dagens Nyheter*, resembled its Swedish colleague in some respects and *The Guardian* in others. The two Swedish papers shared a strong emphasis on the Baltic issues. They were also both sceptical towards Mr. Gorbachev for a fairly long time, even if the liberal paper was more willing to grant the Soviet leader the benefit of the doubt at an earlier stage.

The very first editorial on Gorbachev in *Dagens Nyheter* showed an attitude that was more positive than that of *Svenska Dagbladet*, while still remaining wary:

Let us still be a little bit careful in our expectations concerning this middle-aged man, who has been formed by decades of work in the Soviet system, an established expert on agriculture without any particular successes to point

---

[15] "Dagens Nyheter" = The Daily News.

to. One doesn't reach the top in the Kremlin merely by being suave and charming. Will it really mean anything that the Soviet system now begins to be governed by politicians who have made all of their careers after the times of terror? We can only hope that such a shift in power bit by bit will prove to be of benefit to the common people in the dictatorship that is the Soviet Union ("The great shift in the Soviet Union", *Dagens Nyheter*, 12 March 1985).

In early 1986, *Dagens Nyheter* was the most positive of all the eight papers in this sample concerning how the West should respond to Gorbachev's grand plan for global nuclear disarmament by the year 2000:

Even if one recognizes the Soviet propensity for sweeping formulations and grand gestures in the unrealistic time table, Gorbachev underscores the importance of efficient means of verification, something the U.S. consistently has called for in Moscow's various plans for disarmament. ...
With his latest initiative Mikhail Gorbachev surely tries to influence the West Europeans above all. But it is important to note the possibility that he really wants to contribute to a final global disarmament ("To abolish nuclear arms", ibid., 17 January 1986).

This type of response to the Soviet initiatives, a certain wariness coupled with a willingness to at least test the sincerity of the Soviet leader, strongly resembles the attitude held by *The Guardian*.

In its assessment of the curious rendezvous at Reykjavik, Iceland, between Mr. Gorbachev and President Reagan, the Swedish newspaper expressed disappointment in the failure of the two leaders to reach an arms control agreement. In a way characteristic of *Dagens Nyheter's* treatment of superpower relations during the 1980s, criticism was levelled at both leaders, in a way that may be characterized as "a plague on both your houses". Indeed, the paper was, concerning Reykjavik, even more critical of President Reagan than of the General Secretary.[16] It should be noted that *Svenska Dagbladet*, a conservative paper that generally had a much more positive attitude towards the Reagan Administration's foreign policy than did its Swedish colleague, was also critical of both superpowers in connection with the Reykjavik meeting.

---

[16] See "We have never been so close", *Svenska Dagbladet*, 14 October 1986. The tendency to put a "plague on both your houses" is evident as well in "Confusion in Arms Control", ibid., 19 October 1986; "The War of Expulsion", ibid. 24 October 1986 and "European Security in Vienna", ibid., 4 November 1986. Cf. also "No Helicopters out of Kabul", ibid., 9 January 1988.

The superpower relationship was one of the three main topics on which *Dagens Nyheter's* editorials concentrated during the eventful years of 1987 and 1988. The second topic was the nationalist disturbances in the Soviet Union. The third was the power struggle in the Kremlin and the domestic political strategies of the Soviet leader. This means that little effort was made to assess systematically the extent of the changes in Soviet foreign policy during the 18 months from mid-1987 until late 1988.

Among the editorials in the eight newspapers studied here one can detect several indications of how difficult it was for the analysts to make sense of what was happening in Moscow. One clear expression of this is an editorial from May 1988 in *Dagens Nyheter*:

> For traditional Soviet analysis, the foundations seem uncertain when so much appears to be shifting at the same time. What role is played by these many "discussion clubs"? What does it mean when one has been able to read in the Soviet papers during the last few days that the Molotov-Ribbentrop Pact of August 1939 was a "criminal misjudgement"? Less than a year ago the Pact was still described as protecting Soviet interests and a positive thing for the Baltic states. Mention of the "hegemonic great power ambitions of Stalinism" breaks old taboos ("Gorbachev's test of fire", *Dagens Nyheter*, 24 May 1988).

Given this uncertain attitude towards how one should interpret events in the Soviet Union, it is not surprising that it was difficult to find any really clear-cut analysis in *Dagens Nyheter* about the extent of the changes in foreign and domestic policies. It was possible to detect early on, however, starting in the beginning of 1986, that the liberal Swedish paper felt that Gorbachev's proposals should be taken seriously, particularly in the foreign policy field, even if there might be lingering uncertainties as to the sincerity behind the suggestions.

The uncertainties regarding Gorbachev's sincerity had, in the view of *Dagens Nyheter*, largely disappeared after the Soviet leader gave his celebrated speech to the United Nations General Assembly in early December 1988. That meant that the Soviet leader was by that time putting into practice practical actions in security policy that had previously only been promised ("Gorbachev's Christmas Gifts", ibid., 9 December 1988).

The conclusion can only be that the Soviet leader had by that stage undertaken such changes that the foreign policy of his country had changed fundamentally, in the paper's view. The paper made a distinction, however, between the definite, system-wide policy change, regarding which it still had reservations, and the individual role of Mr. Gorbachev, where its doubts about his willingness to carry out changes had disappeared as 1988 turned into 1989. Without the Soviet leader, there was, even at this point in time, no telling what policy the Soviet Union would conduct ("When Gorbachev's Gesture is Scrutinized", *Dagens Nyheter*, 22 December 1988).

In domestic politics, *Dagens Nyheter* was also fairly positive towards the Soviet reforms. It started comparatively early, however, in pointing to the crucial role that it believed maintaining the Soviet Union as a unified country played for Gorbachev. This is spelled out in an editorial published in November 1987:

> One goal is paramount in all of Gorbachev's efforts: to keep the Soviet Union united. This is at least a vital part of the explanation for aspects that seem strange or downright offensive in his actions, like the treatment of the overly enthusiastic reform supporter Boris Yeltsin or of the Baltic peoples. ...
> As long as the concern for the Soviet empire forces Gorbachev to be an imperialist he lacks the ability to constructively attack all of the very sensitive nationality issues.
> The Soviet leader who shows respect for Baltic strivings makes himself wide open to demands from other parts of the country. Today, Gorbachev does not even dare to take the risk to form his ideas in such a way that allied states in the outer reaches of the empire may have new nationalist impulses. If you take the Balts as an example, Mikhail Gorbachev still has not been able to show any ability at all to free himself from the chains of the past ("To keep the Soviet Union united", ibid., 21 November 1987).

It was hard to find any explanation in *Dagens Nyheter* of why the Soviet leadership embarked upon the reform process in the first place. What there was were a few lines in the final editorial on Mr. Gorbachev when he resigned in December 1991. The gist of this explanation was that the Soviet leader wanted to "liberate" ("His vision was insufficient", *Dagens Nyheter*, 27 December 1991) his own system from a heavy bureaucratic command system and from enormous military expenses, and the world from tension and the fear of war. This explanation, while not very complex, clearly highlighted the importance of the Soviet leader as a person in initiating the reforms. It was, in other words, an explanation of type IV b in the terms applied in this book.

Dagens Nyheter came rather close to issuing a forecast about the ultimate fate of the Soviet Union. In an editorial in December 1988, the paper returned to the previously mentioned theme of how difficult it was to analyse events in the Soviet Union. It added that so much of what would happen in Moscow depended on the person of Gorbachev, which presumably served to make any attempts at forecasting exceedingly difficult ("When Gorbachev's Gesture is Scrutinized", ibid., 22 December 1988).

In September 1989, the paper reacted to a column in the *Sunday Times* that obviously inspired a later editorial in *The Times*, which stated that the Soviet Union would disintegrate in the 1990s. In an analysis that typifies the caution shown on the two Swedish editorial pages, *Dagens Nyheter* neither rejected nor accepted this forecast. It regarded it as food for further thought ("The Shaky Soviet Empire", ibid., 15 September 1989). In March 1990, the liberal Swedish paper went one step further in its foretelling the Soviet future:

> Because even if some temporary reactionary power clique in the Kremlin would dare to attack Lithuania militarily, this will not maintain the Soviet empire intact over time. Without drawing too strong parallels, the recent past of Afghanistan, Romania, and Poland show that bankrupt Soviet Communism, not even with terror and tanks, is able to crush peace loving people ("Psychological warfare around the Baltic Region", *Dagens Nyheter*, 24 March 1990).

The discussion of the predictive efforts of *Dagens Nyheter* illustrates how important the Baltic issues were in its editorials. One interesting example came in February 1988: "To demand sovereignty for Estonia, Latvia and Lithuania after almost forty years, as some exiles do, is still, regretfully, not realistic ("Watchfulness around the Baltic", ibid., 24 February 1988).

The explicit reason given for this was that the paper regarded it as unthinkable for a great power to behave in a way that might encourage other outlying republics to seek increased room for manoeuvre by acceding to the demands of the Balts. In September 1988, it noted that the Baltic nations were "in the process of being rebuilt" ("A Freer Baltic Region", ibid., 14 September 1988). Moscow's ultimate position in this process was, however, still regarded as unclear.

Dagens Nyheter, like most of its counterparts in the other seven newspapers studied here, made a judgement on the conflicting interests that Western nations might have in the stability of Gorbachev's reform program, on the one hand, and the interest that they had in supporting the independence of Lithuania, on the other. While being sympathetic towards the Soviet leader, the newspaper still maintained, "In the struggle of political wills, Sweden should, without reservations, support the Lithuanian people's striving for self-determination" ("Psychological warfare around the Baltic Region", *Dagens Nyheter,* 24 March 1990).

The editorials in *Dagens Nyheter* contained one aspect that was unique to the paper in my sample of newspapers. This was a very personal tone, an attempt to locate the Gorbachev phenomenon very close to individuals living in Sweden, individuals who read the newspaper's editorial page:

> No leader in Moscow has made himself such goodwill as Mikhail Gorbachev. As his restructuring policy and his changed thinking in foreign policy became ever clearer, the outside world with new sympathy began to consider what would happen to his realm. But the pressure against defenceless Lithuania unfortunately raises another, distressingly far-reaching, question: is it in our, Sweden's and others', interest that a great Soviet state be preserved?...
>
> If Gorbachev's reforms have had a hard time taking root, it is better that the Western world know this now rather than postponing the problem out of fear of disturbing the plans of the Soviet leader. If he keeps Lithuania, he is not the one we have been hoping for, not the man of change that we need and that deserves continued respect. ...
>
> A Soviet state that denies Lithuania its freedom and wants to keep everything is not something that we should wish longer life ("Our need of Gorbachev", *Dagens Nyheter*, 23 April 1990).

As noted above, this way of attempting to personalize complex global issues is unique in the material surveyed here. The perspective was not that of the cold-hearted, but supposedly clear-headed detached analyst, as best exemplified by *The Times*, but rather the caring, compassionate individual who was striving for a better world and wondered what position he or she should take and, perhaps, even what he or she could do personally to influence events.

4.4.3 Conclusion: The Swedish Newspapers

The analysis of Soviet affairs under Gorbachev in the two Swedish newspapers illustrates the influence of some of the factors hypothesized in chapter 1. There was a clear tendency for caution in the newspaper material from

Sweden, unwillingness on the part of both papers surveyed to take clear positions on the changes occurring in the Soviet Union. This supports my hypothesis that there is a greater tendency for caution in the analysis carried out in a state that is small and weak of another state that is perceived as much larger and as menacing. This tendency did not necessarily mean that an analyst could not take a strong position on the Soviet Union and developments there. *Svenska Dagbladet* clearly had a very well developed basic view of Moscow. It did demonstrate, however, that there was an inclination for analysts in small, weak, countries to be very hesitant in changing the images they had developed over time of countries that were stronger and that were perceived as menacing. I regard the analysis of Soviet affairs in the two Swedish newspapers as supporting this hypothesis.

The second hypothesis that received support concerns the influence of a strong position for social democracy in a country. It is clear that Sweden was the country of the four that I have analysed that had the strongest element of socialism, or in this case social democracy, in its political culture. I regard the extreme caution shown by the two Swedish papers in predicting, or even clearly assessing, the demise of the Soviet State as support for my hypothesis that a country with a strong "socialist ideology" would be less likely to find that the Soviet State was bound for destruction, as compared to analysts in a non-socialist state.

A third hypothesis, that in a state where social democracy was an important part of the political culture there would be a greater willingness to respond positively to reforms in the Soviet socialist system, also received some support. It could be argued that the editorial attitude displayed by *Dagens Nyheter*, particularly from early 1986 on, exemplified this tendency.

If there were thus some indications of a Swedish foreign policy orientation manifested in the newspapers studied from that country, there was another aspect that was at least as strong in affecting the content of the editorials. That was the ideological aspect, ideological not in the sense of national ideology, which is the main sense in which this concept has been used here. No, here the ideological aspect had to do more with party ideology. It is thus possible to see very strong parallels among the editorial analyses in the conservative newspapers, in particular, in France, Great Britain and Sweden. The three newspapers shared a disdain for a system they regarded as totalitarian. They all subscribed to a realist view of international politics. These two factors, in turn, meant that all three of them were reluctant to take note of changes in Soviet policies, or at least to make any judgement that these changes, even viewed cumulatively, meant that the Soviet system had undergone any fundamental changes. This "party ideological" aspect was most clearly manifested on the conservative side. Even if there were parallels among the three European newspapers on the liberal-leftist side of the political spectrum as well, these were not as strong as they were on the conservative side.

The two Swedish papers' explanations of why Mr. Gorbachev undertook his reforms were not very elaborate. Only *Dagens Nyheter* briefly addressed this issue, highlighting the personal role of Mr. Gorbachev, explanation IV b in table 1.2.

4.5 The U.S. Newspapers

4.5.1 The New York Times

The very first editorial in *The New York Times* on the new Soviet leader gave a condensed version of the paper's view on the Soviet system and on the role of new leaders:

> The Soviet system of government churns with no more flexibility than freedom, a huge and graceless dreadnought riveted with bolts of steel. But the system also possesses the stability of a dreadnought. It functions. ...
> Still, if the generations are starting to change in the Kremlin, the dreadnought is not. The Soviet Union remains an amalgam of secretive bureaucracies; its policies shaped by a collective of old men. Survivors of Stalin's tyranny, they revile even hints of one-man rule, the brash adventurism of a Nikita Khrushchev. Continuity, caution and consensus are the hallmarks of a system revolutionary in doctrine but deeply conservative in practice. Whatever his ambitions, Mr. Gorbachev is unlikely soon to make waves. ...
> A Soviet leader, chosen by a small group, builds power with time and use, and his first years are necessarily devoted to neutralizing rivals ("Soviet Power Passes, Slowly", *The New York Times*, 12 March 1985).

The New York paper saw a system that was very stable and that would be able to turn, if at all, only very slowly. There was, in the view of the editorialist, no reason whatsoever to expect any particular changes in Soviet politics because of the change to the new leader.

As the proposals emanated hard and fast from Moscow during 1985 and early 1986, *The New York Times* in early 1986 voiced criticism not only of the Soviet Union and its leader, but also of President Reagan ("Downhill from the Summit", *The New York Times*, February 28, 1986).

As 1986 came to a close, the paper made a more wide-ranging assessment of Soviet foreign policy and its links to the U.S.

> Propaganda or not, Mr. Gorbachev has a powerful incentive to move now on arms control. It could be very much in his interest to lock in a bipartisan American consensus on arms reductions before President Reagan's successor takes over. That's not just a fanciful view; it's also rooted in a realistic Soviet assessment of American politics. The State Department and the Reagan Administration would do well to hear it out, for it could also be very much in America's interest.
>
> Sure, the Russians are happy when the United States stumbles. Sure, they'll be delighted to exploit the Iran scandal. Posing as peacemaker and compromiser is easy when the other guy is reeling. But propaganda advantages do not strengthen their economy. And that...is Mr. Gorbachev's top priority. That doesn't mean he'll stop playing the power game. It does indicate, however, how he rates his current interests. ...
>
> Soviet strategy seems to assume that if the Soviet Union doesn't get an agreement now, one won't be possible for three years or more. Soviet leaders may not like Mr. Reagan, but they fully appreciate that he is in a stronger position to make a deal than any of his likely successors ("Maybe Not Just Soviet Propaganda. ...", *The New York Times*, 19 December 1986).

This analysis linked the Soviet changes in arms control policy to Moscow's perceived need to strengthen its economy. However, there was no acknowledgement that Soviet foreign policy might have changed for good. It was rather a case of a perceived tactical shift more or less completely geared to the shift from one U.S. administration to another. The emphasis on how closely Soviet policies were linked to U.S. politics is notable. This way of focusing on bilateral relations between their own country and the Soviet Union was very prominent indeed in the U.S. newspapers. It is common for a newspaper to put its own national angle on Soviet developments, but the tendency in the U.S. newspapers was to go further than this. From the way the story was presented in the two U.S. newspapers, it was as if Mr. Gorbachev was doing what he did only because he had to interact with his superpower rival.

In early January 1987, *The New York Times* made a more wide-ranging assessment of glasnost after 21 months of Mr. Gorbachev in power in the

Kremlin ("Some Glasnost Is Better Than None", *The New York Times,* 4 January 1987). In this article, Mr. Gorbachev's goals were portrayed as mainly domestic, the strengthening of both his personal rule and of his country. His other shifts in policy, both foreign and domestic, were explained by how they contributed, directly or indirectly, to these basic goals.

In one aspect, *The New York Times'* analysis of arms control issues resembled the treatment of the same issues in *The Guardian* and *Dagens Nyheter*: it demonstrated a willingness to criticize the policies of both superpowers (see for example "Last Chance in Geneva", *The New York Times*, 15 January 1987).

Mr. Gorbachev was credited with several constructive proposals that the paper regarded as increasing the chances for arms control agreements that would be mutually beneficial, whereas Mr. Reagan was criticized for stubbornness, particularly as it concerned his apparently unbreakable intentions to pursue the SDI project vigorously.

During 1987, the editorials of *The New York Times* covered ever-wider issues in Soviet affairs. One of these concerned how concessions from the West might influence events inside the Soviet Union. The newspaper believed that the fate of Mr. Gorbachev and his reform program was overwhelmingly determined within his own country. The United States could only at the margin influence the chances for success of this reform process. In addition, there was no guarantee that, in the end, the reformed Soviet Union would necessarily be friendlier to the U.S. or to Western interests more generally ("Soviet Reforms, American Interests", ibid., 9 March 1987).

The paper's position on this issue changed somewhat during the Gorbachev years. While it stuck to its view that outsiders could only have a limited impact on Soviet developments, still it urged the West in general, and the U.S. in particular, to support the Gorbachev reforms in several ways (See "America's Stake in Gorbachev's Fate", ibid., 2 July 1989; "Help Who?", ibid., 18 October 1989; "Help Mr. Gorbachev Help the West", ibid., 1 December 1989; "Aid Can Answer A Soviet Question", ibid., 8 July 1990). As the new Soviet policies were seen as ever more valuable for the U.S., so the need for aid to the Soviet leader increased, in the view of the paper.

By the autumn and early winter of 1987, the reform process had achieved so much, and promised to achieve so much more, that *The New York Times* could go far in its characterization of the achievements up to that time:

There are history lessons here, and not only for Russians. A look at the last 70 years shows that the Soviet Union has not been a static place, or Communism an unchanging system — nor did reform begin with Mr. Gorbachev. But he wants to carry it much deeper. He celebrates the Bolshevik Revolution not simply for ritual but to advance his own revolution.

The prospects for this new revolution are utterly unpredictable. Unmistakable, however, is the depth of proposed change. The Soviet system may be a super-bureaucracy but it has produced a leader who himself shakes the world. Those who believe they can deal productively with this Soviet revisionist based on old platitudes need some new vision of their own ("Revolution 1987, Soviet Style", *The New York Times*, 1 July 1987).

There could, in other words, no longer be any doubts that the new Soviet leader had very far-reaching goals. If there could be no disbelief about the wide-ranging nature of the Soviet leader's personal aims, in the paper's view, it was far more difficult to know whether he would be able to carry out his intentions. After two and a half years he had, in the eyes of the New York paper, accomplished a new Soviet "revolution". Where this might end, however, was not possible to predict. The portrayal of Mr. Gorbachev was quite sympathetic, and the basic reason for his reform program was said to be to achieve a strengthening of his own position and of the Soviet system. The concrete aspect of the Soviet system that was most in need of change was, in this analysis, the Soviet economy ("Ten Days That Shook the World", ibid., 1 November 1987).

On the point of diagnosis, of making the assessment as to whether or not the Soviet Union's political system had changed fundamentally, and, if so, at what point in time, *The New York Times* was imprecise, just as were most of the other papers surveyed here.

In the foreign policy sphere, the same sort of imprecision reigned for quite a long period. The speech given by the Soviet leader to the General Assembly of the United Nations in December 1988 was, however, high-lighted by the newspaper as a turning point in the Cold War. Indeed, it led to the conclusion that "[i]n a compelling speech...he proposed, in effect, to abandon the cold war" ("An Invitation the West Can't Ignore", ibid., 11 December 1988. Compare also ibid., "Gambler, Showman, Statesman", 8 December 1988). Mr. Gorbachev was here compared to Woodrow Wilson, Franklin Roosevelt and Winston Churchill, high praise indeed coming from a liberal U.S. newspaper. The Soviet leader was said to be calling for "the basic restructuring of international politics" (ibid., 8 December 1988).

The paper also noted that the unilateral changes in Soviet military forces that the Kremlin leader promised would, if and when they were carried out, significantly decrease the ability of the Warsaw Pact to attack Western Europe.

On 2 April 1989, the paper proclaimed in stark terms, "The Cold War Is Over". Earlier editorials had hinted at the same conclusion, but this was the first time that it was stated so unequivocally. This article was printed after a two-month series on the op-ed page debating this very issue. Together with some other editorials also published in April 1989, *The New York Times* must be viewed as having gone very far towards stating that the Soviet Union had indeed changed for good, notably in foreign policy. The paper explicitly addressed the issue of Mr. Gorbachev's ability to stay in power and answered this question in the affirmative (see in particular "Russian Revolutions", ibid., 30 April 1989).

The New York Times never explicitly attempted to explain why the Soviet Union had embarked upon the great reform program under Mr. Gorbachev. Nor did the paper publish any specific forecasts concerning the fate of the whole reformist enterprise in Moscow.

The special role of the Baltic Republics in the downfall of the Soviet Union was well covered in *The New York Times*, beginning in the fall of 1988:

A year ago, a Lithuanian, Latvian or Estonian citizen who displayed his national flag might have earned 10 months in Siberia. The official myth persisted that the Baltic peoples had outgrown bourgeois nationalism and had become contented citizens of Soviet republics. It wasn't even possible to assert the historical fact that Stalin annexed the Baltic States in 1940.

The recent ferment in the Baltic is thus all the more remarkable. ...

With the chary approval of local Communist leaders, popular movements in all three states now clamour for everything short of full independence. Astonished citizens watch live telecasts of genuine debates in which speakers assail Soviet behaviour, demanding economic autonomy and the right to protect distinctive languages. This may be Mikhail Gorbachev's boldest experiment.

But alas, it remains an experiment, subject to instant reversal ("Not-So-Captive Nations", ibid., 25 October 1988).

The attention the paper devoted to the Baltic Republics, while not negligible, was less than that devoted by the Swedish papers, as well as less than that given by *The Washington Post*.

During the summer and fall of 1989, the dissolution of the Eastern Bloc and the strivings for independence in the Baltic region both increased in pace. Particularly the latter phenomenon posed a problem for *The New York Times* as it was torn between two goals, perceived as possibly conflicting, namely, the stability of the position of Mr. Gorbachev, on the one hand, and support for the independence of the Baltic Republics, in the U.S. long known as "the captive nations", on the other. In contrast to *The Guardian*, which regarded Mr. Gorbachev's survival as a more important interest for the West than at least rapid Baltic independence, *The New York Times* was unable to choose between two objectives it perceived to be equally worthy ("Of Two Minds on the Baltics", ibid., 10 September 10, 1989).

The radical worsening of the Lithuanian crisis that occurred early in 1991, with several civilian deaths resulting from the actions of Soviet troops, finally led to strong criticism from the New York newspaper towards Mr. Gorbachev:

> Yesterday, Mikhail Gorbachev... showed Lithuanians who is who. His predecessors sent tanks into Hungary in 1956, and turned Prague Spring to ice in 1968. When Soviet tanks crush Lithuanian students demonstrating for freedom, the father of glasnost turns his celebrated season of reform into Vilnius Winter. ...
>
> Since coming to power in 1985, Mikhail Gorbachev's daring, realism and flexibility have captured America's imagination and approval. When he uses tanks to crush singing students, and freedom, he instead ignites America's anger and disgust.
>
> Thousands of demonstrators in Vilnius chant "Freedom!" and sing "Tautos Gisme," the Lithuanian national anthem. It's a haunting hymn about home, about a Lithuanian homeland. Today, people around the world mourn and sing with them ("The New Old Face of Tyranny", ibid., January 14, 1991).

As a consequence of this repressive behaviour, the paper also urged the Bush Administration to stop aiding Moscow ("No Aid for a Repressive Moscow", ibid., 15 January 1991).

The final months of the Soviet Union were covered in a way that is remarkable in the sense that the paper for a very long time stuck to the view that the Soviet State was still there to stay. One expression of this tendency was an editorial published in late July 1991, before a summit meeting in Moscow with President Bush, where the paper expressed the hope that the U.S. and the Soviet Union might in the future become "allies" ("Allies", ibid., 28 July 1991).

4.5.2 The Washington Post

There were strong similarities in how Mr. Gorbachev was treated on the editorial pages of the two U.S. papers during his first 18 months in power. An example of this tendency is *The Washington Post's* first editorial on the new leader:

> With the replacement of Konstantin Chernenko by Mikhail Gorbachev, generational change has finally come to the Kremlin. Among those who look on, the tendency has been to confer a greater openness to reform and accommodation on the New Guard, which presumably, unlike the Old Guard, has not been touched by the dark inheritance of Stalinism. But the ostensibly greater energy, education and ambition of the younger generation, plus its lack of first-hand adult exposure to the rigors of the Soviet past, may make its members more formidable competitors, more careless and more prone to risk ("The Kremlin's New Guard", *The Washington Post*, 12 March 1985).

Mr. Gorbachev's new oratory was noted in the capital's newspaper, but the substance of his concrete proposals was dismissed as mainly propaganda. A partial exception was the reaction in *The Washington Post* to Mr. Gorbachev's program for the complete abolition of nuclear weapons by the year 2000, which was presented in early 1986. The Washington paper noted a strong element of propaganda in this case too, but it also identified some aspects of the proposals that might lead to concrete results, notably in the chance it was thought to offer for a slowdown of the nuclear arms race in Europe (see "Mr. Gorbachev's Package", ibid., 17 January 1986 and "The Gorbachev Plan and Europe", ibid., 21 January 1986). *The New York Times* was a nuance more critical towards Mr. Gorbachev's proposals in its main editorial on this topic ("Nuclear Naked", *The New York Times*, 19 January 1986).

In the summer of 1986, *The Washington Post* assessed the foreign policy strategy it believed Moscow was following. In the early analysis of Soviet foreign policy under Gorbachev, as *The Washington Post* took note of a changing policy, it placed its focus on the strategic goals it believed the Kremlin pursued, notably including restraint on U.S. research and development on a strategic missile defence, and a pursuit of a cut in strategic arms ("Mr. Reagan, Mr. Gorbachev", ibid., 22 June 1986).

The paper's assessments of the Reykjavik meeting in October 1986 maintained that this remained the Soviet strategy, adding that Gorbachev wanted to use Western public opinion in his fight against SDI ("Cold in Iceland", ibid., 13 October 1986).

As 1986 drew to a close, *The Washington Post* made an overall appraisal of the Gorbachev reform strategy about one week after the release from internal exile of Andrei Sakharov. Despite the new openness of Soviet politics, the paper noted that "There is no evidence of systemic change" ("Mr. Gorbachev's Gamble", ibid., 30 December 1986).

The General Secretary was, on this analysis, pursuing a reform of the communist system to make it more efficient. There was no intimation here of the radical restructuring that was to come. Nor were there any links made to Soviet foreign policy. What was roughly foreseen, however, was the turmoil in Soviet domestic policies that would follow the riots in Alma Ata in late 1986 (cf. chapter 2.4).

In connection with the Communist Party Conference in the summer of 1988, *The Washington Post* directly addressed the fundamental questions of whether or not the Soviet Union was reformable, and if the answer was yes, how far Mr. Gorbachev had gone after three years in office:

> The question of the century has been whether a full-blown totalitarian system, such as the one imposed by the Communist Party in the Soviet Union, could be transformed or at least substantially changed from within. No answer has yet been given, but the party conference held last week in Moscow demonstrates that the question is still open. ...
>
> But it is also apparent from what has gone on so far, especially in the turbulence of the televised party conference, that movement within totalitarian systems is possible, that history, even under the most thorough of repressive systems, does not come to a halt, that pressures for reform cannot be stamped out forever. And the implication of that is that even if this movement comes to grief or stops far short of what people in the West hope for it, the process will recur in the future — the instincts it has activated in the Soviet Union will always be there ("Moscow's Week That Was", ibid., 3 July 3, 1988).

Despite the caveats issued, *The Washington Post* believed, in other words, that events in Moscow during the first three years of Mr. Gorbachev's rule demonstrated that change in the Soviet Union *was* indeed possible.

By the summer of 1988 it was thus impossible, in the view of *The Washington Post*, to deny that the Soviet leader intended to change the domestic policies of his nation fundamentally. The paper consistently regarded Mr. Gorbachev's foreign policy program as a natural outgrowth of his basic reform strategy.[17] This meant that the approach of the outside world towards the Soviet leader in international affairs should constantly be conditioned upon his domestic position. The question, according to *The Washington Post*, was not whether "Mikhail Gorbachev is for real" ("Ready for Malta", ibid., 30 November 1989).

It was clear by the Malta summit of December 1989, if not earlier, that the Soviet leader was committed to his reform program. The question was whether the Soviet leader would be able to implement his program.

The process of change under way in Moscow, in other words, involved a vast array of aspects of crucial importance to the West generally, and to the U.S. in particular. The very fact that this process of change was overwhelmingly anchored in domestic politics meant, in the view of *The Washington Post*, both that the influence of the outside world was limited and that whatever positive steps the Soviet Union should take in its international behaviour would ultimately always be dependent upon the success of the domestic reform program. This led the paper to suggest that the West had to respond positively to the policies emanating from Moscow but that the basic issue must always be whether indeed the Soviet regime had lasting stability at home. No matter how important and how multifaceted Moscow's changes in foreign policy were, they were always hostage to this basic condition.

By the late spring of 1988 the newspaper stated that Mr. Gorbachev was really serious about altering his country's foreign policy. For *The Washington Post* the Soviet withdrawal from Afghanistan was an important indicator showing that "Mr. Gorbachev is serious about change" and that this occurred in a field of policy even more important than arms control: "foreign societies in crisis" ("Ronald Reagan's Summit", ibid., 29 May 1988).

In connection with the Moscow summit in the early summer of that same year, the paper wrote that the changes in Soviet foreign policy might not be "conclusive" but that they were "pretty close to that" ("Contradictions", ibid., 5 June 1988). *The Washington Post* never did go quite so far as its U.S. counterpart in stating that Soviet foreign policies had indeed fundamentally changed.

In the view of the paper, the reform period in the Soviet Union started because the new leader realized that the system had such economic and

---

[17] See "Mr. Gorbachev's Sensation", *The Washington Post*, 12 December 1988: "It seems evident, however, that the force behind his 'new thinking' is a conviction that the Soviet domestic crisis is so deep and threatening it can no longer be evaded. ... Plainly, Mr. Gorbachev wishes to trim the pace and cost of international confrontation in order to advance his internal perestroika, or restructuring, which entails reversing 70 years of stultification, self-deceit and drift and daring to explore ways that promise the Soviet people a decent life."

social problems that they could no longer be left unattended. The less expansive foreign and security policy aspirations also perceived to be a part of the reform program were, in the paper's view, only there because it was necessary for the Soviet leader to minimize the expenses and the risks attached to a more aggressive foreign policy if the domestic reform program was to have any chance at all of succeeding (see in particular "At the Summit", *The Washington Post*, 6 December 1987).

This explanation put the cognitive qualities of the Soviet leader, explanation IV a, at the very centre. Later, *The Washington Post* added that the outside pressure emanating from the policies of the United States also played a role in the Soviet change of policies ("George Bush, Mikhail Gorbachev", ibid., 1 July 1988). In other words, the paper included an explanation of type I a.

The same way of regarding international politics was displayed by *The Washington Post* in one of several editorials on the Washington summit of December 1987. The superpower relationship was, on this view, bound to remain troubled due to the fundamental differences between the two countries ("A Good Summit", ibid., 11 December 1987).

This was not the very stark realism of *Le Figaro* or *The Times*, but it was, nevertheless, a view of international politics which was firmly anchored in that strand of thinking.

It is hard to escape the conclusion that, for the elite newspapers in this sample at least, complex social and political processes were most readily explainable by what I term the individual level of explanation in table 1.2.

The Washington Post was not one of the papers that made any real effort at forecasting. The events in the Baltic region did, however, lead the paper to speculate, in early 1989, on what this sort of development might lead to:

> The larger fact is that ideologically, economically and politically, Soviet communism is disintegrating, or becoming something else. On this profound and sensitive matter, Mr. Gorbachev cannot be "helped" by well-wishing or anxious outsiders. Nor should he be ("The State of Lithuania", ibid., 20 February 1989).

Again, it was stated that the system was changing profoundly. What this metamorphosis might lead to was, however, left very unclear.

In early 1988, *The Washington Post* identified a new factor in the grand equation that would determine the fate of Mr. Gorbachev's reform efforts: the nationality question. It recognized that this issue had the potential "to undermine Mr. Gorbachev" ("Armenian Pressure", *The Washington Post*, 2 March 1988). The important role that the nationality question would play in the final decline of the Soviet State was here identified as soon as *The Washington Post* addressed the issue.

In early 1989, the Lithuanian crisis began to flare up. In an editorial in February, *The Washington Post* commented on both the specific issue and what it might entail more broadly ("The State of Lithuania", ibid., 20 February 1989). From this point on, and in particular from late 1989 until the summer of 1990, the paper focused very strongly on the issues surrounding Baltic independence. In total, twelve editorials concentrating upon this issue were published between December 1989 and early July 1990. The Washington paper grappled with the question of whether it was the independence of the Lithuanian Republic or the stability of the Gorbachev regime that was most important for the West in general, and for the U.S. in particular. An editorial published in March, tackled the issue head on:

> In the end there can be no alternative to independence for Lithuania, if that is what it wants. ... Any decision by Mikhail Gorbachev to go the Stalinist route and crush the Lithuanian democratic will would inflict huge costs all around but would only postpone Lithuania's liberation. No one can doubt that eventually it will prevail. ...
> The Lithuanians, asking for independence now, are advised by nervous onlookers to wait a bit and take their independence later. But it would be more appropriate and fair for onlookers to advise the Soviet leadership to sweeten its offer to the Lithuanians, and meanwhile to call off the tanks. The Lithuanians, practising non-violence, are asserting their independence. The Soviets are using crude displays of force to enforce Soviet law on an illegally seized foreign country. There is no moral equivalence here. No doubt concessions are difficult and painful for Mr. Gorbachev. But surely he understands the requirement for any new relationship between the republics and the center to be voluntary. That principle is at the heart of his reform, isn't it? ("The Lithuanian Alternative", ibid., 28 March 1990.)

On the continuum running from an emphasis for support on Lithuanian independence to a preference for the stability of Mr. Gorbachev and his reform process, *The Washington Post* came much closer to supporting the Lithuanians. Its U.S. counterpart was very explicit in pronouncing itself as being "of two minds", in other words in the middle, on the issue. *The*

Washington Post, in addition to being pro-Lithuanian independence, was more critical than *The New York Times* of the actions taken by Mr. Gorbachev as the crisis deepened regarding Lithuania in the spring of 1990 ("Call Off the Tanks", *The Washington Post*, 3 April 1990).

The criticism of Mr. Gorbachev's actions regarding Lithuania's steps towards its declaration of independence was strong, stronger than in *The New York Times* and much stronger than in *The Guardian*. Additionally, where *The New York Times* praised President Bush for his even-handedness in the Lithuanian crisis, *The Washington Post* was critical: "President Bush is proceeding very gingerly in his support of Lithuania and its right to choose its own future. Understatement can be useful in diplomacy, but beyond a certain point the message becomes inaudible" ("The Lithuanian Case", ibid., 25 April 1990).

4.5.3 Conclusion: The U.S. Newspapers

The two newspapers chosen to represent the United States in this book are the two liberal, establishment papers from the East Coast. There were, as should be expected, strong similarities between their analyses of Soviet affairs. There was also a similar limitation: neither of them produced any forecast that foretold the Soviet collapse.

One further aspect that the two papers had in common can be characterized as a U.S. foreign policy orientation. This was the tendency to see developments in the Soviet Union as directly caused and influenced by events and processes in U.S. politics. It is not surprising to see that the media in one superpower believed that their own country's policies were of importance to decisions made in the other capital. Still, the belief in the strength and directness of this link was stronger and more manifest that I initially supposed would be the case.

There were also some differences between the two newspapers, however. One of these concerned the diagnosis of the situation. *The New York Times* was the more explicit of the two in making the assessment that the Soviet Union had changed its foreign policy for good, which was made by April 1989. *The Washington Post* never went quite as far as this, but was willing to concede that important changes had occurred by mid-1988.

A second difference had to do with developments in the Baltic Republics. Both papers focused on this issue, but *The Washington Post* did so to a much greater degree than did its counterpart in New York.

Overall, the two U.S. newspapers were more similar in their views than they were different. In this case, it was hard to detect any ideological differences, in the party political sense. Instead, the results of this analysis are that these two papers represented a U.S. view of the world, and of the Soviet Union in particular, that was to some extent distinct from that of the other six newspapers scrutinized here.

4.6 Conclusion

Two broad assumptions guided my expectations concerning the newspaper editorials on developments in the Soviet Union under Mikhail Gorbachev. One had to do with what I called foreign policy orientation, or the historical, political and cultural outlook that each country brings to its encounters with the outside world. This hypothesis led to the expectation of clear differences in the newspaper analysis of the matter at hand. The disagreements would, following this expectation, be between newspapers in different countries, whereas papers published in the same country were anticipated to have largely similar views.

The second assumption had to do with media-specific factors. Here the tendency was assumed to be that the newspapers would have a strong inclination to cover the material in a similar manner due to the fact that they are all Western media working in market economies and could thus be expected to be subjected to the same type of circulation and other types of pressures. In addition, there was the further pressure to publish material that resembled that of other international newspapers on a story that was truly of global interest.

My analysis shows that the second hypothesis did not receive much support. This is, of course, if one excludes the general fact that all eight newspapers gave prominent coverage to events in the Soviet Union under Gorbachev. For the newspapers in one of the countries there was, however, one aspect that clearly distinguishes their analysis of Soviet developments from that typically recorded in the other countries. There was, in other words, strong evidence supporting my assumption of the existence of a foreign policy orientation that was quite distinctive in the U.S., which led newspapers to analyse Soviet affairs as more or less determined by a necessity to respond to events and processes in the United States. Even if the conservative papers in Sweden and the United Kingdom also emphasized the importance of the U.S. in pressuring the Soviet Union and Mr. Gorbachev,

Table 4.1   Results of the Newspaper Analysis

Newspaper	Why did Mr. Gorbachev start the reform process?	Does the paper present any forecast?
Le Figaro	II b: economy inefficient; III: nomenclature's wish to improve living standard;	Yes, March 1990;
Le Monde	—	No;
The Times	I a: pressure from US; II b: inefficient economy; IV b: Gorbachev as leader;	Yes, November 1989;
The Guardian	II b: inefficient economy;	No;
Svenska Dagbladet	—	No;
Dagens Nyheter	(IV b: Gorbachev as leader);	No;
The New York Times	—	No;
Washington Post	IV a: rethinking by Gorbachev; I a: pressure from US;	No;

( ) = indicates an implicit rather than explicit explanation

there was not nearly the same tendency to regard Soviet politics as more or less an extension of what happened in Washington. It is important to try to be precise here. What I claim is not, of course, that the role of the United States was unimportant to the events of the Gorbachev years, either in my personal reading of these events or in the assessment of the six newspapers outside the U.S. that I studied. What I do claim, however, is that in the newspaper material surveyed here it was only in the U.S. that an editorialist — to illustrate the general tendency — could come up with the idea that the detailed policies pursued by Mr. Gorbachev were influenced by the detailed phases of the U.S. presidential election cycle.

It is notable that this foreign policy orientation manifested itself both in the official assessments made by the politicians and in the newspaper material. It cannot be said that there was any sense that the politicians with their analyses determined what was written in the U.S. newspapers. It was rather the case that politicians and editorialists alike shared the same foreign policy orientation, a foreign policy orientation that in this respect set the U.S. apart from the other three countries analysed in this book.

Aside from this aspect of foreign policy orientation, which meant that the views of the two newspapers from the U.S. were essentially the same in an important respect, the material showed several cases of fairly strong differences between the analyses published in one newspaper in one country, and the other paper from the same country. In my analysis, this was largely explained by another type of factor, not initially specified in this study. This is the ideological factor. Earlier in this book, this term was used to indicate a sort of national political heritage, where the main beliefs about international politics and one's own country's role in these affairs were believed to have been shared across the most important parts of the political spectrum. What is indicated here, however, is ideology in the narrower sense of party politics.

The party political ideology is particularly strong in its accounting for the similarities found in the Soviet analysis of the three conservative European newspapers studied here — *Le Figaro* in France, *The Times* in the United Kingdom and *Svenska Dagbladet* in Sweden. One of the similarities was the initial image the editorial pages of these three newspapers presented of the Soviet system, and to some extent of the international system as well, as the reform period started. The three editorial pages had a world-view characterized by the term "realism" in the study of international relations. In other words, they regarded the state as the only important actor to consider in international affairs; they saw no type of actor above the state — there was international anarchy — and, in this context, power and traditional security policy were crucial. They saw the Soviet State as totalitarian, in a way that was strongly reminiscent of the analytic model in Sovietology bearing that name. It was a state where all power was concentrated in the Communist Party, where no other power centres existed and where change in the system was out of the question. The Soviet political system could not, on this view, be reformed, it could only disappear.

The consequences of these shared views were not important enough to produce strong similarities in all other respects. *The Times* was, in one sense, the most logical of the three in its analysis. True to its belief in realism, the conservative British newspaper identified strategic pressure from abroad, especially the U.S., as being behind, first, the start of the Gorbachev reform process, and, second, as bringing about the eventual collapse of the Soviet State. It is notable that *Le Figaro*, which shared many characteristics of its analysis of Moscow with *The Times*, did not follow the British newspaper in giving U.S. pressure a crucial role in accounting for the start of the Soviet reform process. It is hard to overlook the fact that the two newspapers on this point tended to display their differing foreign policy orientations, with *The Times* naturally focusing on the role of the U.S., and *Le Figaro* being less inclined to highlight Washington's role.

The analysis in this book concerns how various actors diagnosed what was happening in the Soviet Union, how they explained what had happened and whether or not they issued any forecasts about the likely Soviet future. On the first of these questions it is hard to detect any clear pattern that could explain how the newspapers reacted. One characteristic aspect shared by most newspapers on this issue was that they seldom were very explicit and definite in stating that the Soviet Union had indeed changed for good, particularly with respect to foreign policy, and that the West ought to take this into account in its policies. In this respect, the newspaper editorials in the elite newspapers were very different from the politicians' statements surveyed in chapter 3. The politicians took it as one of the tasks of diplomacy to publicly announce when they made the assessment that one crucial factor in their foreign policy environment had indeed changed for good. The newspaper editorials, in contrast, had a much stronger tendency to make their diagnosis in terms of, on the one hand, the fact that there were important changes, but, on the other, that one couldn't know whether Mr. Gorbachev's personal intentions (doubted by few) would ever be thoroughly implemented institutionally throughout the Soviet system.

It is notable that when it came to stating unequivocally that Soviet foreign policy had changed for good, it was two very different papers that did so: *Le Figaro* in France and *The New York Times* in the U.S. It is difficult to find any more overarching explanation for why this was so.

On the explanatory issue, the newspaper editorials tended to explain why Mr. Gorbachev started the reform process in terms of mainly two levels of explanation: the State level, level II, and the individual level, level IV. On the former question, the five newspapers that really addressed this issue tended to concentrate on the state-level explanation. The Soviet State, on this view, had such problems by mid-1985 that the new Soviet leadership simply had to attempt to reform it fundamentally.

The final overriding research question here concerned whether or not any forecasts, or even predictions, were issued by the actors analysing the Soviet Union during the period between 1985 and 1991. In the case of the eight newspapers surveyed here, there were indeed two cases of well-developed forecasts grounded in systematic reasoning. These assessments came from the two newspapers that probably held the most negative views of the Soviet system as my analysis started in 1985: *Le Figaro* in France and *The Times* in Great Britain. It is hard to avoid the suspicion that it was easier for an analyst who held the view that his object of study represented a despicable political system to forecast that this system might collapse than it would be for an actor with a less value-laden assessment of the Soviet system.

A second possible explanation for the similarity of the two papers in terms of their correct forecast of the Soviet system's eventual demise is the historical legacy of the two nations that they represent. In other words, it would appear to be more likely for a newspaper in a nation that had had an empire, and had seen it collapse, to identify a similar process elsewhere than it would typically be for a newspaper from a country without this historical experience. Since France and Great Britain shared this historical experience, one can assume that conservative newspapers from these countries — with their presumed tendency to be conscious of the lessons of history — were more likely to recognize a collapsing empire than newspapers from countries without this historical legacy would be. If the two possible explanations for an increased tendency to see impending collapse are brought together: Is an analyst who holds a very negative view of a system and also sees historical parallels between this system and the decline of his or her own state all too likely to find analogies for this to be regarded as the result of non-biased analysis? It is impossible to answer this question conclusively here. The fact that it looms so large must, however, be regarded as sufficiently important to cast a doubt over the legitimacy — in a stricter, academic, sense — of prognoses that are issued by analysts with these two types of bias.

Chapter 5
The Sovietologists

5. 1 Introduction

The Sovietologists are evaluated in three respects. The first is *prediction*. To what extent should it be the task of social scientists to try to forecast the outcome of complex social processes? Is trying to look into the future an appropriate task for academics? It is clear that far from all scholars, even in my own discipline of political science, would identify this as an appropriate task for scientific endeavour. Even less can it be said that scholars from other disciplines, such as those analysed alongside political science in this work — that is, economics and history — necessarily set themselves this goal. The historians very seldom do so, while the economists might be more inclined to.

Still, it cannot be denied that, for some social scientists, the ideal has been to arrive at a science where one can predict the future developments of political and other social processes. This is why this aspect is included in this book. The Sovietologists covered here are assessed as to whether or not they attempted to either forecast or, more demandingly, predict what was going to happen to Soviet politics after Mr. Gorbachev came to power. If they did attempt to make such predictions, the accuracy of these attempts has been appraised.

The second issue in this chapter concerns *explanation*. Even if scholars in the social and human sciences disagree as to whether or not they should attempt to predict future occurrences, few would deny that it is one fundamental purpose of their respective disciplines to explain what has happened to basic issues under analysis. As mentioned in chapter 1, this book explores issues that contain one very crucial explanatory question. It has to do with the start of the process of change in Soviet domestic, and more important for this study, foreign policy. The explanatory problem can be stated in the following way: *What explains the start of the fundamental process of foreign policy change in the Soviet Union, initiated around the time of Mr. Gorbachev's accession to power in 1985, and greatly accelerating from 1988 on?*

There is a third issue that is specific to the Sovietologists. It has to do with the tendency of social scientists, in particular, to use analytic models as a basis for their analyses. In this chapter I evaluate whether or not the scholars used a specific model of analysis in formulating their understanding of the Soviet system. This aspect is most interesting in the cases where it can be surmised that a scholar has so strongly adhered to the model in question that it has hampered his or her analysis of the extent of changes in the Soviet Union under Gorbachev. Could it be that one explanation for the difficulties some Sovietologists had in correctly assessing both the depth of the Soviet reforms and their implications for the future of the Soviet system had to do with the very models they used in their analyses of that system?

5.2. Sovietologists in the Four Countries

5.2.1 France

In the case of France, I have elected to study two political scientists and two historians. One of the political scientists is *André Besançon*. The second political scientist, at least that is the closest we can come to a classification, is *Pierre Hassner*.[1] The first historian is *Hélène Carrère d'Encausse*. She has been working for many years as a *professeur à l'Institut d'Études Politiques* in Paris. In the 1990s she became a member of the Academie Française. The other historian is the late *Alexandre Bennigsen*. Bennigsen worked during most of his career at CNRS in Paris and at the Ecole des Hautes Études en Sciences Sociales, also in Paris.

5.2.1.1 Alexandre Bennigsen

> Barring a major crisis - such as a foreign war - the present status quo in the Soviet Union will be uncompromisingly preserved for as long as possible. The final, inescapable, violent crisis will be delayed, but for how long? (Bennigsen, with Marie Broxup, 1983, p. 125.)

Alexandre Bennigsen specialized in the history of Soviet Muslims. As illustrated in the quote above, from a book he wrote with Marie Broxup in 1983, Bennigsen viewed the Soviet System as doomed to disintegrate. In the terms applied in this book, this is a forecast, however imprecise, to

---

[1] In his reader containing examples from 40 years of writing, published in 1995, Pierre Hassner writes "[A]près 1955, j'ai quitté la philosophie pour les relations internationales..."; *La violence et la paix: De la bombe atomique au nettoyage ethnique* (Paris: Éditions Esprit, 1995), p. 9.

this effect. A further motive for regarding it as a correct forecast is that Professor Bennigsen pointed out one of the fundamental reasons that indeed contributed strongly to the end of the Soviet Union. It could be argued that this prognosis belongs to what Goldmann calls "sooner-or-later theories". What makes me regard it as a correct forecast is the fact that it accurately identifies one plausible cause of the Soviet collapse. Even if the national question in the western part of the Soviet Union was even more important, unrest in republics with a large proportion of Islamic people also contributed to the instability of the Soviet empire.

In a second book published in 1986, which he co-authored with S. Enders Wimbush, Bennigsen made a nuanced analysis of the problems that the Soviet State faced concerning the integration of Soviet Muslims into their empire:

> One might argue...that Soviet muslims are mostly becoming well integrated economically into the Soviet system, and that they are developing a stake in that system which makes dissent unlikely. There can be little doubt that many Soviet muslims have prospered under Soviet rule, although it is a false comparison to suggest that they have done better under tight Russian control than their counterparts just across Soviet borders, most of whom are free to exercise political and economic choices that are unknown to Soviet muslims. A study of the history of decline of multinational empires should dictate prudence in accepting that economics is such a powerful integrator. It is certainly one factor which helps to bind minorities to a large imperial state, but as experience has shown, it is unlikely to be the main one or even a very important one. Similarly, other measures of "socialisation," such as linguistic indicators, educational equalisation, the frequency and ethnic composition of mixed marriages, similarities or dissimilarities of family habits, and the international composition of the labour force, should be treated with caution as evidence of Soviet muslim "integration" or commitment (Bennigsen and S. Enders Wimbush, 1986, p. 31, note omitted).

The authors continued their analysis by noting that there were several factors which "will make Soviet ethnic management of the Islamic community within its borders more difficult in the years ahead" (ibid.).

In one of his last publications before his death in June 1988, Professor Bennigsen made a general assessment of the role and future of Muslims in the Soviet Union:

> After the Alma-Ata riots, it is no longer credible to believe that a "Soviet" way into the future is possible if it requires the abolition of Islam in the

USSR. Although Soviet dogma has insisted for nearly seventy years that Islam must be eliminated in the course of producing the "New Soviet Man," all evidence points to just the opposite having happened: Islam has strengthened and Marxism-Leninism has failed to inspire and to satisfy. The Soviet "melting pot" does not work, and there is little evidence to convince observers that it ever will. Islam — either as an active religion or a body of culture — has successfully thwarted Russian attempts to assimilate Muslims and, consequently, to assure the biological symbiosis of the Islamic community with the Russian one. From Afghanistan and Iran, Soviet muslims receive the message that Soviet power is not invincible, that mighty empires can be brought to bay. Islam is the challenger in the USSR as elsewhere, and it is likely that the future will find Muslims of the Soviet Union on the offensive. More active challenges to Russian rule from this increasingly dynamic quarter cannot be ruled out (Bennigsen, 1988, pp. 785-786).

The rest of Bennigsen's writings consist mostly of specialized writings on Sufism and other, at least for this book, esoteric matters. As stated above, Professor Bennigsen died in June 1988, which makes it impossible to carry the analysis any further (see Bennigsen, Henze, Tanham, Wimbush, 1989, p. vii).

Alexandre Bennigsen was a scholar who, during the whole period in which his publications were studied, made clear that he rejected the claims by the Soviet State that it had created a new society in which old nationalities had disappeared in favour of a new "Soviet man". In particular, Bennigsen concentrated on the role of Soviet Muslims in this regard. To this writer, it is obvious that Bennigsen was correct in this respect. He also made a forecast to the effect that this inability of the Soviet system to integrate the many peoples would lead to the system's "violent end". It is probably true that Bennigsen somewhat overestimated the role of the Islamic peoples in bringing about the collapse of the Soviet State, but in general his point about the inability of the Soviet system to integrate the non-Russian peoples was very well taken.

5.2.1.2 Alain Besançon

The West misunderstands the Gorbachev reaction for several reasons:
• The discrepancy between Soviet words and Soviet actions is greater now than perhaps ever before. ...We have the impression of important change in the Soviet Union; we are under the impression that we know something about this country, when in fact we know as little about it as ever, less even than in the past. We know about the Soviet regime what they want us to know about it, and nothing else.

• Westerners imagine that Gorbachev only pretends to believe in Leninism. In fact, everything in his speeches points to his having no other doctrine. ...

• Westerners can never get used to the idea of a uniform, atomized, and voiceless society. They project onto Soviet "society" structures analogous to our own, a political life implicitly similar to the one in democracies. ...Most of the time our analysis only reproduces the mythology exuded in the official Soviet line (Besançon, with Françoise Thom, Spring 1987, p. 27.)

Alain Besançon in 1987 took part in an assessment of Soviet politics published in the American journal *National Interest,* where he published an article together with the journalist Françoise Thom. There, two questions were posed to several Sovietologists. The general one was "What's happening in Moscow?" The more specific question was "Will Gorbachev succeed?" On the latter point, the authors' answer was:

"Will Gorbachev succeed?" is an ambiguous question. If it means, will the Soviet people become free and prosperous citizens, as some Westerners naively believe, let us be blunt: that is not his goal. If the point is to regain control of the apparatus, Gorbachev stands a serious chance of succeeding. But this attempt to destroy the underground economy and to revitalize the state sector is destined to fail: the more he fights against "illegal income," the less the Soviets will work and the greater will be the deterioration of the "human factor. ..."

There are two possible sorts of secondary effects of Gorbachevism: we could witness an unleashing of terror from below, accompanied by a freezing-up of the economic machinery. That is not very likely. A more plausible outcome is that the Gorbachev program will bog down and the USSR will be quietly "re-Brezhnevized" (ibid.).

Besançon's basic view of the Soviet system was revealed in the final words of his advice to Western governments regarding what to do in response to what only appeared to be, in his eyes, changes in the Soviet system: "...the West will approach an objective it has lost sight of since de jure recognition of the USSR: putting an end to the fiction of the legitimacy of that regime."[2] Of the Sovietologist models presented in table 1.1., Besançon can most aptly be described as subscribing to the totalitarian model, without, however, being totally wedded to the Anglo-Saxon version of that model. Indeed, the

---

[2] Ibid., p. 30. On Besançon's own experiences with the French Communist Party, see his volume of memoirs: *Une Génération* (Paris: Juillard, 1987, passim). He was a militant Communist from 1951 to late 1956.

French Sovietologists, while of course being part of the larger category of Western academics studying the Soviet system, do not wholly conform to the practices of the scholars from the U.S. and Britain. This is one of the problems for the writer who tries to assess the workings of Sovietology after the fact.

In a French volume entitled *Après Gorbatchev* published in 1990, Besançon returned to his characterizations of the Soviet system:

> Il me semble qu'on rend mieux compte des faits de ces cinq dernières années...en considérant que ce dirigeant communiste a été promu et a agi en vue de résoudre cette crise, d'empêcher cette décomposition, de sauver ce régime, quitte à l'adapter aux nouvelles conditions, sans le changer substantiellement. C'est dans cette assumption...que je me pose la question célèbre: Gorbatchev peut-il réussir?
> Je suis loin d'en être certain. Je suis donc pessimiste de point de vue de Gorbatchev, et optimiste du mien, parce que je souhaite la fin de ce régime... On devine aujourd'hui que l'action de Gorbatchev s'incrit dans un plan d'ensemble qui a été élaboré avant lui. ...
> C'est probablement dans les milieux des K.G.B., professionellement mieux informés de l'état réel des choses, que naquit le grand dessein. Il fut mis en œuvre par Andropov et continué par Gorbatchev.[3]
> It seems to me that one better understand the events of the last five years...if one considers that this Communist leader was promoted and has acted with the aim of solving this crisis, of stopping this decline, of saving this regime, ended up by adapting it to new circumstances without making any substantial changes. It is from this assumption...that I ask myself the famous question: can Gorbachev succeed?
> I am far from certain that he can. I am thus a pessimist from Gorbachev's point of view, and an optimist from mine, because I want this regime to end. We are today learning that Gorbachev's actions should be seen in terms of a larger plan that was drawn up before him. ...
> It is probably within the ranks of the KGB, which was professionally better informed about the real state of things, that this grand plan was born. It was set in motion by Andropov and continued by Gorbachev.

One interesting aspect with this quote is how Besançon returned to the ambiguous question of what constituted "success" for Gorbachev. It would be possible for observers to have different views when assessing whether

---

[3] Alain Besançon: "Les Atouts de Gorbatchev: Une Évaluation" in *Après Gorbatchev*, Présenté par Jean-Marie Benoist and Patrick Wajsman (Paris: La Table Ronde, 1990), pp. 59-60. Notes omitted. A longer quote from this text is included in appendix 4.

or not Gorbachev was successful in his policies. This depended on how the individual observer defined "success". If the definition was that Gorbachev would be considered successful if he was able to start to reform the Soviet Union, he was successful, at least to some extent. If the criterion by which the Soviet leader should be judged was, rather, on the extent to which he was able to implement changes, in particular concerning the functioning of the Soviet economy, then Gorbachev was unsuccessful, even spectacularly so. If, finally, one were to judge Gorbachev according to the most overarching criterion — was Gorbachev able to reform the Soviet system and preserve the superpower status of that system? — then the judgement has to be more negative still. To attempt to reform a system and then to cause its total collapse is, to be sure, the most spectacular failure imaginable.

It was on this very point that the attitude of the Sovietologist to the very character of the Soviet system became so important. For those Sovietologists who regarded the system positively, or in an academic, dispassionate way (if such a perception was indeed even possible), the two first aspects of "success" were legitimate ways of judging the Soviet system. For those who regarded the system as fundamentally illegitimate, and here Besançon is a prime example, then the first two criteria for judging success were irrelevant. The 18 Sovietologists I studied were very different indeed in their judgements of the character of the Soviet system. They ranged from those who were at least to some extent positive, such as the British economist Alec Nove, to those scholars who — at least ostensibly — subscribed to a neutral or perhaps dispassionate view, such as the political scientist Jerry Hough in the U.S., over to those who were totally negative towards the legitimacy of the system, where Besançon is one example,[4] and the Swedish economist Stefan Hedlund is another. Apart from these cases, which are probably the easiest to characterize in terms of their basic views of the Soviet system, the other Sovietologists all held perspectives which are more problematic to characterize. One aspect of my assessment of each Sovietologist is thus an attempt to capture the essence of that scholar's fundamental view of the Soviet system.

Later in the chapter from the French anthology assessing perestroika after five years, Besançon returned to the question of what he expected would be the outcome of all this. He was clear on the point of prediction:

---

[4] "Gorbachev peut-il réussir? Je suis loin d'en être certain. Je suis donc pessimiste du point de vue de Gorbachev, et optimiste du mien, parce que je souhaite la fin de ce régime." "Can Gorbachev succed? I am far from certain. I am pessmistic from Gorbachev's point of view, but optimist from mine, because I want this regime to end." Besançon, (1990)"Les Atouts de Gorbatchev: Une Évaluation", p. 59.

"Je ne fais point de scénario" (Besançon, 1990, p. 59). According to him, the fundamental goals of Soviet foreign policy never changed, at least up to 1990. What changed were the means by which the leadership tried to reach these goals.

Alain Besançon viewed the Soviet reform process as a result of rethinking. He identified the basis of this rethinking as the KGB, which somehow passed its ideas on to the political leadership. Even if he never published any real forecast, the future he indicated for the Soviet Union, writing sometime around the turn of the year 1989/1990, was a bleak one indeed. He labelled the question of the restive nationalist republics as "insoluble", it cannot be solved, "les échéanges fatales" (ibid., p. 83) can simply be postponed.[5]

Besançon's explanation of why the reform process was started is a rare case of the bureaucratic explanation, level III, in the terms of table 1.2. He based his explanation on a bureaucratic elite within the Soviet system, rather than on either the state itself or the leader.

Besançon is one of the Sovietologists who failed to address all of the research questions that are posed in chapter 1 of this book. What determined his way of analysing the Soviet Union was his immense distaste, indeed his loathing, of the Soviet system. He addressed only my second research question, why did the reforms start, and then only in a cursory fashion. As stated, the probable reason for his failure to address the question of when the reforms had changed the character of the Soviet system was the fact that he regarded the Soviet system as illegitimate. For this reason, the question of the reformability of the system was illegitimate for Alain Besançon. His assessments of the changes under way in the Soviet Union during Gorbachev's time in power were to some extent marred by his apparent inability to acknowledge the possibility of any real changes inside the system. In this sense he comes at least close to being an example of a specialist on the Soviet system whose belief in a model clouded his analysis of the possibilities for change. On the other hand, his negative beliefs concerning the impossibility of reforming the system can be said to have been proved correct with the collapse of the state in 1991. This makes it hard to regard his analysis as being all too wedded to a misguided model.

---

[5] The attentive reader will note that this is very close to what Alexandre Bennigsen wrote. The difference between Bennigsen and Besançon in this respect, and the reason why the latter is not classified as having issued a correct forecast, is that Besançon explicitly states that Gorbachev by the time of his 1989/1990 analysis still had the possibility to obtain "du moins...un sursis". In other words, Gorbachev still had the chance to obtain at least a postponement of the demise of the Soviet State. Ibid. p. 59.

5.2.1.3 Hélène Carrère d'Encausse

> Ce que prouvent ces crises, c'est que l'URSS n'est pas une famille totalement unie où toutes les differences se sont effacés, et où les sentiments d'appartenance à un sol et à une culture sont essentiellement des souvenirs. Ce crises prouvent que le *peuple soviétique* est encore un conglomérat de peuples. Et ce qu'il y de diverses, c'est que les crises les opposent *explicitement* au pouvoir central. Dans leur désir d'imposer leurs aspirations, c'est vers le pouvoir central qu'il se tournent, c'est lui qu'ils s'efforcent de convaincre ou d'intimider. Ces crises ont en définitive en commun de se situer à l'intérieur du système politique soviétique, de se poser dans les termes et par rapport aux valeurs que sont ceux de l'URSS. Ces crises affectent-elles l'ensemble du système? En apparence non. Si l'on se fie aux données visibles — manifestations ouvertes de désaccord —, il est clair qu'une partie importante de la societé non russe en est preservé. C'est le cas, semble-t-il, de la société musulmane, nombreuse et dynamique. Est-elle l'élément stabilisant du système qui compenserait les crises constatées ici? Ou bien cette stabilité recouvre-t-elle une crise latente d'une autre dimension, plus redoutable encore à la cohésion de l'ensemble?" (Carrère d'Encausse, 1978, p. 271.)

What these crises prove is that the U.S.S.R. is not a united family where all differences have disappeared, and where sentiments of belonging to one piece of land and one culture are essentially memories. These crises prove that the *Soviet people* is still a conglomerate of peoples. And the differences that exist are that the crises make these peoples *explicitly* oppose the central power. In their desires to realize their aspirations, they turn to the central power, it is it that they try to convince or intimidate. These crises definitely have in common that they are situated within the Soviet political system, that they are raised within the terms and the values of the U.S.S.R. Do these crises affect the whole of the system? Apparently not. If one relies on obvious signs — open manifestations of opposition —, it is clear that an important part of non-Russian society remains loyal. This seems to be the case with the numerous and dynamic Muslim society. Is it the stabilising element of society which compensates for the crises noted here? Or is it rather the case that this stability hides a latent crisis of another dimension, even more threatening to the cohesion of the whole system?

The most prolific writer of the four French Sovietologists analysed here is *Hélène Carrère d'Encausse*. From 1978 to 1992, she published 11 substantial books, all covering Soviet affairs, although not all are relevant for this study. To assess this Sovietologist fully, I have regarded it as impossible to overlook her 1978 volume, *L'empire éclaté,* in which she covered the issue of nationalities in the Soviet Union. While this book very clearly established this issue as very problematic for the Soviet State, it did not contain any prediction that it would lead to the downfall of that state, not really even a forecast in my terms. What the "nations" wanted to reach, according to the author, was not full sovereignty but greater room for manoeuvre inside the system: "Ce que les nations réclament, sous des formes diverses, ce n'est pas la destruction du système existant, mais l'élargissement à l'intérieur de ce système de leurs privilèges nationaux et des avantages qu'elles peuvent en tirer" (Carrère d'Encausse, 1978, p. 335) "what the nations reclaim, in different forms, it is not the destruction of the existing system. but the widening of their national privileges and the advantages that they may draw from this within current system". The author's summing up at the very end of the book perhaps best captures the flavour of the basic argument:

> En soixante ans, le régime soviétique a accompli des transformations considérables dans la societé. Sans doute, se heurte-t-il à des nombreaux problèmes. Mais il est clair que, de tous les problèmes auxquels il doit faire face, le plus urgent, le plus irréducible, c'est celui que posent les nations. Et comme l'Empire auquel il a succedé, l'État soviétique semble incapable de sortir de l'impasse nationale (ibid., p. 342).
>
> In sixty years, the Soviet regime has accomplished considerable transformations within society. Without a doubt it faces numerous problems. But it is clear that of all the problems that they face, the most urgent, the most insurmountable, is that of the nations. And like the Empire that it succeeded, the Soviet State seems incapable of escaping from the national impasse.

In other words, the nationalist issue was a long-term one that the Soviet system had to live with. There was no solution to be found to the stalemate that had been created. The problem was, however, nowhere in the book defined as being so large as to threaten the very survival of the system.

Carrère d'Encausse did not focus on Soviet foreign policy to any great extent in her analyses of the Gorbachev years. In a book published in 1986 there were, however, some passages that indicate that the French Sovietologist believed in a Soviet foreign policy that had its own logic:

> Pétrification du système politique, piétinements de l'economie d'une part, et dynamisme exceptionelle de l'action externe, de l'autre, sont-ce là des réalités compatibles? Pourtant, c'est bien ainsi que l'U.R.S.S. a traversé la seconde moitié des années 70. Qu'en conclure? Sinon que la politique étrangère de l'U.R.S.S. peut avoir une autonomie, une dynamique propre. Qu'elle n'est pas obligatoirement le reflet des problèmes internes, ni dépendante de l'état des dirigeants (Carrère d'Encausse, 1986, p. 359).

Petricfication of the political system, stagnation of the economic system on the one hand, and the exceptional dynamism of foreign policy, on the other, are these compatible realities? In any case, that is how the U.S.S.R. traversed the second of the 1970s. What can we conclude from this? What else but that the foreign policy of the U.S.S.R. may have an autonomy, a dynamic of its own. That it is not necessarily the reflection of internal problems, nor dependant on the state of the leaders.

Carrère d'Encausse's belief in the separate role of foreign policy for Soviet politics was further underlined in the final words of the volume just quoted, where she stated that whatever the problems of Brezhnev's reputation at the time of her writing in the mid-1980s, he was assured of his place "au panthéon de la géopolitique" (Carrère d'Encausse, 1986, p. 379).

In a volume published in 1990, Hélène Carrère d'Encausse indicated where she believed one could find at least part of the explanation for the start of the reform process:

1986: Andreï Amalrik ne s'est trompé que de deux ans. L'U.R.S.S. si puissante découvre alors en un instant que cette puissance n'est qu'un mythe et que les réussites constantes dont elle se prévalait ne recouvraient qu'une faillite générale. A l'origine de cette révélation, on a coutume de penser qu'il y eut un homme: Gorbatchev. En réalité, il y eut aussi un événement: Tchernobyl. Venu en pouvoir en 1985, Gorbatchev sait que la puissance de son pays dissimule bien des faiblesses. Mais il considère aussi que le bilan comporte deux réussites incontestables: l'Empire intérieur, l'Empire extérieur. Il s'attache à reconstruire cette puissance, à accélérer le progrès en s'appuyant sur ces deux points forts de l'heritage: le *peuple soviétique* et la partie de l'Europe économiquement et militairement intégrée à la communauté soviétique. ...
L'explosion, que l'on ne peut longtemps cacher à la societé, impose a Gorbatchev un tournant politique radical, la fin du mensonge (Carrère d'Encausse, 1990).
1986: Andrei Amalrik was not off by more than two years. The U.S.S.R. which is so powerful discovers now in an instant that this power is no more than a myth and that the constant successes that it boasts of only cover a general breakdown. A the origin of this revelation it is common to think that there was a man: Gorbachev. In reality, there was also an event: Chernobyl. Having come to power in 1985, Gorbachev knew that the power of his country well hid several weaknesses. But he thought also that the balance showed two incontestable successes: the internal Empire, and the external Empire. He set out to reconstruct this power, to accelerate progress by leaning on these two strong points of his heritage: the *Soviet people* and the part of Europe economically and militarily integrated with the Soviet Community. ...

The explosion, which could not kept secret from society for any long time, forced Gorbachev to undertake a radical political change, the end of lying.

Although it was not a precise explanation, this statement identified two factors that must be regarded as part of Carrère d'Encausse's explanation of this process. The first element is Gorbachev himself. The French Sovietologist regarded him as absolutely crucial to the start of the reform process. Exactly how this was so, however, was never spelled out in the material I have studied. The second element in her explanation is clearer: the "explosion" in Chernobyl. In this case Carrère d'Encausse included a causal element: Chernobyl "imposed" on Gorbachev an end to the lying that, in the French Sovietologist's view, had been at the very core of the Soviet system up to that time. I classify these two explanations for the changes in Soviet policy as IV b, the great-man theory, and II a, domestic structures.

Later in the same volume, Hélène Carrère d'Encausse returned to the issue of the nationalities. In this section, she stated that the problems she identified in the late 1970s had by 1990 come into the open. This was still in the form of an assessment of a situation, however; it was in no way a forecast (Carrère d'Encausse, 1979, pp. 189-190).

Hélène Carrère d'Encausse, despite her reputation in some circles as having foretold the end of the Soviet empire, nowhere presented a forecast, much less a prediction, in the terms I have presented in section 1.3.2 of this book. A qualification is that this assessment of course applies only to the material I have studied (cf appendix 2a). Her 1978 book *L'empire éclaté* simply did not contain any forecast to the effect that the nationalist issues would cause the Soviet empire to collapse.[6] It was only in *La gloire des nations ou la fin de l'Empire soviétique*, published in late 1990, that the French Sovietologist stated that the Soviet Union was in a process that would end in its collapse. In my conception, this was stated at too late a stage to qualify as a correct forecast.

---

[6] It should be noted here that my assessment of this work is based on the French original. Randall Collins claims that in the U.S. version, printed in 1979, Carrère d'Encausse went so far as to predict that when the non-Russian population of the Soviet empire exceeded the number of Russians in the early 21st century, the state would collapse. The French original contains no such claim. It is tempting to speculate, however, that when Carrère d'Encausse wanted to publish in the U.S. she succumbed to the pressures for "prognoses" that was so strong in U.S. Sovietology. See Randall Collins: "Prediction in Macrosociology; The Case of the Soviet Collapse", *American Journal of Sociology*, Vol. 100 (May 1995), pp. 1552-1593, at p. 1575.

Hélène Carrère d'Encausse does not really base her analysis of the Soviet Union on any of the four models of Sovietology presented in table 1.1. This despite the fact that she is a professor of political science. This is thus not a scholar who let her fundamental academic views cause her to disregard the breadth and depth of the changes wrought by Gorbachev.

Carrère d'Encausse was a perceptive analyst of Soviet affairs during the period in focus in this book. She put much emphasis on the nationalist issues in her publications, prominently including her 1978 book *L'empire éclaté*. My view that this cluster of issues was one of the prime causes of the Soviet collapse strongly contributes to my positive view of her as an analyst. Carrère d'Encausse did not directly address my three research questions to any great extent, however. Of the three, she was most explicit on the explanation of the causes behind the change in Soviet policies. It was — in her view — the new Soviet leader, first, and the Chernobyl disaster, second, that led to the start and perhaps also the acceleration of the Soviet reform process. In the material that I was able to find, Carrère d'Encausse never explicitly addressed the extent of the changes that had already occurred under Gorbachev, as she saw them. Even more surprising is perhaps the finding that the correct forecast that she did issue came late in the autumn of 1990. Even if my cut-off point for forecasts, 18 months before the collapse of the Soviet State, can be discussed, still Carrère d'Encausse did not issue any early forecast, much less any clear predictions, to the effect that the Soviet Union would disintegrate before that time. It must be added that she issued forecasts in some French materials that I have been unable to unearth, but my conclusion stands at least for the material detailed in appendix 2a in this volume.

5.2.1.4 Pierre Hassner

> Indeed, it might be said that what used to be the most predictable element of the international system has become the most unpredictable, yet it still provides us with the trend that allows the safest long-range prediction, the death of Marxism-Leninism. The exhaustion of its legitimacy and the avowal of defeat by the leading elites of the major communist states in the face of economic failure and social decay seem as inevitable as any ideological trend can be (Pierre Hassner, 1990, p. 20.)

The philosopher and political scientist *Pierre Hassner* wrote mostly about matters that are somewhat peripheral for this study during the relevant period. Several of his chapters in edited volumes, as well as his articles, analysed the making of French Soviet policy, rather than making any direct analyses of Soviet behaviour. Still, parts of his writings are clearly relevant here. In these, Hassner early on stressed the basic stability of Soviet politics:

> One may even imagine, under the new Soviet leadership, bolder attempts at détente abroad and reform within. But one may safely predict that these attempts will, once again, find their limits in the primacy of control (Hassner, 1984, p. 313).

One of Hassner's most interesting pieces, from the perspective of this book, was published in the fall of 1988. In this article, Hassner underlined the reactive nature of Gorbachev's actions. He began, in true dialectical fashion, by stating his credo about the "two missions of government":

> Every government has a twin mission: relations with its own people and relations with other states. In the case of a totalitarian regime, particularly if it is communist, there is a structural conflict between the dynamics of the system and both the demands of civil society and those of the international order. Moreover, given that Gorbachev neither wants nor is able to impose impenetrable barriers between these two missions, the interior and the exterior of his regime are themselves constantly interacting, sometimes positively, sometimes negatively. The result is a genuinely triangular relationship between the Soviet government, Soviet domestic factors, and the external world.
>
> Gorbachev strives simultaneously to control and manipulate this relationship and he succeeds in giving the impression of constantly holding the initiative in the face of divided or paralyzed adversaries. ...Thus, one might well ask: is Gorbachev truly looking for a real compromise with societies of the East and West? Does he acknowledge their aspirations in order to adjust to certain fixed realities? Or does he acknowledge them in order to conquer them and to reestablish control and the totalitarian initiative.
>
> An answer seems nearly impossible to discern (Hassner, 1988, pp. 75-76).

On foreign policy in particular, Hassner was sceptical about the extent of real change:

> To date, real and irreversible changes in Soviet foreign policy are still too few and tentative to erase completely the impression that behind the changed outward appearances are traditional Soviet international policies and goals. Gorbachev has, however, broken with traditional positions in a number of important areas (ibid., pp. 100-101; for a longer quote from this article see appendix 4).

For Hassner, much had changed in the Soviet Union by mid-1988, even in foreign policy. It was unclear to him, however, whether these foreign policy changes had really altered the core of the long-term Soviet goals. In explaining the changes that had indeed occurred by that time, Hassner highlighted the importance of the state's economic difficulties while he simultaneously always underlined the manipulative nature of Soviet politics. In this latter respect, Mr. Gorbachev was, to Hassner, no path breaker; he was instead a traditionalist. In a key formulation in the article, Hassner gave his basic explanatory view: "Gorbachev is neither an anonymous product of an unchanging system nor a heroic reformer won over by liberal values. Above all, he ought to be seen as 'the grand coopter', concurrently the agent and the instrument of a dialectic mixing both adaptation and manipulation" (ibid., p. 95).

When Hassner returned to the issues of the reformability of the system roughly two years later, probably writing in late 1989, much had changed. What used to be stable, up to the mid-1980s at least, had by that time become the opposite. Indeed, Hassner even ventured a prediction about the future of Marxism-Leninism, as illustrated in the first quote in this section. There can be no doubt whatever that Hassner included the fate of the Soviet Union in the forecast. Another attempt, made about six months later, to make forecasts about the Soviet future, was roughly of a similar character. It correctly forecast that a new, democratic Russia could only appear out of the 1990 Soviet turmoil after "'a time of troubles'" (Hassner, 1990c). In other words, Pierre Hassner, in the terms specified in section 1.3.2 of this book, made a correct forecast concerning the coming demise of the Soviet Union. The first such forecast was written around the turn of the year 1989/1990.

In his explanation of why the Soviet reform process started, Pierre Hassner combined the importance of the economic slowdown and the political use of this excuse as a means to further long-term Soviet goals.

Hassner addressed all three of the questions posed at the start of this book in his analyses of the Soviet system under Gorbachev. He assessed the extent of the changes to policy, including those of foreign policy. He remained sceptical, however, about the breadth of these changes for at least three years. Hassner found the reasons behind these policy changes in explanation II b, the socialist economy. To this he added, however, the way in which the Soviet leader used this weakness for other purposes as well. Lastly, Pierre Hassner forecast the demise of the Soviet Union about two years in advance.

5.2.1.5 Conclusion: The French Sovietologists It is hard to detect any particular French Sovietological angle on analysing developments in the Soviet Union, based on the examination of the four writers studied here. The French Sovietologists seemed, rather, to be focusing on topics that interested them as scholars, and, in the case of André Besançon, on a system that he obviously detested.

The two historians, Alexandre Bennigsen and Hélène Carrère d'Encausse, shared a strong focus on the importance of nationalist issues for the weakness that they both saw in the Soviet State. A crucial difference between the two was, however, that for Bennigsen this problem complex led him to prophesise that the weakness to which the composition of nationalities directly led was a weakness that would, in the end, prove fatal for the Soviet system. Though it was fairly imprecise, his formulation to this effect in 1983 is here classified as a correct forecast. Professor Carrère d'Encausse never made such an explicit linkage between the nationalities question and the end of the Soviet empire, as far as I have been able to establish. Her books from the late 1970s and early 1980s established a strong and unmistakable view of a petrified system, with many problems that led her to regard it as unreformable. Not until late 1990, however, did she publish a prognosis to the effect that the Soviet system would disintegrate. This prognosis was issued at a late stage, however, at a time when the decline of the system had become too obvious, in my assessment, to allow me to classify it as a correct forecast.

If Alexandre Bennigsen can be regarded as having issued a correct forecast concerning the end of the Soviet Union, this was even truer of Pierre Hassner. Hassner moved from a basic view emphasizing the stability and unchangeability of the system, which lasted at least until mid-1988, to a view that encompassed a stated belief that the system was on the way to collapse by late 1989.

On the question of diagnosis, the French Sovietologists varied strongly in their assessments of when the Soviet system had really changed, whether in domestic or in foreign policy. One can detect a tendency for them to remain sceptical of whether or not Mr. Gorbachev's reforms really touched the fundaments of the system for a fairly long time. Indeed, up until 1989 there is no example of any of the three[7] French Sovietologists clearly stating that Gorbachev's Soviet Union was different from what the country had been before. Indeed, André Besançon remained very sceptical on this issue well into 1990.

---

[7] Only three because Professor Bennigsen died in the summer of 1988.

On the explanatory question of why the reform process started, three of the French scholars provided answers. They were Besançon, Carrère d'Encausse and Pierre Hassner. For Hélène Carrère d'Encausse, the explanation for the start and the subsequent acceleration of the reform process was to be found in two factors: Gorbachev as an individual and the processes started after the nuclear disaster at Chernobyl. The new leader was finally able to break with a tradition of stagnation. Chernobyl served to strengthen and radicalize a process of greater openness that the new leader had already started. Chernobyl's role in this process was crucial for Carrère d'Encausse. After this event, the Soviet leadership was never again able to conceal the secrets that had for so long been hidden from the Soviet population.

For Alain Besançon, the Soviet reform process was based on rethinking. This was, however, not done by Mikhail Gorbachev but by the KGB, which was in close contact with, first, Yuri Andropov and, then, Mikhail Gorbachev. Pierre Hassner saw the reasons behind the Soviet reform process as two strongly linked factors. One was the undeniable fact of a severe economic crisis. The second was the political use to which the Soviet leadership put this crisis in trying to influence the West to believe in Moscow's willingness for reform, while it still, conceivably, tried to reach its old, timeless, foreign policy goals. Hassner was, however, uncertain as to whether or not the foreign policy goals had indeed changed during the early years of Gorbachev.

Three of the four French Sovietologists focused on truly fundamental problems for the Soviet State, two of them, Pierre Hassner and André Bennigsen, going so far as to forecast the system's demise. At the very least this shows that some representatives of French Sovietology were able to identify the cracks in the Soviet system and to draw conclusions from this. My results indicate that the analysis of the Gorbachev years in France was a very well informed one, in the elite media as well as among Sovietologists. It is not possible to tell from this limited study whether this is a tendency that is true more generally of the way that these two actors look at the outside world from their French vantage point. The indication that my results provide of a general tendency to view the outside world in a way that lacks fundamental biases and that does not hesitate to explore the longer-range consequences of their analyses raises the question of whether this may be true more generally for French analysis of foreign policy. Any more definitive assessments of this will have to await results from further comparative research into how the French experts view the outside world, on their own and in comparison with their counterparts in other countries.

5.2.2 Great Britain

Two of the British Sovietologists included here are political scientists: *Archie Brown* and *Alex Pravda*. One is a military historian: *John Erickson* and the final one was an economist, the late *Alec Nove*.

5.2.2.1 Archie Brown

> As general secretary, Gorbachev has played a major role in the radicalization of the political reform agenda, but at every stage he has had to carry his Politburo colleagues with him. He began as the most radical member of the Politburo he inherited and, quite apart from the extent to which some of his own views have developed, could not have proposed to that body in 1985 some of the things he advocated in 1987, 1988, and 1989. With the emergence of *glasnost*, competitive elections, and a legislature in which radicals have been given a forum for public protest, Gorbachev and the progress of *perestroika* now have liberal as well as conservative critics. While in some ways this makes life tougher for the Soviet leader, on balance it is to his political advantage. He can play the role of a centrist, albeit one clearly leaning to the liberal side of the center, while taking on board more of the policies of the liberal critics than of their conservative counterparts. ...Gorbachev...has in mind a Soviet Union that in the year 2000 will be far more democratic and markedly more efficient economically than ever before. His problem is getting from here to there, for the problems of the transition period are horrendously difficult. ...
> How long the Soviet population will give credence to a leadership that does not produce concrete economic results remains a moot point (Brown, 1989 b, pp. 126-127).

It seems very right to start with *Archie Brown*, as he was one of the Sovietologists who first focused on Mikhail Gorbachev as a new type of Soviet leader. Brown's early article in *Problems of Communism*, published in mid-1985, was one of the very first scholarly pieces published on the new Communist party boss, and as such it was a trendsetter. Brown, a professor of politics at Oxford University, maintained his interest in Gorbachev and published a new major study on him — *The Gorbachev Factor* — in 1996.

In his article in *Problems of Communism* Brown presented an analysis of the new Soviet leader, which started by saying that "the choice of Gorbachev is of exceptional significance for the Soviet Union and — given the country's role in international affairs — for the rest of the world" (Brown, 1985, p. 1). The British Sovietologist went on to note that the climate for "policy innovation" (ibid., p. 17) in the Soviet Union was better in the mid-1980s than it had been in the past. The possibilities for change were highlighted in the economic and political domestic spheres, as well as in foreign policy. In the latter respect, Brown was fairly precise:

> ...Gorbachev seems determined to improve the Soviet Union's external relations on several fronts. ...Given Gorbachev's acknowledged ability to argue the Soviet case flexibly and reasonably, and without either dogma or script, the Soviet Union can well afford to be much more active diplomatically than it has in the recent past.
>
> Gorbachev, who has made the journey from kolkhoz to Kremlin in record time, is about as likely to question the foundations of a system that enabled him to rise from humble origins to the highest office in the land as an American president who rose from log cabin to White House would be to question the wisdom of the Founding Fathers (Brown, 1985, p. 23).

Archie Brown's 1985 analysis of Gorbachev, coming three years after the British Sovietologist first mentioned the Soviet leader in an article already in 1982, is suffused with a sense of the importance and dynamism of the new leader in the Kremlin. Professor Brown clearly belonged to the school of Sovietologists for whom the system was reformable, and Gorbachev was the man to do it. Note also, however, the limits within which Brown believed, in 1985, that these reforms would be likely to stay.

Brown's continued interest in the developments in the Soviet Union during the period under study here makes it possible to follow the evolution of his analysis quite closely. Writing in the second half of 1986, Brown dismissed those analysts who denied that there was indeed a process of economic reform under way in the Soviet Union. He stated that the analogy between the economic reform process during Gorbachev's first eighteen months in power, and that of the aborted economic reform under Kosygin in the mid-1960s, was wrong on several grounds. The attempts at reform under Gorbachev were, in his view, much more serious (Brown, 1986/87, pp. 63-65). On foreign policy he wrote in the late summer of 1986:

> It is undoubtedly true that at present there is more coordination and complementarity between Soviet domestic and foreign policy than has been the case at times in the past. But while domestic economic pressures and priorities play a part in determining current Soviet foreign policy objectives, they are not the whole story. Foreign policy changes are also being made on their own grounds and reflect Soviet security concerns and some new thinking on international politics. ...In addition to these important personnel shifts, Gorbachev has undeniably made innovations in Soviet policy toward

Western countries. The extended unilateral moratorium on nuclear testing is a case in point, as was the package presented by the Soviet Union at the Reykjavik summit. Particularly noteworthy is the Soviet acceptance of the 'zero option' — the elimination of all intermediate-range nuclear weapons in Europe (Brown, 1986/87, p. 70).

For Archie Brown, it was thus clear that important changes in Soviet foreign policy had taken place by the end of 1986. Brown also, in a characteristic way, took a swipe at other Sovietologists, who were less willing to concede that there had been important changes in Soviet policies by that time:

Nothing I have said should be taken to suggest that the Soviet Union is about to embrace a form of democracy that would be recognized as such in Western Europe or the United States. But to rule out of court or to dismiss as trivial change over time from quasi-totalitarianism to authoritarianism to the beginnings of a more enlightened authoritarian regime is an abdication of responsibility on the part of scholars and policymakers. Western observers who respond in this manner to change in the Soviet Union tend to be carrying more ideological ballast than is to be found these days in the arguments of some of the better Soviet scholars and political analysts (Brown, 1986/87, p. 83).

Still, even Archie Brown conceded that, at least as of late 1986, the changes, while not insubstantial in his view, "are not necessarily irreversible. But the shifts that have occurred, and seem likely to continue, do need to be reckoned with" (ibid., p. 84).

In 1987 Brown characterized the Soviet reform process as a "period of political struggle". The reformers themselves were, to Brown, uncertain about how far the "reform process will go" (Brown, 1987, p. 146).

On the issue of the reversibility of the reform process, Brown remained cautious, but was somewhat more optimistic in mid-1987 about the chances for its success than he had been six months earlier: "There is reason for at least hope that by [the turn of the century] the reform of the Soviet system will have made it qualitatively better than it has been hitherto and that opportunities will have arisen (which should not be passed by) for a more constructive relationship with the West" (ibid., p. 151).

Writing in 1989, Brown underlined his view that Gorbachev didn't have any fixed plan for the reform process when he came to power (Brown, 1989a, p. 186-187). In a second article written the same year, Brown returned to his old theme about other Sovietologists having misread the breadth of the Soviet reform process. While he conceded that Gorbachev, by mid-1989, had lost popularity at home, this "has not undermined his power" (Brown, 1989b, p. 117). Indeed, the British professor went on to observe, with apparent admiration, that Gorbachev had been able to strengthen his position against the conservative Communists who, in Brown's analysis, tried to stop the Soviet leader's reform process. In his conclusion to this part of the analysis, the British Sovietologist went further with a forecast about the coming years, which ended: "Gorbachev's consolidation of power at the top of the party and state hierarchy, together with the process of institutional change, have probably secured for reformers in the Soviet leadership several more years in which to make some improvements in living standards to accompany and reinforce political progress" (Brown, 1989b, p. 127).

In late 1989, in a revision of the article just quoted, Archie Brown characterized the evolution of his views under the impression of what had been happening in Moscow:

> As recently as late 1986, while emphasizing the significance of the political developments already under way, I could characterize the change (itself an important one) in the post-war Soviet Union as movement from "quasi-totalitarianism to authoritarianism to the beginnings of a more enlightened authoritarian regime." In the last two-and-a-half years, the Soviet system has developed beyond that. It is now indeed a more enlightened authoritarian regime and one, furthermore, which already contains some significant elements of political pluralism and of democratisation (Brown, 1990, p. 57; note omitted).

Archie Brown gave his views on why the reform process started in earnest under Gorbachev on several occasions, emphasizing four factors. The first was the sorry state of the Soviet economy, where the trends were much worse than they had been in the mid-1960s. The second factor concerned perceptions. Here the personal role of the new leader was underlined. The Soviet leader had, according to Brown, analysed the situation and grasped the extent of the problems. In his 1996 book, *The Gorbachev Factor*, Brown elaborated on this explanation in an interesting chapter on the role of ideas in the Soviet transformation (ibid., pp. 89-129). The role of cognitive factors, of learning, was here underscored. Brown included not just the new ideas of Mr. Gorbachev himself, but also the role of the international institutes where "new thinking" to some extent originated. Professor Brown stressed the overwhelming importance of the Soviet leader as an individual to the extent that he regarded Mr. Gorbachev himself as having been a prerequisite to the start of the Soviet reform process. Without Mr. Gorbachev, in other words, there would have been no Soviet reform process of anything even approaching the magnitude attempted during the second half of the 1980s (Brown, 1990, p. 309, 317). The third explanation highlights the balance of power inside the Soviet power apparatus. There is a difference, according to Brown, between a chairman of the Council of Ministers, such as Kosygin in the 1960s, and a General Secretary of the Communist Party, like Gorbachev, pressing for reform. The position of the latter official was much stronger in the Soviet system than was that of the former. The fourth explanation is that the situation in Eastern Europe was, in the mid-1980s, seen as an inspiration for reform by the new Soviet leadership (Brown, 1986/87, p. 65).

Brown's analysis of the causes behind the start of the reform process, and of its development, was suffused by the notion that this was an evolutionary process. Gorbachev was aware of the need for reform from the beginning, but as time and events went on, he became progressively more radical in his views on the extent of the reform that was needed (Brown, 1996, pp. 155-160).

From this article, one can deduce that Brown saw the causes of the reforms as essentially emanating from two of the levels of analysis presented in table 1.2. The first is the state level, level II. Here Brown included both the failings of the Socialist economy, explanation II b, and the peculiarities of the totalitarian system, explanation II a. The second is the individual level, level IV, where the cognitive learning processes of Mr. Gorbachev himself, as well as of the leadership more broadly, were identified. It should be remembered that Professor Brown expressly stated that the Soviet leader, as an individual, was a necessary condition for the start of the reform process. In other words, the British Sovietologist included both explanation IV a, cognitive factors, and the individual characteristics of the Soviet leader, explanation IV b. The role of the international institutes, which is mentioned in particular in *The Gorbachev Factor,* adds a flavour of a level III explanation, that is, it points to the role of a bureaucratic apparatus, but this factor is not as developed as are the explanations on the other two levels.

In his magnum opus on the Soviet leader, Professor Brown also explicitly addressed the question of why the Soviet leadership under Mr. Gorbachev embarked on a radically new foreign policy, which was gradually manifested during the Soviet leader's years in power. In this assessment, the British political scientist contrasts two broad explanations: "the Gorbachev factor" and the "Reagan factor". Professor Brown comes down squarely in favour of the former. It was, in other words, the new Soviet leader, his rethinking, and the consequences flowing from this that explain the Soviet changes in foreign policy. The influence of the external pressure administered by the Reagan Administration was, on this view, marginal as compared to the internal factors (Brown, 1996, pp. 226-230).

Archie Brown's analysis of Mikhail Gorbachev and his policies was nuanced and, in many ways, insightful. Brown obviously held the Soviet leader in high regard, even after the collapse of the state. He was clearly willing to note the changes in the Soviet Union. Brown was, however, careful about not going too far in stating that the Soviet Union had indeed changed for good at any stage. It was characteristic of most of the Sovietologists, even the ones who were quite willing to note the immensity of the changes that they saw in Soviet politics, to continue to issue warnings to the effect that one could not be certain that the changes would be lasting. Brown, furthermore, provided a fairly complex explanation for the changes that he saw in Soviet policies. He also presented a separate explanation for the changes in Soviet foreign policy.

It is notable, finally, that despite the many insights into Soviet events that, to this author, characterized Brown's writings, he was unable to foretell that the experiment would end in collapse. Is it too bold to speculate that one reason behind this could have been his too exalted view of the Soviet leader? Was Archie Brown perhaps a direct contrast to those Sovietologists who "foretold" the end of the Soviet Union because they wanted this to happen? Archie Brown was clearly not wedded to any rigid model of Soviet politics that made it hard for him to grasp the breadth and depth of changes in the system under Gorbachev. Instead, his high regard for Gorbachev as leader clouded his judgement in some respects, particularly as it concerned the Soviet leader's ability to control the dynamics of change and the subsequent decay that resulted from the reforms commenced in 1985.

5.2.2.2 John Erickson

> I think he is a shrewd man. I think he has lots of things going but I do not regard him as being one of the brightest of the bright. I don't think he is. Sorry, but that's my own view. I think he sees things very dimly as to what he wants to do. He is a very witty man – he is very accomplished, but that does not amount to being a bright man. I think he is very quick on his feet. I will accept that too. I think he understands the need to present images but I see nothing in Gorbachev's remarks or speeches or anything that conveys to me the impression that he really has what one might call the aptitude to run their society (Erickson, 1986, p. 22).

Professor *John Erickson* is a military historian based at the University of Edinburgh. His specialties included the Soviet Union in the Second World War and the role of the military in Soviet politics. In the second half of 1986, Professor Erickson expressed a rather low estimation of the Soviet leader and of his ability to run his country as illustrated in the opening quote in this section.

John Erickson, in the same series of conversations, also stated his belief that it was not possible to create an "efficient power" (ibid., p. 26) in the Soviet Union without changing the very structure of the system. On the question of whether it was possible for the scholar to predict what would happen to the Soviet Union under Gorbachev, the British professor was very modest:

> My own guess is, I think Gorbachev is going to have to be careful. I don't think he will last very long, but that is a guess. I have been completely wrong plenty of times (Erickson, 1986, p. 24).

Concerning foreign and security policy, Erickson believed, in the fall of 1986, that it was important for Gorbachev to reach some successes. In particular, he singled out a wish in the Soviet polity for better relations with the U.S., including an agreement on strategic nuclear arms that was close to Soviet demands. A second foreign policy goal that he identified was a wish for a re-entry of the Soviet Union into the Middle East as an equal power to the United States. A third goal mentioned was the "regulation of the relationship with China on terms that are acceptable to the Soviet Union" (ibid., p. 26).

In 1990 Professor Erickson was prepared to grant that Gorbachev's "political initiatives and arms control proposals are...attempts at a fundamental 'systems shift', with the aim in the short-to-medium term of adjusting the 'correlation-of-forces' more in the Soviet favor, or less to the Soviet disadvantage" (Erickson, 1990, p. 144).

John Erickson did not provide any explanation for why the Soviet reform process started in the mid-1980s. Erickson thus belonged to that group of Sovietologists who did not focus to any great extent on the changes wrought by Mr. Gorbachev on the Soviet system. Indeed, he was the scholar of the 18 included in this book who had the least interest in Soviet changes from 1985 through 1991, according to my research. The main explanation for this seems to me to be that this was a scholar who focused on issues other than foreign and domestic policy in the Soviet Union.

5.2.2.3 Alec Nove

> Therefore, the lack of any powerful social group that favors reforms is one of the main obstacles to their introduction. Economists alone are not enough, especially because they are disunited. One may then ask: Why has reform been in the air, why is it still worth discussing, as we have been doing?
> The answer surely is this. The system is not working efficiently and cannot do so. The intentions of the party and state leadership are not being carried out. They desire an effectively functioning economy, producing more and better, no longer dependent on massive imports of grain or of the latest technology, with the producers responding to the requirements of other managers and of the consumers. Supplies should be arriving punctually and be of the right specifications. Plans should be balanced, materially and financially. All this the leaders repeat over and over again. Gorbachev has been particularly eloquent about the urgency of the need for change, several times deploring the failure to tackle the task in a determined and comprehensive manner (Nove, 1986, p. 328).

Alec Nove was professor of economics at Glasgow University, and for several years he was Director of the Institute of Soviet and East European Studies. He died in 1994. Throughout his distinguished career, Professor Nove was a prolific writer on the Soviet economy.[8] His basic view was that the Soviet system could indeed be reformed, without necessarily leading to any collapse of the system.[9] To him, the fundamental flaw of the Soviet economy was "the over-complexity of centralized planning, the sheer impossibility of coping with the informational and decision making tasks which the model concentrates at the centre" (Nove, 1982, p. 25). Nove's positive attitude towards the reformability of the Soviet economy was also apparent in his views about Mikhail Gorbachev and the latter's willingness to pursue genuine reform of the Soviet system. Alec Nove identified this inclination on Gorbachev's part more than one year before the latter's accession to power (Nove, 1984, p. 97).

For Alec Nove the explanations for the start of the reform program were fairly simple as shown in the first quote in this section. It is hard to find an explanation that more directly and precisely places the causes behind Gorbachev's reforms at explanatory level II b.

---

[8] It should be noted that the reference list on the Sovietologists surveyed for this book contains only those references for Professor Nove that deal with matters other than strict economics. Given his large production, this does not pose any problems for my analysis.

[9] Professor Nove discussed his views of the Soviet System, in comparison to the U.S., in a polemic against Jeane Kirkpatrick in "The Scope and Scale of Good and Evil", *Society*, (March/April 1985), pp. 12-17.

In the third edition of his major work, *The Soviet Economic System*, published in 1986, Nove went so far as to characterize the first year of the new Soviet leader's speeches as indicating a "radical-sounding program"(Nove, 1986, p. 336), but he did not label its implementation as equally far-reaching. Professor Nove's caution on the extent of the economic reforms continued into 1987, when he noted that Gorbachev had stated that things would be "different". It was, in the British Professor's view impossible to tell how different it would be: "I have no crystal ball, and cannot foretell the future" (Nove, 1987, p. 452). Alec Nove thus did not see it as his task to try to venture forecasts about what would happen to the Soviet economy that he studied so closely for so many years. It is not possible to identify in Nove's writings anything approaching a forecast about the Soviet Union's coming demise.

By 1987, Professor Nove was convinced that "large-scale reforms are intended" (ibid., p. 185) and he criticized those Western politicians who were unwilling to concede this. In 1989, Alec Nove was still more convinced of the breadth of the reforms attempted by Gorbachev, in the economic sphere as well as in the political:

> It should be clear, then, that the Soviet leadership is indeed trying to introduce radical reforms in the economy, and equally it should be clear that this process has been slow and uneven. There are...three reasons for this: First, opposition, much (but not all) of it due to vested interests and privileges; second, the sheer practical difficulties of implementing the desired changes; and third, the gaps and ambiguities in the reform model itself (Nove 1989a, p. 472).

At the same time, Nove introduced, for the first time, a note of caution in his analysis about the possible future of the Soviet reform process in an article from the fall of 1989. The situation, he wrote, was "deteriorating — political[ly] as well as economic[ally]" (ibid., p. 474). Nove also indicated the risk of failure in this context. In another publication, published at roughly the same time, he pointed to the uncertainty surrounding the ultimate goals that the Soviet reformers may have had with their program. He wrote: "I am not sure that they know" (Nove, 1989b, p. 231) as a response to this question. In 1990, Professor Nove's analyses of the Soviet situation turned progressively gloomier.

On the surface at least, Alec Nove presented straightforward explanations of the causes behind the reform process. He explained it with reference to the sorry state of the Socialist economy in the Soviet Union, and it is thus an explanation at level II b in the terms of my table 1.2.

Alec Nove was one of the Sovietologists who clearly and eloquently highlighted what is now, 10 years after the fall of the Soviet State, regarded as one of the major reasons for the collapse of the system: the flaws in the economic system. It should be noted, however, that while Nove identified the importance of these flaws as causes for the start of the Soviet reform process, he did not take the second step and identify these flaws as being serious enough to be a likely cause of the system's demise. In this sense, Nove, together with some of the other Sovietologists studied in this book who are also economists, was correct in identifying economic issues as being one important cause of the Soviet reforms. At the same time, he never made the point that these problems were so intractable that they might, in the end, cause the system to collapse. On the contrary, particularly during the early Gorbachev years, Nove believed that the Soviet system was eminently reformable. It is also evident that Nove did not base his analysis on any rigid model of Soviet politics.

5.2.2.4 Alex Pravda

> Gorbachev assessed the legacy of *zastoi* [stagnation] in terms of systemic crisis (officially called "pre-crisis") and launched under the label *perestroika* a strategy of economic and political modernisation. Critically important for the purposes of our analysis is the fact that Gorbachev conceived and pursued this strategy as modernisation by way of opening up in both the domestic and international arenas. To a greater extent than any previous Soviet modernising leader Gorbachev has sought radically to restructure the economic and political system in a Western orientation by exposing the USSR to greater international influence and involvement. The degree and pace of openness has varied between policy areas. It took less time and effort, for instance, to make headway in security and foreign policy than in domestic affairs. Progress in the international dimension helped advances at home. Defusing East-West tension has contributed to creating a more favourable climate for domestic democratisation, the progress of which has aided Soviet international credibility. Under *perestroika* there is not merely congruence but also to some extent symbiosis between open strategies at home and abroad (Pravda 1990a, p. 213).

Alex Pravda first addressed the Soviet reform process in a chapter published in 1988. This chapter, probably written by the end of 1986, only noted that a process of change was under way, and otherwise underlined the fluidity of the situation at that stage, noting that, both domestically and in foreign policy, "the policy record...is...mixed (Pravda, 1988, p. 245).

By late 1989 Alex Pravda had concluded that Mikhail Gorbachev had indeed changed both Soviet foreign and domestic policy in a fundamental way:

> Since assuming office and assessing the legacy of *zastoi* [stagnation] in terms of systemic crisis, Gorbachev has pursued a comprehensive, radical and highly activist policy of "opening up" on both domestic and international fronts — the strategy of perestroika. Gorbachev is the first Soviet leader to see the salvation of the Soviet Union in a strongly Westernizing strategy rather than a temporary tactic. He is the first to consider the USSR to be in a systemic crisis sufficiently grave to warrant revolutionary change and at the same time the first to have sufficient confidence to attempt this by exposing the Soviet Union to outside influences and involvement...(Pravda, 1990b, pp. 2-3).

In Professor Pravda's analysis there was no hesitation to classify the changes initiated by Mikhail Gorbachev in the domestic sphere as revolutionary. The Soviet leader had, on this explanation, "learned" that the system did not work, that it needed to be reformed. This is an explanation of the reform process that belongs to the individual level, level IV a, cognitive psychology and learning, in the terms of my table 1.2. The very state of the Soviet economy, explanation II b, must also be added.

In the same piece, Alex Pravda gave his views on the linkages between foreign and domestic policy under Gorbachev, as well as on what made the Soviet leadership initiate the reform process in the first place:

> As the process of perestroika has developed in ever more radical directions, so the links between its domestic and international components have thickened. Domestic perestroika has broadened from economic to political reform (and reform on both those fronts has become progressively more radical), while foreign policy has gone from efforts to re-establish détente to the determined pursuit of entente and a qualitatively new involvement in the international system. ...On the one hand, declining international standing certainly contributed to the initial decision to undertake radical domestic change, which in turn required a neo-détentist policy in order to obtain international tranquillity. On the other hand, democratizing reforms within the Soviet Union have contributed substantially to the creation of a non-threatening and more acceptable image abroad which remains essential to the successful pursuit of Gorbachev's more cooperative foreign policy strategy (Pravda, 1990b, p. 3).

For Pravda, the foreign policy of the Soviet State had undergone enormous changes by the turn of the year from 1989 to 1990. Professor Pravda was thus one of the Sovietologists studied in this book who most clearly assessed the extent of Soviet foreign policy change.

As the situation in Moscow worsened in the first half of 1990, Pravda tried to sketch the possible avenues down which future developments would be likely to travel. His piece can perhaps be classified as a hedged forecast. It also illustrates the difficulty in attempting to foretell what was going to happen to the Soviet future, even when making the judgement in 1990 (Pravda, 1990d, p. 47).

Alex Pravda has not, to this author's knowledge, published any piece specifically assessing why the reform process started in the Soviet Union. His analysis of domestic developments published in the fall of 1990 suggests the main elements he would likely use to put together such an explanation. This includes the fact that, in Pravda's conception, perestroika was clearly an attempt "to introduce revolutionary change from above" (Pravda, 1990d, p. 46). Since the Soviet system contained a large bulk of bureaucracy "in the middle", Gorbachev tried to mobilize support for policies of reform from below. "Predictably, these efforts...developed their own momentum. ...." In addition, "[t]he deterioration and decay of the economic fabric...reinforced and in turn...made worse the second set of problems — those linked with declining governability, the declining ability of Moscow to enforce its policies and simply to control events" (ibid., p. 46).

Alex Pravda's analysis of Soviet affairs during the Gorbachev years belongs to the category of dispassionate, insightful analysis into complex political processes. Pravda displayed no strong biases of any kind, nor did he subscribe to any inflexible model of Soviet politics. He is one of the few Sovietologists in my sample who explicitly stated, in late 1989, that both Soviet domestic and foreign policy had changed drastically. This was fairly late, but it was also emphatic. In his explanations for these changes, Pravda highlighted the Soviet leader in a way that suggested a cognitive explanation, type IV a, and, also, the sorry state of the Soviet economy, type II b.

5.2.2.5 Conclusion: The British Sovietologists Put very generally, the design of this book is founded on the assumption that there are three broad factors that might explain variations in the contents of the analysis of the Soviet Union undertaken by any actor outside that country. The first has to do with what I call foreign policy orientation, by which I mean a perceptual lens on the outside world that is shaped by shared historical, geographical, political and other elements within a particular nation. The second group of factors comprises the individual perceptual lenses. Each actor saw the Soviet Union as she or he did because of various personal traits. The third group concerns professional aspects, meaning that depending on whether one was a journalist or a Sovietologist, for example, one would be expected to have a tendency to assess the Soviet Union in a particular way.

This analysis of British Sovietologists points squarely to the second of these explanatory factors. There is no influence of anything resembling a British foreign policy orientation in the writings of the four Sovietologists studied here. Nor is it possible to regard these analyses as based on professional similarities. Instead, I found four very distinct ways of approaching what was happening in the Soviet Union during the second half of the 1980s. To characterize the basic views of the three British Sovietologists with the most clearly etched standpoints: Archie Brown believed that Mikhail Gorbachev was a unique leader, without whom no reform process could have been undertaken in Moscow; John Erickson stated his belief that Gorbachev was a mediocre leader, incapable of ruling his complex system; and Alec Nove based his views on a structural analysis of the system, in which the leader played a role but where larger societal forces were what decided the outcome.

When it comes to the explanation for the start of the reform process, only Brown, Nove and Pravda addressed this issue. They all included the individual-level explanation; in particular they focused on cognitive factors. Mr. Gorbachev, in their view, understood the need for a thoroughgoing reform of the Soviet economy. All three also pointed to the dismal state of the economy in itself as a factor that more or less caused the Soviet leadership to undertake a reform project.

On the issue of whether or not the Soviet system could be reformed, there was disagreement. Brown, Nove, and, to some extent, Pravda, believed that it could be reshaped. Erickson clearly did not.

None of the four British Sovietologists gave any real attention to the question of whether or not the specialist on the Soviet Union should have as a goal to be able to forecast what will happen to their object of study. Alec Nove stated unequivocally that he did not regard such prognostication as being possible for him to undertake. Archie Brown, John Erickson and Alex Pravda did, however, engage in fairly loose prognoses, mostly of a very speculative kind. None of them went so far as to make any more precise forecast. This means that there were clear differences between the French and the British Sovietologists on the aspect of prognoses. Two of the French specialists made forecasts foretelling the Soviet system's demise, while none of the four British scholars did so. My sample is too small to draw any definite conclusions regarding this, but perhaps I may venture the supposition that French scholars in the human and social sciences are more likely to attempt to look into the future than are their British colleagues. Whether this assumption has any validity into other areas than Sovietology will have to await further empirical analysis.

The British Sovietologists differ from some of their U.S. colleagues in the sense that the British scholars showed no inclination to adhere to fixed views of the Soviet system through which they interpreted, or in extreme cases even distorted, developments. This means that in neither of the two medium-sized Western nations analysed here did their specialists show a tendency that may be characterized as uniquely based in the U.S.: an adherence to models even after the fundamentals of those models have been invalidated by empirical events.

5.2.3 Sweden

In Sweden, Sovietology was represented in several academic disciplines. The authors selected here include one historian, two economists and one political scientist. Two of these four Sovietologists, the historian *Kristian Gerner* and the economist *Stefan Hedlund*, have co-operated on several publications, including two major volumes published in England and the U.S. in 1989 and 1993. Even though their views were very similar in many respects on the issues analysed in this book, they are treated separately.

5.2.3.1 Anders Åslund

> Gorbachev remains one of the most radical reformers in the Soviet leadership. His ideological speech in December 1984 revealed his radicalism, and there does not appear to be any good reason to dispute it.
>
> The General Secretary has pushed a broad agenda of both economic and political reform, but he tends to single out one or a few major issues at a time. Like any clever politician he does not reveal more of his political agenda than is good for him. As long as Gorbachev belongs to the most radical wing of the leadership, we cannot establish how far towards marketisation and democratisation he wants to go.
>
> Gorbachev appears to thrive on decision-making. Rather than accepting a stalemate, he forms a sufficiently broad alliance to be able to promote some kind of action, even if it barely complies with his own purposes (Åslund 1989b, p. 185).

In hindsight, it appears remarkable that Mikhail Gorbachev could receive so much acclaim for the economic policies that he pursued from 1985. From our current perspective, it appears all too evident that his rule was characterized by an unprecedented confusion in economic policies. Virtually every mistake that could be made was made. The Gorbachev administration carried out a massive destruction of the old Soviet system. In history, Gorbachev will go down as one of the greatest destructors of evil, while he failed in all his many attempts at construction. Gorbachev's great achievement was that he swiftly and relatively peacefully broke down one of the most centralized and ruthless systems the world has seen to date (Åslund 1993, p. 184; note omitted).

Anders Åslund is an economist. His academic career has been spent in Sweden, Great Britain and in the United States. Åslund's first article of relevance for this study was published in a Swedish anthology in 1988. In this chapter, Åslund discussed both the difficulties inherent in reforming Socialist economies of the Soviet type and the program that Gorbachev had been carrying out during his first 30 months or so in power:

> The world has seen many attempts to reform an economy of the Soviet type. Some progress has been made, but the most striking thing is how small the extent of progress is. Most attempts at reform have been limited or abandoned after some time. Thus, Western discussion concerning reforms in Soviet-type economies is characterized by deep pessimism. ...
> It is difficult to avoid being impressed by the strong political will, skill and the courage that Gorbachev has manifested since the Party Congress in 1986. His actions seem to be guided by Lenin's maxim: two steps forward, one step back. A large number of economic policies have already been undertaken, but it is still unclear how far Gorbachev wants to go in his reforms. He advances step by step. ...
> The practical results of the reform process are less impressive than the political will. It took more than two years before Gorbachev's Politburo produced a coherent reform program. The actions of reform already taken are very inconsistent, even if judged by Soviet standards. This indicates strong political resistance at all levels...(Åslund, 1988, pp. 86, 142-144).

This section clearly illustrates one central characteristic of Anders Åslund's early analysis of Soviet affairs: his admiration for Gorbachev as an individual and as a politician. At the same time, the Swedish economist was from the beginning clearly aware of the enormous task that Gorbachev faced as he tried to reform the Soviet system.

In 1989, Åslund published the book that made him famous throughout the Sovietology field and even beyond: *Gorbachev's Struggle for Economic*

Reform (1989b). This is an analysis of the policies carried out by the Soviet leadership in the economic sphere during the first three and a half years under Gorbachev. He tackled the explanatory puzzle highlighted in this book head on:

> Why did perestroika start? By its own standards, the Soviet regime did well in domestic politics, and in foreign policy until about 1980. The outstanding weakness was the economy. Economic growth had declined sharply in 1979 and stayed at a low level. Military demands are likely to have dramatized the need for an economic revitalization. The rapid US arms build-up, characteristic of the Reagan administration, posed a serious challenge to the Soviet Union. ...
> Thus, a combination of economic problems and strains in foreign policy led to perestroika (Åslund, 1989b, pp. 13.-14).

Åslund's explanation of the start of the reform process was, quite naturally given his profession as an economist, centred on the failings of the socialist economy in the Soviet Union. In addition to including explanation II b, Professor Åslund also incorporated foreign policy in a way that, to this author, indicates an explanation of type I a. In other words, he regarded the weakening of the Soviet power base as a cause behind the start of the reform process.

Åslund also characterized the policy style and the convictions of the Soviet leader in the 1989 book, as illustrated in the first quote in this section.

Åslund was also very explicit when it came to identifying the obstacles to reform that the Soviet leader had to overcome. He identified nine such problems that Gorbachev had to find a way around if he wanted to accomplish thorough reform of the Soviet system: 1) "top-level resistance"; 2) "the bureaucracy"; 3) "popular resistance"; 4) "inflationary pressures"; 5) "the absence of any form of market for capital and equity"; 6) "national unrest"; 7) "unrest in the most reformist East European countries, notably Hungary and Poland"; 8) "the CMEA trade system"; 9) "the paucity of Soviet statistics" (Åslund, 1989b, pp. 186-189). One only needs a glance at this list to understand that the hurdles that Gorbachev had to clear in his attempts to achieve a thorough economic reform of the Soviet system were very difficult indeed. At the same time, Åslund's analysis was impressive in this respect; he identified most – if not all – of the many problems underlying the immense difficulties that the leadership faced in their attempts to achieve economic reform in the Soviet Union. It is on this point that the special quality of the best analysis of the system by economic Sovietologists stands out: they were indeed able to make a penetrating assessment of both the reasons behind the Soviet problems and of the intractability of their resolution. In what may be called the "problem analysis" of the predicament of the Soviet Union in the second half of the 1980s, Anders Åslund appears to have been the most insightful, but other economists such as Alec Nove and Marshall Goldman also made important contributions. It is notable, however, that this splendid analysis was nowhere accompanied by equally impressive prognostications. I shall return to this issue in my concluding observations on Åslund's writings.

The above does not mean that Anders Åslund refrained entirely from issuing forecasts. He concluded his book on Soviet economic reform from 1989 by sketching three possible scenarios for the future:

> Three scenarios appear as the main options for the 1990s. We shall discuss them in order of probability. The first scenario is *radicalized economic reform with far-reaching democratization.* ...The second scenario is a *reactionary* or neo-Stalinist attempt to improve the Soviet system by a bit more repression, harder discipline and greater centralization than under Brezhnev. ...This might be seen as a Ligachev or military option. It would be the most obvious choice if Gorbachev is ousted.
> Our third scenario is *Brezhnevite*: to muddle along the old lines without much more repression and without major economic or political reforms. ...As public awareness evolves, more and more Soviet citizens are likely to turn their backs on this alternative. ...The worse we consider the state of the Soviet economy, the more likely either of the two first scenarios become. ...
> What we are seeing is a society in a severe bind, but it is trying to avert its apparent fate and recover as a great power. It remains to be seen whether this attempt will succeed, but it appears far more serious than any other Soviet attempt at reform since the 1920s (Åslund, 1989b, pp. 194-95).

Åslund thus attempted a very loose form of forecasting. He went so far as to identify the first scenario as the most likely to occur, but the caveats were so many that it is impossible to state that he made one specific forecast about the likely Soviet future.

Another publication by Åslund that was much discussed was his analysis of the weakness of the Soviet economy, as seen in revised GNP figures. The title — "How Small is Soviet National Income" (Åslund, 1989c) — gives an indication of the main result of the article published in 1989. This was that Soviet national income was much smaller than had previously been thought in the West. Åslund estimated that Soviet national income was less than a third of that in the U.S., which, among other things, indicated that the burden of the military build-up that the Soviet Union was still carrying out at the time was, and had been, much more costly for the system than had previously been believed.

True to its character as a scholarly work of economics this article contained no political conclusions. In two newspaper articles, published in *The Washington Post* in August 1989 and January 1990, Åslund discussed the political consequences of his findings more directly. His prognostications never became more precise than this, however:

> The Soviet economy is deteriorating more rapidly than most Westerners realize. ...A crisis clearly lies ahead: The question is whether it will be a revolution or counterrevolution (Åslund, 1990).

In 1991, Åslund published two articles in *Problems of Communism* in which he analysed the further problems of the Soviet attempts to reform their economy. The assessment of Gorbachev and his policies was by that time much harsher than it had been earlier:

> Looking back at Soviet economic policy during the second half of the 1980's, it is difficult to avoid the impression that virtually every possible mistake has been made. At present, *perestroyka* has proven to be an utter economic failure. ...
> It is very likely that September-October 1990 will stand out as a crucial turning point for Gorbachev from both a political and an economic point of view. Whatever the faults of the Shatalin program, it signified an understanding of the needs for a radical change of economic system and the forging of a new kind of relationship among the constituent republics of the Soviet Union. ...
> In September of 1990, President Gorbachev possibly had the option of a tentative resolution of the national crisis together with an initial cure of the economic crisis. However, he failed on both accounts, because he was not prepared to accept a diminution of his own power, the weakening of the Union, and large-scale privatization. The window of hope closed in October. After such a spectacular failure, Gorbachev can expect little mercy in his country or in history (Åslund, 1991a).

For Åslund, the leader who had shown such bravery and skill during his first years in power now found himself in the midst of disaster in the latter part of his Kremlin period, at least in terms of strict economic reform. Åslund did not assess the question of the reformability of the Soviet system to any important extent. The whole tone of his writings, however, indicated that he did indeed believe that it was possible to reform the system.

Anders Åslund displayed an acute ability to pinpoint the economic problems of the Soviet Union in the late 1980s and early 1990s. His talent for clarifying the extent of these problems are, to this author, the clearest examples of the ability of the economists surveyed in this book to make a correct problem analysis of one of the crucial, indeed fatal, weaknesses of the Soviet system. The political scientists who assess their writings after the fact can easily point out that these economists failed to draw clear political conclusions regarding the long-term viability of the system itself from these insights. In a sense it is unfair, however, to evaluate economists and their research with criteria constructed from the view of political science. If seen from the perspective of the academic discipline to which he belongs, economics, Anders Åslund's writings are admirable – at least to the political scientist assessing from outside the discipline – in their ability to clarify the extent of the Soviet troubles in the economic sphere as these looked in the second half of the 1980s.

5.2.3.2 Kristian Gerner

> Gorbachev realised that the country's situation was difficult. He tried to reform the Soviet system. The first practical result was a new self-image that made the entire Soviet project seem like a giant failure. In the Soviet press, one could read that instead of wealth, misery had been created; instead of integration between the peoples, there had been violent clashes; instead of the people ruling, there had been mafias and dictatorship. When Gorbachev began acting as a reformer it became clear that hardly anybody either within or outside the country believed that Soviet citizens, who had become accustomed to being treated as passive subjects, could save the system using their own strengths. All hope was placed on the new leader, that he as a strong-man, as a magician, might solve everything. If Gorbachev's policies failed, the country would become a developing nation and start on the road towards disintegration. If his policies were successful, it would be the triumph of an authoritarian dictator and the final proof that the Soviet system was the negation of political democracy. The alternatives at the end of the 1980s seemed to be either a number of successor states or a strong Russian power. In any case, it was possible to envision the end of the Soviet era and the beginning of the post-Soviet one (Gerner, 1989a, pp. 7-8).

Kristian Gerner has worked mostly at the University of Lund, Sweden, but from the mid-1990s on he has been based at another eminent Swedish

University, that in Uppsala. Gerner has by no means focused exclusively on Soviet and Russian matters. Indeed, his professor's chair in Uppsala is specialized in Central and Eastern Europe. Nevertheless, Gerner has had a substantial production on Soviet affairs, and his was an influential voice in the Swedish debate on relations with the Soviet Union, which makes his inclusion here a very natural one. He was also something of an iconoclast in the Swedish debate on the Soviet Union during the Cold War years. One expression of this is the fact that the Soviet side of a co-operative exchange of Swedish-Soviet historians specializing in Scandinavian history denied him a visa to a conference in the Soviet Union in 1986. This was done with the explicit consent of the Swedish leader of his country's delegation.[10]

In his two first publications, both published in 1986 and both co-authored with Stefan Hedlund, Gerner was very sceptical regarding the extent to which Mikhail Gorbachev intended to carry out any real reforms in the Soviet Union, at least in the economic sphere. Indeed, their analysis of Gorbachev's behaviour at the 27th Communist Party Congress in February 1986 focused on the fact that the Soviet leader "did not dare to mention the Russian word *Reforma*" (Gerner and Stefan Hedlund, 1986b).

One of Gerner's main interests in Soviet and East European affairs has been nationalist and ethnic questions. On this topic, he was very early in pointing out the potential explosiveness of this issue for the future of the Soviet empire:

> Both in the Soviet Union and in Eastern Europe, ethnonationalism has been politicized. Whereas the undemocratic political system and the excessive forces of repression available to the rulers make open articulation of demands and political aggregation of interests difficult, it seems obvious that different social and economic problems are being increasingly viewed through the prism of ethnonationalist feelings. Thus the vitality of ethnonationalism in the Soviet Union and Eastern Europe can be said to have made a mockery of the expression "proletarian internationalism". In this sense, the whole Soviet bloc has entered a post-Communist stage (Gerner, 1987b).

Gerner was prescient in pointing to the importance of nationalist issues to the coming instability in the Soviet Union this early (1987). He even went so far as to introduce a term that would increasingly be used by him in the coming years: "post-communism" (or "post-sovietism"). The idea was not developed on this first occasion, but it already made clear Gerner's

---

[10] For Kristian Gerner's version of this episode see Gerner, 1989a, pp. 283-297.

basic view that the Soviet system had utterly failed in creating any Soviet national feeling, or, even less, any belief in "proletarian internationalism" among the larger population.

In 1988, Gerner explicitly assessed Gorbachev's foreign and security policies. He acknowledged the existence of "new thinking", but was, at the same time, very nuanced in his appraisal of the extent to which this really meant fundamental changes in the basic Soviet foreign and security policy:

> Both in the old version concerning peaceful coexistence and in its modernized version, new thinking should be regarded as a means of security policy with the purpose of making the outside world accept the Soviet Union's control over its rimland, from the Finnish Bay and the Elbe in the West to Afghanistan in the South and the Kuriles and Japan in the East. ...One important change in Soviet foreign policy under Gorbachev...is to be found in the difference between the old and the new party program. It is now much more heavily underlined than in Khrushchev's party program from 1961 that it is necessary to coexist with capitalism for the foreseeable future (Gerner, 1988a, pp. 227 and 229).

In Gerner's analysis, the Kremlin was by no means ready to abdicate as a superpower in 1988; instead it was continuing its basic strategy of seeking equivalent political status with the U.S., even though some of the means to reach this goal had changed (ibid., pp. 225-226). By 1988, Kristian Gerner thus identified non-trivial changes in Soviet foreign policy. He explicitly stated, however, that the fundamental goals remained the same.

One aspect of Kristian Gerner's writings on Soviet affairs needs to be highlighted: his very negative view of the Soviet system. The following quote from his review of Gorbachev's book on *Perestroika* in early 1988 illustrates this:

> Gorbachev's book is very superficial, lacks any binding concrete goals, hardly has even rudimentary explanations of causes and fails to identify any individual as responsible for the small faults that are pointed out in the country of socialist example. The book just about lacks any analysis of social processes and characterizations of individuals. All foreign politicians, businessmen and writers that Gorbachev has met are, to be sure, dutifully recorded, but this is only a form of name-dropping of the kind that one meets with individuals in the academic sphere in the West, who want to believe that the politicians listen to them. The type is well-known from Arthur Koestler's book 'Call-Girls'. That we encounter the problem here indicates that the author has an inferiority complex or that he is trying to convince his

sceptical comrades that he is an important man of the world, someone they should fully support. The reader may decide for himself which interpretation is the most disturbing (Gerner, 1988f).

It is hard to imagine an assessment of the Soviet leader that is more contrary to that of Archie Brown. The latter was, together with Jerry Hough in the U.S., the Sovietologist of the 18 experts surveyed for this book who presented the most positive appraisals of the Soviet leader.

Gerner's further writings on the years of Gorbachev continued to concentrate to a large extent on ethnic issues. While he never went so far as to make any precise prediction that the Soviet empire was going to collapse due to nationalistic unrest, I regard the gist of his writings on these issues as a forecast, in the terms specified in chapter 1, that this was indeed going to happen.

> Gorbachev's first years in power not only meant the disappearance of "Soviet Man." They also meant that the Soviet Union was polarized on ethnic grounds. ...What is interesting for the future in the dissolution of the concept 'Soviet' is how the reconstruction of the different national identities will take place and how small the new entities will be. ...What can the Russians, Moscow, do to keep the empire united? Will it carry out a diversified policy, such as giving wide sovereignty to the Balts and keep strict controls over the Turks? ...Will the Russians voluntarily give up their empire? ...Seventy years after the founding of the Soviet Union the questions should be posed in this way. There are no simple, clear answers. But one thing is known. There is no way back to a Russian-dominated, centrally controlled Soviet Union other than by force (Gerner, 1989b, pp. 7-8).

This excerpt, together with several other passages from Gerner's publications, can only lead to the conclusion that from 1989 on, he forecast that the Soviet Union would be dissolved due to ethnic unrest (Gerner and Stefan Hedlund, 1989a, pp. 381-382; Gerner, 1989a, p. 22; idem. 1990e, p. 54). It should be added that this doesn't mean that Gerner was able to foretell all the important events in Soviet politics during the tumultuous years between 1985 and 1991. For instance, he was very wrong when, in early February 1988, he wrote that he did not believe that the Soviet Union would really leave Afghanistan (Gerner, 1988a, p. 222). The final announcement from Gorbachev of the withdrawal came on February 8, 1988 (Garthoff, 1994, p. 735). It does mean, however, that the essence of Gerner's analysis of the development of Soviet affairs from 1989 clearly indicated that he regarded the system as headed for collapse.

Gerner did not delve very deeply into the question of why Mikhail Gorbachev started the process of reform. What little he wrote on this issue is perhaps best caught in the following quote: "Gorbachev's primary purpose is to get the economy, which is in crisis, back on its feet again in order to create conditions for the Soviet Union to maintain its position as a military superpower" (Gerner, 1989b, p. 7; idem, 1989a, pp. 7-8). This is an explanation based on a realization, on the part of the Soviet leader, that the economy was in crisis. What mattered to Gerner was the cognitive explanation, the fact that the Soviet leader himself had understood that the system had grave problems and that he needed to do something about it. This is, in the terms of my table 1.2, an explanation at level IV a. The new Soviet leader, in Gerner's view, ultimately caused the rethinking that took place. The objective condition of the Soviet economy, explanation II b, is the second part in his overall explanation of the policy changes under Gorbachev.

Kristian Gerner and Stefan Hedlund provided a separate explanation for the changes in Soviet foreign policy under Gorbachev. While this issue is clearly linked to the overall picture, it merits attention:

> While many of the policies implemented by Gorbachev were marked by confusion and contradictions, we may nevertheless identify two crucially important principles that guided policy-making throughout. One was the realization that a revitalization of the Soviet economy would not be possible to achieve without the help of the West. The other was the equally vital realization that such help would not be forthcoming as long as the countries of the West viewed the Soviet Union as a threat to their own security. Consequently, the first order of the day was to alter Western perceptions, an endeavour in which the new management would prove rather successful (Gerner and Hedlund, 1993, pp. 29-30).

In the conception of two Swedish Sovietologists, the Soviet leadership, as a logical consequence of the reasoning presented above, had embarked upon a strategy to reach agreements to lower the level of armaments spending. This was — in the view of Gerner — intended, in turn, to create a "breathing spell" during which the Soviet Union could regain its economic strength and once again take its rightful place as an unquestioned superpower. Again, we see here an explanation where the new Soviet conduct perceived by the analysts is explained by cognitive factors. In their view, the leadership — perhaps only the supreme leader himself — had realized that if the Soviet system were to have any chance to reach the fundamental goal of a stronger economy, it needed to co-operate with the West. The West — following this logic — would only be prepared to co-operate with a state that it perceived as non-threatening. Hence, Moscow had to change its behaviour in foreign and security policy as well, although the two Swedish Sovietologists were not at all convinced that this change would be permanent.

Gerner's analyses of the Soviet Union under Gorbachev led me to two conflicting conclusions. On the one hand, Gerner was one of the Sovietologists that I have studied who most clearly forecast that the system was collapsing, and he also identified what I regard as one of the main causes of that collapse, national issues. On the other hand, Gerner plainly had a very negative view indeed of the Soviet system. His views were so negative that it is possible to assume that he might have been all too willing to accept what he regarded as indications of Soviet collapse. Kristian Gerner turned out to be "correct" in his forecast of Soviet collapse, but is it possible that his extreme scepticism towards things Soviet predisposed him so strongly towards a finding in this direction that the academic value of his forecast is at least tainted? This is one of general questions that need to be further addressed in the concluding sections of this book.

5.2.3.3 Stefan Hedlund

> Since Soviet citizens during the last few years have been so heavily influenced in terms of their values and ideals it is impossible for the Soviet Union to return to the ways of old. Gorbachev's "revolution from above" has caused Soviet socialism irreparable damage. Whatever happens to *perestroika* and *glasnost,* the end result — for better or for worse — will be a very different entity from the Soviet Union that we have grown used to. Speculations regarding the possible character of this new creation should at present be delegated to the department of hazard and crystal balls (Hedlund, 1989b, p. 22).

As mentioned in the section above, Kristian Gerner co-authored several articles and two books with *Stefan Hedlund*. The two scholars, consequently, had similar views in many respects. Particularly during the first year of Gorbachev's rule there were, however, differences in their analyses. One difference between the two was that Hedlund in 1985 published several articles, particularly in *Svenska Dagbladet,* in which he wrote, "All the way from top to bottom, the System is totally insured against any form of important change" (Hedlund, 1985a). A few months later, Hedlund focused on the issue of whether there was a crisis in the Soviet economy in 1985:

Do we face a threatening collapse? A total breakdown of the Soviet system? This type of prognostication is, in my view, of the same scientific calibre as Soviet forecasts about the rapidly approaching collapse of capitalism. ...It is definitely not my view that the growing economic problems threaten the Soviet *system*. ...But there is a large difference between *systemic crisis* and *regime crisis*. ...[The Soviet system] has earlier proven to be able to handle much more difficult crises than the present one...But if we think in terms of degree and direction of change, we see the situation in a different light. It may be possible to endure hardships if one knows that the situation will improve. ... Clearly smaller difficulties may, however, be insupportable if one notices an ongoing deterioration, with no hope that the trend will change. Such a development may cause a *regime crisis* and it is much more fruitful to regard the Soviet worries from this perspective than in terms of a threatening total collapse (Hedlund, 1985c).

For Hedlund, there was, in other words, no crisis on the horizon that threatened the essence of the Soviet system itself in 1985. There were, however, large problems, particularly in the economy, which could eventually have led to a regime crisis, as distinct from a systemic crisis. In addition, Hedlund in this piece, as on other occasions, distanced himself from attempts at prognosticating the Soviet future (Hedlund, 1989b, p. 22). There was only one real exception to this rule in the material that I have found, which was when Stefan Hedlund in 1990 discussed the future of the Soviet system in terms of three scenarios (Hedlund, 1990a, pp. 59-87).

Hedlund continually published articles on Soviet politics during the second half of the 1980s. He was very sceptical about the degree to which Gorbachev was able, or perhaps even willing, to carry out any real reform of the Soviet system. A typical formulation, this time from 1988, is:

In Western media the new-Soviet catch terms *glasnost* and *perestroika* have to an ever larger extent become seen as equalling reform, even economic reforms. Unfortunately, one may with reason claim that this view lacks any foundation in reality, at least if by reform one means lasting changes of Soviet society (Hedlund, 1988a, p. 36).

Later in the same year, Hedlund returned to the state of the "reform process":

After nearly four years of wide-ranging rhetoric concerning the need for immediate and lasting changes in the Soviet economy, and after important changes in the leadership, Gorbachev's *perestroika* still hasn't led to any real results. As the information about the deficiencies increases, the list of problems calling for an immediate solution gets ever longer. It is no longer possible to doubt that time is now running out, that Gorbachev's own political future, as well as that of economic reform, hangs on an ever-thinner thread. The power struggle in the Kremlin gets more and more public and the Soviet attempts to deny speculation about political struggles become ever less credible (Hedlund, 1988b, p. 433).

In late 1988 or perhaps very early in 1989, Hedlund changed his mind about whether Gorbachev had indeed started a process of real reform:

> In the beginning of 1987, I wrote an article called "Gorbachev's Unfinished".
> ...In this piece I was very sceptical about the chances of actually implementing very much needed reforms of the Soviet economy... Against the background of events after that date, I now regard it as appropriate to disavow my previous pessimism. A pessimistic attitude contains, after all, some hope that positive changes can occur. I now emphasize that there is no such chance. A death watch over Gorbachev's *perestroika* by no means indicates that it is *in principle* impossible to carry out reforms of "really existing socialism". The point is rather that there — in most so-called Eastern bloc states — seems to exist a cyclical phase in which it only rarely occurs that all of the forces necessary for a serious attempt at reform are in alignment. The coming to power of Gorbachev seems to indicate such an occurrence, but after almost four years of inconsequential (economic) policy this chance now seems spent (Hedlund, 1989b, pp. 13-14).

To Hedlund, the turn of the year 1988 to 1989 meant that the Soviet Union as it was before 1985 had been irrevocably changed by Gorbachev's policies. It was, however, idle to speculate what this change might eventually result in (ibid., p. 22). It was, at the same time, clear to Hedlund that the Soviet leader had lost control of the reform process.

Only once in his numerous publications on Soviet affairs between 1982 and 1996 did Professor Hedlund really attempt to forecast future Soviet developments. This was in a chapter for a book published as part the cyclical process of the Swedish debate, and the eventual decision, on national defence policy. This process contains several steps; the relevant one for this book is that the government, or least the committee designated to analyse defence problems, commissions Swedish academics to write on developments of relevance to Swedish security policy. In this context, Hedlund published a chapter in 1990 where he discussed three possible futures for Soviet development: 1) "Continued development"; 2) "Builddown, but with sense"; 3) "Quick dismantling".[11] The first possibility was that the purpose of the reforms was simply to strengthen Soviet power. The chance of this occurring was, to Hedlund, very small. The second possible development was "to accomplish wide-ranging economic, political and cultural autonomy for different nationalities and regions within the Soviet Union" (Hedlund, 1990a, p. 81). The chances for the success of such a process was, as for the first scenario, very small. The third scenario was one in which Soviet development had entered a stage where it was no longer possible to control what would happen. If, following the logic of this scenario, the "nationalist revolt reaches the Ukraine, the game is over for the Russians" (ibid., p. 85). Hedlund merely sketched these three scenarios in his chapter; he never made any forecast that one of them was more likely than the other, even if there is an implicit preference for the third alternative.

In a newspaper article published the same year, Hedlund went further in his negative prognostications regarding the probable Soviet future. His views on the Soviet system are obvious from these lines. They were also very close to those held by Kristian Gerner:

> De facto there is no more Soviet Union, no Soviet Communist Party, no Comecon and no Warsaw Pact, but just a very small and rapidly diminishing power-political pond, where the last Bolsheviks dabble in the water and try to pull each other under the surface, under the cheering of kremlologues and other specialists on soothsaying in the West. Today the largest frog is named Gorbachev. What will be the case tomorrow is totally dependent on whether there is still any water to splash (Hedlund, 1990c).

Stefan Hedlund is one of the 18 Sovietologists included in this volume who held a very negative view indeed of the Soviet system. This creates a problem for my assessment in that a scholar who has a truly negative view of his object of study tends always to believe that the outcome of what is happening will also be negative. One case where this tendency may create a problem for me is where the scholar may be believed to be inclined to conclude that the large reform process initiated by Gorbachev could lead only to negative results. If the scholar has this general view, he or she may be said to have a bias towards concluding that the system can only end in disaster and collapse.

---

[11] As any Swedish reader will understand, this is a humorous allusion to the three alternatives in the Swedish referendum on the future of civilian nuclear power in the country, which was held in 1980.

It is obvious that there are important similarities in several respects in the analyses of the Gorbachev years written by Kristian Gerner and Stefan Hedlund, and not just because they published several pieces together. There are, however, also important differences between them in this respect, differences that are significant enough on the question of prognostication to lead me to classify them in different ways. Gerner is regarded as having forecast the demise of the Soviet state in a correct way, whereas I do not classify Hedlund in this way. There is one main reason for this difference in assessment. This is that Stefan Hedlund was, with one single exception, very negative indeed towards any attempts by scholars to foretell the future developments of complex political processes. He equated this with the Soviet habit of foretelling the coming collapse of capitalism. Gerner has, to my knowledge, published no such denunciation of all attempts at prognostication.

5.2.3.4 Lena Jonson

> The Soviet power structure is in the process of breaking down...Gorbachev's policy has been to try to reform while at the same time as long as possible to avoid challenging the Party's power position. This has meant that his reforms have been seriously hindered and his conservative orthodox opponents have forced him into compromises and retractions.
> Gorbachev has great tactical abilities and he is now trying to manoeuvre the Party away from its position of monopoly and let other political forces free. He is strengthening the power of the State, of the various popular assemblies, and is establishing strong presidential power. If Gorbachev is allowed to carry out this policy, it may result in a peaceful dismantling of the Soviet system (Jonson 1990c, p. 63).

Lena Jonson is an associate professor of political science who has been primarily based at the Swedish Institute for International Affairs in Stockholm for several years. She specializes in Soviet, and now Russian, affairs, broadly defined. She characterized Gorbachev's reform strategy this way in the second half of 1987: "To accomplish a modernization and effectivization of the Soviet economy, he tries to activate Soviet society" (Jonson, 1988, p. 12).

In a manuscript completed in March 1989, Lena Jonson tackled the question of whether the changes in Soviet security policy during four years of Gorbachev's leadership indicated lasting, fundamental change:

Does this mean that Moscow under Gorbachev has abandoned Brezhnev's purpose to advance the Soviet Union's political positions beyond the borders given by the power-political boundaries of post-war Europe? Experts seriously debate the answer to this question. Should Gorbachev's policies be regarded as a lasting change of course or as 'peredyshka', that is, a temporary lull before the next phase of Soviet expansion?

We can't answer this question regarding Moscow's long-term strategic goals for Europe. What these goals are depends not only on Gorbachev's ambitions, regarding which we lack complete information, but also on his political opponents in Moscow. The struggle for power in the Kremlin will continue and its outcome is impossible to foretell.

What we can state is that Moscow today offers an opening to better relations and an increased exchange between East and West in Europe (Jonson, 1989a, p. 30).

Thus Lena Jonson's assessment of the Soviet reform process was, by mid-1989, that it was impossible to make any detailed assessment of where the Soviet reform process may end. Indeed, she had an attitude that can only be characterized as cautious concerning the possibility of making any forecasts about matters as complex as basic developments in the Soviet Union.

In early 1990, Jonson saw the risk of total disintegration in the Soviet Union as a result of Gorbachev's reform policies (Jonson, 1990c, p. 47). She presented this in a way that approached a forecast that the Soviet system would not survive the Gorbachev reform era. It was, however, not sufficiently precise to be classified as a forecast here.

In an essay for the Swedish defence committee in 1990, Lena Jonson made clear that she believed that Gorbachev had by that time fundamentally changed Soviet foreign policy. There had, however, appeared a new uncertainty: could these changes be maintained in a period of great internal instability? (Jonson, 1990b, pp. 121-123). Lena Jonson characterized these alterations in Soviet foreign policy as multidimensional. In her view, not only means but also important goals in Soviet foreign policy had changed by late 1989.

Lena Jonson approached the two main questions in this book in a cautious way. Not until the end of 1989 did she state unequivocally that Soviet foreign policy under Gorbachev had fundamentally changed. Note, however, that most of the other Sovietologists were even more careful on this point: they tended to hedge their assessments instead of flatly declaring that Soviet foreign policy had indeed altered. Jonson was even more cautious in attempting to foretell what would happen to the Soviet experiment. She brought up the issue, but mainly in the form of mentioning that other colleagues were discussing it, not by clearly stating any viewpoint of her own.

Lena Jonson's analysis of the Soviet Union under Gorbachev displayed no obvious biases of any kind. She was careful about making prognoses, but did state that the Soviet Union had, in her assessment, changed its foreign policy by late 1989.

5.2.3.5 Conclusion: The Swedish Sovietologists   It is hard to detect any specific national traits in the Swedish Sovietologists' analyses of the Soviet Union. In this respect they resemble their British colleagues. The analyses of Soviet affairs published by the Swedish scholars seem to have been mainly influenced not by their nationality but by their basic views of the Soviet system. It is unavoidable to point to the very strong parallels between Kristian Gerner and Stefan Hedlund in this respect. The two specialists shared a very strong dislike, if not detestation, of the Soviet system. Where they differed was perhaps mostly in the very elaborate views that Hedlund expressed in 1985 about how the system was totally insured against any type of real change. These were views that Kristian Gerner never mentioned.

There were no such strongly distinguishing characteristics for the other two Swedish specialists, with the partial exception of Anders Åslund. Åslund's analysis was, up until 1991, very positive regarding Gorbachev and his personal role in the Soviet reform process. By 1991, however, the image Åslund projected to his readers of the Soviet leader had changed drastically. The leader who, between 1985 and into 1990, was portrayed as bold and inventive, bent upon restructuring his society, had by late 1990 changed — in the view of Anders Åslund — into a leader who presided over a system where, in the economic sphere "virtually every possible mistake has been made" (Åslund, 1991a, pp. 30, 40).

When it comes to detecting when and whether the Soviet system had changed fundamentally, domestically or with respect to foreign policy, there was no consensus among the Swedish Sovietologists. Lena Jonson was very cautious on this matter, and she never took a firm position. Anders Åslund concentrated on economic matters. While he painted a vivid picture of the breadth of the reform program, he remained sceptical of where the practical results might lead. Kristian Gerner moved from a position that was very sceptical about the extent of reforms during the early years of Gorbachev's rule to a position where, by early 1989, at the latest, he was aware that the Soviet system had changed to such an extent that the transformation was becoming uncontrollable and had entered a process of inevitable descent into collapse. This perspective allowed for no positive assessment that Soviet policies, whether in the domestic or in the foreign policy sphere, had changed for the better in any sense. For Gerner, it appears, the Soviet system could only go from bad to worse, and any positive development within the framework of that system was by definition impossible. Stefan Hedlund's analysis resembled that of Gerner in several respects, but differed in others. In particular, Hedlund's early analysis of the "unchangeable Soviet system", together with his disdain for "looking into the crystal ball" made it difficult to assess him in terms of the few attempts at prognoses that he did publish. I settled for not regarding the thrust of his analysis as indicating that the Soviet system would collapse.

All four Swedish Sovietologists addressed the reasons behind the changes in Soviet policy. Lena Jonson merely mentioned in passing the role of the economy for the start of the reform process. Anders Åslund, as an economist, as expected pointed to the problematic Soviet economy as a vital reason behind perestroika. Åslund added pressure from the United States, however, in explaining why the reform process got under way. Kristian Gerner was not very interested in explaining why the reforms started, but what little he had to say underlined the importance of cognitive factors, the realization by Gorbachev that the system needed to be reformed. Indeed, Gerner's explanation of the start of the Soviet reform process was centred on level IV a, the cognitive explanation. Gerner also included the disastrous Soviet economic situation, explanation II b. Stefan Hedlund, in the articles and books he wrote by himself, consistently took such a negative view of the possibilities for change in the Soviet Union that he never really tried to explain the reasons behind what was otherwise universally recognized as an important reform process emanating from Moscow after 1985.

The second dimension on which I analysed the Sovietologists concerns their fundamental views on the meaningfulness of making prognoses about the Soviet Union, and whether, if they did issue such prognoses, these turned out to be correct. On this question, there were important differences between the four Swedes. Lena Jonson explicitly stated on several occasions that she would not enter into speculation about where developments might lead in the future. Anders Åslund expressed a belief in the value of presenting scenarios, but he did not go any further than to present three possible futures for the Soviet economic reform effort, in a fashion that did not classify as a prognosis. The position of Stefan Hedlund on this question is somewhat paradoxical. On the one hand, he was on several occasions dismissive about the meaningfulness of trying to speculate about the likely future of processes under way in the Soviet Union. On the other hand, he also presented three possible scenarios for the Soviet future in a book chapter in 1990. It was thus never really clear what his position was on the possibility of foretelling the Soviet future. Kristian Gerner was one of the most prescient of all the 18 Sovietologists analysed here. He never explicitly tackled the question of whether it was meaningful to make prognoses, as far as I can see. Still, there was an aspect of his writings from about early 1989 on such that, taken together, they conclusively prove to this author that Kristian Gerner made a correct forecast that the Soviet Union was on the way to disintegration. He made no attempt to make a strong positivistic prediction to the effect that the "Soviet Union will collapse in two years". There was, however, a solid analysis of the disintegrating processes under way in a system that was clearly portrayed as being bound for oblivion.

One aspect of Anders Åslund's writings is striking. This was the clarity of what could be called his problem analysis: his ability to identify the enormity of the economic problems of the Soviet State. This incisive analysis was not followed by prognostications in the fashion regarded as ideal by some political scientists and perhaps sociologists. This indicates that perhaps my research design, which is based on the logic of a problem analysis followed more or less naturally by diagnosis, may be more suited to studying the work of individuals in specific strands of the social sciences, such as perhaps some sociologists and political scientists, whereas academics from other disciplines, such as economics, do not follow the "logic" that I have attempted to ascribe to them.

5.2.4 The United States

One of the problems of research design in this assessment of how the outside world evaluated Mikhail Gorbachev and his policies was how to choose Sovietologists to represent the four countries. There were two separate ways to handle this issue. One solution, which I toyed with for a long time, was to select the same number of Sovietologists from each country to simplify comparison between the academic analyses of the Soviet Union within the four countries. Another solution was to distinguish between Sovietology in the United States, on the one hand, and Sovietology in the other three countries, on the other. The reason that I settled on the second alternative was that Sovietology in the U.S. was a much larger discipline than in any of the other countries. Even if there were many Sovietologists in the United Kingdom as well, still the field was much larger in the United States. My final choice was thus to study four Sovietologists each in France, Sweden and Great Britain, and six in the United States. One important additional reason to have a larger number representing the United States is that it was there that what came to be called "revisionism", an alternative way of analysing the Soviet system in an academic way, was most important. In my sample, *Jerry Hough*, professor of political science at Duke University and a fellow at the Brookings Institution in Washington, D.C., represents this way of studying Moscow during the whole period in question.

The six U.S. Sovietologists selected include three political scientists, two historians and one economist. Apart from a breadth of academic disciplines, I have attempted to include, as stated above, one revisionist. The most famous of the six U.S. scholars is *Zbigniew Brzezinski* who, aside from his academic career, worked as National Security Adviser to President Jimmy Carter from 1977 to 1981. During his academic career, Professor Brzezinski has worked at Columbia University and at the Center for Strategic and International Studies (CSIS), which until 1987 was affiliated with Georgetown University (Nygren, 1992, pp. 147-149). In addition to his academic scholarship, Professor Brzezinski has written many other pieces on Soviet affairs, including articles in the largest U.S. newspapers. These articles have also been perused, to the extent that I was able to find them, and they are included in the analysis when they give new information that is relevant to my analysis here.

The second political scientist in my sample is Professor *Seweryn Bialer*. Bialer is, like Brzezinski, of Polish origin. Professor Bialer has spent most of his academic career at Columbia University. The third political scientist, as mentioned, is Professor Jerry Hough. The first of the two historians is Professor *Alexander Dallin*. Dallin worked at Columbia University and at Stanford University. He retired in the mid-1990s and he died in 2000. The other history professor is *Richard Pipes*. Like two of his political science colleagues in this sample, Professor Pipes was born in Poland (Nygren, 1992, p. 205). Professor Pipes has spent most, if not all, of his academic career at Harvard University, from which he has now also retired. Finally, Professor *Marshall I. Goldman* is an economist. Professor Goldman has worked in the Boston area as professor at Wellesley College and as an associate, some of the time an Associate Director, of the Russian Research Center at Harvard University.

5.2.4.1 Seweryn Bialer

> The economy is not going to go bankrupt, and it is capable of delivering the necessary minimum of sustenance to the population. It can support the upkeep of its military machine. The crisis does not mean rebellious behavior on the part of the working class. It does not mean that large professional groups will join the movement of open dissent. It does not mean that we will witness a visible decline of Soviet ambition to expand its power and influence in the international arena. It does not imply an inability to provide the minimum resources necessary for the support of the nation's international status. Finally and most importantly, it does not presage fundamental disunity among the leadership and the functional elites, nor their loss of will to preserve the existing system. ....
> Obviously there comes a point at which a crisis of effectiveness becomes a crisis of survival. One should stress, however, that the present situation may last for a very long time before signs appear that the survival of the system is endangered (Bialer 1986a, p. 169).

Seweryn Bialer regularly published articles and books of relevance to this study during the whole period from 1982, in connection with Brezhnev's death, until the end of 1991, with the final lowering of the Soviet flag over the Kremlin. Bialer's writings during the early period indicated his assessment of a superpower "in an ascendant phase of great-power ambitions to which the messianic traditions of Russian nationalism and revolutionary Marxism-Leninism add virulence" (Bialer and Joan Afferica, 1982/83), p. 257). Bialer believed, in 1982, that the Soviet leadership that took power after Brezhnev would continue this policy.

In 1985, writing with Joan Afferica in *Foreign Affairs*, Professor Bialer assessed what to make of the first signals out of Moscow indicating reform:

> The first, and simplest, possibility accepts available evidence at face value. Gorbachev, while a reformer, remains persuaded of the system's unfulfilled potential and does not regard radical reform as essential. He will introduce many policy and organization reforms, streamline the system. ...He will not become a proponent of "market socialism."
> A second possibility concedes that Gorbachev and his comrades believe they can improve the system without radical reforms but expects to convince them by the late 1980s or early 1990s that only radical reforms can reverse Soviet decline. At that point Gorbachev, already well consolidated in power, will attempt to build a coalition capable of achieving a radical transformation.

A third possibility assumes that Gorbachev aims to undertake radical reform. An oligarchic leadership, however, is ill suited for initiating and executing major reforms of structures, procedures, or even policies. Singular determination and unrelenting pressure from a very powerful leader are required for even moderate success, given the strong and widespread opposition to fundamental change at all levels. Until Gorbachev achieves such power, he cannot openly advocate radical reform. ...

To judge which possibility best reflects or predicts Soviet realities goes well beyond knowledge conveyed by primary sources. The first option is probably the most accurate, but intuition and study of the system suggest that the third is likely as well. (Bialer and Joan Afferica, 1982/83, p. 257).

This clearly shows a social scientist who believed that it was the task of the scholar to try to foretell the basic developments within his area of expertise.

In 1986, Seweryn Bialer published a major work on Soviet politics tellingly entitled *The Soviet Paradox: External Expansion, Internal Decline*. In this book, Bialer ventured several more forecasts, not all of them very prescient. The crux of his argument is as follows:

While most of the utopian dreams of the original Bolshevik Revolution have been discarded or become a hollow ritual, the universalistic claims have largely expanded with the growth of military capabilities. This then is the Soviet paradox of today and of the foreseeable future, which both its leaders and the West have to face squarely in the 1980s: internal decline coupled with awesome military power directed toward external goals (1986a, pp. 133, 169, 171) .

In 1986 Bialer thus appeared to believe less in fundamental changes in the Soviet Union than he did the year before. He presented several forecasts. These were all very cautious about the extent of the Soviet reform process.

In his next relevant publication, Seweryn Bialer went much further in his assessment of the Soviet situation: "In the fall of 1987, the Soviet Union had become the most interesting country in the world. What is happening there is nothing less than a gigantic experiment, now only in its infancy" (Bialer,1988a, p. 231).

In foreign affairs, the policy area of greatest interest for this book, Professor Bialer was very explicit in this piece written in late 1987 or early 1988:

It is probable that the decade from 1985 to 1995 will mark an end to the cycle of strategic armaments that began after the Second World War and has continued unabated for more than 40 years. The domestic and international pressures on both superpowers are likely to be strong enough to lead them in this direction. ...
Gorbachev's foreign policy is still evolving; the most important and difficult decisions have still to be made by the Politburo. ...
Predictions are always risky. The one thing that can be predicted with certainty, however, is that even if he is firmly in control, the General Secretary's course of action in the coming years will not be one of unrelenting pressure and forward movement, but will involve instead as many tactical zig-zags and feints and retreats as straight-forward advances. If this evaluation of Gorbachev himself after his first three years in office is accurate, if his commitment to radical reforms and determination are genuine, then the retreats will be only temporary. But the changes he has introduced are nonetheless reversible (Bialer, 1988b, pp. 459, 468-469, 483).

For Seweryn Bialer, it was thus from the second half of 1987 until the first half of 1988 that the process of Gorbachev's reforms changed character. What in 1986 could have been regarded as a wish to avoid fundamental reforms of the Soviet system was in early 1988 to be regarded as a process whereby Mr. Gorbachev was aiming to undertake just such reforms. While Seweryn Bialer still did not regard the changes already undertaken at that stage as irreversible, it is obvious that by early 1988 he perceived a global actor that was behaving very differently in international affairs than before, and it was an actor that would — in his view — continue to act very differently. He regarded this process, together with domestic pressures within the United States, as presaging a very different bilateral relationship between the superpowers in the future, a future in which the strategic armaments race would be much less rapid and pronounced than had been the case up to that point in time.

After a visit to Moscow in April 1988, Professor Bialer underlined that, despite the many new steps undertaken by the Gorbachev leadership, the process was "still very much reversible" (Bialer, 1988c, p. 241). He also wrote, "I do not expect Gorbachev to be ousted in the foreseeable future (which in a revolutionary period can mean no more than two to three years)" (ibid., p. 238). In a book published together with Michael Mandelbaum in 1989, Bialer also ventured the forecast that "Even so determined a reformer as Gorbachev is unlikely to permit the kinds of arrangements in Poland that the Poles themselves would find wholly satisfactory" (Bialer and Michael Mandelbaum, 1989, p. 196).

On the issue of diagnosing the extent of Soviet changes after three or four years of Gorbachev's rule, Bialer was thus always nuanced. On the one hand, he acknowledged that very important things had indeed happened; the Soviet Union was behaving very differently in the international sphere also, as compared to before Gorbachev's coming to power. On the other hand, Bialer constantly entered the proviso that there existed a risk that the Soviet leadership might be overthrown, thus underlining the provisional quality of the changes.

In 1989, Professor Bialer presented his most thorough explanation of the origins of the Soviet reform process, in the domestic field as well as in foreign policy. For Bialer it was not enough to seek the explanation simply in the domestic conditions of the Soviet Union, though he regarded such factors as crucial. For him, there were three domestic causes behind the reform effort and two international causes. These causes were not unrelated. The three domestic causes were the following: "first, the domestic performance of the Soviet system during the Brezhnev era; second, the new and necessary conditions of Soviet economic growth under contemporary circumstances; and third, the changed nature of Soviet society and the conditions of its stability" (Bialer, 1989 (1992), pp. 283-284). To these three domestic factors were added related international factors. The first was the tendency of the Soviet leadership to measure the domestic performance of their system against that of the developed capitalist countries. Their realization, gradually from the end of the 1970s on, that the Soviet Union, by this measure, was falling well behind its Western competitors was one important cause of the reform process. Professor Bialer labelled this factor "psychological" (ibid., pp. 287-288). The second factor was a similar realization on the part of the Soviet elite, during roughly the same period, that they were losing ground in terms of military strength as well, in their competition with the United States (ibid., pp. 289-290). In other words, this is an explanation of the Soviet reform process which includes levels II a, the domestic structure; II b, the deficiencies of the socialist economy; I a, the structure of the international system; and IV a, cognitive aspects among the Soviet leadership as a whole. Seweryn Bialer thus presents a multifaceted explanation of Soviet change, as perhaps befits a professor of political science.

During 1990, as the Soviet system began to disintegrate, Professor Bialer — a prolific writer on Soviet affairs throughout the 1980s — published less. He returned in 1991 in a volume edited with Robert Jervis: *Soviet-American Relations After the Cold War*. For Bialer, writing in the second half of 1990, Soviet developments could at that stage be perceived as leading inexorably towards the collapse of the Soviet system (Bialer, 1991, pp. 98, 103). Judging with the criteria that I employ in this book, this means that Bialer was not able to issue a correct prognosis of Soviet collapse until the downward spiral had become more or less visible to all knowledgeable observers. Still, Bialer was one of the Sovietologists who did indeed fore-tell the Soviet Union's demise more than one year, but less than eighteen months, ahead, thus raising the question of whether my cut-off point at June 1990, as the latest a forecast can be issued to be regarded as correct, is the best conceivable option.

My assessment of Seweryn Bialer is that he was an insightful Sovietologist who was able to identify at a reasonably early stage that the changes in the Soviet system were crucial, even if he was for a long time careful about mentioning the risks for a reversal of regime. A crucial part of his analysis of the Soviet system was, however, an image of immobility that characterized his portrayal of the Soviet system in his 1986 book. As has been seen, this did not prevent Bialer from noting that important, indeed crucial, changes had occurred in the Soviet system. It is very likely indeed that the model to which Bialer subscribed, which regarded the Soviet system as one characterized by a self-sustaining elite, made it more difficult for him to see that the process of change and dislocation under way during the latter Gorbachev years was bound to end in a collapse of the system. I also believe that the fact that Bialer's scholarship was to a large extent identified with his belief in the "immovable superpower" of the mid-1980s meant that his role and influence as a Soviet scholar declined, particularly as the Soviet system neared its end. At the very least, it is possible to note that his production declined from about 1990 on.

5.2.4.2 Zbigniew Brzezinski

One is thus entitled to be doubtful that genuine success - which can be called option 1 - is in store for Gorbachev's *perestroika*. Other options must, therefore, be considered. These include:

Option 2: Protracted but inconclusive turmoil.

Option 3: Renewed stagnation, as *perestroika* runs out of steam.

Option 4: A regressive and repressive political coup, in reaction to either Option 2 or 3.

Option 5: Fragmentation of the Soviet Union, as a consequence of some combination of the above.

Of these options, the most likely alternative for the next several years seems to be Option 2, but with a high probability that *perestroika* will gradually lose some of its momentum in the face of internal obstacles. Growing domestic turmoil or eventually renewed stagnation could in turn prompt some renewed efforts on behalf of heightened social and political discipline. The latter could even lead to a military dictatorship, especially if the party proves to be too complacent either in the promotion of change or in the maintenance of order (Brzezinski 1989a, pp. 100-101; emphasis supplied).

Zbigniew Brzezinski, like his colleague Seweryn Bialer, was a prolific writer on Soviet affairs throughout the years analysed here. Professor Brzezinski had a very clear view of the Soviet Union as a world power, which he spelled out in an article in *Encounter* in 1983. According to him, "the expansionism of the Soviet imperial system is a unique organic imperative produced by the sense of territorial insecurity on the part of the system's Great Russian national core" (Brzezinski, 1983a, p. 10). The role of the "Great Russian national core" (ibid.) in turn, meant that any evolution of the Soviet system into a more pluralistic shape was not likely in the foreseeable future. For Brzezinski, the Soviet Union in the 1980s was thus a state that was doomed to be expansionist and that, at the same time, was very unlikely to develop in a democratic direction for a long time to come.

The basic view that Brzezinski held of the Soviet Union made it logical to expect that his initial reactions to the Gorbachev succession would be very sceptical. This was indeed true, as shown by an article in *The Washington Quarterly* in 1985:

> When a group of rather senile and quite elderly Politburo members agreed that Gorbachev would be promoted over some of his peers...it was because they saw in him a significant element of continuity as well as intelligence and energy. He was chosen not to undo the system with which the most senior statesmen were associated, but, rather, to rejuvenate and revitalize it. That is not the same thing as being a reformer at home. Nor does it foretell significant departures in Soviet foreign policy (Brzezinski, 1985b, p. 32.)

However, in this first assessment Brzezinski did not exclude the possibility that the new Soviet leader might turn out to be a reformer.

As the signs from Moscow that something new was indeed afoot there multiplied, Brzezinski remained sceptical. He wrote about the "theatrical flavor" (Brzezinski, 1987d, p. 10) of Gorbachev's foreign policy during the first 18 months in office. In addition, Brzezinski characterized the Soviet leader as a

...totally new type of Soviet leader, in that he is the first one in the entire history of the Soviet Union who has not seized power by himself, but was instead selected by his predecessors. ...In that sense his power is far less personal and more an expression of a certain institutional consensus. ...And it is an open question whether his reforms can successfully penetrate a system that is so notoriously resistant to change – and to do so in the face of a *nomenklatura* that so jealously guards its privileges and levers of control over the system (Brzezinski, 1987a, pp. 12-13; emphasis supplied).

In May 1988, President Reagan went to Moscow for a summit. This was six months after the conclusion of the INF Treaty. During the meeting, President Reagan stated that he no longer regarded the Soviet Union as an "evil empire". Professor Brzezinski's assessment was less optimistic than that of the President:

The Cold War is not over, and the empire is still evil. ...

The summit, however, did underline two important changes in the character of that continuing Cold War, and they deserve serious comments. The first is that the West is now on the offensive, ideologically and even politically, in the Cold War. The cause of human rights...has put the Soviet leaders on the defensive and they have been forced gradually to make concessions. ...

The summit's second change in the character of the Cold War pertains to military stability...the President's comments, eagerly seized on by Secretary Gorbachev, have contributed to the further undermining of nuclear deterrence as the basis for military stability in the Cold War (Brzezinski, 1988a).

When it came to diagnosing the extent of the changes in the Soviet Union, Brzezinski was one of the scholars who remained very sceptical. In a sense, he never ever stated that the system had changed for good. To my mind, this was because Zbigniew Brzezinski regarded the Soviet Union as a political system that could not be reformed, but could only be changed by means of a system collapse. The logic by which Brzezinski arrived at these conclusions is presented below.

Zbigniew Brzezinski's most interesting publication, from the perspective of this study, is his book *The Grand Failure: The Birth and Death of Communism in the Twentieth Century* published in 1989. In this volume, he gave an overall assessment of the Soviet reform process and made forecasts about its likely future. On the very first page of the book, Brzezinski made some of his essential points in characteristic style:

This is a book about the terminal crisis of communism. ...Prospering only where it abandons some of its external labels, communism will be remembered largely as the twentieth century's most extraordinary political and intellectual aberration.
The argument in this book is developed in six parts. The first argues that the key to communism's historic tragedy is the political and socioeconomic failure of the Soviet system. The second examines in more depth the current Soviet attempts to reform and revitalize that system and concludes that success is less likely than continuing internal decay or turmoil (Brzezinski, 1989a, p. 1).

In his analysis of the development of Gorbachev's domestic reform program, Brzezinski underlined the way that it moved "through several tactical stages" (ibid., p. 42). What began as a rather limited public discussion of previous and current deficiencies of the Soviet system gradually moved — partly through the responses within Soviet urban centres to the first stages, which created new impulses for reform — to culminate, in Brzezinski's 1989 analysis, in the Party Conference in July 1988. There, Gorbachev placed political reform ahead of restructuring (ibid., p. 58). This meant that the Soviet Union had "a revisionist General Secretary in the Kremlin", which, in turn, had "momentous [implications]" (ibid., p. 64). This led to new levels of debate in the Soviet polity, which raged far and wide on issues seldom, if ever, before touched upon during the Soviet Union's existence.

The entire domestic process of reform, as of the late summer of 1988, was summed up in the following fashion:

> All these interlocking debates created a dynamic effect. The quest for economic renewal generated pressures for democratization, which in turn threatened the party's monopoly over power and formal beliefs, thereby opening the doors to competing appeals of religion and nationalism, and even posing the danger of protracted and perhaps even intensifying Soviet disunion. That these debates were actually occurring, and that they were no longer confined to the inner sanctums of the party, was particularly significant for three reasons:
> First, it represented a remarkable break with established political norms. ...
> Second, it posed a danger to the integrity of the Marxist-Leninist doctrine and even potentially to the unity of the Soviet Union. ...
> Third, it discredited Soviet communism specifically and, by inference, communism in general (Brzezinski, 1989a, pp. 93-94).

This analysis led to the forecasts about the likely future for the Soviet Union printed in the very first quote of this section. Zbigniew Brzezinski is thus a very clear example of a social scientist who made forecasts regarding his area of expertise. The fashion in which he did so was imprecise; it was precisely "forecasting" and not "prediction" in the terms specified in chapter 1. Even if one can detect nuances in which his prognostications were incorrect, I regard the gist of his prognosis as being on the mark. In the first quote in this section, Brzezinski was able to accomplish just about the ultimate that the social scientist, in this author's estimation, can accomplish when it comes to looking into the crystal ball: he discussed alternative future developments in a way that is based on solid research and deep insights into the political processes under analysis.

The problem with Brzezinski's approach, from my perspective, is once again that here is a scholar who detests the system that he analyses. Isn't there a problem of bias with respect to a scholar who could, with some exaggeration, be said to be waiting for indications that the system that he despises is about to collapse? To put it in the bluntest way possible: is the fact that Zbigniew Brzezinski was able to foretell the end of the Soviet Union a triumph of dispassionate, insightful, scholarly analysis or just wishful thinking coming true?

In his investigation of Soviet developments, Brzezinski was more precise in his analysis of domestic aspects than he was concerning foreign policy. In the latter sphere, it was the relationship between Moscow and Eastern Europe that occupied him most, which was connected to his repeated assessments of the question of whether or not the Cold War had ended or was ending (Brzezinski, 1989e and idem., 1989b). Brzezinski clearly realized that momentous changes had occurred in Soviet foreign policy, at the very least by the summer of 1988, but he never discussed the issues in those terms. What concerned him was, rather, the policies that the West, and in particular the United States, ought to pursue in response to the Soviet changes. Gorbachev's celebrated address to the United Nations in December 1988, for example, was characterized as asking "for an armistice in the cold war, which he knows the Soviet Union has been losing" (Brzezinski, 1989b. Cf Garthoff, 1994, pp. 365-368).

For Brzezinski, the explanation of why the Soviet Union entered a process of reform in the mid-1980s contained two causes. The first was based in level IV a, cognitive psychology and learning. In this first element of an explanation, the Politburo's members realized that the system needed a new leader in order to remain strong. The second explanation was really based on the same level, but at this later stage in the reform process, Brzezinski focused on the Soviet leader as an individual, explanation IV b.

Zbigniew Brzezinski thus combined what can be termed an impressive ability to look into the crystal ball concerning the coming fall of the Soviet Union, with a detestation of the very existence of that system. While such detestation of the system may indeed induce a tendency to see signs of decline where none exist, developments in this case proved Brzezinski right.

5.2.4.3 Alexander Dallin

> ...my own inclination is to distrust both conspiracy theories and flukes, and to be suspicious of all manner of determinism and inevitability, mysterious "essences" and broad *a priori* philosophical schemes. It is far better, I would maintain, to examine the empirical evidence without prejudging the case (Dallin 1992b, p. 281; emphasis supplied).

Alexander Dallin retired in the mid-1990s from his chair as professor of International History at Stanford University, and he died in 2000. During his long career, Dallin served as the Director of the Russian Institute at Columbia University and then as Director of the Center for Russian and East European Studies at Stanford (Holloway and Naimark, 1986, p. 1).

In a chapter published in 1985, Dallin spelled out his basic views of Soviet foreign policy as he saw it at that stage:

> In my view there is no ideological imperative for the Soviet Union to expand or seek conflict abroad. ...
> There is in fact no master plan for Soviet practitioners to follow, no blueprint that would tell Soviet officials what to do next, no "timetable of aggressiveness"...Despite the widespread tendency to interpret Soviet behavior as the extension of prerevolutionary Russian practice, I see little merit in invoking historical antecedents to explain Soviet policy. ...Historical determinism is as treacherous a guide as economic or technological determinism (Dallin, 1985b, pp. 67-70).

The contrast between Dallin's analysis of Soviet foreign policy and that espoused by Zbigniew Brzezinski could hardly be any clearer.

In a chapter written with Gail Lapidus in 1987, Dallin explained his views of why the Soviet reform process began under Gorbachev:

> This reassessment may be seen as the product of several converging trends already visible in the last Brezhnev years but increasingly visible in the early 'eighties. Among other things, these trends served to undermine the Soviet leaders' confidence that the international "correlation of forces" continued to shift to Moscow's advantage.

First and foremost were the enormous strains produced by the slowing growth of the Soviet economy. ...The economic slowdown, coupled with increasing instances of poor management, corruption, and incompetence, sharpened the widespread concern of the Soviet elite over the ultimate viability of the Soviet economic model at a time when the gap between its output and that of the West was widening instead of shrinking, when China was repudiating the Soviet model, and when Japan was overtaking the Soviet Union as 'number two.'...

In the 1980s, the Soviet Union also faced a less benign international environment. Events in Poland provided visible evidence of the vulnerabilities of its East European empire and the realization that reducing its costs might well threaten its stability and the certainty of control. In the Third World, the Soviet Union's military and economic support had produced dubious and transient gains in areas it could not control, while jeopardizing, in the view of some critics, the more important relationship with Washington...Finally, the collapse of détente made it clear — or should have — that the assumptions underlying the general line of Soviet foreign policy in the 1970s were shattered along with it (Dallin and Gail Lapidus, 1987, pp. 241-242).

Alexander Dallin's explanation for the start of the Soviet reforms thus included several elements. One was "rethinking" on the part of the elite, explanation IV a. Another was domestic economic problems, explanation II b. The third element was explanation I a, an international system in which the Soviet position was less strong than before.

In the same chapter, Professor Dallin and his co-author noted that Gorbachev had "brought a new dynamism to Soviet foreign policy..." (Dallin and Gail Lapidus, 1987, p. 245).

Writing in 1987, Dallin went to the root of the problems with which this book is concerned: how could the interested observer know whether or not what was going on in Moscow really was transforming Soviet foreign policy:

For the American observer, it has been a matter of genuine difficulty to decide whether the Gorbachev regime has introduced anything substantially different or new into the calculus that produced Soviet foreign policy. ...

In fact, the evidence is not so clearcut as an observer might wish. It is not that the words coming from Moscow have been unpromising; rather, the issue concerns the uncertain relationship between words and intentions, between words and behavior, between words and reality, sometimes even between one set of words and another. ...

In examining Soviet foreign policy since Gorbachev took over in March 1985, we can most readily trace the changes in personnel. ...

And yet none of this proves that the substance of Soviet foreign policy objectives has actually changed — that the reorganizations and replacements of personnel amount to more than a tactical or superficial change. Moreover, not all of the old-timers in Moscow have (yet) been moved out (Dallin, 1988a, pp. 212-214).

In 1988, Professor Dallin went further in his assessment of Soviet changes in foreign policy under Gorbachev. He noted that

...the fundamental orientation has begun to change. It has been remarked that for Stalin, Soviet security was essentially a function of everyone else's insecurity. For Gorbachev, Soviet security presupposes a sense of security not only for the allies of the Soviet Union but also for its adversaries: as he remarked, there can be no "security for the USSR without security for the United States." True, that rhetoric remains to be translated into consistent conduct; yet the gulf between past and present concepts informing Soviet policy could scarcely be more profound (Dallin, 1998d, p. 606; cf Dallin, 1998b, pp. 99-113).

In addition to his explanation of why the general process of Soviet reform started, Professor Dallin also provided an explanation for "new political thinking" in foreign policy specifically. This interpretation linked perceptions of internal problems, on the part of decision makers, with relations with the outside world. On the domestic side, the problems in the Soviet economy and the relationship between state and society were in focus. On the foreign policy side, Dallin highlighted, first, the fact that the domestic weaknesses led to a realization on the part of the leadership that their country was more fragile than they had imagined. Second, the need for domestic changes meant that the Soviet Union had a great interest in international stability while these changes were being carried out. Third, the need for resources for domestic development meant that funds needed to be transferred from foreign and security policy to domestic affairs (Dallin 1992, p. 74).

In another paper published in 1988, Dallin touched upon the question of whether or not it was possible to foretell what would happen to the Soviet reform process:

A sense of balance requires adding that, even if the reforms were to be fully carried out, the Soviet Union would presumably remain an authoritarian one-party state, with a powerful secret police, with collectivized agriculture, and with a political culture that tends to make Soviet political and social mores significantly different from those of Western "bourgeois" societies. At the same time, it is important not to dismiss the impact or the significance of the changes wrought since the Gorbachev team took over, and even less those they are pledged to introduce: they represent the best prospect yet of moving the Soviet Union toward becoming a more open and modern society (Dallin, 1988c, pp. 6-7).

Later in the same article, Dallin added:

> For many years there was a widespread assumption in the West that "nothing could happen" in the Soviet Union and, in particular, in Soviet politics. Recent developments have given the lie to this argument, but the speed and scope of the change since Gorbachev became General Secretary have surprised even those who had long challenged it. ...
> ...Whether or not Gorbachev survives in power cannot be predicted. That is a question entirely distinct from the prospects of his policies of reform. What is clear is that, at best, he will face a difficult uphill struggle. Of course he has repeatedly shown himself to be a very adroit actor and fighter, and possesses the advantages of incumbency and fame (ibid., p. 21).

In his diagnosis of the changing situation in the Soviet Union, Alexander Dallin in many ways resembled Seweryn Bialer. There was, on the one hand, a willingness to accept that important changes were going on in the Soviet system. Dallin was probably more willing to accept that it was indeed possible to change the Soviet system, without this necessarily leading to any system collapse, than was Bialer. At the same time, both scholars repeatedly underlined that, while changes had indeed occurred, there was a clear risk that these could always lead to the fall of the Soviet leadership under Gorbachev, which might in turn lead to the reversal of all of the changes. In this sense, both scholars displayed a clear willingness to accept that important changes were indeed occurring in Soviet foreign as well as domestic politics in the second half of the 1980s. At the same time, they took care to underline what they regarded as the provisional character of these changes.

Alexander Dallin explicitly refrained from making any specific forecasts regarding the probable future of Gorbachev or of his policies of reform. He noted — in an assessment published in the first half of 1988 — that there would be problems for Gorbachev in his attempts to carry out the policies of reform that the Soviet leader had undertaken. He published no discussion of whether or not it was possible in principle to issue forecasts — as far as I have been able to establish; instead he simply noted that the situation after three years of Gorbachev's rule was so unclear as to make any attempts to see into the future impossible in practice. Dallin's analyses of Soviet events during the period under study strike me as unbiased and insightful. Perhaps because he was a historian he refrained from trying to forecast what would happen to Gorbachev's Soviet Union. In all other respects, however, Dallin's analysis strikes me as close to the ideal of unprejudiced scholarship.

5.2.4.4 Marshall I. Goldman

> ...attempts to introduce economic and industrial reform to revitalize the economy could set off uncontrollable political and economic forces. This then is the Soviet dilemma. It may be inappropriate in the Soviet context, but this dilemma brings to mind an old Chinese proverb: "He who rides the tiger is afraid to dismount." The present situation is bad, but the consequences of a reform may be even worse. The need then is for leadership that is prepared to face the tiger and find the treacherous road that runs between the extremes of no change and too-radical change. Based on how previous leaders have handled change, there is not much room for optimism (Marshall Goldman 1983, p. 182).

Marshall I. Goldman has for a long time been professor of economics, with tenure at Wellesley College. At the same time, he has been Associate Director of the Russian Research Center at Harvard University for more than 15 years (see Nygren, 1992, p. 208 and Goldman, 1991/92, p. 9).

Professor Goldman's first major work of direct interest to this book was published in 1983: *The U.S.S.R. in Crisis: The Failure of an Economic System*. The first page of the main text gave a clear view of his assessment of the Soviet system as it functioned in the early 1980s:

> The Soviet Union is facing a very serious crisis. This crisis is the result of the Soviet Union's failure to adapt its economic planning model to meet the country's radically changed economic needs. ...While the Soviet model performed well in the early years of the country's industrialization, it has proven to be unresponsive, if not inappropriate, to the needs of a more mature economy, and, in recent years, it has failed badly. This failure was inevitable, given the type of economic model that was chosen (Goldman, 1983, p. 1).

In this book, Goldman also expounded on whether or not it was possible to make predictions about what would happen in the Soviet Union.

In view of Goldman's behaviour in this realm a few years later, his views are of interest:

> Making predictions may be bold, but it is also foolhardy. ...It is difficult to make predictions about politics and economics in the West, it is even more dangerous to make predictions about the U.S.S.R. Just to decipher what has already or is now happening in the Soviet Union is enough of a challenge. Even the best informed may be unable to anticipate key trends (Goldman, 1983, p. 4).

Marshall Goldman thus moved between insights into the coming trials and tribulations of the Soviet system in its changes in the domestic economy, on the one hand, and his dismissal of the possibilities for scholars to foretell the future, on the other. This basic uncertainty seems to me to characterize Goldman's writings. On the one hand, the pressures of U.S. Sovietology induced him to try to forecast what would happen in Moscow. On the other, he seems, at the same time, to have maintained a strong scepticism about how far one might reach as a scholar in such attempts.

For Goldman, the Gorbachev reforms started and ended with the Soviet leader's attempts to improve the Soviet economy. A typical quote, which connected economic reforms with other issues, gives the gist of his early analysis:

> While economic reform was his number one priority, Gorbachev soon recognized that economic reform would have to be accompanied by political and social reforms. In fact, almost everything Gorbachev has done recently seems designed to promote his economic reforms. For example, arms control is essential if he is to reduce Soviet military expenditures and to increase investment in light industry and consumer goods. Similarly, a policy he came to call '*glasnost*' and democratization is needed to curb abuses of power, to reduce alienation among the workers, and to win the support of the intellectuals, which Gorbachev must have if he wants the Soviet Union to be a serious contender in the race for high technology (Goldman, 1987a, p. vi).

Goldman was, from the beginning, very aware of the deep difficulties that Gorbachev and his associates faced when they tried to reform the Soviet economic system:

> To the outside observer, Gorbachev's continued emphasis on human failings and narrow parochialism makes one wonder whether Gorbachev understands that the difficulty in reforming the Soviet economy is not just a consequence

of human frailty. That certainly is a problem, but a bigger dilemma, one that tends to bring out what seems to be so much Soviet resistance is that the system itself is at fault. In other words, it is not enough to select the best managers and engineers, train them in the most advanced technique, and instill in them a passion for service to the state. This will have little long-range effect if, once the experts start to work, they find that the machinery they have to work with is ill-designed and obsolete, that the incentive system leads the work force to shoddy production, and that their suppliers are more highly rewarded when they supply poor quality, ill-suited goods than when they deliver high-quality, appropriate products (Goldman, 1987a, p. 256).

Even though Marshall Goldman believed that Gorbachev and his leadership needed to institute basic reforms in the Soviet economy, he still did not believe that the Soviet system, by 1987 at least, was in any terminal crisis. Gorbachev pursued détente with Washington during this period, in Goldman's view, not to prevent any collapse of the system, but to facilitate the success of his economic program (ibid., pp. 261-262).

For Marshall Goldman, a decisive step in Gorbachev's reforms was taken, or at least it was highlighted by the Soviet leader's speech to the UN General Assembly in December, 1988:

> Mikhail S. Gorbachev had something for almost everyone last week in New York. In a single speech, Gorbachev sought to solve what appeared to be the near-intractable dispute between East and West while at the same time offering some needed support for perestroika and his effort to revitalize the Soviet Union's economy. Others have discussed extensively the international effect. But the internal implications in some ways may be equally far-reaching.
>
> From the day he assumed the post of general secretary in March, 1985, Gorbachev's obsessive concern has been to revitalize his country's economy. Almost everything else is designed in some way or another to facilitate the realization of that goal. Thus, whatever their intrinsic merits, glasnost and democratization are intended to win popular support for the economic-reform effort. By calling for criticism of waste, incompetence and corruption, Gorbachev hopes to show Soviet workers that society will not tolerate the type of favoritism and elitism that characterized so much of the Brezhnev era (Goldman, 1988b).

Goldman's analysis of Gorbachev in power was based on the fundamental view that the new Soviet leader intended to try to reform the Soviet economy. It seems that this emphasis meant that Goldman never explicitly tackled the question that was so important for so many other analysts, and that is so crucial to this book, namely, were the changes limited or fundamental? And further, could the analyst determine that the changes had moved from one stage to another, from tinkering at the edges, as it were, to fundamentally restructuring the system, if the analyst even accepted that the Soviet Union could be reformed? For Marshall Goldman, it seems, the crucial question was never *when* could it be determined that the U.S.S.R. had indeed changed fundamentally, whether in domestic or foreign policy. For him, the crucial question was, instead, would Gorbachev be able to implement the reform program that he undoubtedly was intent on completing? Consequently, what I call the diagnostic question in chapter 1 simply cannot be answered in the case of Marshall Goldman.

Marshall Goldman is unique among the Sovietologists I have studied for this book in two respects. First, he was one of the few who really ventured a clear prediction about the future of Gorbachev and his reforms. Second, he wrote in one of his books that he saw his role as not simply that of an analyst of Soviet affairs, in particular economic affairs. In addition to being a scholar, Goldman purported to give advice to the Soviet leadership and believed that, at the very least, they would listen to his words and read his book. None of the other 17 Sovietologists in this work had both of these characteristics.

The occasion for Professor Goldman's prediction was a hearing before the Commission on Security and Co-operation in Europe on Implementation of the Helsinki Accords called "Glasnost: The Soviet Policy of 'Openness'", held in Congress on March 4, 1987. At the end of his statement, Marshall Goldman said:

> In other words, he's moving so fast that Gorbachev is worried whether or not he'll be able to pursue it. My own prediction is that he won't last 4 years (Goldman, 1987b, p. 27).

As stated above, such an attempt to predict what would happen to the Soviet Union under Gorbachev went against Marshall Goldman's own views about the difficulty of predicting the future of the Soviet Union, which he expressed in his book from 1983. I have found no specific explanation in his works for this apparent change of views concerning the fruitfulness of trying to foretell political developments in the Soviet Union. My own belief, however, as I have stated before, is that the extra-academic pressures on U.S. Sovietologists to produce policy-relevant forecasts found a clear victim in Marshall Goldman.

As noted in chapter 1, there are two aspects to the prognostic research question that I ask of my analysts. The first is: were they able to foretell the fall of Gorbachev as an individual leader? This is the simpler of the two prognostic dimensions as there were historic precedents — in particular the fall of Khrushchev in 1964 — from earlier Soviet times of this happening. The fall of Gorbachev as an individual leader was thus always possible from the perspective of several, if not most, of the Sovietologists in this study. The second dimension of the prognostic side of my analysis is, however, the crucial question: was any analyst able to predict, or forecast, the fall of the Soviet system itself? Marshall Goldman's statement was thus a prediction concerning the simpler of the two dimensions, the personal fate of the Soviet leader. There is not even a hint that his prediction concerns the wider system. On the crucial point — the very survival of the system — Marshall Goldman's prediction thus cannot be classified as being correct.

In his book *What Went Wrong with Perestroika*, first published in 1991, Marshall Goldman commented upon his own prediction, and more widely upon the difficulties of making such predictions. One of the aspects that he highlighted was the tendency by him and his fellow Sovietologists to make attempts to look into the crystal ball that were hedged and that may have pointed in different directions at different times (Goldman, 1991(1992), p. 124, including note).

The other unique aspect of Professor Goldman's writings about the Soviet Union was, as mentioned, that he believed his task to be something more than just a scholarly analysis of Soviet affairs. Writing in the preface to the original edition of *Gorbachev's Challenge*, published in early 1987, Marshall Goldman spelled out his views in this respect:

> After years of having been attacked for our comments about the Soviet Union, I now find it gratifying that some of our views are apparently receiving serious attention in Moscow itself. This book is an effort to examine the challenges that face Gorbachev. In addition to all the old problems, he now must also deal with the need to master what we have come to call high technology. ...
>
> It may be presumptuous, but this study is meant as a guidebook for him and thus ends with a series of suggestions about the steps he might profitably take (Goldman, 1987a, Preface (to original edition): pp. xvi- xvii).

For Goldman, the role of the scholar studying the Soviet Union could thus have included the task of giving advice to the Soviet leaders themselves. There are indeed indications in the scholarly literature that Gorbachev and his entourage read and listened to Western experts to an extent far beyond anything before their time in Soviet history (Archie Brown, 1996, pp-115-117). Still, for an individual scholar to believe that his own writings might possibly influence the course of Soviet decision making, or even the country's very historical development, can only be characterized as presumptuous.

Marshall Goldman was not very clear on the explanatory problem with which this book is mainly concerned. On the question of why did the reform process start, it is still possible to piece together an explanation that essentially consisted of two factors. The first was that the origin of the entire process of new policies in the Soviet Union lay in the state of the Soviet economy.[12] The second was that a necessary condition for the initiation of basic policies that aimed at rectifying the Soviet economy was the person of Mr. Gorbachev himself. Goldman believed that, without Gorbachev as an individual, such important reforms would never have been undertaken (Goldman, 1991 (1992), pp. 66-68). For Goldman, the start of the Soviet reform process could thus be explained at level II b, the failings of the Socialist economy, and level IV b, the individual leader and his ability to undertake important new reforms. There was no sense of the importance of cognition and learning when Goldman discussed Gorbachev's individual role for the Soviet reform process.

5.2.4.5 Jerry Hough

> In my judgment, Gorbachev is a Cossack firmly mounted on his horse, wreaking havoc on the old boyars who have few defenses. His willingness to show strikes and national demonstrations on television, to let the speakers at the Congress of People's Deputies run wild and to permit competitive elections is the strongest evidence that the Soviet people are nowhere near a revolutionary stage. Gorbachev has been far too cautious in the way he has handled his consolidation of power within the party to have allowed these things if there was the slightest chance that they would get out of control (Hough, 1989e, p. 3).

As stated in chapter 1, Sovietology in the United States has often been characterized as containing two generations with very different outlooks, if one confines oneself to assessing the discipline up to the early

---

[12] This basic point is fundamental to Goldman's analysis. See for example *Gorbachev's Challenge*, p. 3.

1980s, when the Sovietologists that interest me for this study must have been active in order to be of possible interest for analysis. The first generation thus comprised the traditionalists, who studied the Soviet Union as if it were a totally unique system — a system that could only be analysed by instruments uniquely suitable to it. The second generation of Sovietologists in the U.S., to continue this somewhat simplified overview, broke with the consensus that so strongly characterized the first generation of Sovietologists. For these scholars — the revisionists — the Soviet Union was, to put it somewhat crudely, just another political system that could and should be studied by employing the same theories and models that social scientists applied to other political systems. With some simplification, five of the U.S. Sovietologists in my sample — Bialer, Brzezinski, Dallin, Goldman and Pipes — all belong to the traditionalists. This makes it necessary to include at least one who was explicitly a revisionist, which is the main reason for including Professor *Jerry Hough* in this book.

Jerry Hough took his Ph.D. in political science at Harvard in 1961 and entered the faculty of Duke University in 1973, where he has subsequently remained as a professor of politics (Nygren, 1992, pp. 206,209). At the same time, Hough has for many years been affiliated with the Brookings Institution in Washington as non-resident fellow. Hough is one of the Soviet scholars — Hélène Carrère d'Encausse is the most pertinent other example — for whom it is necessary to start assessing their writings before 1982, when my regular analysis starts.

In the case of Jerry Hough, the early publication is *How the Soviet Union is Governed*. This is an extensively revised and enlarged edition by Hough of Merle Fainsod's classic study *How Russia is Ruled,* from 1953. One passage from the very last pages of this volume is of great interest to the themes of this book:

> When scholars have often been so unsuccessful in their predictions of the Soviet future, when academics specializing on the western countries...generally eschew prediction, when many consider the long-range planning by the State Department's Policy Planning Board largely irrelevant because of the impossibility of taking all contingencies into account, the temptation is extremely strong to hypothesize that our fascination with predicting the Soviet future reflects our lack of knowledge of that system rather than our knowledge of it. The temptation is equally strong to break with tradition and to write a book without a concluding chapter on the future.
>
> Nevertheless, general interest in the future remains strong, especially within the United States government, and if others are analyzing the subject, one can hardly resist making his own contribution to the dialogue (Hough and Fainsod, 1979, pp. 557-558).

This is a very good expression of what I would call the U.S. Sovietologist's dilemma during the Cold War. On the one hand, he or she was aware of the immense difficulties inherent in trying to foretell what would happen to so complex and obscure a political system as that in the Soviet Union. Indeed, the attempts at constructing scenarios on relevant issues in the State Department were probably widely derided in U.S. academic circles. At the same time, the pressures on the Sovietologists to take part in "the guessing game" were next to irresistible. As is shown in this chapter, Jerry Hough was not able to resist those pressures; perhaps he never really wanted to.

After Mr. Gorbachev came to power, Hough was one of the earliest of the Sovietologists studied here to find signs of important change in Soviet policies. One indicative quote comes from a newspaper article published just after Eduard Shevardnadze become Soviet Foreign Minister, replacing the old stalwart Andrei Gromyko:

> The selection of Mr. Shevardnadze changes the situation drastically. The simultaneous announcement of two major trips — the summit meeting and Mr. Gorbachev's planned trip to France — and the selection as foreign minister of a man who has no ties to Mr. Gromyko is a clear sign that Mr. Gorbachev intends to be his own Foreign Minister. ...
>
> ...Mr. Gorbachev is saying something important with the Shevardnadze appointment: It is a dramatic sign he wants a break with old ways of thinking and old policies. (Hough, 1985a).

It is obvious from this very first quote that Hough believed that the Soviet Union could indeed change. Hough is one of the Sovietologists whose assessment of Moscow under Gorbachev it was possible to follow over time as he regularly published articles and books during the period under study. Moreover, his articles appeared regularly in three of the most prestigious newspapers in the United States: *The New York Times*, *The Washington Post* and *Los Angeles Times*. It is a nearly constant theme in these articles that "Soviet Times They Are A'Changing", as one article published in the *Los Angeles Times* in early 1986 was headlined. Hough maintained a strong emphasis on personnel changes in the Soviet leadership — in the Politburo and the Central Committee — and noted what he perceived to be the crucial importance of these changes for Gorbachev's ability to carry out his plans in practical policies (Hough, 1986d).

This means that in a conventional sense, Jerry Hough never really answered the question of when the changes in the Soviet Union — whether in the domestic or in the foreign policy sphere — had become fundamental. In another sense, however, the question of the changes that occurred in Soviet policies under Gorbachev form the very foundation of Jerry Hough's analyses during the first years of the new leader's rule. An article published in *The New York Times* in early 1987 made clear the wide ramifications of Soviet change that Hough saw as more than possible:

> It is hard to say how far the changes in policy and system will go. Mr. Gorbachev's reforms will be like the New Deal, only more fundamental, and no one could judge the ultimate meaning of the New Deal by what President Franklin D. Roosevelt had done by 1934.
> But with the broadly educated Soviet population eager for reintegration with the West, and a leader determined to catch up with the South Koreas or even advanced countries, the change is likely to be more drastic than we anticipate (Hough, 1987c).

The explanation behind Gorbachev's reforms was, to Jerry Hough, a simple one: the need to reverse economic decline in order to remain a superpower. From this perceived necessity to reform the Soviet economy flowed other changes, such as those in foreign policy, more or less naturally.[13] At least implicitly, Hough also included an element of elite rethinking here, explanation IV a. When he made his analyses of the Soviet reform strategy Hough often employed one of the very central approaches of political science as an academic discipline — comparative analysis:

> All countries — including the United States at the turn of the century, Japan in the 1950s and the 1960s, and South Korea and Taiwan today — pass through a stage when they change from low-quality, simple products to more sophisticated and high-quality ones. Russia should have made the transition several decades ago. It is extremely unlikely that the economic reform will bring Soviet technology to world levels as quickly as Gorbachev hopes, but the Soviet Union is at the stage of development where the progress will come much more rapidly than we expect (Hough, 1988b, p. 200).

---

[13] Hough explains his views on the reasons behind the changes in Soviet policies best in *Opening up the Soviet Economy* (Washington, DC: Brookings, 1988).

This comparison between the Soviet Union under Gorbachev and several of the Asian "Tigers" was characteristic of Hough's analysis throughout the years that the Soviet leader held power. For Hough, the most apt comparison for Gorbachev's Soviet Union — in particular from 1987 until about 1990 — was indeed with the Asian Tigers:

> Indeed, the main effect of the establishment of genuine democratic institutions would be to give increased power to the middle-aged and elderly — those who had the most reason to fear and oppose economic reform and who would otherwise be powerless. Because of this prospect, some analysts (most notably Marshall Goldman) have seen an insuperable conflict between democratization and economic reform in the Soviet Union. Since democratization, in their view, is essential for economic progress, they have regarded Gorbachev's position as hopeless. However, the very premise of this argument is false. The most rapid economic growth in recent years has come in authoritarian or dictatorial regimes such as Chile, Taiwan, South Korea, and Singapore that have suppressed popular demands, not those that have gone a more populist or Peronist route. Why should the Soviet Union be different? (Hough, 1990c, p. 654)

This quote contains three elements crucial to Hough's way of analysing Soviet developments in the Gorbachev years. The first was his employment of the comparative method, a method that very much misled him as the objects with which he chose to compare the likely prospects of Soviet economic developments were obviously not appropriate. Second, Hough made a point of contrasting his analysis of Soviet events with that of other Sovietologists, such as Marshall Goldman in the quote above. Third, Hough was, in his analysis, always clear on the point that Gorbachev was not — as many seem to have believed — attempting to introduce democracy into the Soviet Union. Hough was consistent in pointing out the authoritarian character of the Soviet leader.

On the issue of making a prognosis of what would happen to the Soviet experiment under Gorbachev, Hough was the Sovietologist who was most spectacularly wrong. The essence of Hough's mistakes in this regard can perhaps be summed up as an overemphasis on the superlative skills that Gorbachev showed in the political game that went on within the traditional Soviet power structure during his years in power.[14] These skills, in Hough's

---

[14] "Over the decades my most abiding scholarly interest has been the structure of power in the Party and the relationship of cadres policy to it. I have followed these issues with meticulous care, and Gorbachev's sophistication in this realm, often at the most detailed level, has always struck me as extraordinarily impressive", Hough, 1991d, p. 94.

analysis, were so immense and so important that most other analysts tended to overestimate the risks of Soviet collapse strongly, a collapse that Jerry Hough for a long time more or less refused to identify as a risk. While Hough made penetrating and stimulating analyses of Gorbachev's latest moves in the leading Soviet circles, he failed to notice that the entire Soviet system was collapsing. A metaphor that comes to mind is that Hough saw Gorbachev as an incomparable manager of the deck chairs on the Titanic, but he failed to notice that the whole ship was sinking. More broadly, it is evident that Hough's belief in the applicability of modernization theory to the Soviet system under Gorbachev prevented him from grasping that the system was in terminal decline from 1989 on.

A crucial argument in Hough's attempts to look into the Soviet future was his emphasis on the importance of the multinational character of the Soviet empire and how Gorbachev would be able to use this very character to hold the State together. This argument first appears in Hough's analysis in the autumn of 1987:

> The one factor that will save Gorbachev over the next 15 years is the multinational character of the country. Intellectuals who would demonstrate for meaningful elections and workers who would demonstrate for free trade unions are likely to be restrained by fears of what such possibilities would mean in the Ukraine, in the Baltic states and in central Asia. They will fear that real democratization would lead to separatist movements in the non-Russian republics and perhaps the break-up of the union (Hough, 1987e).

This basic argument retains a place in Hough's analysis when it comes to his assessment of the likely Soviet future almost until Gorbachev is finally deposed:

> Legislative elections are scheduled for 1994 and presidential elections for 1995. Gorbachev wants to be able to say in 1994 and 1995: 'Remember how bad 1990 was? You gave me great powers. Are you better off than you were four years ago?' He wants the memories of 1990 to be as exaggerated as possible, and he wants his electoral opponents to be identified with extreme measures — especially the breakup of the U.S.S.R.
> My own belief is that Gorbachev's position will be very strong in the mid-1990s; the agricultural and services reform that worked in China and Hungary should work in the Soviet Union. Industrial reform will be much more difficult, but that is not Gorbachev's immediate worry (Hough, 1991b).

The last example I found presenting elements of what Hough regarded as the crucial reasons why Gorbachev would remain in power for years and would also be able to hold the Soviet Union together was in an article published in April 1991:

> Those who have said for four years that Mikhail Gorbachev's overthrow is imminent, that economic reform has collapsed and that Gorbachev has gone from failure to failure in foreign policy have been at it again in recent weeks.
> And, instead, as the predictable "compromise" with the republics demonstrates, Gorbachev has been in the process of bringing Boris Yeltsin and the republics to heel, accelerating economic reform and successfully integrating his country into the Western economy and military structure. Gorbachev's so-called failure in Japan was a crucial move in his domestic chess game (Hough, 1991c).

While this analysis contains details that are very hard to put into their context now, as of this writing nearly ten years after the fact, it is still possible to remember how the situation in the Soviet Union was portrayed in Western media in the winter and spring of 1991. The near-universal analysis outside the Soviet Union at this time was of a country in very serious decline, a country in which there was domestic strife both within the realm of politics itself and within other sectors, such as labour, added to which there were public demonstrations. In this situation, one of the acknowledged U.S. academic experts on Soviet affairs discussed not the decline of the system, but the likely electoral chances of the Soviet leader in elections that were scheduled to take place some three and four years, respectively, after the point at which Jerry Hough was writing.

There is something remarkable about the extent to which Jerry Hough got it wrong when he tried to make prognoses into the Soviet political future from 1987 through 1991. Not only did he fail to issue by mid-1990 — as my perhaps too-restrictive analytical scheme requires — any prognosis to the effect that the Soviet Union would collapse, he actively derided those who did issue such forecasts. Hough grossly overestimated the lingering importance of Gorbachev's manoeuvrings within the Soviet power apparatus, and simultaneously in practice ignored the importance of the decline of the broader political, social and economic system within which this decline occurred. The explanation for why Hough could end up clinging to the belief that the Soviet system would survive long past the point when it shouldhave been obvious to an expert like him that it would likely collapse must, to my mind, be found in the fundamental analytic model that he applied to his study of the reform process under Gorbachev: modernization theory. The quotes included here clearly illustrate Hough's tendency to equate the Gorbachev reforms with processes carried out earlier in countries such as South Korea. With the admitted benefit of hindsight, the application of this model to understanding the "progress" of Gorbachev's reforms, particularly in the socio-economic sphere, was spectacularly unsuccessful.

It is possible that Jerry Hough's perception of himself as a corrective to the old guard of Sovietologists, as the true social science scholar of the Soviet Union in a sea of "anti-Soviet traditionalists", also contributed to his tendency to cling to some of these ideas long after developments on the ground should have convinced him that they were outdated. Hough was thus able to combine deep, indeed probably unique, insights into the inner workings of the Soviet system, with great mistakes in his assessments of broader characteristics of the viability of the system. The Soviet Union was never comparable, in any meaningful politico-economic sense, to the Asian Tigers, as Jerry Hough believed. The more apt comparison is, rather, to be found in that awful phrase sometimes employed by polemicists in the U.S. to other economies asserted not to be working: "basket-case economy".

5.2.4.6 Richard Pipes

Since Mikhail Gorbachev came to power, the Soviet Union has been far less aggressive in its foreign policy pronouncements. Desperately seeking foreign aid to shore up a collapsing economy, it has projected with all the propaganda means at its disposal the image of a country that requires peace and defense-budget cutbacks. Such professions and certain steps, largely symbolic, have had the desired effect of blurring the perception of the Soviet Union as an aggressive, hostile power...

How genuine is the change in Soviet foreign policy? Take defense expenditures. Moscow has finally released what it claims to be its true military budget. The 77 billion ruble figure announced earlier this year is about half of what U.S. experts believe to be actual defense appropriations... There are at least two reasonable explanations for the discrepancy between Soviet professions and performance. One is that Moscow regards the present period as a breathing spell, to restore its flagging economy and popular morale, before resuming a worldwide offensive. The other is that the leadership is so beholden to its generals, especially in the view of growing internal unrest, that it cannot afford to alienate them with cutbacks in appropriations and foreign commitments.

Whichever explanation is correct, world stability and peace are nowhere as close as much of world opinion would like to believe. The Kremlin's professions of peaceful intent, and certain steps carefully calculated to mollify the West, do not alter the fact that Soviet military activities at home and abroad under Mr. Gorbachev have proceeded pretty much as they did under Leonid I. Brezhnev (Pipes, 1989b)

Richard Pipes was Baird Professor of History at Harvard University, a chair from which he retired in the mid-1990s. He has been director of the Harvard Russian Research Center. During the first two years of the Reagan Administration, Professor Pipes served as Senior Soviet Specialist on the National Security Council. Richard Pipes was born in Poland in 1923 (Nygren, 1992, pp. 100-101, 205, 210).

In a 1984 book Professor Pipes gave his basic views of the Soviet system, and of its fundamental policies and aspirations, a year or so before Gorbachev came to power:

These crises, which include declining rates of growth, the emergence of an uncontrolled "second" or free economy, widespread corruption, political dissent, and the demographic decline of Slavs, cannot be overcome by repressive measures: they confront these regimes with the necessity of thoroughgoing internal reforms. The author concludes from this evidence that a growing discrepancy is emerging between the global aspirations of the Communist elite and the means at its disposal, that this elite is finding it increasingly difficult to pursue its global ambitions and to maintain intact the Stalinist system. While the Soviet government is in no danger of imminent collapse, it cannot forever "muddle through" and will have to choose before long between reducing its aspirations to worldwide hegemony and transforming its internal regime, and perhaps even find it necessary to do the one and the other (Pipes, 1984a, pp. 12-14; cf, Pipes, 1986a, p. 279).

The foreign policy of the Soviet Union was presented in a similarly stark manner:

What is the objective of Soviet and Soviet-type expansionism, and by what means is it pursued?
As concerns the objective, no one familiar with Communist theory can entertain much doubt. It is the elimination, worldwide, of private ownership of the means of production and the "bourgeois" order which rests upon it, and its replacement with what Lenin called a "worldwide republic of soviets."...

These objectives, it needs stressing, are not a distant, unfocused hope, as is the case with the synthetic "national goals" that issue from time to time from committees of distinguished Americans appointed for the purpose, but a concrete expectation and an operative principle (Pipes, 1984a, pp. 49-50).

Despite these views, Professor Pipes did not believe that the Soviet system was unreformable. He also believed that such internal reforms, if implemented, were bound to have implications for Soviet international behaviour (Pipes, 1984b, pp. 47-61).

In 1985, Pipes assessed the Helsinki Final Act 10 years after its signing in an op-ed piece in *The New York Times*:

The Soviet Union won important psychological and moral victories with the signing of the Helsinki accords 10 years ago. What the West gained is by no means apparent. ...
The net effect of these provisions has been to promote on the [European] Continent a sense of complacency — an illusory security quite at odds with the Kremlin's military preparations. ...
The other Soviet success has been of a moral nature. What could Western statesmen have had on their minds when they solemnly agreed to clauses committing the Soviet Union to "respect human rights and fundamental freedoms, including the freedom of thought, conscience, religion or belief" as well as the right of peoples to "self-determination"? These statesmen knew that Moscow would not — indeed, could not — abide by such premises, for to have done so would have caused the subversion of the Soviet regime and the dissolution of its empire. Whether they realized it or not, therefore, they prostituted Western values by tacitly confirming Moscow's view that human rights are nothing but "bourgeois hypocrisy" (Pipes, 1985).

As the Soviet reforms began, Pipes acknowledged them, and explained them as a need to deal with an internal crisis, particularly an economic crisis (see Pipes, 1986c). He did not believe, however, that the Soviet reforms really meant that Soviet foreign policy was being changed in any important way.

By 1988, the demonstrations had begun in various parts of the Soviet Union. Pipes presented a warning of what this might mean for the future stability of the country in a newspaper article published in March:

In the three years since Mikhail S. Gorbachev and his team took charge, the Soviet Union has experienced a succession of unauthorized demonstrations of increasing size and violence. ...

Clearly, sooner or later Moscow will have to acknowledge that in a world in which islands like the Seychelles with 67,000 inhabitants enjoy national sovereignty, the 45 million Ukrainians or 14 million Uzbeks will not remain content to live forever under colonial rule. Perestroika will have to deal with the problem of decentralizing the state structure to give the republics, at the very least, meaningful autonomy and transforming a pseudo-federation into a genuine federal union.

From Moscow's point of view, the gravest danger is that the ethnic disturbances may spill into Russia proper. The Great Russians, whose political culture is dominated by the legacy of centuries of serfdom, tend to be more docile when subjected to firm authority. But when they perceive that authority to weaken they are likely to explode in uncontrollable anarchy that sweeps all before it.

Time is catching up with communist Russia in many ways. Moscow has eased censorship in deference to the rise of public opinion, and it is about to carry out major reforms to bring the economy into step with that of the industrial democracies. But, quite unexpectedly to itself, it has now been forced to confront a domestic problem that it had believed firmly under control: its imperialism and the spirit of nationalism that it evokes among its victims (Pipes, 1988a).

While this assessment does not quite measure up to being a forecast, in the fairly strict sense introduced in chapter 1 of this book, still it has to be acknowledged that Professor's Pipes was very much on the mark in his way of trying to look into the future of the Soviet Union as a result of the domestic disturbances from late 1986 on.

If Richard Pipes was thus willing to acknowledge that truly fundamental processes were taking place in the Soviet Union domestically by early 1988, he did not believe that the country's foreign policies were undergoing any similar changes. The title of a newspaper article published in *The New York Times* on October 9, 1989 — cited in the first quote in this section — really catches the essence of the history professor's views: "The Russians Are Still Coming". Professor Pipes identified a chasm between the Soviet Union's official statements on its foreign policy and its actual behaviour. The military activities, he writes, "at home and abroad under Mr. Gorbachev have proceeded pretty much as they did under Leonid I. Brezhnev" (Pipes, 1989b).

This was an assessment of the extent of changes in Soviet foreign and security policies that can only be regarded as incorrect. By the autumn of 1989, the Soviet Union had withdrawn from Afghanistan, it had agreed to destroy of one class of nuclear weapons — the INF missiles, it was acquiescing the transformation going on in several of the Warsaw Pact nations. To state at this late stage that the country's military activities were essentially the same as they were under Leonid Brezhnev is, in this author's estimation, the only clear example of a scholar studied here exhibiting the fundamental error of attribution. In other words, in this instance Professor Pipes let his distaste for the Soviet system, in essence his classification of that system as the enemy, determine the character of his analysis. For the experts and *cognoscenti* of U.S. Sovietology this is not a surprising result. Yet, in a broader, comparative sense Richard Pipes' views of Soviet foreign policy are still very notable

5.2.4.7 Conclusion: The U.S. Sovietologists The analysis of six Sovietologists from the United States shows very wide differences in their analysis of what was happening in the Soviet Union, what had caused the reform process, and whether it was possible to foretell what would happen. In other words, the foreign policy orientation that I looked for as an explanation of the main reasoning of the analysts of the Soviet Union does not seem to fit at all in the case of U.S. Sovietologists. Neither can I find that the fact that they belonged to the profession they did, Sovietology, accounted for the gist of their analyses. They are far too different for the latter to be true. Given my perspective, only one way of explaining the structure of their analysis remains: the personal one. Each of the six U.S. Sovietologists, in this view, saw the Soviet Union in a distinct light. The contents of their analyses are explained by their personal characteristics as scholars and as individuals rather than by any other overriding structural explanation.

My analysis of the six U.S. Sovietologists also indicates the only clear case of the fundamental error of attribution that I have encountered in the material investigated for this book. This came when Professor Richard Pipes in the late autumn of 1989 stated, in essence, that Soviet security policies under Gorbachev had not really changed. Given all that had happened in Soviet foreign and security policy at that stage, I regard this analysis as a manifestation of Professor Pipes' classification of the Soviet Union as an "enemy" rather than the result of any scholarly analysis.

If Richard Pipes may be classified as a scholar who was anti-Soviet and who, largely because of this fundamental negativism towards the Soviet system, was wrong in important aspects of his analysis, there is at least one other example of a prominent U.S. Sovietologist who also was manifestly wrong on one of the basic issues of this book, but in another respect, and based on a fundamentally different perspective. This was Jerry Hough, who displayed a very high estimation indeed of Mr. Gorbachev's political skills during at least six of the roughly six and a half years that Gorbachev stayed in power. This meant that Hough tended to overestimate strongly the staying power of the Soviet leader, as well his ability to keep the Union together. Indeed, Hough's admonitions to other scholars — issued in early 1991 as the decline of the Soviet system should have been fairly obvious, yet saying that others were mistaken to think that the result might be Soviet collapse — are a remarkable testament to how even an acknowledged expert can be terribly wrong about central aspects of his area of expertise. Hough himself commented in 1979 on the pressures that U.S. Sovietologists felt to issue prognoses about likely Soviet developments, given the great interest in the matter in political and media circles, and this despite the fact that most of them knew that such prognostications were very uncertain indeed. To put it crudely, Jerry Hough failed to follow his own admonition to be careful about issuing prognoses about future Soviet developments and instead succumbed to the political pressures for future-oriented punditry that he had admonished against in 1979. The main explanation for Hough's failure to see the extent of the disintegration of the Soviet system even as late as early 1991 was, in my view, that he stuck to the application of a clearly inadequate analytic model, modernization theory, for far too long. It is clear today that the Soviet Union had very few similarities with Singapore and South Korea in the socio-economic field. It should have been clear even in 1991 that this was so.

My general conclusion is that U.S. Sovietology, at least if one judges from these six scholars, was influenced by politicization during the Gorbachev years. Scholars who had different perspectives on the Soviet Union, for example, Jerry Hough and Richard Pipes, felt a need not only to espouse their academic views in the public arena, but also to sharpen the contrasts between their analyses and those of other scholars to the extent that crucial elements of the analyses became clearly distorted. Indeed, Hough and Pipes illustrate the general tendency quite well. They came to the study of the Soviet Union from diametrically opposing general standpoints, and since they felt so passionately about their subject, and also about their subject's importance to the foreign policy of their country, they tended to exaggerate crucial aspects of their analyses in a public discussion that can only be characterized as shrill and one-sided. Exaggerations and simplifications such as Hough and Pipes presented cannot be said to have contributed to the extent that one might have expected of two such eminent scholars to any informed policy discussion about issues of central importance to U.S. foreign and security policy, that is, the relationship with the other superpower.

The participation of scholars in such a debate in a democracy is an ideal that to some extent underlies my whole approach in this book. It should be added that this unfortunate tendency towards simplification and exaggeration was most notable in Hough and Pipes, and that the other four U.S. Sovietologists — Bialer, Brzezinski, Alexander Dallin and Marshall Goldman — displayed little, if any, of this tendency.

I detected one other peculiarity in the positions taken by the Sovietologists regarding the role that they thought they should rightfully play in the public debate on relations between the U.S. and the Soviet Union. This was when Marshall Goldman, an economist, wrote that he was pleased that his analyses of Soviet economic development not only played a role in the scholarly discourse on Soviet developments, and in the public debate in the U.S. on these issues, but they also provided input into the economic policy debate in the Soviet Union. I find it troubling that an academic, a specialist in the political and economic developments in another country, should strive for a role in the policy-making process of that country. Such an aspiration seems to me to be another case in which the academic ideals of dispassionate, thorough analysis risk being compromised by external factors that are irrelevant to the fundamental cause of good academic scholarship.

Finally, Seweryn Bialer displayed some similarity to Jerry Hough in his inability to realize that the Soviet Union was disintegrating from about 1989 onwards. The explanation as to why Bialer made this mistake is to my mind the same one as for Hough: the application of an academic model or theory that in the end proved inapplicable. For Hough the theory was that of modernization, for Bialer that of a system which would remain stable because it was based on an elite that tended to generate its own survival through the recruitment of ever more candidates.

5.3 Conclusion

One of the charges levelled at academics specializing in international relations as the Cold War ended, as the East European countries broke free of the Soviet Union and that country itself collapsed, was that they had been unable to foretell what was going to happen. A similar charge has been levelled against the Sovietologists. They were also, it has often been said, unable to warn the world that the state that they had studied so intently for so many years was about to expire. One of the purposes of this book is to examine the extent to which this charge against the Sovietologists was correct. I have thus considered whether or not the Sovietologists regarded it as a worthwhile enterprise to try to foretell the Soviet future. If they regarded such an aspiration to be worthwhile for an academic to undertake, I have also assessed whether they were able to make a correct forecast, or, more demandingly, a correct prediction about what was going to happen.

A second purpose of my analysis of the Sovietologists is to compare their assessments of the changes in policy undertaken by Gorbachev. Did they regard these as being fundamental, particularly in the field of foreign policy, and if they did, when did they state so publicly? The assessment on this score was linked to a fundamental dimension on which I also compared all the Sovietologists: was the Soviet system possible to reform fundamentally? Or, alternatively, was the system of such an essentially flawed character that any attempt to reform it would inevitably sooner or later result in its collapse?

A third purpose was to consider the explanations that the Sovietologists presented for why Mr. Gorbachev had started his process of policy changes in Moscow. In assessing the Sovietologists' explanation for this question, I developed a classificatory scheme (see table 1.2). Is it possible, I asked myself, to learn anything about the general problems of explanation in the human and social sciences from this case that is both politically relevant and interesting from the academic aspect?

Fourth, I am interested in the tendency of at least some scholars, particularly in the social sciences, to apply theories and analytical models to their objects of study. Could this tendency provide an explanation for at least some of the mistakes of analysis and prediction that the Sovietologists made?

There were great differences among the scholars concerning prediction and whether this was a meaningful or even possible activity for Sovietologists. There is one group comprising seven specialists[15] who regarded it as appropriate and meaningful for scholars to try to foretell the future. In addition, Professor Alexandre Bennigsen, who did not explicitly address the question of the feasibility of predictions, nevertheless issued a forecast, and so I classify him in this group as well. There is a second group consisting of five scholars[16] who did not explicitly take a standpoint on this issue. Some of

---

[15] The scholars who explicitly stated that they believed that it was possible to predict/forecast the Soviet future were John Erickson, Alex Pravda, Anders Åslund, Seweryn Bialer, Zbigniew Brzezinski, Marshall Goldman and Jerry Hough. Alexandre Bennigsen is not quite clear on this point, but because of his explicit forecasts, made on several occasions, I have classified him as belonging to this group.

[16] The Sovietologists who refrained from discussing whether or not forecasting was feasible in principle, but still issued at least forecasts were: Hélène Carrère d'Encausse, Pierre Hassner, Archie Brown, Kristian Gerner and Richard Pipes.

the scholars in this group still ventured what may be called loose forecasts. Finally, there was a third group of Sovietologists, five[17] individuals, who explicitly stated either that they did not regard it as appropriate for academics to try to make forecasts, or that they themselves would not undertake any such prognostications. Even within this group I found some examples of scholars who, although they regarded foretelling as something of an illegitimate exercise for academics, still ventured some imprecise forecasts on occasion. Stefan Hedlund is the most prominent example. First, he very explicitly derided attempts at making predictions about what would happen in Soviet politics, then, in 1990, he took part in just such an exercise.

I have found only one attempt at an outright prediction in my material, in the sense that the speaker identified both a discrete event or process and a time frame within which this was prognosticated to happen. That was when Marshall I. Goldman, at a hearing of the Committee on Security and Co-operation in Europe before the U.S. Congress in March 1987 predicted that "[Gorbachev] won't last 4 years" (Goldman, 1987b, p. 27). This prediction was not put into any larger, tightly reasoned framework. The essential point is, however, that the prediction dealt only with the limited question of the survival of Gorbachev himself. Soviet leaders as individuals had fallen before. The really difficult prediction concerned the collapse of the entire Soviet system. On this dimension, Professor Goldman never issued any prognosis to the effect that he believed that the system would collapse as a result of the Gorbachev reforms.

The category of forecasts includes the work of scholars who did not predict any precise future state, but rather declared that the future would *probably* look a certain way, or presented three or four possible scenarios. I found several academics who can be characterized as having issued such forecasts. Three of the scholars who were most prescient in this sense were Kristian Gerner from Sweden, Zbigniew Brzezinski from the U.S. and Pierre Hassner of France. In Gerner's publications I found, starting as early as 1987, a clear tendency to write about "post-sovietism" when he discussed the future of Soviet affairs. This was not just a loose inclination, but it was made more precise in several pieces published by the Swedish Sovietologist. Likewise, Zbigniew Brzezinski wrote about the "Birth and Death of Communism in the Twentieth Century" (Brzezinski, 1989a) in 1988/1989, in an accurate way.

---

[17] The five who explicitly denied either the general feasibility of forecasting the future of the Soviet Union, or stated explicitly that they would not attempt to do so were: Alain Besançon, Alec Nove, Stefan Hedlund, Lena Jonson and Alexander Dallin.

Pierre Hassner, after emphasizing the stability of the Soviet system during several years, had changed his mind by the end of 1989 when he wrote that the socialist systems, clearly including the Soviet Union, were doomed. He made this forecast even more precise during the first months of 1990.

A fourth scholar who issued a forecast that raised the question of what precisely constitutes an accurate forecast was the late Professor Alexandre Bennigsen. Bennigsen, in 1983, confidently stated that the end of the Soviet Union, in a crisis caused by nationalist feelings among the non-Russian Republics, was inevitable. The timing of this unavoidable crisis was, however, not at all clear from Professor Bennigsen's writings. Here we have a scholar whose prognostication might, in other words, illustrate what Kjell Goldmann calls "sooner-or-later theories" (Goldmann, 1992, p. 88). The other aspect that is debatable about Professor Bennigsen's way of looking into the future is his identification of the failure of the Soviet State to integrate the Muslim population into the system as so crucial as being a direct and sufficient cause of the fall of the state. It is difficult for a non-specialist in Soviet politics, even nearly ten years after the system's collapse, to assess the extent to which the undeniable fact that the Soviet Muslims were not very integrated into the Soviet "Union" was a direct cause of the collapse. I personally believe that it contributed to the end of the system, but it is not possible to assess the correctness of Professor Bennigsen's prognoses on this point conclusively. Specialists on the Soviet collapse also seem to agree that this was to a larger extent caused by instability in some of the Western Republics — such as the Baltic Republics and the Ukraine — rather than in any Muslim-dominated Republics.

There is a fifth scholar whose writings also indicated that he believed that the Soviet Union was in decline: Kristian Gerner's Swedish colleague, Professor Stefan Hedlund. In this case, however, I don't find the analysis to be as consistent as it was in the cases of Gerner, Brzezinski and Hassner, in particular. Professor Hedlund also started his analysis of the Gorbachev years by confidently stating that "the system is totally ensured against change" (Hedlund, 1985a). Hedlund was, however, a second case where the ultimate judgement was hard to make on the question of whether or not his analysis contained any correct forecasts about Soviet collapse by the stipulated time of mid-1990.

Another scholar who quite early identified what I personally regard as one of the main causes of the Soviet collapse, the nationalist issues, was Hélène Carrère d'Encausse. Her 1978 work *L'empire éclaté* had a very suggestive title, and an interesting general thrust. Nowhere in this book, or in any of the other writings by Carrère d'Encausse that I have studied, was there, however, any more precise forecast presented. The understanding that I got from her book was that the problem of nationalism was insoluble and that the Soviet Union would have to grapple with it indefinitely. It was explicitly stated, however, that what the diverse nationalities strove for was greater autonomy within the Soviet Union. This, in my assessment, is something clearly less fundamental than the outright fall of the Soviet empire.

In her 1990 book *La gloire des nations ou la fin de l'Empire soviétique*, Carrère d'Encausse, in a very perceptive manner, analysed the spiral of decline that was, by then, clear to most interested observers. This book was published only a little more than one year before the collapse of the Soviet State, however, which means that I did not classify it as containing a correct forecast regarding the future of that state. This result indicates, however, how difficult it is to determine a time period during which a prognosis must have been issued in order for it to be regarded as correct. If my requirement is relaxed from 18 months before the collapse of the regime in Moscow to 12 months, then Hélène Carrère d'Encausse, at least, should also be included in the category of scholars who were indeed prescient. Indeed, the fact that the French Sovietologist very early identified the crucial issue of nationalism as one cause of likely Soviet troubles makes classifying her as having issued correct forecasts even more plausible.

There were also examples of Sovietologists whose attempts at prognoses were demonstrably off the mark. Jerry Hough in this regard made the most prominent mistakes. Hough insisted well into 1991 that Gorbachev was still able to control the Soviet system and would be able to prevent the collapse of the Soviet Union. This is an example of the tendency of some social scientists to utilize analytical models when studying their objects even after such models have become demonstrably inapplicable. Please note that the present writer — also a social scientist — is by no means negative to the application of theories and models; on the contrary. Still, the use of such analytic devices must also be critically assessed in a project such as the current one.

My overall assessment of 18 Sovietologists on the issue of their ability to forecast the coming fall of the Soviet Union is still that a politician, or interested citizen, who intently followed the academic analysis of Soviet affairs would not have been able to learn therefrom, with anything even approaching certainty, that the Soviet system was going to collapse in the early 1990s. At the same time, it must be noted that the scholars were divided on whether or not it was a legitimate scholarly exercise to undertake the attempt to foretell where Soviet developments might indeed lead. This issue even meant that some scholars, Jerry Hough and Stefan Hedlund come to mind, were of two minds on whether or not the Sovietologist should indeed venture any forecasts. Both of them have published material to the effect that attempting to forecast the Soviet future was an exercise that was fruitless because the system was so difficult to comprehend and there were so many variables involved that it would be impossible to succeed even if one tried. At the same time, both of these Sovietologists still issued prognoses during the Gorbachev years.

The main results of my analysis of the writings of 18 Sovietologists in assessing their use of forecasting are thus inconclusive. There were individual scholars whose views clearly indicated, well beforehand, that the Soviet system was on the way to extinction. There was, however, nothing even approaching a consensus among Sovietologists — whether these are seen in each individual country studied here or as a whole profession — on the two crucial issues regarding predictions: was the exercise legitimate at all during the existence of the Soviet Union, and was it possible to foretell that the system would collapse. It is notable that after the event there are several scholars who claim that they did indeed foretell what was going to happen. This author has looked at scholars outside the 18, at least to some extent, and has been unable to find anyone who fulfils the criteria stipulated in chapter 1 for a correct prediction at least, and probably also for a forecast.[18]

At this point, it seems necessary to enter another aspect into the discussion. This is the extent to which foreign and security policies, and defence policy as well, in France, Great Britain, Sweden and the United States are based on "scenarios" concerning what is likely to happen to aspects deemed crucial for their international policies. To be able to issue scenarios, the politicians and the diplomats who create them need inputs. This

---

[18] To take just one example one of the Sociologists — Randall Collins — in the special issue of *American Journal of Sociology* "Symposium on Predictions in the Social Sciences" (Vol. 100 (May 1995), pp. 1520-1626) claims that through his use of "geopolitical theory" he successfully predicted the demise of the Soviet State in publications printed in the 1980s. For several reasons I remain unconvinced that Collins did indeed succeed in what he claims he accomplished. One reason is that I do not believe that it is possible to regard an approach, such as the one Collins applies, with a time frame of 30-50 years, as sufficiently precise to enable assessment by scientific methods. This risks falling into the "sooner-or-later" trap. Cf. Collins "Prediction in Macrosociology; The Case of the Soviet Collapse", in the special issue of *American Journal of Sociology* (pp. 1552-1593). See also Edgar Kiser "What Can Sociological Theories Predict? Comment on Collins, Kuran, and Tilly" in the same issue (pp. 1611-1615) and K. Goldmann (1992) : "Bargaining, Power, Domestic Politics, and Security Dilemmas".

creates pressures on scholars with relevant specialities. The Sovietologists obviously belonged to this category during the period under study. The scholars in all four countries were under pressure to produce prognoses about future Soviet developments, pressures that few academic specialists were able to deflect, even if they wanted to. One conclusion that I draw from this study of Sovietology is that it was very difficult indeed to make predications about social and political processes as complex as the ones that happened in the Soviet Union. I find no reason to believe that this should be any easier ten years after the demise of that state.

To the extent that scenarios in foreign and security policy are based on the very loose prognoses that do exist, great caution is warranted in constructing the scenarios, and, subsequently, in basing important aspects of national policy on such scenarios. Another conclusion is that academics should be wary of strong political pressures that induce them to try to look into a future that they believe is impossible to foretell.

On the question of the reformability of the Soviet system, the scholars took all kinds of different positions. Some stated that they were convinced that the Soviet system could be reformed. One surprising member of this group was Richard Pipes, well known for his strongly anti-Soviet views. Professor Pipes believed, however, that nothing was totally stable, whether in nature or in human affairs.

This view on whether or not the Soviet system could be reformed was directly tied to what I called the diagnostic aspect of my analysis in chapter 1. In other words, when did the scholar in question classify the changes undertaken by Mr. Gorbachev and his leadership as being fundamental, as opposed to merely ephemeral? For scholars who regarded the Soviet system as an illegitimate political construction, this question was not of any interest at all, since such a system, in their view, could not be reformed; it could simply muddle along until it collapsed at some unspecified time in the future. There are several examples in this book of scholars with this basic view of the Soviet Union. One of the most pronounced examples is André Besançon of France; another is Stefan Hedlund in Sweden. There are some other scholars who are close to this view, without quite embracing it. In this second group, the scholars were still able to contemplate that the Soviet system might have been reformed. This group includes Kristian Gerner in Sweden, and Zbigniew Brzezinski and Richard Pipes in the U.S.

Having said this, the results of the analysis of when the scholar stated that the Soviet Union had indeed changed hardly turned up any sensational results. To most of the scholars the interesting question was not when the

Soviet Union had really changed to any great extent, but rather whether or not Mr. Gorbachev would be able to implement the reforms to which he was very widely perceived to be personally committed. I detected no nationally based difference in the timing for when the scholars stated that the Soviet Union had changed.

Most scholars surveyed in this study attempted to explain the main issue explored in this study: why did the reform process start in the Soviet Union in the mid-1980s? The most important single explanation for these academics was the inefficiency of the socialist economic system, which was mentioned by ten of the specialists. Another important explanation for this was what I call the cognitive explanation, in this case mainly that the Soviet elite had realized that their system was facing severe problems and needed far-reaching reform.[19] Six experts mentioned this. It is notable that only one of the Sovietologists raised explanation 1 a, pressure from the United States, as a cause behind the Soviet changes. This was a fairly prominent explanation for the conservative newspapers, as well as for the U.S. and U.K. governments.

What is perhaps most notable about these explanations of the policy changes in the Soviet Union under Gorbachev is the important role played by explanations on the individual level, level IV in my table 1.2. In particular, several scholars highlighted the role of cognitive factors, of rethinking by either Mr. Gorbachev himself or by a broader Soviet elite, as a cause behind the moves in Soviet policies that started in 1985. This gives further support to the belief in a more general trend where cognitive factors have gained an increased role in social and human sciences during the last decade or so.

One of the questions I have studied in this chapter was whether or not any analyst displayed the fundamental error of attribution. In other words, were there any instances when any of the Sovietologists presented judgements of Soviet affairs that were clearly influenced by their personal views of that system, in this case consisting of an enemy image? Any judgement on this score has to depend upon a personal assessment by the scholar making the determination of when Soviet foreign policy had really changed for good. As made clear in chapter 1.6.2 of this volume, I regard the time by which this has occurred as March 1988.

---

[19] It should be mentioned that it is in some cases difficult to classify the explanatory logic of the scholar correctly. The most important difficulty occurs when the scholar mentions both one or more "objective" problems facing the Soviet Union, and in the same context notes the importance of rethinking on the part of the elite.

Only one of the 18 scholars studied in this book can be regarded as manifesting the fundamental error of attribution. This was when Professor Richard Pipes, in October 1989, stated that Soviet military policies under Gorbachev were essentially the same as they were under Leonid Brezhnev. I regard this as a case where the Sovietologist's image of the Soviet Union as an enemy influenced his judgement of the magnitude of Soviet foreign policy changes. To be sure, those who followed Sovietology during the Cold War regard this as a fairly uninteresting result, since the basic views of Professor Pipes were widely known at the time among specialists. In a broader sense — that of evaluating a whole sub-discipline — I still regard it as interesting that one of the most prominent members of an academic profession could have publicly espoused such views so late in the Soviet reform process. For me, this result further underlines the very peculiar character of Sovietology, where even truly fundamental disagreements on absolutely vital points existed to the end.

An additional comment on the analysis of the Soviet Union carried out by 18 eminent specialists is to express amazement at the enormous differences in so many aspects of their diagnoses, their explanations as well as their prognoses of what might happen politically in that country. As a non-specialist in Soviet affairs, I have more than once asked myself whether these 18 scholars were even writing about the same country, so vast were the differences among their assessments

A further question I asked myself was whether or not the use of theories and analytic models by social scientists may have contributed, in some cases, to failures to understand the breadth and depth of the Soviet reform process or to realize that the system was bound to collapse. I found two cases among the Sovietologists where I believe that such a tendency was displayed, both in the United States. Of the two, I believe that the case of Jerry Hough was the most clear-cut. Hough consistently applied modernization theory to his analyses of the Soviet reform process and to his assessments of the likelihood of success. There can be no doubt whatever that this application of the theory was incorrect and unsuitable. Less clear-cut, but still wrong at least on the margin, was the belief held by Seweryn Bialer that the Soviet Union was governed by an elite that had a strong tendency to remain stable because it was able to constantly recruit new talent into the pool of the elite. Even if there might have been something to the model in at least partially assessing the workings of the Soviet system, Bialer clearly overestimated its importance for functioning so as to stabilize Moscow into an indefinite future.

One additional question in this assessment of eighteen Sovietologists was to find explanations for these wide divergences between their analyses. It is hard to find any national traits in the analyses of the Soviet Union made by the specialists in the United Kingdom, in Sweden and in the United States. In essence, with few exceptions these 14 specialists made particular analyses of Soviet affairs, analyses that seemed to differ due to their views of the subject matter, the Soviet Union, and also due to their party political ideologies.

In the case of the French specialists, however, there were some national traits to the analyses. It does not seem an overstatement to say that in the case of the French Sovietologists, I found the most developed ability to identify the enormous problems that the Soviet Union had to deal with, as well as the greatest willingness to make prognoses. Among French specialists, and to some extent among the French elite media, one can thus detect a willingness to delve fairly deeply into foreign political processes that are of potential importance to French foreign policy.

Whether this French tendency to probe deeply into the affairs of the Soviet Union was, or even more, if it still is, characteristic of other aspects of French foreign policy as well is a question that will have to be answered by future studies.

This assessment of the analytic abilities of eighteen specialists in clarifying several aspects of Soviet developments in the period from 1985 to 1991 offers few clear-cut answers to the question of how the interested layperson can identify the superior expert who is able to make sense of complex current events, to explain their causes, and perhaps also to foretell what will happen. One aspect that comes to mind is that economists such as Anders Åslund and Marshall Goldman were very successful in clarifying the extent of Soviet economic problems, both as the Gorbachev period started and as the reforms began to be talked about and then gradually implemented. Does this indicate that economists tend to be superior to other academics in the social and human sciences when it comes to identifying fundamental problems in nations that tend to become destabilized?

The economists did not, however, follow these analyses of important problems with any specific prognoses. As mentioned above, this comment may, however, be viewed as the way the political scientist tries to make his criteria fit the analyses made by specialists from other disciplines, in this case economics. In the verbal debate about the inability of scholars to foretell the demise of the Soviet Union, one sometimes encounters the view that "the economists had it right early on". This analysis indicates that such a way of characterizing economic research on Soviet behaviour is to some extent true if one looks at the analysis of the extent of Soviet problems by the mid-1980s and a few years later. In this respect, several economists were able to identify colossal weaknesses in the Soviet economy by the mid-to late 1980s.

If the issue is whether or not the economists were able to foretell the Soviet demise, the judgement must be different. I really cannot find any correct forecasts, much less predictions, by Sovietologists specializing in economic issues, that the Soviet Union was going to collapse. The only exception, and that case is hard to decide, was the Swedish Sovietologist Stefan Hedlund. He held a very negative view indeed of the Soviet Union in general, and of the new General Secretary in particular. This raises the question of how we are to judge the accuracy of a prognosis that was, in a sense, the personal wishes of the analyst come true. Since he, in this case, wanted the Soviet system to collapse, perhaps he was inclined to issue forecasts to this effect at regular intervals. Was this really a correct prognosis according to the definition presented in chapter 1 of this book? I believe that it was not.

An overall result of this assessment of Sovietology in four countries during the final years of the existence of the object of study is of a discipline that was very diverse indeed. Every effort has been made to include some of the most eminent scholars in each of the countries studied. What is striking are the very large differences that existed between these scholars on the issues under analysis here. These differences, to be sure, were much larger in several respects than just the nuances and shades that are to be expected of experts in the same field. In this case there were chasms between the scholars regarding questions of the character of the Soviet State and whether or not it was worthwhile to foretell the Soviet future; if prognoses were issued, these differed in important respects. Finally, there were enormous differences in opinion regarding whether or not the state was really reformable. The very diversity of the discipline makes it extremely difficult to assess the success or failure of Sovietology as an academic discipline. The discipline was to such an extent characterized by fundamental disagreements, even during what were really its last years of existence, that it is hard to be categorical about its essence.

Chapter 6
Conclusion:
To Analyse the Collapse of a State

6.1 Introduction

In its broadest sense this book assesses how three types of observers in four countries understood and analysed a very rare occurrence in the modern international system: the collapse of a state, a state that was classified as a superpower. This way of stating the analytical issue indicates two factors that illustrate how difficult it is to get such an assessment right. The first factor is that the very concept "state", with its connotations as one of the fundamental building blocks of the international system, indicates stability. The state system has been ever more stabilized since its inception after the Treaty of Westphalia in 1648, and particularly so in the 20th century, with the growth of international co-operation, most developed after the establishment of the United Nations in 1945.

Thereafter, it has been a very rare occurrence indeed that a state has collapsed. This very fact means that there is a kind of bias inherent in my assessment: it must be very difficult to foretell such an event. Since it is so difficult, it is not surprising that so many analysts failed to predict the collapse of the Soviet system. Indeed, it would have been very strange if the opposite had been the case and several of the analysts had been able to foretell what would happen. The second factor supporting this conclusion is that the Soviet State was conceived to be a very powerful one. The notion of "superpower" connotes even more strongly the ideas of stability and longevity than does the simple concept "state".

While the question of prediction, or forecast, is the most spectacular one that this book touches upon, the analysis of the Soviet Union under Gorbachev also raises several other issues. In this final chapter I explore five additional issues. The first has to do with the concept of foreign policy orientation. By this I mean the historical experience, political culture and other aspects that form the common perceptual lens through which politicians and other interested observers in a given country view the outside world. There are two aspects that I explore regarding this dimension in this final chapter. The first is: *is there such a thing as a foreign policy orientation that is reflected in the material analysed in chapters 3, 4 and 5 of this book?*

Did the politicians in France, Great Britain, Sweden and the United States view events in the Soviet Union in distinct ways due to the fact that they had varying foreign policy orientations? If so, did newspaper editorialists in elite newspapers also exhibit this tendency and/or did the Sovietologists write in a way that resembled the analysis presented by the politicians?

If the answer to the first fundamental question is yes, then the second question is, did this foreign policy orientation really count when it came to the matter at hand in this book; in other words did actors in the four countries diagnose the situation in the Soviet Union differently; did they explain events in that country in distinct ways, or make prognoses about what was going to happen, in ways that can be accounted for by the foreign policy orientation in their country? Alternatively, perhaps, did the foreign policy orientation exist but not really matter for the analysis of the Soviet Union?

A second aspect tackled here concerns perceptual variables, in particular the fundamental error of attribution. *Did the analysis of Soviet events under Gorbachev illustrate the working of the fundamental error of attribution?* In other words, is it possible, with the admittedly enormous benefit of hindsight, to state that the analysis of the Soviet Union during the last six years of that country's existence was in any way affected by the tendency of analysts to regard that country as an adversary? If so, there would be concomitant effects in underestimating the capability of that system to change and the tendency to explain away any actions that could be regarded as indications of positive intentions as simply being diversionary manoeuvres of an evil system? Since this factor is presumed to work solely on the individual level, its application is here reserved for the analysis of the Sovietologists.

A third theme of this final chapter concerns two concepts at the very centre of positivism, *explanation* and *prediction*. In this respect, the treatment in this chapter centres on the analysis of the academics who made it their profession to study the Soviet Union — the Sovietologists. *How did the Sovietologists explain the start of the Soviet reform process around 1985?* Do these explanations have anything more general to say in accounting for social and political events and processes? Do they represent a success for a perspective on political processes that is focused on the causal explanation, or, by contrast, is this a case where other methods of elucidation, based on perspectives other than positivism, might more effectively explain what happened in Moscow during those momentous years?

An even clearer assessment of positivism can be made in terms of the second concept, that of prediction. Does the case of the Soviet Union's collapse indicate that the positivist ambition, as exemplified in the study of international relations, to be able to foretell the future of social and political events is a fruitless one? What does it mean to "predict" something, as illustrated by the fate of the Soviet Union?

A fourth aspect is the use of models and theories, particularly in social scientific research. Are there lessons to be learned about the application of theories and models to the political processes in the Soviet Union during its final six years of existence? What — if anything — does this case say about the perennial problem in social science of finding, sometimes even constructing, and then applying theories and models to empirical political processes? Put another way, can the use of theories and models make it harder to understand the very events that they are intended to clarify?

A final theme in this concluding chapter is that this book has analysed the very first stage in what has become a transformation of the European security system. Looking back some twelve years from the time of this writing to the spring of 1988, the changes that have occurred since then are truly enormous. The Soviet Union and the Warsaw Pact are no more. NATO has enlarged, with three new members who were previously members of the Warsaw Pact. The European Union has resolved to start negotiations for membership with thirteen new states, three of which, Estonia, Latvia and Lithuania, were formerly republics in the Soviet Union. This book concludes with some reflections on what this study of the first stage of that revolution in the system of European security can teach us about how to understand and analyse political change.

6.2 Foreign Policy Orientation

The concept of foreign policy orientation is a tricky one. What does it mean when one says that a country exhibits such a tendency? In addition, if there is such a tendency, what does that signify for the way foreign events and processes are analysed in the country in question? Is there some causal mechanism at work here, by way of which the foreign policy orientation of a certain country strongly influences how the elites in that country view the world around them? Questions such as these have been studied in two dissertations at the Department of Political Science, Stockholm University.[1]

---

[1] See A. Robertson (1992): *National Prisms and Perceptions of Dissent*, Ph.D., diss. (Stockholm: Department of Political Science, Stockholm University) and K. Riegert (1998): *'Nationalising' Foreign Conflict: Foreign Policy Orientation as a Factor in News Reporting*, Ph.D. diss. (Stockholm: Department of Political Science, Stockholm University,).

To quote one result from one of these books: "The external orientations of Britain and the FRG clearly differed...in ways affecting the climate of opinion in which views about international affairs in general and INF deployments in particular were formed and disseminated."[2]

The analysis in this book gives further support to the basic notion of foreign policy orientation. As presented in section 1.4, I have operationalized the notion of foreign policy orientation as it applies to the analysis of the Soviet Union undertaken in France, Great Britain, Sweden and the United States. Broadly stated, there was fairly strong support for the existence of a specific foreign policy orientation in the analysis presented by the politicians, some support for it in the analysis in some of the newspapers, and no support for its existence in the analyses presented by the Sovietologists.

Foreign policy orientation played a very small role concerning the diagnosis of the situation in the Soviet Union in respect to foreign policy. In other words, a Swedish politician did not make the assessment that Soviet foreign policy had markedly changed at any different point in time than did his British counterpart. In all four countries, the politicians issued the statement that the Soviet Union had changed in its international behaviour during 1988. The only case that differs somewhat from the others in this respect is the U.S. This is probably best explained by the system of elections in that country. The fact of the U.S. presidential elections in November of 1988, and of the caution of the new President during his first few months in office, affected the public analysis of the Soviet Union in Washington so as to introduce more caution in the public statements after the Moscow summit of May-June 1988. For about a year after this meeting, official U.S. assessments were of a clearly more bland and cautious character than had been the case during the year before the Moscow summit.

Foreign policy orientation played an important role in accounting for the differing explanations offered by representatives of the four governments for why Mr. Gorbachev started the reforms. Here the self-perception of U.S. policy makers as representing the strongest power internationally meant that they tended to explain both of these events as largely caused by the policies of the United States. The British government, which was the one most closely allied with Washington during the period in question, had a similar explanation, in particular for the first of these two questions. The governments in Paris and Stockholm, by contrast, did not include the aspect of pressure from the United States upon Moscow as having contributed to the start of the reform process.

---

[2] Robertson, 1992, p. 267. "External orientation" in the quote is essentially the same concept as my "foreign policy orientation".

In this case, the explanatory perspective presented by the representatives of the U.S. government was fairly closely mirrored by the analyses published on the same questions in the editorial pages of two U.S. newspapers, *The New York Times* and *The Washington Post*. In other words, in explaining the causes behind both Mr. Gorbachev's reform policies and the demise of the Soviet system, the two U.S. newspapers exhibited what is here called a U.S. foreign policy orientation.

The analyses by the representatives of the United States displayed yet another aspect of that country's foreign policy orientation, namely, that of an open and explicit debate on security policy. The possible effects of this debate on the contents of the analysis of the Soviet Union should not be exaggerated, but it is clear that the number of statements, as well as the detail of the analysis presented in those statements, was much more developed in the United States than it was in any of the other three countries.

A further indication of foreign policy orientation came from the French material. This was most clearly manifested when the French Foreign Minister, on the occasion of Mr. Gorbachev's visit to Paris in October 1985, noted that it was significant that the Soviet leader made his first state visit outside the Warsaw Pact nations to France. This statement obviously reflected the foreign policy self-perception of the representative of a country that has, particularly since the presidency of Charles de Gaulle, regarded its role in international relations as a very distinct one. It should be noted that this tendency, like the one concerning the breadth and depth of foreign and security policy debate in the United States, are aspects that are of interest for the analysis of these two countries more generally, but the extent to which either of them really influenced the analysis of the Soviet Union undertaken in these two countries during the period in question here is less clear. Indeed, the evidence for a particular French foreign policy orientation is not overwhelming. This author's understanding of the French approach to international affairs still leads me to regard it as having manifested itself in the analysis of Mr. Gorbachev, but it is clear that other analysts may question this assessment.

The question of the striving of the Baltic Republics for greater self-determination and, ultimately, for independence has been especially focused. The differences found in this respect have not been very important in the case of the politicians. Representatives of all four countries came to support the wishes of the people in the Baltic Republics, but the emphasis given to this issue in the official material was greatest in Sweden and the United States. The differences were somewhat greater in the newspaper material.

Here, the two Swedish and the two U.S. newspapers gave thorough, and very sympathetic, coverage to the struggle of the Baltic Republics to break free from Moscow. The French and the British newspapers allotted somewhat less space to these issues, and three of them were also clearly sympathetic towards the Balts. *The Guardian* in Great Britain, however, expressed clear irritation over the "impatient" Balts who, in the view of the British paper, threatened more important developments, namely, the chances for success of Mr. Gorbachev's entire reform enterprise. This case illustrates how foreign policy orientation can influence the views of a newspaper. The plight of the Baltic Republics was clearly less than central for the paper than the aspirations of Mr. Gorbachev. *The Guardian* also maintained a positive attitude regarding the chances of success for the Soviet leader's policies for a very long time.

The concept of foreign policy orientation has, in other words, proved valuable in accounting for some aspects of the analysis made by the politicians, in particular, from the four countries analysed here. The same concept could also, although to a smaller extent, account for some systematic traits in the analyses presented by some of the newspapers in my sample. The influence of this type of factor should not be exaggerated, however. It played some role in explicating the general approach to international affairs exhibited by, for example, French officials. It was most directly relevant to my analysis in the explanation for the changes that the Soviet Union underwent, in two respects, during the period from 1985 until the end of 1991. The first occasion was when the new Secretary General of the Communist Party, Mikhail Gorbachev, started changing Soviet policies in several respects, notably foreign policy, some time after his coming to power in March 1985. The second change, or rather transformation, was when the Soviet Union collapsed in December 1991. It is significant that, for both issues, both U.S. politicians and the editorials in the two U.S. newspapers surveyed here, *The New York Times* and *The Washington Post,* emphasized the role of their country and its policies in more or less forcing the Soviet Union to change.

It also significant that there were important similarities in the analysis of particularly the first question, that of the new Soviet policies, by both the British politicians and by the conservative British paper in my sample, *The Times*. In both cases, the role of the United States in pressuring the Soviet Union is highlighted as one important reason behind the start of the Soviet reform process. An interesting contrast here is that *Le Figaro*, the French conservative newspaper — which was in so many other respects very similar to *The Times* in its analysis of Soviet affairs — did not mention the influence of pressure from the United States at all in its explanation of the start of the Soviet reform process. I regard this as a reflection of the important difference of relations between the country that the paper represents, on the one hand, and the United States, on the other. For Great Britain, the relationship with the United States, particularly as it concerned security issues, was crucial. For France, its independent posture in foreign and security policy was one vital aspect of its foreign policy orientation, thus making its representatives less likely to note any particular influence emanating from pressure from the United States upon the Soviet Union.

The comparison between Britain and the U.S. in explaining the changes in Soviet policy after 1985 showed the limits of existing similarities between the foreign policy orientations of the two countries in terms of assessing Soviet affairs. To U.S. politicians, as well as for the two newspapers, it was obvious that the United States and its policies had a direct and important influence on what was happening in the Soviet Union. This conviction seemed to be largely shared by the Conservative British politicians in power during the period studied and by the conservative British newspaper. There was no consensus in Britain regarding the importance of the United States in forcing change in the Soviet Union, however, since *The Guardian* never mentioned this factor.

The case of the analysis of Soviet affairs during a momentous six-year period has shown that the concept of foreign policy orientation can account for some of the differences in the ways analysts in different countries approached the examination of important events outside their own nation. In this case, this factor did not play any significant role concerning what I call the diagnostic element, that is, when the analysts in the respective countries stated that Soviet policies had indeed changed for good. It did play a role, however, in the explanations offered for why Mr. Gorbachev's reform policies started. It is perhaps significant that it was in the case of the most important power, the United States, where this factor seemed to be most significant.

This book, together with previous research, indicates that the foreign policy orientation of a country serves as a prism through which representatives of that country perceive the outside world. Further study of the more precise circumstances under which this might work, and the extent to which it may do so, seems warranted.

6.3 The Role of Perceptions

Since the publication of Robert Jervis' book *Perception and Misperception in International Politics* in 1976, the importance of perceptions and cognitions has been analysed in the study of international relations. This book has assessed the influence of such factors. In particular, I have tried to appraise the extent, if any, to which the fundamental error of attribution was at work in the analyses presented by any of the Sovietologists in my sample. As conceived here, this tendency is manifested when an analyst looks at an object that he or she regards as an adversary or an enemy. Any actions undertaken by that object of study which might otherwise be perceived as friendly are then typically explained as diversionary manoeuvres simply intended to mask the evil character of the adversary. As this tendency is hypothesized to work strictly at the level of the individual, I have not attempted to apply it to the other two categories of analysts; many influences apart from individual characteristics are at work in accounting for why the politicians say what they say, or why the editorialists print the analyses they do.

It is not easy to go from the general statement that such a thing as the fundamental error of attribution might exist to the empirical study of this phenomenon. In this book I have, I believe, encountered this tendency at work on one occasion. This was when Professor Richard Pipes, in a newspaper analysis published in the early autumn of 1989, stated that the "Russians are still coming". Professor Pipes asserted that Soviet military policies were still, at that late date, essentially the same as under Leonid Brezhnev. As spelled out in section 1.3.2, I regard it as unmistakable that by February-March of 1988, Soviet foreign and security policy had changed for good. This was after Moscow, for the first time, had agreed to destroy one whole class of nuclear weapons in the INF Treaty, and after it had agreed, also for the first time — with the withdrawal from Austria in 1955 as an arguable precedent — to withdraw from a country it had classified as belonging to its sphere of influence, Afghanistan. To state about 18 months after these two facts that the Soviet Union was essentially the same actor in international security policy as it had been under Leonid Brezhnev is, to this analyst, a reflection of the enemy image that Richard Pipes held of the Soviet Union, not the result of dispassionate academic analysis. I have stated before that this result is no surprise for the scholar who followed Sovietology during the Cold War, as Professor Pipes was a prominent specialist whose views were widely known. From the perspective of this book, in the sense of an assessment of Sovietology more broadly, I still find it remarkable that such a knowledgeable expert would cling to such views so late in the game in Moscow.

It is to be noted that this was the only case where I have found indications of the fundamental error of attribution at work in my material. It is not clear what this means for the study of the fundamental error of attribution in the way that individuals perceive other nations. It cannot be said that the workings of this tendency have been firmly established here, or that it has conclusively been proven that it is without influence. The most apt conclusion is probably that the fundamental error of attribution is worthy of further study, but that such a study should be undertaken only on very specific material, in which the individual perceptions of leaders and other analysts can be directly investigated. In this respect, the interesting book by Deborah Welch Larson[3] is one example of how this could be carried out; the likewise suggestive study by Daniel Heradstveit[4] is another.

The analysis of the Sovietologists in this book seems to point more generally to the need for further study of the importance of perception for the understanding of how at least scholars approach the analysis of other countries. Particularly during the period while the Soviet Union still existed, there were enormous differences, in almost all conceivable respects, between the analyses offered by the experts on the Soviet Union. I find it very difficult to believe that perceptions, seen broadly, do not account for some of the variance between the analyses offered by the Sovietologists during this period.

6.4 Explanation and Prediction

6.4.1 Explanation

As was made clear from the outset, this book has evaluated the analysis of events in the Soviet Union from a premise that can most correctly be characterized as positivist. I have looked for causal explanations behind the changes in Soviet policy. In addition, I have also assessed the extent, if any, to which the academics working on Soviet affairs saw it as their task to try

---

[3] D. W. Larson (1985): *Origins of Containment: A Psychological Explanation* (Princeton, NJ: Princeton University Press).
[4] D. Heradstveit (1979): *The Arab-Israeli Conflict: Psychological Obstacles to Peace* (Oslo: Universitetsforlaget).

to predict the future, and, if they did, the extent to which the prognoses they issued could be regarded as correct. In this section, the wider implications of my book in these respects are discussed.

I believe that the explanations provided by the Sovietologists do indeed indicate that the previously quoted statement: "At its core, real explanation always involves causal inferences" (G. King, R. Keohane, S. Verba, 1994, p. 75, note 1) still has considerable validity for the study of international relations and foreign policy.

The explanations offered for the two puzzles in this book — first for the start of the Soviet reform process and, second, for the Soviet collapse — do not yield any startling results. The academic experts surveyed here presented analyses that exemplify all of the categories that I illustrated in table 1.2. The non-functioning Soviet economy was the explanation most often put forward to account for the start of the reform process. The fact that the totalitarian system proved impossible to reform was the most important explanation for the collapse of the state offered by the Sovietologists. The Soviet economy also figured prominently in the second explanatory case, as did mistakes made by Gorbachev as leader. Gorbachev's personal role, and the role of the leader more generally, was also one of the most important reasons offered for why the reform process started in the first place.

It could be claimed that the cases that I have utilised here to evaluate whether or not the positivist enterprise still retains any relevance for the study of international relations in the first years of the 21st century are cases of a special kind, which made them particularly suitable for causal attempts at explication. I believe this claim to be correct. There is no assertion made here that positivism, in the sense of a search for causal explanations for social and political events and processes, is to be preferred in all realms of social science. To make just one illustration, it is my belief that the European integration process, centred on the European Union, typically involves political processes where the positivist explanatory logic is much less applicable. These processes are — to my mind — so complex that any simplified causal models cannot explain them. In the case of European integration, other approaches such as the ones indicated by the term "process tracing" are more likely to prove fruitful. What I am asserting, though, is that for explicating some events and processes, the approach called positivism still has much to contribute.

6.4.2 Prediction

A second aspect of the positivist credo, at least as applied to the field of international relations, has been that social scientists should strive to foretell the future of the events and processes that they are studying. Indeed, it has been claimed that such aspirations are part of the very essence of social science. I have evaluated the success of the 18 Sovietologists in my sample in this respect.

In my assessment of the degree of success or failure in foretelling events and processes in the Soviet Union I have attempted to be as precise as possible. One reason for this precision is that I believe that any real appraisal of the Sovietologists' study of the Soviet Union has to be based on precise and specific criteria in order to be scientifically sound. There have, in my view, been all too many assertions made regarding the inability of social science to foretell the end of the Soviet Union, and/or the end of the Cold War, without any basis in empirical investigation founded on strict academic rules of method. Chapter 5 in this book is intended to fill this gap, at least partly. I do not claim to have answered conclusively whether or not Sovietology was able to foretell the end of the Soviet Union, but I do claim to be able to say with more certainty than before whether any of these 18 Sovietologists were able to do so. My sample should also be sufficiently large to warrant some generalization across the discipline of Sovietology. My method, my criteria and my material are all explicit, which makes it possible to evaluate and question all three.

I have elected to distinguish between *prediction* and *forecast*. By the former, I mean an assertion that contains a time frame in which the event being foretold is predicted to occur within a specified time period. This is distinguished from a forecast, which is a looser type of statement where the scholar nevertheless, by the thrust of his or her statement, makes clear that he or she believes that a certain event or process is likely to occur. In other words, I regard the difference between the specificity of a prediction and the looser forecast as being crucial for the ability to assess the success of attempts at foretelling the future. To put it differently, what distinguishes the two versions of foretelling is the "certainty" of prediction versus the probabilistic nature of forecasts. I believe the distinction to be vital,[5] and

---

[5] See, on this point, J. R. Freeman and B. L. Job (1979): "Scientific Forecasts in International Relations: Problems of Definition and Epistemology", *International Studies Quarterly*, Vol. 23, No.1 (March), pp. 117-118; J. L. Gaddis (1992/93): "Theory and the End of the Cold War", *International Security*, Vol. 17, No. 3 (Winter), p. 2 and C. F. Doran (1999): "Why Forecasts Fail: The Limits and Potential of Forecasting in International Relations and Economics", *International Studies Review*, Vol. 1, Issue 2 (Summer), pp. 12-14.

that it is essential to look for both in assessing this aspect of, in particular, the social sciences. To my mind, both the precision of the scholar making the assessment of the success of foretelling, and the distinction between the two versions, are equally important if the "test" is to be a thorough one.

This book, particularly as it concerns the Sovietologists, has shown that there was only one case of a specific prediction in the material surveyed. This prediction was not, however, directed at the likely future of the Soviet Union, but rather related the personal future of Mr. Gorbachev. This means that Marshall Goldman's statement of March 1987 that he did not believe that the Soviet leader would last four years in office is of less interest for my purposes. Another aspect that, to this author, further lessens the value of the statement by Marshall Goldman is that he was clearly one of the Sovietologists who, in the political atmosphere of a Cold War between the United States and the Soviet Union in the 1980s, tended to blur the distinction between academic analysis and policy-relevant assertions. As demonstrated by Bertil Nygren (see Nygren, 1992, pp. 74-82 and 154-175 in particular), the role of many Sovietologists based in the U.S. was a peculiar one during the latter part of the Cold War, in particular. Given the immense importance that the U.S.-Soviet relationship was perceived to have in the U.S. polity, the tendency towards politicization of the study of Sovietology, already existing in the U.S., can be said to have increased with the coming to power of Mr. Gorbachev. I regard Marshall Goldman as one of those Sovietologists for whom the role of commentator on policy matters was a very important one during the period under scrutiny here. To put it more precisely, I cannot escape the suspicion that Marshall Goldman's assessments of Soviet affairs, in particular when they were as public as a congressional hearing, were clearly influenced by a wish to be classified as an "interesting Sovietologist, valuable on the media circuit".

There were also four cases of forecasts, which were of a more probabilistic character than predictions, to the effect that the Soviet Union was in decline and was bound to disintegrate. In addition, two of the newspapers, both with conservative ideologies, *The Times* of London and *Le Figaro* in Paris, both forecast the dissolution of the Soviet empire well before the event took place. The fundamental question is, what do this attempted prediction and these (to me) acceptable forecasts mean for the aspiration that a social scientist should attempt to forecast the future? Do they mean that such aspirations have been proven valid by the example of the collapse of the Soviet Union? Do they, instead, mean that it is very problematic to state that one has indeed been "correct" in prognosticating the end of something that one obviously detests, as was manifestly the case with most of those analysts who were able to foretell that the Soviet Union was going to disintegrate?

To my mind, four of the six analysts[6] who prophesied the end of the Soviet Empire were very critical indeed of the Soviet system. This raises the question of whether their assessments can really be seen as the triumph of dispassionate analysis or, rather, as the foretelling of a future that they strongly wished to come true. The very existence of this important doubt makes me inclined to believe that the academics' forecasts, admirable as they are, cannot be regarded as strong support for the social scientific aspiration of reaching the ability to predict. It would be going too far, however, to assert that this negativism towards the Soviet system completely negates the value of these four correct forecasts. The two academics displayed a very sophisticated understanding of the system, and the editorial pages of the two conservative papers were remarkably prescient. As is so often the case, it could perhaps be said that the Soviet Union was, in this case as well, a very special example.

Two cases of forecasts remain to be assessed. They were written by the late Alexandre Bennigsen, in 1983, and by Pierre Hassner, in 1989 and 1990. In the first case, Professor Bennigsen wrote the following, in a book co-authored with Marie Broxup:

> Barring a major crisis — such as a foreign war — the present status quo in the Soviet Union will be uncompromisingly preserved for as long as possible. The final, inescapable, violent crisis will be delayed, but for how long? (Bennigsen with Marie Broxup, 1983, p. 152.)

This was but the most explicit formulation by a scholar who clearly viewed the Soviet empire as a system that was bound to implode. I have not been able to find any more detailed reasoning by Professor Bennigsen that amplifies his view on this matter at any length. It is not possible, however, to issue any caveats about this forecast as I have done for the previous forecasts and the single prediction. To put it crudely, Professor Bennigsen was convinced that the multinational Soviet empire was a state structure that was bound to collapse, and eight to nine years after issuing this prognosis he was proven right. His precision in terms of time frame is disturbingly reminiscent of what has been called the "sooner-or-later" trap. On the other hand, his analysis is at least close to the mark in terms of identifying one of the vital reasons why the Soviet system did eventually collapse: its inability

---

[6] In this first category, I place Kristian Gerner, Zbigniew Brzezinski and the editorial pages of *The Times* and *Le Figaro*. It is more difficult to characterize Pierre Hassner or André Bennigsen in this clear-cut way.

to integrate non-Russians into the state. It has been argued in the scholarly debate on how to explain the fall of the Soviet Union that, to the extent that national issues played a role in accounting for the demise of the state, this was more because of the actions of the Western Republics, such as the three Baltic Republics and the Ukraine, than it was because of the actions of Republics dominated by Muslims. While this, to my mind, diminishes the value of Bennigsen's forecast to some extent, it does not eliminate it completely.

The second scholar who was able to foretell the fate of the Soviet Union, and whose scholarship is not shot through by an explicit anti-Sovietism, was Pierre Hassner. Professor Hassner had, by late 1989, changed his previous view that the socialist system in Eastern Europe, and particularly in the Soviet Union, was the most immovable of systems. By that time, he regarded what he called "the death of Marxism-Leninism" as "inevitable" (Hassner, 1990a, p. 20). This was a correct forecast that fulfils all the requirements I have specified in chapter 1 of this book. Professor Hassner, born in Romania, to me represented the Sovietologists who, growing up with a Marxist perspective, retained at least important elements of this thinking during their careers as mature scholars. I find it impossible to accuse Pierre Hassner of any anti-Sovietism that may be conceived to cloud his judgement.

One additional result that is of overall interest for this book is the position taken by the U.S. Sovietologist Jerry Hough. Hough not only did not issue any prognoses to the effect that the Soviet Union was going to collapse; he explicitly derided those analysts who did say this well into 1991. There are, to my mind, two explanations for this obvious lack of foresight in Professor Hough's analysis. The first is that Hough's undeniably excellent understanding of the inner workings of the Soviet political system led him to overemphasize what he perceived to be Gorbachev's unsurpassed mastery of the intricacies of that system. Hough seems to have looked too closely at the micro aspects of the Soviet political process while for too long ignoring the accumulating evidence that, in a macro sense, the whole political system was collapsing. The other explanation for Hough's analysis belongs to the following section on the role of theories and models in assessing Soviet developments.

To this scholar, this assessment tells us to be very careful, and very humble, about our ability to make prognostications about future developments in politics. I agree with James Rosenau's appraisal that "We look ahead in probabilistic terms and any claim to knowing exactly what will happen is sheer pretense" (Rosenau, 1997, p. 17). None of the 18 scholars that I have analysed was able to predict, based on a scholarly analysis, what was going to happen to the Soviet Union. There were a few — it is arguable how many — who reached the level of "looking ahead in probabilistic terms". To my mind, that is the limit of what scholars can do when analysing international relations and foreign policy.[7] We can make the parameters within which political developments are likely to develop somewhat clearer. We may also be able to exclude developments as impossible, or at least extremely unlikely. However, to strive for the ability to make prognoses is, in my view, a task that will prove fruitless. I am also very doubtful as to whether we really ought to have such aspirations.

6.5 The Use of Theories and Models for Empirical Analyses

Theories and models are used in different ways by scholars from all three disciplines represented among the Sovietologists assessed in this book — history, economics and political science. Given the explicit perspective of political science that is applied here, the evaluation of the role of theories and models for diagnosing, explaining and predicting events in the Soviet Union is done using the methods of this discipline. The question is whether the use of such analytical devices can be seen to have had a detrimental influence on the analyses presented by any of the 18 Sovietologists in my sample, in any of the crucial three respects just outlined.

There are two such cases, both of them Sovietologists working in the U.S. The case of Jerry Hough is, to me, the most clear-cut one. Hough believed that the Soviet Union was — to put a bit more crudely than he would perhaps have accepted — a system that could and should be studied using the analytical instruments of modern social science. One basic method that Hough used was thus comparative politics, where the political and economicprocesses in the Soviet Union were explicitly assessed in comparison to those of other countries that — in Professor Hough's estimation — had gone through similar political and economic processes. The cases most often used for comparison where those of the East Asian "Tigers", some five or six countries that had experienced rapid

---

[7] For an argument that the collapse of the Soviet Union was impossible to foretell due to "the contingent nature of the outcome" see W.C. Wohlforth (1998): "Reality Check: Revising Theories of International Politics in Response to the End of the Cold War", *World Politics*, Vol. 50, No. 4 (July), pp. 650-680. The quote is from p. 669.

economic growth and at least some democratic development as well during the 1970s and 1980s. The most prominent examples used by Jerry Hough were South Korea and to some extent Singapore.

The second element in Hough's analysis was the use of modernization theory, where the examples just mentioned were surmised as following the same path from a not very developed economic system, with reforms being added and then the economy "taking off". Hough saw South Korea as the most apt comparison for the Soviet Union under Gorbachev. It is very obvious in retrospect that both of these analytical devices were, if not completely wrong, then at least not very applicable. This seems particularly true of modernization theory. Hough's statements about where the economic reforms in the Soviet Union would lead the country were persistently wrong, and he continued to issue forecasts that were far too optimistic in terms both of economic and political developments well into 1991.

The second case of what I believe to be a somewhat misguided use of a social-scientific model is less clear-cut: Seweryn Bialer's use of a version of elite models. Bialer believed for a very long time that the Soviet system was characterized by stability, a stability that was largely due to the particulars of the elite, and the recruitment process into that elite, in the Soviet Union. Even if the use of this model did not lead Bialer as far wrong as modernization theory led Jerry Hough, still the stability identified by Bialer was not the most appropriate view of the Soviet Union of the late 1980s. It is notable that in both cases the problems with the use of the analytical devices occurred most prominently when it came to the ability to see how far the changes might lead; in other words, they affected the dimension of prediction.

I believe it to be significant that the only two cases of an exaggerated reliance on theories and models that I found among the 18 Sovietologists concerned U.S. scholars. This is not to say that no Sovietologist in any other country utilized theories and models; on the contrary. The Swedes Kristian Gerner and Stefan Hedlund used theories, particularly in their 1989 work *Ideology and Rationality in the Soviet Model: A Legacy for Gorbachev*. British Sovietologists Archie Brown and Alex Pravda also allude to relevant theories and models in their publications. In none of these cases, however, was any theory or model used in such a way that its application served to lead the analyst to overlook crucial elements in the empirical processes they studied because these elements did not fit easily into the model.

This author is in this respect — regarding the unfortunate utilization of theories and models to the study of international relations by U.S.

scholars in political science — reminded of one other case where I get the sense of a similar misapplication. This has to do with some elements of the study in the U.S. of political processes in the European Union. It is striking how U.S. political science scholars, in their books and scientific papers during the last decade or so, have presented analyses of events in the EU that, to this author, have been singularly off the mark, precisely because of the use of models with a purportedly general application. These models have typically been developed in the study of politics in the United States. Their application to the study of the EU strikes me as often incorrect, due to the fact that models of rationality are to my mind seldom, if ever, fruitfully applied to the study of a multifaceted, amorphous polity such as that of the European Union. There is of course no way of really assessing whether this impression is correct or not, at least at the present stage of EU development.

It should be added that none of the above should be taken as a belief on the part of this author that theories and models are inapplicable to the study of international relations. On the contrary, I am a firm believer in the application of these analytical devices to this endeavour. What this assessment indicates, however, is that the misguided use of theories and models can lead the scholar to the wrong analysis. To the extent that theories and models purport to clarify empirical processes, they must simply be applicable to the cases under study. When this application is misguided, the analysis will suffer. I argue that this was the case for two Sovietologists in this study. It is clear that these are not the only two cases of modern social science where such an assessment is true.

6.6 The Limits of Expertise: Analysing the Evolving European Security Structure

This book has looked at the first stage of what was to become a transformation of the European security system. A structure that in 1985 seemed locked in concrete tumbled completely during a period of less than 10 years. Many scholarly books and articles have been published on what happened from 1985 onward. There are fewer studies that, like this one, attempt to evaluate how politicians, editorialists and academics in other countries reacted to the processes that Mikhail Gorbachev came to symbolize in 1985. To me, the study of the process of change in the European security structure is a vital and extremely multifaceted task for scholars. This book is a contribution to the study of the first stage of that process of change: the analysis of Gorbachev's foreign policy.

My study started from the question of whether or not different countries had diverse ways of looking at the outside world — distinctive foreign policy orientations — and, if they did, whether this mattered for how they assessed important events in the world. I further assumed that the first stage of a political reaction in a country to external shifts was a stage in which there would be a public interplay between political officeholders, editorialists in elite newspapers and the academic experts on the issues at hand — in this case the Sovietologists. I wanted to find out if it was indeed the case that these three categories of analysts were all influenced by the same foreign policy orientations, or if other factors were at work in determining the contents of their analyses. As an academic long fascinated with the rather peculiar brand of scholarship that Sovietology seemed to represent to me, I also wished to delve deeper into some of the issues surrounding that discipline. These issues have been widely discussed in the scholarly as well as the public debate on the success or failure of scholars to anticipate, as well as to explain, what was happening in the Soviet Union while it happened, and to account for these events after the Soviet State had been dissolved in 1991. Were any of these experts able to foretell what was going to happen to policies in Moscow, I asked myself? How did these scholars explain what was going on in Moscow while it happened and afterwards?

The results of my book appear to me to be more interesting with respect to the assessment of the scholarship than with respect to foreign policy orientation. In the latter respect, I have found clear indications that this somewhat amorphous concept explained some of the characteristics of how analysts in different countries vary in their analyses of events abroad. These differences should not be exaggerated, however, and they were not important when it came to the timing of when analysts stated that Gorbachev was really different; that he had really changed Soviet foreign policies. This all happened in the second half of 1988 or early 1989. The timing of this nearly universal assessment seems possible to explain, at least partly, with reference to the international role of the media. To put it crudely, since everyone was saying that Gorbachev was different, he must really have been different.

Foreign policy orientation is more interesting, judging from my results, if we concentrate on how analysts in different countries explain the causes of changes in foreign countries. It is no coincidence, if seen from this perspective, that U.S. politicians and editorialists underlined the importance of their own country in inducing the Soviets to change policies. Nor is it any coincidence that the Conservative British government, as well as the editorial page of a prominent conservative paper in London, to a large degree supported this interpretation. Further, the same tendency seemed to be at work when none of the French analysts, in either the political or the editorialist category, highlighted the role of the United States in this respect. In other words, analysts in different countries who participated in the more elitist foreign policy debate were influenced by their country's foreign policy orientation in explaining how other countries changed their (foreign) policies.

It seems clear that such differences may pose problems when, for instance, governments of various countries wish to co-ordinate their foreign and security policies more closely. If the representatives from two, let alone more, countries cannot really agree on how to explain the basic characteristics of the world around them, it seems problematic to expect that they will be able to agree on solutions to common problems and positions to be taken with respect to other actors around them.

This tendency would seem to be at work, at least to some extent, in two contexts in the Europe of the early 21st century. One of these contexts is the European Union, whose fifteen members are striving towards at the very least a more developed parallelism in their foreign, and now increasingly also their security, policies. The results of this book suggest that even countries sharing many traits do demonstrate quite different analyses of the world around them. Such differences are not a good basis on which to construct common solutions to foreign policy issues.

The second context is probably even more relevant to the analysis in this book. I refer to the enlargement of NATO. This is a process that has completed one stage, and where another stage is under active consideration for 2002. One crucial variable in the equation that politicians, and other participants, debate about this process is the reaction of Russia, the successor state to the Soviet Union, to the expansion of NATO ever closer to that country's borders. The questions then become: how will Russia react to this process, and what will this reaction, in turn, mean for the long-term chances for stability in the European security system? It seems clear that any analysis of such questions would require the ability to forecast the future developments in Russian foreign policy, as well as in the broader European security system. One school of thought, the official one, perhaps best represented by the U.S. and the German governments, insists that this process will lead to the extension of the zone of stability into more sectors of the European continent. The Russian reaction, on this view, will be handled in a constructive way by including Russia in various pan-European, as well as more regional, co-operative projects. The most prominent among these is the NATO-Russia Permanent Joint Council.[8] This school of thought can be illustrated by quoting from one of many speeches by Secretary of State Madeleine Albright on this topic during 1997 and early 1998:

> ...a larger NATO will make America safer by expanding the area of Europe where wars do not happen. By making clear that we will fight, if necessary to defend our new allies, we make it less likely that we will ever be called upon to do so.
> Is central Europe in immediate jeopardy today? It is not. But can we safely say that our interest in its security will never be threatened? History and experience do not permit us to say that. ...[9]

Another school of thought, perhaps most prominent in the debate in the United States, argues that NATO expansion will, instead, ultimately lead to dangerous consequences for the stability of the European security system. Professor Michael Mandelbaum of Johns Hopkins University represented this second strand of thought:

> NATO expansion is the equivalent of the Gulf of Tonkin that authorized the war in Vietnam. ...Like the commitment to Vietnam, if NATO expansion is launched we will be unable to go backward, because we can't expel these countries; unable to go forward, because the Europeans are not ready to expand NATO to the Russian border; and unable to stay where we are, because we have vowed to expand NATO to the Russian border and not to do so would be to draw a new dividing line in Europe.[10]

Once again, we see a wide-ranging debate concerning the fluid security situation in Europe. Once again, politicians and academics have issued forecasts about complex developments that have an air of certainty to them. And once again, Russia, the successor state to the Soviet Union, is prominently involved in these prognostications. This book does not pretend to be any guide to the future of NATO. But if the scrutiny in this book about

---

[8] For the text of the Founding Act on Mutual Relations, Cooperation and Security between NATO and the Russian Federation see "http://www.nato.int/docu/basictxt/fndact-a.htm".

[9] Secretary of State Madeleine Albright, statement to the Senate Foreign Relations Committee, February 24, 1998, as retrieved from the State Department's homepage on the Internet: "http://secretary.state.gov/www/statements/1998/980224.htm".

[10] Professor Michael Mandelbaum as quoted in Thomas L. Friedman: "Gulf of Tonkin II", *The New York Times*, March 31, 1998.

a previous stage of analysis of the developments in security policy in Europe has come to any clear result, it is at least this: politicians, as well as academics, would do well to be quite humble when they attempt to foretell the likely consequences of different developments or policies. Neither scholars nor politicians have the analytic instruments to be able to predict what will happen to international politics and foreign policy. On the margin, the odd scholar might be able to issue forecasts that will be largely correct.

The crucial question, however, is how are we to determine which scholar has the correct analysis and the correct prognoses? At this time (summer 2001), it is probably best for the non-committed observer to regard both of these beliefs concerning the future of security in NATO with equal scepticism. The decision to enlarge NATO was taken in 1997, and the three new members, Hungary, Poland and the Czech Republic, entered formally in 1999. The most negative forecasts issued by the opponents of NATO enlargement have been at least tentatively proven to be overstated. The question of NATO enlargement lives on with a new decision to come in late 2002. Perhaps the question of Russian reactions is not quite as acute as it was during the first enlargement, but in essence the two schools of thought still exist.

This caution about the limits of expertise seems to be valid in the two senses previously applied in this book. To my mind, it works for the interested layperson looking for the True Expert, in whom one can place trust in the depth and reliability of her analysis. It works also in the case of the politicians who look for the academic specialist to make good input into the policy-making process. This is not to say that all of the politicians do look for such specialists, just to say that when they do, there are no clear criteria by which to decide who is and who isn't a genuine expert.

The overall conclusion of this book is by no means that one should disregard expertise, whether in the true academic context or in the case of politicians and laypersons. There are, to be sure, many knowledgeable experts in many fields of international relations at work in all four countries surveyed in this book. The conclusion is rather that in whatever setting one tries to evaluate the quality of their diagnoses, their explanations and their prognoses, one should be aware that there are clear limits to expertise, in particular when it comes to forecasting. At most, it is possible to sketch the probable routes along which developments will move in complex international policy processes. It is even more possible, for the non-biased analyst, to identify that something important has indeed happened in such circumstances. It is easier still, after the fact, to construct plausible explanations for what has happened, even in multifaceted processes. But there is no self-evident criterion to use when one tries to find the most reliable expert in social and political affairs.

Appendix 1
The Sovietologists

France

Alexandre Bennigsen, historian, employed at Centre National de la Recherche Scientifique and École des hautes études en Sciences Sociales, both in Paris; died June 1988;
Alain Besançon, political scientist, employed at École des hautes études en Sciences Sociales Paris;
Hélène Carrère d'Encausse, professor of political science, employed at the Institut d'Études Politiques, Paris, member of l'Académie française;
Pierre Hassner, first philosopher, later international relations (political science), employed at Fondation National des Sciences Politiques, Paris.

Sweden

Anders Åslund, professor of economics, employed at the Stockholm School of Economics, later at the Carnegie Endowment for International Peace, Washington, DC;
Kristian Gerner, professor of history, first employed at the University of Lund, later at the University of Uppsala;
Stefan Hedlund, professor of economics, first employed at the University of Lund, later at the University of Uppsala;
Lena Jonson, political scientist, first employed at the University of Gothenburg, later at the Swedish Institute for International Affairs.

Great Britain

Archie Brown, professor of political science, Oxford University;
John Erickson, military history, University of Edinburgh;
Alec Nove, professor of economics, Glasgow University; died 1994;
Alex Pravda, political scientist, Oxford University.

United States

Seweryn Bialer, professor of political science, Columbia University, retired;
Zbigniew Brzezinski, professor of political science, Columbia University, National Security Adviser to president Jimmy Carter, 1977-1981, Center for Strategic and International Studies (CSIS);
Alexander Dallin, professor of history, first at Columbia University, later at Stanford University, died 2000;
Marshall Goldman, professor of economics, Wellesley College, and Russian Research Center, Harvard University;
Jerry Hough, professor of political science, Duke University, fellow the Brookings Institution;
Richard Pipes, professor of history, Harvard University, retired.

Appendix 2
Empirical Material

2A Publications by the Sovietologists

Åslund, A. (1988), "Många små steg: En planekonomi under omdaning (Many Small Steps: A Planned Economy Under Reconstruction)", *Den Sovjetiska Utmaningen: Reformer och politik under Gorbatjov (The Soviet Challenge: Reforms and Politics Under Gorbachev).* Edited by Arvidsson, C. and Fogelklou, A. Stockholm: Norstedts, pp. 86-144.

Åslund, A. (1989a), "Can the Soviet Union Be Saved?", *The Washington Post.* August 14, p. A13.

Åslund, A. (1989b), *Gorbachev's Struggle for Economic Reform.* London: Pinter.

Åslund, A. (1989c), "How Small is Soviet National Income?", *The Impoverished Superpower: Perestroika and the Soviet Military Burden.* Edited by Rowen, H.S. and Wolf, C. San Francisco, CA: Institute for Contemporary Studies, pp. 13-61.

Åslund, A. (1990), "Gorbachev Governing on Razor's Edge", *The Washington Post.* January 28, p. C01.

Åslund, A. (1991a), "Gorbachev, *Perestroyka*, and Economic Crisis", *Problems of Communism.* Vol. XL, pp. 18-41.

Åslund, A. (1991b), "The Soviet Economy After the Coup", *Problems of Communism.* Vol. XL, pp. 44-52.

Åslund, A. (1992a), "A Critique of Soviet Reforms", *The-Post Soviet Economy: Soviet and Western Perspectives.* Edited by Åslund, A. London: Pinter, pp. 167-180.

Åslund, A. (1992b), "Russia's Road from Communism", *Daedalus.* 121, pp. 77-95.

Åslund, A. (1993), *The Former Soviet Union in Transition: Study Papers.* Washington, DC.: U.S. Government Printing Office, pp 184-195.

Bennigsen, A. (1988), "Unrest in the World of Soviet Islam", *Third World Quarterly.* Vol. 10, pp. 770-786.

Bennigsen, A. and Broxup, M. (1983), *The Islamic Threat to the Soviet State.* London: Croom Helm.

Bennigsen, A., Henze P. B., Tanham G. K. and Wimbush S. E. (1989), *Soviet Strategy and Islam.* New York: St. Martin's Press.

Bennigsen, A. and Wimbush S.E. (1985), *Mystics and commissars: Sufism in the Soviet Union.* London: Hurst.

Bennigsen, A. and Wimbush S.E. (1986), *Muslims of the Soviet Empire: a guide.* London: Hurst.

Besançon, A. (1987), *Une generation.* Paris: Juillard, 1987.

Besançon, A. (1990) ,"Les Atouts de Gorbatchev: Une Evaluation", *Apres Gorbatchev.* Edited by Benoist, J.-M and Wajsman, P. Paris: La Table Ronde, pp. 59-110.

Besançon, A. and Thom F. (1987), "What's Happening in Moscow", *The National Interest.* No. 8, pp. 27-30.

Bialer, S. (1983a), "Realism Toward Salvador, Nicaragua", *The New York Times.* March 6, p. Section 5, p. 19.

Bialer, S. (1983b), "Our Soviet Policy: No Either/Or We Need a Mix of Detente, Containment and Confrontation", *The Washington Post.* June 26.

Bialer, S. (1983c), "The Soviets Really Need Their Nukes: They'll Never Give Up What Gives Them Power", *The Washington Post.* May 8.

Bialer, S. (1984a), "A Wounded Russian Bear Is Dangerous. Reagan's Soothing Words Won't Help Moscow May Prefer a New Cold War", *The Washington Post.* January 22.

Bialer, S. (1984b), "Kremlin, Insecure, Might Increase Risks", *The New York Times.* February 5.

Bialer, S. (1985a), "The Rise of a Red Star. How Gorbachev Seized the Kremlin's Brass Ring", *The Washington Post.* March 17.

Bialer, S. (1985b), "Gorbachev's Tightening Grip on Power", *The New York Times.* July 14.

Bialer, S. (1986a), *The Soviet Paradox: External Expansion, Internal Decline.* New York: Knopf.

Bialer, S. (1986b), "Gorbachev's Preference for Technocrats", *The New York Times.* February 11.

Bialer, S. (1987), "Gorbachev's Move", *Foreign Policy.* No. 68, pp. 59-87.

Bialer, S. (1988a), "Gorbachev's Program of Change: Sources, Significance, Prospects", *Gorbachev's Russia and American Foreign Policy.* Edited by Bialer, S. and Mandelbaum, M. Boulder, CO & London: Westview, pp. 231-299.

Bialer, S. (1988b), "The Soviet Union and the West", *Gorbachev's Russia and American Foreign Policy.* Edited by Bialer, S. and Mandelbaum, M. Boulder, CO & London: Westview, pp. 457-490.

Bialer, S. (1988c), "The Yeltsin Affair", *Politics, Society, and Nationality Inside Gorbachev's Russia.* Edited by Bialer, S. Boulder, CO & London: Westview, pp. 91-120.

Bialer, S. (1989), "Domestic and International Factors in the Formation of Gorbachev's Reforms", *Journal of International Affairs.* 42, pp. 283-297 as reprinted in *Articles on Russian and Soviet History, 1500-1991: Volume 14: The Gorbachev Era* Edited and with an Introduction by Dallin, A. (New York & London: Garland Publishing, 1992), pp. 31-45. (The reprint is an exact copy of the original article.)

Bialer, S. (1991a), "Is Socialism Dead?", *Soviet-American Relations After the Cold War.* Edited by Bialer, S. and Jervis, R. Durham, NC and London: Duke University Press, pp. 98-106.

Bialer, S. (1991b), "The Death of Soviet Communism", *Foreign Affairs.* Vol. 70, pp. 166-181.

Bialer, S. and Afferica J. (1982/83), "Reagan and Russia", *Foreign Affairs.* Vol. 61 pp. 249-271.

Bialer, S. and Afferica J. (1982), "The Bear Doesn't Dance To Our Tune", *The New York Times.* December 12.

Bialer, S. and Afferica J. (1985), "The Genesis of Gorbachev's World", *Foreign Affairs.* Vol. 64 (1985), pp. 605-644.

Bialer, S. and Mandelbaum M. (1989), *The Global Rivals: The Soviet-American Contest for Supremacy.* London: I.B. Tauris & Co. Ltd.

Brown, A. (1985), "Gorbachev: New Man in the Kremlin", *Problems of Communism.* Vol. XXXIV, pp. 1-23.

Brown, A. (1986), "Change in the Soviet Union", *Foreign Affairs.* Vol. 64, pp. 1048-1065.

Brown, A. (1986/87), "Soviet Political Developments and Prospects", *World Policy Journal.* (Winter), pp. 55-87.

Brown, A. (1987), "Gorbachev and Reform of the Soviet System", *Political Quarterly.* April/June, pp. 139-151.

Brown, A. (1988), "The Soviet Political Scene: The Era of Gorbachev?", *Gorbachev and the Soviet Future.* Edited by Lerner, L. and Treadgold, D. W. Boulder, CO: Westview, pp. 21-43.

Brown, A. (1989a), "Power and Policy in Time of Leadership Transition", *Political Leadership.* Edited by Brown, A. London: Macmillan, pp. 163-217.

Brown, A. (1989b), "Policy Change in the Soviet Union", *World Policy Journal.* (Summer), pp. 469-501 as excerpted in *The Soviet System in Crisis: A Reader of Western and Soviet Views.* Edited by Dallin, A. and Lapidus, G. W. Boulder, CO: Westview, 1991, pp. 116-129,.

Brown, A. (1990), "Perestroika and the Political System", *Perestroika: Soviet Domestic and Foreign Policies.* Edited by Hasegawa, T. and Pravda, A. London: Sage, pp. 56-87.

Brown, A. (1992a), "Introduction", *New Thinking in Soviet Politics.* Edited by Brown, A. London: Macmillan, pp. 1-11.

Brown, A. (1992b), "New Thinking on the Soviet Political System", *New Thinking in Soviet Politics.* Edited by Brown, A. London: Macmillan, pp. 12-27.

Brown, A. (1996), *The Gorbachev Factor.* Oxford/New York: Oxford University Press.

Brzezinski, Z. (1983a), "Tragic Dilemmas of Sovet World Power", *Encounter.* December, pp. 10-17.

Brzezinski, Z. (1983b), "2 Missions, Common Strategy", *The New York Times.* January 30.

Brzezinski, Z. (1984a), "The Future of Yalta", *Foreign Affairs.* Vol. 63, pp. 279-302.

Brzezinski, Z. (1984b), "Moving from standoff to an interim accord", *The New York Times.* January 29.

Brzezinski, Z. (1985a), "Linking Two Crises", *The New York Times.* October 6.

Brzezinski Z. (1985b), "Overview of East-West Relations", *The Washington Quarterly.* Vol. 8, pp. 31-37.

Brzezinski, Z. (1986a), *Game Plan. How to Conduct the U.S.-Soviet Contest.* Boston, MA/New York: Atlantic Monthly Press.

Brzezinski, Z. (1986b), "Reagan is Leaving an Ominous Legacy in Foreign Policy", *The Washington Post.* October 5.

Brzezinski, Z. (1987a), "The U.S.-Soviet relationship: paradoxes and prospects", *Strategic Review.* Vol. 15, pp. 11-18.

Brzezinski, Z. (1987b), "Marxism: old order in disorder", *The Los Angeles Times.* October 18.

Brzezinski, Z. (1987c), "The Crisis of Communism: The Paradox of Political Participation", *The Washington Quarterly.* Vol. 10, pp. 167-174.

Brzezinski, Z. (1987d), "National strategy and arms control", *The Washingon Quarterly.* Vol. 10, pp. 5-11.

Brzezinski, Z. (1988a), "It's premature to bury the cold war. (influence of Moscow summit)", *The Los Angeles Times.* June 5.

Brzezinski, Z. (1988b), "Entering the Age of Defense: After 70 Years of Offensive Supremacy, the Tide of War Has Turned", *The Washington Post.* October 2.

Brzezinski, Z. (1989a), *The Grand Failure. The Birth and Death of Communism in the Twentieth Century.* New York: Charles Scribner's Sons.

Brzezinski, Z. (1989b), "A proposition the Soviets shouldn't refuse. (Is the Cold war over?)", *The New York Times.* March 13.

Brzezinski, Z. (1989c), "Will the Soviet empire self-destruct? Four scenarios for failure", *The New York Times Magazine.* February 26.

Brzezinski, Z. (1989d), "The Wall Falls: If Gorbachev Keeps Moving, America Should Help Out", *The Washington Post.* November 12.

Brzezinski, Z. (1989e), "Ending the Cold War", *The Washington Quarterly.* Vol. 12, pp. 29-34.

Brzezinski, Z. (1990), "For Eastern Europe, a $25 Billion Aid Package", *The New York Times.* March 7.

Brzezinski, Z.(1991a), "The Taiwan solution. (Should the Soviet Union Be Saved?)", *The Washington Post.* March 4.

Brzezinski, Z. (1991b), "Help the new Russian revolution.... (Soviet Union seeks economic aid)", *The New York Times.* July 14.

Carrère d'Encausse, H. *L'Empire éclaté.* Paris: Flammarion, 1978.

Carrère d'Encausse, H. *Le Grand Frère.* Paris: Flammarion, 1983.

Carrère d'Encausse, H. *Ni paix, ni guerre: Le nouvel Empire soviétique ou du bon usage de la détente.* Paris: Flammarion, 1986.

Carrère d'Encausse, H. *Le grand defi: Bolcheviks et nations 1917-1930.* Paris: Flammarion, 1987.

Carrère d'Encausse, H. *Le malheur russe: Essai sur le meurtre politique.* Paris: Fayard, 1988.

Carrère d'Encausse, H. *"L'U.R.S.S. Eclatée", Après Gorbatchev.* Edited by Benoist, J.-M. and Wajsman, P. Paris: La Table Ronde, 1990, pp. 111-136.

Carrère d'Encausse, H. *La gloire des nations ou la fin de l'Empire soviétique.* Paris: Fayard, 1990.

Carrère d'Encausse, H. *Victorieuse Russie.* Paris: Fayard, 1992.

Dallin, A. (1982), "Soviet and East European Studies in the United States", *Soviet and East European Studies in the International Framework.* Edited by Buchholz, A. Berlin: Berlin Verlag, pp. 11-31.

Dallin, A. (1985a), *Black Box: KAL 007 and the Superpowers.* Berkeley: University of California Press.

Dallin, A. (1985b), "Some Lessons of the Past", *Shared Destiny: Fifty Years of Soviet-American Relations.* Edited by Garrison, M. and Gleason, A. Boston, MA: Beacon Press, pp. 59-81.

Dallin, A. (1986a), "The Legacy of the Past" , *The Gorbachev Era.* Edited by Dallin, A. and Rice, C. Stanford, CA: Stanford Alumni Association, pp. 1-9.

Dallin, A. (1986b), "A Soviet Master Plan? The Non-Existent "Grand Design" in World Affairs", *The Gorbachev Era.* Edited by Dallin, A. and Rice, C. Stanford, CA: Stanford Alumni Association, pp. 167-177.

Dallin, A. (1988a), "U.S.-Soviet Relations: Trends and Prospects", *Gorbachev and the Soviet Future.* Edited by Lerner, L. and Treadgold, D.W. Boulder, CO: Westview, pp. 207-225.

Dallin, A. (1988b), "Gorbachev's Foreign Policy and the "New Political Thinking" in the Soviet Union", *Gorbachev's Reforms: U.S. and Japanese Assumptions.* Edited by Juviler, P. and Kimura, H. Hawthorne, NY: Aldine de Gruyter, pp. 97-113.

Dallin, A. (1988c), "Reform, 'Repentence' and Resistance: Soviet Politics in the Gorbachev Era", *The Gorbachev Reform Policy.* Oslo: Norwegian Institute of International Affairs, pp. 4-22.

Dallin, A. (1988d), "Soviet Approaches to Superpower Security", *U.S.-Soviet Security Cooperation: Achievements, Failures, Lessons.* Edited by George, A., Farley P. J. and Dallin A. New York/Oxford: Oxford University Press, pp. 603-617.

Dallin, A. (1989), "Reform in Russia: American Perceptions and U.S. Policy", *Reform in Russia and the USSR: Past and Prospects.* Edited by Crummey R.O. Urbana, IL: University of Illinois Press, pp. 253-266.

Dallin, A. (1992a), 'New Thinking in Soviet Foreign Policy', *New Thinking in Soviet Politics.* Edited by Brown A. Houndmills: Macmillan, pp. 71-85.

Dallin, A. (1992b), "Causes of the Collapse of the USSR", *Post-Soviet Affairs.* Vol. 8, pp. 279-302.

Dallin, A. and Lapidus, G.W. (1983), "Reagan and the Russians: United States Policy Toward the Soviet Union and Eastern Europe", *Eagle Defiant: United States Foreign Policy in the 1990s.* Edited by Oye, K., Lieber R. J. and Rotchild, D. Boston, MA/Toronto: Little, Brown, pp. 191-236.

Dallin, A. and Lapidus G.W. (1987), "Reagan and the Russians: United States Policy Toward the Soviet Union and Eastern Europe", *Eagle Resurgent: The Reagan Era in American Foreign Policy.* Edited by Oye, K., Lieber, R. J. and Rothchild, D. Boston, MA/Toronto: Little, Brown, pp. 193-254.

Erickson, J. (1986), *Conversations with John Erickson.* Edited by Thomas, R. E. Austin, TX: Texas A&M University System.

Erickson, J. (1990), "Perestroika and the Soviet Army", *Soviet Union 2000: Reform or Revolution?* Edited by Laqueur, W. New York: St. Martin's Press, 1990, pp. 135-148.

Erickson, J. (1996), *The Collapse of Communism, The End of the Cold War: Or, How to Interpret Change?* Edinburgh: Unpublished paper.

Gerner, K. (1985), "Finlandisera Baltikum (Finlandise the Baltic Republics)", *Svenska Dagbladet.* August 16.

Gerner, K. (1986a), "The Bolshevik Order and Russian Tradition", *Nordic Journal of Soviet and East European Studies.* Vol. 3, pp. 21-44.

Gerner, K. (1986b), "Hotet mot det ryska Norrland (The Threat against the Far North in Russia)", *Svenska Dagbladet.* February 24.

Gerner, K. (1987a), "Hatets ideologi (The Ideology of Hatred)", *Judisk Krönika.* 55 pp. 6-8.

Gerner, K. (1987b), "Nationalities and Minorities in the Soviet Union and Eastern Europe", *Nordic Journal of Soviet and East European Studies.* Vol. 4 , pp. 5-30.

Gerner, K. (1988a), "Tänka nytt och leva med kapitalismen: Sovjetisk utrikespolitik under Gorbatjov (Thinking anew and living with Capitalism: Soviet Foreign Policy Under Gorbachev)", *Den Sovjetiska Utmaningen: Reform och politik under Gorbatjov (The Soviet Challenge: Reform and Politics Under Gorbachev).* Edited by Arvidsson, C. and Fogelklou, A. Stockholm: Norstedts, pp. 177-230.

Gerner, K. (1988b), "Nationaliteter och minoriteter i Sovjetunionen (Nationalities and Minorities in the Soviet Union)", *Sovjet Under Glasnost (The Soviet Union During Glasnost).* Edited by Ignats, U. and Hammar, M. Gothenburg: MH Publishing, pp. 49-61.

Gerner, K. (1988c), "Glasnost och mijödebatten i Sovjet (Glasnost and the Debate on Ecology in the Soviet Union)", *Sovjet Under Glasnost (The Soviet Union During Glasnost).* Edited by Ignats, U. and Hammar, M. Gothenburg: MH Publishing, pp. 80-87.

Gerner, K. (1988d), "Moscow and the Surrounding World: Perceptions of

Gorbachev and His Entourage", *Nordic Journal of Soviet and East European Studies.* Vol. 5, pp. 193-226.

Gerner, K. (1988e), "Commentary: Internal Consequences of the Reform Process with Emphasis on Demographic and Ethnic Relation", *NUPI Report.* No. 115, pp. 57-78.

Gerner, K. (1988f), "Gorbatjovs trista 'lilla svarta' (Gorbachev's Boring "Little Black Book")", *Svenska Dagbladet.* January 2.

Gerner, K. (1988g), "Sovjetstatens skuldkonto (The Debt Account of the Soviet State)", *Sydsvenska Dagbladet.* February 1.

Gerner, K. (1989a), *Svårt att vara ryss. På väg mot postsovjetismen. Sex essäer om ryska identitetsproblem. (Hard to be a Russian. On the Road to Post-Sovietism. Six Essays on Russian Identity Problems).* Lund: Bokförlaget Signum.

Gerner, K. (1989b), "Etnisk identitet och Sovjetunionen (Ethnic Identity and the Soviet Union)", *Invandrare & Minoriteter*, pp. 3-8.

Gerner, K. (1989c), "Rysshatet ökar i Sovjetunionen (The Hatred of Russians is on the Rise in the Soviet Union)", *Sydsvenska Dagbladet.* June 13.

Gerner, K. (1990a), "Domen mot Gorbatjov blir hård! (The Judgement On Gorbachev Will be Harsh!)", *Civila Försvarstidningen.* 53, pp. 6-7.

Gerner, K. (1990b), "Ryssland och Europa — en ny Samlevnadsmodell (Russia and Europe — a new model for Co-existence)", *Finsk Tidskrift.* Vol. 4, pp. 217-233.

Gerner, K. (1990c), "Nationalismens återkomst (The Return of Nationialism)", *Judisk Krönika.* Vol. 4, 11-14.

Gerner, K. (1990d), "Efter Sovjetunionen (After The Soviet Union)", *Svensk Tidskrift.* Vol. 77, pp. 350-355.

Gerner, K. (1990e), "Ukraina och Vitryssland på väg mot postsovjetismen (The Ukraine and Bielorussia on the Road to Post-Sovietism)", *Svensk Tidskrift.* Vol. 77, pp. 53-59.

Gerner, K. (1990f), "Larm om nöd i ryska imperiet (Alarm about suffering in the Russian Empire)", *Sydsvenska Dagbladet.* December 10.

Gerner, K. (1991), "Katastrofen går mot sin fullbordan (The Disaster is approaching its final completion)", *Sydsvenska Dagbladet.* April 29.

Gerner, K. (1995), "Från Gorbatjovs Soviet till Gorbatschows Ryssland: Konsten att lösa upp ett imperium (From Gorbachev's Soviet Union to Gorbatschow's Russia: The Art of Dissolving An Empire)", *Nordisk Alkoholtidskrift.* 2, pp. 1-11.

Gerner, K. and Hedlund S. (1986a), "Att måla om ett tåg (To repaint a train)", *Svensk Tidskrift.* Vol. 73, pp. 410-416.

Gerner, K. and Hedlund, S.(1986b), "Det gamla vanliga resultatet (The Same Old Result)", *Svenska Dagbladet.* July 31.

Gerner, K. and Hedlund, S. (1987), "Slutet på en epok (The End of an Epoch)", *Svensk Tidskrift.* Vol. 74, pp. 454-459.

Gerner, K. and Hedlund, S. (1989a), *Ideology and Rationality in the Soviet Model: A legacy for Gorbachev.* London and New York: Routledge.

Gerner, K. and Hedlund, S. (1989b), "Byråkratisk mekanism för naturens förintande (Bureaucratic Mechanism for the Extermination of Nature)", *Sydsvenska Dagbladet.* March 14.

Gerner, K. and Hedlund, S. (1993), *The Baltic States and the End of the Soviet Empire.* London/New York: Routledge.

Goldman, M.I. (1983), *U.S.S.R. in Crisis: The Failure of An Economic System.* New York/London: Norton.

Goldman, M. I. (1985), "Will Gorbachev be Brezhnev II?", *The New York Times.* March 12.

Goldman, M. I. (1986a), "Sakharov: Now a Symbol of Change. Gorbachev Runs Risk in Nudging Soviets Toward "Reform"", *The Los Angeles Times.* December 21, Section 5, p. 5.

Goldman, M. I. (1986b), "The Grim Toll of Chernobyl: A Threat to Soviet Economic Reform", *The New York Times.* May 4, Section 3, p. 2.

Goldman, M. I. (1987a), *Gorbachev's Challenge: Economic Reform in the Age of High Technology, 2nd edition.* New York/London: Norton.

Goldman, M. I. (1987b), "Statement of Marshall I. Goldman", *Implementation of the Helsinki Accords. Hearing Before the Commission on Security and Cooperation in Europe. One Hundreth Congress, First Session. Glasnost: The Soviet Policy of "Openness".* Washington, D.C.: U.S. Government Printing Office, pp. 24-30.

Goldman, M. I. (1987c), "A Preview of Coming Attractions: With Conservatives on the Attack, Can Gorbachev Hang On?", *The Los Angeles Times.* November 19.

Goldman, M. I. (1987d), "Gorbachev's Plan: An Experiment in Chaos?", *The New York Times.* August 2, Section 3, p. 3.

Goldman, M. I. (1988a), "Wide Bitterness at Gorbachev's Glasnost Shouts Through", *The Los Angeles Times.* April 28.

Goldman, M. I. (1988b), "Gorbachev Gambles That Success Is Measured in Plumbing, Not Missiles", *The Los Angeles Times.* December 13.

Goldman, M. I. (1989), "Gorbachev Shows Off, But Soviets Wonder 'Where's the Beer?,'" *The Los Angeles Times.* September 22.

Goldman, M. I. (1990), "Gorbachev's Other Crisis", *The New York Times.* April 22, Section 4, p. 27.

Goldman, M. I. (1991 (1992)), *What Went Wrong with Perestroika,* updated edition. New York: Norton.

Goldman, M. I. (1991), "Reformer or Apparatchik?", *The New York Times.* May 12, Section 7, p. 9.

Hassner, P. (1984), "Le Totalitarisme Vu De l'Ouest", *Totalitarismes.* Edited by Hermet, G. Paris: Economica, pp. 15-41.

Hassner, P. (1985), "Communist Totalitarianism: The Transatlantic Vagaries of a

Concept", *The Washington Quarterly.* Vol. 8, pp. 17-29.

Hassner, P. (1986), "Europe between the United States and the Soviet Union", *Government and Opposition.* pp. 17-35.

Hassner, P. (1988), "Gorbachev and the West", *The Washington Quarterly.* Vol. 11, pp. 95-103.

Hassner, P. (1990a), "The Priority of Constructing Western Europe", *Europe and America Beyond 2000.* Edited by Treverton, G. New York/London: Council on Foreign Relations Press, pp. 18-35.

Hassner, P. (1990b), "Conclusion "Democrature" et "Refolution" ou la transition bouleversee", *Vents d'Est.* Edited by Gremion, P. and Hassner, P. Paris: Presses Universitaire de France, pp. 115-134.

Hassner, P. (1990c), "Europe beyond partition and unity: disintegration or reconstitution?", *International Affairs.* Vol. 63, pp. 461-475.

Hassner, P. (1995), "Introduction", *La violence et la paix. De la bombe atomique au nettoyage ethnique.* Edited by Hassner, P. Paris: Editions Esprit, pp. 7-20.

Hedlund, S. (1985a), "Systemet är helförsäkrat mot större förändringar (The System is totally ensured against greater changes)", *Svenska Dagbladet,* March 18.

Hedlund, S. (1985b), "Sorti, protest och stabilitet i Sovjetunionen (Exit, Protest and Stability in the Soviet Union)", *Ekonomisk Debatt.* Vol. 7, pp. 481-489.

Hedlund, S. (1985c), "Sovjetunionen är inte i kris (The Soviet Union is not in a crisis)", *Svenska Dagbladet.* October 6.

Hedlund, S. (1985d), "Längtan tillbaka till Stalintidens lag och ordning (A Wish to Return to the Law and Order of the Stalin Epoch)", *Svenska Dagbladet.* October 9.

Hedlund, S. (1986), "Ideologi, liturgi och sovjetisk politik (Ideology, lithurgy, and Soviet politics", *Statsvetenskaplig Tidskrift.* pp. 89-97.

Hedlund, S. (1987a), "Gorbatjovs ofullbordade (Gorbachev's Unfinished)", *Ekonomisk Debatt.* pp. 93-100.

Hedlund, S. (1987b), "En man med tänder av stål...eller en rysk Kennedy? (A Man with Teeth of Steel...or a Russian Kennedy?)", *Expressen.* November 6 .

Hedlund S. (1987c), "Om glasnost och perestrojka i det sovjetiska jordbruket (On Glasnost and Perestroika in Soviet Agriculture)", *Svensk Tidskrift.* Vol.74, pp. 341-347.

Hedlund, S. (1987d), "Långsiktig strategi för förändring i Sovjetunionen (A Long-term Strategy for Change in the Soviet Union)", *Svenska Dagbladet.* January 11.

Hedlund, S. (1988a), "Glasnost och perestrojka — i stället för reform? (Glasnost and Perestroika — Instead of Reform?)", *Sovjet Under Glasnost (The Soviet Union During Glasnost).* Edited by Ignats, U. and Hammar, M. Gothenburg: MH Publishing, pp. 36-43.

Hedlund, S. (1988b), "Om glasnost och den pluralistiska ignoransen (On Glasnost and Pluralist Ignorance)", *Svensk Tidskrift.* Vol. 75, pp. 433-440.

Hedlund, S. (1988c), "Stordåd eller apati (Great Deeds or Apathy)", *Sydsvenska Dagbladet.* December 4.

Hedlund, S. (1989a), *Private Agriculture in the Soviet Union.* London and New York: Routledge.

Hedlund, S. (1989b), "Gorbajtovs fullbordade (Gorbachev's Completed)", *Ekonomisk Debatt.* pp. 13-22.

Hedlund, S. (1989c), "En Marshallplan för miljön i Östeuropa (A Marshall Plan for the Environment in Eastern Europe)", *Svensk Tidskrift.* Vol. 76, pp. 114-121.

Hedlund, S. (1989d), "Apokalypsens flyktingar (The Refugees of the Apocalypse)", *Sydsvenska Dagbladet.* November 13.

Hedlund, S. (1989e), "Miljökatastrof i Sovjet (Ecological Disaster in the Soviet Union)", *Tiden.* pp. 175-184.

Hedlund, S. (1990a), "Postsovjetiska interiörer (Post-Soviet interiors)", *Säkerhetspolitiska perspektiv inför 90-talet — nio åsikter (Perspectives on Security Policy in the 1990s — Nine Views).* Edited by Landahl, P.-A. Stockholm: Folk och Försvar, pp. 59-87.

Hedlund, S. (1990b), "Perestrojkan i Sovjet snubblar vidare (Perestroika in the Soviet Union stumbes on)", *Ekonomisk Debatt.* pp.13-23.

Hedlund, S. (1990c), "Glöm Gorbatjov! (Forget Gorbachev!)", *Svenska Dagbladet.* July 29.

Hedlund, S. (1990d), "Svälten i Ryssland drabbar Baltikum (Starvation in the Soviet Union Strikes the Baltic Republics)", *Sydsvenska Dagbladet.* December 2.

Hedlund, S. (1991a), "Gorbatjov har sålt sig till djävulen (Gorbachev has sold himself to the Devil)", *Sydsvenska Dagbladet.* January 16.

Hedlund, S. (1991b), "Sovjet på väg mot katastrofen (The Soviet Union on the Road to Disaster)", *Svensk Tidskrift.* Vol. 78, pp. 8-16.

Hedlund, S. (1991c), "Alltmer splittrad bild av krisens Sovjet (An Increasingly Confusing Image of the Soviet Union in Crisis)", *Svenska Dagbladet.* July 4.

Hedlund, S. (1991d), "Felaktigt och reaktionärt (Incorrect and Reactionary)", *Vårt Försvar.* Vol. 102 , pp. 16-17.

Hedlund, S. (1992a), "Dödsruna över perestrojkan (An Obituary over Perestroika)", *Efter Sovjet: Tankar kring ett imperium i upplösning (After the Soviet Union: Thought about a Disintegrating Empire).* Edited by Hedlund, S. Stockholm: Nerenius och Santérus, pp. 87-106.

Hedlund, S. (1992), *Öststatsekonomi (The Economy of the Warsaw Pact States).* Lund: Dialogos.

Hough, J. and Fainsod, M. (1979) *How the Soviet Union is Governed.* Boston: Harvard University Press.

Hough, J. (1985a), "Shifts in Soviet Foreign Policy, Maybe", *The New York Times.* July 10.

Hough, J. (1985b), "Let's Make a Deal: For Once, We Have a Summit, When Both Sides Badly Need Arms Cuts", *The Washington Post*, October 20.

Hough, J. (1986a), *The Struggle for the Third World: Soviet Debates and American Options*. Washington, DC: Brookings.

Hough, J. (1986b), "Soviet Times They Are A'Changing", *The Los Angeles Times*. January 24.

Hough, J. (1986c), "Gorbachev Cools to Revolutions, Warms to Industrializing Third World", *The Los Angeles Times*. February 13.

Hough, J. (1986d), "Gorbachev: Fashioning a Pedestal for Mikhail the Great?," *The Los Angeles Times*. February 24.

Hough, J. (1986e), "Something Will Change in the Soviet Union", *The Washington Post*. March 15.

Hough, J. (1986f), "Western Press, Government Smear Soviets", *The Los Angeles Times*. May 11.

Hough, J. (1986g), "Our Hopeful Summit Talk May Be Wishful Thinking", *The Washington Post*. August 24.

Hough, J. (1987a), "Moscow Deals From Strength in Afghanistan", *The Los Angeles Times*. January 16.

Hough, J. (1987b), "Grim Fairy Tales About Gorbachev", *The Los Angeles Times*. February 5.

Hough, J. (1987c), "New Deal in Moscow", *The New York Times*. February 13.

Hough, J. (1987d), "Gorbachev Isn't Khruschev: Yes, He's a Reformer; But No, He Isn't Going to Be Dumped", *The Washington Post*. February 22.

Hough, J. (1987e), "Squeeze on Gorbachev Is From Liberals", *The Los Angeles Times*. November 5.

Hough, J. (1987f), "The Tentacles of Soviet Reform", *The New York Times*, November 18.

Hough, J. (1987g), "Expectations May Be Lower Than Merited: Interests of U.S. and Soviets Now Permit Serious Agreement", *The Los Angeles Times*. December 4.

Hough, J. (1988a), *Opening up the Soviet Economy*. Washington, DC: Brookings.

Hough, J. (1988b), *Russia and the West: Gorbachev and the Politics of Reform*. New York: Simon and Schuster.

Hough, J. (1988c), "The Europeanization of Gorbachev", *The New York Times*. April 8.

Hough, J. (1988d), "Around the Kremlin, Days of High Drama", *The Los Angeles Times*. April 26.

Hough, J. (1988e), "We're far From a Summit Worth Celebrating", *The Los Angeles Times*. May 20.

Hough, J. (1988f), "Gorbachev's Lame Ducks: Why the Soviet Leader Needs to Purge the party's Has-Beens", *The Washington Post*. June 26.

Hough, J. (1988g), "Turmoil Hides Soviet Economic Shifts", *The Los Angeles Times*. June 27.

Hough, J. (1988h), "Signal-Readers Forget That Our Own Are Hash", *The Los Angeles Times*. October 4.

Hough, J. (1988i), "The Message to America Is That the Soviets Can Go It Alone", *The Los Angeles Times*. December 9.

Hough, J. (1989a), "Soviet Vote Shows Resiliency, Not Fragility", *The Los Angeles Times*. March 31.

Hough, J. (1989b), "Bush's Losing Soviet Strategy: By Misreading Gorbachev's Power and Aims, We May Outfox Ourselves", *The Washington Post*. May 21.

Hough, J. (1989c), "Gorbachev Sees Vein of Opportunity to be Mined From Worker Unrest", *The Los Angeles Times*. July 25.

Hough, J. (1989d), "...but is Driven by Soviet Needs", *The Los Angeles Times*. August 24.

Hough, J. (1989e), "The Politics of Successful Economic Reform", *Soviet Economy*; pp. 3-46.

Hough, J. (1989f), "Gorbachev's Politics", *Foreign Affairs*. Vol. 68, No. 5, pp. 26-41.

Hough, J. (1989g), "Gorbachev's Agenda For the 90's", *The New York Times*. December 31.

Hough, J. (1990a), "Why Gorby Is Defying The Pundits' Predictions", *The Washington Post*. February 11.

Hough, J. (1990b), "O, What a Worldwide Mess Lithuania Would Put Us In", *The Los Angeles Times*. April 27.

Hough, J. (1990c), "Gorbachev's Endgame", *World Policy Journal*. Vol. VII, No. 4 (Fall), pp. 639-672.

Hough, J. (1990d), "Shevardnadze and 3 Scenarios", *The New York Times*. December 21.

Hough, J. (1991a), "Soviet Radicals Want Us to Feel They're the Only Decent Guys in Town, *The Los Angeles Times*. January 4.

Hough, J. (1991b), "Soviet Dictators – And Democrats: From the Beginning, Gorbachev Was More — and Less — Than We Imagined', *The Washington Post*. February 17.

Hough, J. (1991c), "Moscow's Master of Timing", *The Los Angeles Times*. April 26.

Hough, J. (1991d), "Understanding Gorbachev: The Importance of Politics", *Soviet Economy*. Vol 7, No. 2., pp. 89-109.

Jonson, L. (1988), "Historiska erfarenheter av sovjetisk förnyelse (Historical Lessons of Soviet Change)", *Sovjet Under Glasnost (The Soviet Union During Glasnost)*. Edited by Ignats, Ü. and Hammar, M. Gothenburg: MH Publishing, pp. 9-14.

Jonson, L. (1989a), "Gorbachev och Europa (Gorbachev and Europe)", *Världs-politikens Dagsfrågor*. Stockholm: Swedish Institute of International Affairs.

Jonson, L. (1989b), "Motsägelsefull: Sovjetisk politik i Nordeuropa (Contradictory: Soviet policy in Northern Europe)", *Internationella Studier.* Vol. 2, pp. 14-20.

Jonson, L. (1990a), "What's In Store for Northern Europe in the Gorbachev Era?," *Gorbachev and Europe.* Edited by Harle, V. and Iivonen, J. London: Pinter Publishers, pp. 130-152.

Jonson, L. (1990b), "Inrikespolitik i sovjetisk utrikespolitik (Domestic Politics in Soviet Foreign Policy)", *Säkerhetspolitiska perspektiv inför 90-talet — nio åsikter (Perspectives on Security Policy For the 1990s — Nine Views).* Edited by Landahl, P.-A. Stockholm: Folk och försvar, pp. 121-141.

Jonson, L. (1990c), "Det Sovjetiska Maktsystemet inför sönderfall (The Soviet System of Power Facing Collapse)", *Sovjets sammanbrott (The Break-Down of the Soviet Union).* Edited by Hammar, M. and Melander, T. Gothenburg: MH Publishing, pp. 47-66.

Jonson, L. (1991), "Russia and Europe: The Emergence of a New Russian Foreign Policy", *Yearbook 1990-91: Towards a New European Security Order.* Edited by Huldt, B. and Herolf, G. Stockholm/Gothenburg: Swedish Institute of International Affairs/MH Publishing, 1991, pp. 173-191.

Jonson, L. "Ryssland"'(1995), *Utländska Politiska System (Foreign Political Systems),* 7th ed. Edited by Lindahl, R. Stockholm: SNS, pp. 205-235.

Nove, A. (1982), "USSR: economic policy and methods after 1970", *The East European Economies in the 1970s.* Edited by Nove, A., Höhmann, H.-H and Seidensechter, G. London: Butterworths, pp. 17-44.

Nove, A. (1984), "Whither the Soviet Economy?," *The Washington Quarterly.* (Spring), pp. 84-99.

Nove, A. (1985), "The Scope and Scale of Good and Evil", *Society.* (March/April), pp. 12-16.

Nove, A. (1986), *The Soviet Economic System, 3rd ed.* London: Unwin & Hyman.

Nove, A. (1987), ""Radical Reforms", Problems and Prospects", *Soviet Studies.* Vol. XXXIX , pp. 452-467.

Nove, A. (1989a), *Glasnost in Action: Cultural Renaissance in Russia.* Boston, MA: Unwin Hyman.

Nove, A. (1989b), "The Problems of Perestroika: Portrait of an Economy in Transition", *Dissent.* (Fall), pp. 462-474.

Nove, A. (1991), "Reforming the Soviet Economy", *Dissent.* (Winter), pp. 9-11.

Nove, A. (1992), *An Economic History of the USSR, 3rd ed.* London: Penguin.

Pipes, R. (1983), "Putting the Brakes on a War Machine", *The New York Times.* August 21, Section 3, p. 2.

Pipes, R. (1984a), *Survival Is Not Enough: Soviet Realities and America's Future.* New York: Simon and Schuster.

Pipes, R. (1984b), "Can the Soviet Union Reform?", *Foreign Affairs.* Vol. 63, pp. 47-61.

Pipes, R. (1985), "Assessing the Helsinki Final Act, 10 Years After: A Loss for the West", *The New York Times.* August 1.

Pipes, R. (1986a), "Dealing with the Russians: The Wages of Forgetfulness," *U.S.-Soviet Relations: The Next Phase.* Edited by Horelick, A. L. Ithaca, NY and London: Cornell University Press, pp. 276-287.

Pipes, R.(1986b), "Call Iceland What it Was — A Trap. We Can Still Negotiate with Soviets but not at Expense of SDI', *The Los Angeles Times.* October 21.

Pipes, R. (1986c), "Why Hurry Into a Weapons Accord?," *The New York Times.* October 10.

Pipes, R. (1988a), "For the Last Empire, the Clock is Ticking", *The Los Angeles Times.* March 15.

Pipes, R. (1988b), "Western Aid Shouldn't Precede Visible Reform by Soviets", *The Los Angeles Times.* June 16.

Pipes, R. (1989a), *Russia Observed. Collected Essays on Russian and Soviet History.* Boulder, CO/San Francisco, CA/London: Westview.

Pipes, R. (1989b), "The Russians Are Still Coming", *The New York Times.* October 9.

Pipes, R. (1990), "Soviet Army Coup? Not Likely", *The New York Times.* November 20.

Pipes, R. (1992), "The Past on Trial: Russia, One Year Later", *The Washington Post.* August 16.

Pipes, R. (1995), "Misinterpreting the Cold War", *Foreign Affairs.* Vol. 74, pp. 154-160.

Pipes, R. and Weiss, S. (1988), "The Record of "Team B"", *The Washington Post.* August 21.

Pravda, A.(1988), "Ideology and the Policy Process", *Ideology and Soviet Politics.* Edited by White, S. and Pravda, A. London: Macmillan, pp. 225-252.

Pravda, A. (1990a), "The politics of foreign and security policy", *Developments in Soviet Politics.* Edited by White, S., Pravda, A. and Gitelman, Z. London: Macmillan, pp. 207-227.

Pravda, A. (1990b), "Introduction: Linkages between Soviet Domestic and Foreign Policy under Gorbachev", *Perestroika: Soviet Domestic and Foreign Policies.* Edited by Hasegawa, T. and Pravda, A. London: Sage, pp. 1-24.

Pravda, A. (1990c), "Introduction: pre-*perestroika* patterns", *Soviet-British Relations since the 1970s.* Edited by Pravda, A. and Duncan, P. J .S. Cambridge/New York: Cambridge University Press, pp. 1-16.

Pravda, A. (1990d), "Stumbling Toward Soviet Democracy", *European Affairs.* Vol. 4, pp. 46-50.

Pravda, A. (1992), "Soviet Policy Towards Eastern Europe in Transition: The Means Justify the Ends", *The End of the Outer Empire: Soviet-East European Relations in Transition, 1985-90.* Edited by Pravda, A. London: Royal Institute of International Affairs/Sage, pp. 1-34.

Pravda, A. and Duncan, P. J. S. (1990), 'Conclusion: Soviet-British relations under *perestroika*', *Soviet-British Relations since the 1970s*. Edited by Pravda, A. and Duncan, P. J. S. Cambridge/New York: Cambridge University Press, pp. 232-256.

Appendix 2B

Editorials Analysed in the 8 Newspapers

	1985	1986	1987	1988	1989	1990	1991
Le Monde	26	47	33	52	38	55	59
Le Figaro	13	11	37	33	35	32	md
The Times	33	55	51	64	67	60	64
The Guardian	29	37	43	23	26	47	39
Svenska Dagbladet	45	77	67	74	41	48	42
Dagens Nyheter	42	61	54	56	48	59	61
The New York Times	37	39	70	55	47	59	61
The Washington Post	32	44	46	49	51	59	49

md= missing data

Sources for the Politicians' Speeches

France: *La Politique Étrangère de La France*, Paris. Published by the French Foreign Ministry 6 times per year;

Great Britain: 1) *Survey*: Official Journal published by the Foreign and Commonwealth Office;
2) *Hansard*: Parliamentary proceedings from the House of Commons.

Sweden: *Utrikesfrågor* (Foreign Policy Issues): Yearbook issued by the Swedish Foreign Ministry.

United States: 1) *Department of State Bulletin*: Monthly journal issued by the Department of State until the end of 1989;
2) *Department of State Dispatch*: Journal issued by the Department of State since 1990.

Appendix 3
Important Speeches by the Politicians

1. France

M. Jean-Bernard Raimond, Foreign Minister, April 20, 1988:

'Les soviétiques veulent réformer leur système de gestion économique et sociale parce qu'ils ont pris conscience de ce que leur pays a accumulé un retard considérable. Mais, pour l'instant, toutes les réformes restent inscrites dans les cadre du système marxiste léniniste.

Pour ma part...je pense que pour transformer réellement le système et le rendre efficace, il faudra à un moment donné remettre en cause sa nature même. Et quand ce moment-là sera arrivé, les dirigeants soviétiques auront à répondre à ces questions: est-ce que c'est possible?...Des gens très compétents nous disent souvent: tout cela est voué à l'échec, un système marxiste-léniniste est condamné à l'immobilisme, il ne peut pas évoluer.

Personnellement, je ne vois pas les choses ainsi. Je crois, au contraire, et l'Histoire en témoigne, que tous les systèmes peuvent changer...Aussi je pense vraiment que, dans l'avenir, le système soviétique changera. Même si en Union soviétique il est des courants qui s'opposent aux réformes. Ils changeront, eux aussi, parce qu'il n'y a pas d'alternatives. ...

Les nouveaux dirigeants ont considéré qu'ils avaient hérité de leurs prédécesseurs un certain nombre d'erreurs. Il y en avait deux, notamment, deux erreurs majeures: le déploiement des SS 20 et la guerre d'Afghanistan. Ils ont corrigé, ou ils sont en train de le faire, ces deux erreurs. Mais ils ne tiennent pas compte d'une troisième, celle de Staline, qui fut l'extension du système marxiste-léniniste en Europe centrale.

En Union soviétique il existe, qu'on le veuille ou non, un consensus fondé sur le nationalisme. Il peut y avoir des problèmes des nationalités, comme on le voit en Arménie ou dans les anciens États baltes, mais il n'en demeure pas moins que ce consensus existe.

Or il en est bien différemment dans les pays d'Europe centrale...Précisément parce que ces pays ne connaissent pas le même consensus que l'Union soviétique et que, profitant de l'évolution de leur système, ils s'empresseraient d'échapper à la tutelle de leur protecteur.

Les dirigeants soviétiques qui sont clairvoyants le comprennent bien. Et comme ils veulent à la fois réformer leur pays mais ne pas perdre le contrôle de leur empire, ils ressentent la nécessité de maintenir, voire de renforcer, la puissance de l'Union soviétique, non pas seulement en Europe de l'Est mais dans toute l'Europe. C'est pourquoi je crains que les années à venir ne soient très difficiles pour les Occidentaux'.[1]

---

[1] Jean-Bernard Raimond, *Politique Etrangère*, 20 April 1988, p. 66.

The Soviets want to reform the system by which they administer their economic and social system because they have understood that their country has accumulated a considerable retardation. But, for the moment, all the reforms are undertaken within the Marxist-Leninist system.

For my part...I believe that to really transform the system and to make it efficient, they one day have to question its very nature. And when that moment arrives, they Soviet leaders have to respond to this question: what is possible?...Very competent people tell us this very often: all this is bound to fail, a Marxist-Leninist system is bound to immobilism, it cannot change.

Personally, I do not see things that way. I believe, on the contrary, and History shows us this, that all systems can change...Thus I think that, in the future, the Soviet system will change. Even if there exist in the Soviet Union forces who are opposed to change. They will also change, because there are no alternatives. ...

They new leaders have thought that they inherited a number of errors from their predecessors. There were two majors errors: the deployment of the SS-20 and the War in Afghanistan. They have corrected, or they are in the process of correcting, those two errors. But they do not count a third, that of Stalin, which was the extension of the Marxist-Leninist system to Central Europe.

In the Soviet Union there exists, whether you want it or not, a consensus founded on nationalism. There may be problems with nationalities, as we have seen in Armenia or in the former Baltic Republics, but still this consensus exists.

It is, however, very different in the countries of Central Europe. ...Just because these countries do not subscribe to the same consensus as the Soviet Union, and because of the evolution of their systems, these countries hasten to escape the tutelage of their protector.

The Soviet leaders who are forward-looking understand this well. And because they want, at the same time, reform their system but not lose their empire, they feel the need to maintain, even reinforce, the power of the Soviet Union, not only in Eastern Europe but in all of Europe. That why I fear that the coming years may be very difficult for the West.

2. **Great Britain**
-

3. **Sweden**
-

4. **The United States**
Secretary of State James Baker III, May 4, 1989:

These great changes, however, are not the only realities of the Soviet Union today. There is an uneasy and, I might add, a not always peaceful coexistence between the slogans of the new thinking and the reality of both Soviet capabilities and Soviet actions. We must all, I think, face the fact that the Soviets continue to pose a significant military threat to Western interests. Even after the unilateral Soviet reductions in Europe take place, the Warsaw Pact would retain a two-to-one edge in tanks and artillery. ...

For all the talk of "defensive defense," Soviet military exercises still continue to show a marked inclination for taking the offensive. For all the talk of openness, the Soviets have yet to publish a real defense budget — a budget that would reveal what the Soviets really are spending on defense; a budget that would provide a guide to Soviet defense production; a budget, in effect, that would show the direction of future Soviet defense plans. ...

For all the talk of a common European home...the European house remains divided by Soviet force. If there is ever to be a true "common European house," the Soviets must no longer prevent the residents from moving from room to room. ...

So the reality of Soviet change...is both promising and problematic. How do we address the very serious difficulties remaining on the agenda, while giving due credit to the remarkable progress that has been made in the past few years. ...

Our foreign policy has to be based on an understanding of change in the Soviet Union, but it cannot wholly rely on that change to produce the results that we want. Our actions, of course, will play an important role in shaping the future of U.S.-Soviet relations. Our policy has got to be to press forward with our agenda, to test the application of Soviet new thinking again and again. ...

Indeed, new thinking in Soviet foreign policy gives us an unique opportunity to take Moscow at its word...across all areas of U.S.-Soviet relations. Are the Soviets really prepared to recognize the constraints of an interdependent world? Is Moscow ready to abandon the quest for unilateral gain? Can military confrontation really be replaced by political dialogue and even by cooperation? Will the slogans of new thinking be translated into enduring action?

The only way to answer these questions is to test the new thinking on issues that go beyond the recent intense focus on human rights and arms control.[2]

II. Secretary of State James Baker III, Statement to the Senate Finance Committee, October 4, 1989:

The causes for these failures [of previous reform efforts] give us a better idea of what conditions may be necessary for perestroika to succeed. I believe these conditions include:

1. Top-level political support;
2. Clear recognition of the need for economic changes;
3. An openness that permits the rethinking of ideology and economic theory so as to justify change;
4. A conducive international environment;
5. Consistency in the design and implementation of reforms; and
6. Ability to counter the power of the antireform bureaucracy.[3]

---

[2] Secretary of State James Baker, *Department of State Bulletin*, May 4, 1989, pp. 37-38.

[3] It should be noted that these points, on the support necessary for the economic reforms to succeed, are taken almost verbatim from a work by one of sovietologists analyzed here Anders Åslund: *Gorbachev's Struggle for Economic Reform*. This fact is noted in the *Department of State Bulletin*. See *DSB*, October 5, 1989, p. 26.

Even these conditions may not totally suffice, for the reformers are taking on Russian as well as Soviet traditions. This society did not experience many important Western movements - neither the Reformation nor the Renaissance touched this borderland of Europe. It is rent by divisions among many nationalities. These splits are exacerbated by a growing movement of strikes. Openness may bring conflict as well as progess.

The first four conditions for a successful reform effort are probably present. But the fifth and sixth pose real challenges for President Gorbachev. At this point, the real dangers to perestroika are:

A poorly designed and nomcomprehensive program, reflecting compromises among top leaders or the lack of top-level appreciation of the need for changes;

Poor implementation due to bureaucratic opposition;

Public opposition due to the loss of benefits from the old system before the advantages of the new system kick in; and

Failure to win a constituency for the reform due to uncertainty about its staying power and legal protections.

Given the magnitude of the challenge, it should not be surprising that perestroika has turned out not to be one reform program but an amalgam of many. It is an ongoing experiment, relying on a fair amount of "seat-of-the-pants" logic. It has reflected compromises made necessary by the Soviet system of collective leadership. It has incorporated contradictions because different factions pressed alternative solutions. These compromises and contradictions have created

ambiguities, which in turn have opened opportunities for bureaucratic reinterpretations and obstructions. This lack of an internally consistent, comprehensive, and integrated reform program — while understandable — remains a major, ongoing weakness.
...

I believe a combination of four factors convinced the Soviet leadership of the need for reform.

The first was the overall decline in economic performance. ...

A second factor promoting reform was the decline in the competitive position of the Soviet economy. The gap between the U.S.S.R. and the West was growing, not narrowing. Even more shocking, the Soviets could see the newly industrializing economies surging forward. ...

The military implications of Soviet economic failure were a third reason for reform. The Reagan Administration's military buildup proved difficult to counter without drawing off an even greater share of civilian resources and increasing the already heavy defense burden. ...

The fourth factor was the emergence of new leadership in the Soviet Union. This leadership represented a new generation. ...

As of late 1989, perestroika has been comprised of a grab bag of economic reforms. Some are striking changes from Brezhnev's economic system. Unfortunately, not much has worked — at least as measured in terms of economic performance.

The political changes, however, have been exceptional. Gorbachev has decided that he needs to change the political system to support economic reforms. Yet glasnost also opens up the failures of the Marxist system for the world and Soviet citizens to see. The lessons of early failures are clear.

1. The old Brezhnev model was totally discredited.

2. The Andropovian moral discipline fix was a bust.

3. G.D.R.-type streamlining efficiency didn't work.

4. Piecemeal reforms of enterprises and industrial organization couldn't be successful as long as they operated in a system hostile to private initiative, competition, markets, and profits.

5. Even the agricultural sector — the leading edge for the Hungarians and the People's Republic of China — was impervious to reform.

There was, however, a positive lesson as well: Reform must be comprehensive — economically and politically — to have a reasonable chance of success. A comprehensive program might take a number of forms, each involving different risks. I divide comprehensive strategies into three categories:

One-shot radical reforms all at once, the "big bang" approach, perhaps after some groundwork is laid.

Gradual changes but sequenced carefully to enable reforms to take hold; or major transformation by sector.

Each strategy requires a shift from the ad hoc adjustment of the past. And there's the rub. It will be exceedingly difficult for a collective leadership to develop a comprehensive effort. This should be no surprise. It is hard for our decentralized political system to develop comprehensive programs too. But our basic political and economic systems work. The Soviet Union's does not. And many members of the Soviet political leadership remain ideologically resistant to the necessary reforms. ...

I don't consider it my place to offer detailed prescriptions to the Soviets. Their society is vastly different from ours. I would not presume to know the political and ideological constraints. And there is much we still don't know about what goes on there. But a few economic points stand out to me personally.

First, market price reform is the key. ...

Second, there is a reasonable case that price reform cannot proceed until the Soviets have stabilized the value of the ruble. The massive deficits financed by printing rubles and the large number of rubles chasing too few goods have led Soviet citizens to prefer real assets to monetary assets of declining value. ...

Third, market prices and macro-economic stabilization measures will not suffice in the absence of macroeconomic reforms in industrial organization. Enterprises and cooperatives must be free to compete. Monopolies must end. ...

Fourth, the Supreme Soviet must establish legally certain property rights. ...

Fifth, the Soviet Union will have to move carefully in substituting tax and regulatory policies for confiscation and production directives. ...

Finally, the Soviet Union will need to develop a 'safety net' that protects those who cannot fend for themselves in the changed economic environment. ...

These six tasks are a tall order for perestroika. But even this brief analysis points out the interrelationships among necessary reforms. Action on any one element standing alone will not suffice. The pieces must fit together if the new economic machine is going to work. ...

Gorbachev has not been deterred by the failure to produce economic results. To the contrary, his recourse when facing obstacles — as we saw again this summer — is to use problems to further consolidate his authority. Then he takes steps to press political and economic reforms further. He does not fold; he does not call. He raises the stakes.

Nevertheless, Gorbachev and his allies still must operate as members of a collective leadership with very different notions of what reform means. So the leadership decisions are often compromises. The results are often confusing.

This ad hoc policy development process is a severe handicap when the objective is to overhaul a society's attitudes toward work, competition, property, responsibility, and freedom. Policy is often incoherent. People remain uncertain. No one really knows what the future will bring.

It would be a mistake, however, to conclude that the challenges are too daunting or that the impediments to success are too great. So far Gorbachev has secured greater power over the years, and he reveals every intention to "stay the course". The jury is still out on whether he will succeed or fail.

III. Secretary of State James Baker III: Speech to the Foreign Policy Association, New York, October 16, 1989.[4]

We are in a time of rising promise. Relations with the SU have improved considerably since 1985, when MG launched what he called *perestroika* — a total restructuring of Soviet society, including Soviet foreign and defense policies. ...

There are two reasons why we think that the prospects for a lasting imrprovement in U.S.-Soviet relations are better than ever before. First, we in the West have demonstrated through our strength, unity, and fidelity to our values that democracy and free market economies work and work well together. Second, the alternative vision advocated by the SU has failed to produce either prosperity or an attractive society. Simply put — freedom works! Communism doesn't!

As a consequence of the failure of their system, the Soviets, led by Mikhail Gorbachev, have begun the process of reform and rebuilding called *perestroika* — including the restructuring of Soviet-American relations — to succeed. We have reached this conclusion not because it is our business to reform Soviet society or **keep a particular Soviet leader in power** — we can really do neither — but because *perestroika* promises Soviet actions more advantageous to our interests. Our task is

---

[4] *DSB*, pp. 10-14.

Our task is to search creatively for those points of mutual U.S.-Soviet advantage that may be possible — and many more may be possible because of *perestroika*.
...

I think it is important ot begin by understanding the origins of *perestroika*. First and foremost, it is a Soviet response to a rapidly changing world in which they see themselves increasingly hard pressed to compete economically, technologically, politically, and militarily. The exponents of *perestroika* see their country as rich in natural resources and human talent but stifled by the legacy of stagnation — a system incapable of producing the economic progress and political legitimacy which Soviet citizens have the right to expect. ...

Thus the very logic of *perestroika* requires that the Soviets themselves must solve their own problems in a comprehensive, organic way. Not only must the economic system be reformed but the political and legal systems too. *Perestroika* is, therefore, different than earlier, failed attempts at reforming the state Lenin founded and Stalin built. ...

Nor are Soviet problems susceptible to rescue from abroad through abundant Western credits. ...As Ed Hewett, a Western expert on the Soviet economy, has put it "...however strong Western feelings may be about the possible outcomes of this reform effort, Western policymakers should see that their "influence" on this process can be no more than modest".

This self-reliant and radical nature of domestic *perestroika* has become even more crucial as the reforms have encountered increasing difficulties. ...

Perestroika may have reached a turning point where the bets will have to be redoubled again. Consumer shortages are not likely to be relieved nor productivity increased without the incentives of a stable currency, free and competitive markets, private property, and real prices. ...

Finally, the systemic, organic nature of *perestroika* takes it beyond the category of an exclusively domestic reform. ...

And that is where we come in. Fascinating as domestic change in the Soviet Union may be, we are mainly affected by the way the Soviet Union approaches the rest of the world.

Here, too *perestroika* promises a radical reform. ...

Yet for all the expansion of their military forces and their efforts to establish beachheads around the globe, the Soviet bought neither greater security nor lasting success.

Indeed the lessons of the 1970s learned by today's Soviet leadership appear to contradict fundamentally the rose-colored view of the Brezhnev era. Gorbachev and his group of 'new thinkers' now speak of the following lessons.

— The Brezhnev military buildup brought greater insecurity instead of increasing security. Soviet actions — such as the deployment of the SS-20s in Western Europe, for example — provoked Western responses, making the correlation of forces less favorable to Moscow, not more.

— The military buildup also bankrupted the economy. ...

— Security could not be achieved unilaterally, only multilaterally.

— Military and political gains in the Third World were expensive, and the shallow successes were nearly always fleeting.

— Regional conflicts could escalate and produce undesired confrontations. Possible gains in were not worth the risks inherent in such situations.

These are the lessons the Soviets speak of having learned from Brezhnev's failures, theoretical lessons that have shaped the new thinking and *perestroika.*

But while in theory they have learned these lessons, they have not put them all into practice by any means.

In defense policy and arms control, the Soviets have shown greater understanding of the need to promote mutual security. In both conventional and nuclear arms control talks, the Soviets have shifted their positions to correspond more closely with long-held Western assumptions about preventing war and producing greater stability. ...

In regional conflicts, the picture is very mixed. The Soviets have withdrawn from Afghanistan. And they fostered the settlement in Angola. But, overall, Moscow appears less willing to make hard choices on the regional questions than on arms control. We've seen a surge in Soviet arms shipments to Afghanistan and Ethiopia; in Cambodia, Soviet shipments this year are already twice as high as all of 1988; and Soviet bloc arms continue to end up in Nicaragua. ...

What explains this mixed record? Some analysts, invoking past disappointments, argue that the Soviets are engaged in a mere *perestroika* [sic!] - a breathing space until Leninism is strong enough to do battle once more with capitalism. Others, invoking future hope, argue that the new thinkers are so consumed by domestic concerns that old thinking still holds sway over certain aspects of foreign policy.

But to me, it reveals something else. I find a certain parallel between the course of Soviet domestic *perestroika* and new thinking in Soviet foreign policy. Domestically, as Gorbachev has sought to turn theory into practice, his program has altered and evolved. And just ast the Soviets have come face-to-face with domestic dilemmas that must now be resolved if progress is to be made, so they will come face-to-face with the need for further change in their foreign policy.

Domestically we can have but a small direct impact on how the Soviets resolve their dilemmas. But in foreign and defense policies, through a prudent search for points of mutual advantage, we can more readily shape and alter the calculus so that the Soviets face up to the contradictions between the new thinking and old habits. In arms control, the Kremlin has made some politically difficult choices and in some areas selected the path of mutual progress. Now we must also shape the Soviet calculus so that Moscow chooses the path of progress in regional conflicts.

In the course of our search for mutual advantage, we must not succumb to a false optimism that *perestroika* in Soviet foreign policy has gone far enough and that we can rely on the new thinking to take account of our interests.

It would be an equally great blunder to ignore the possibility that *perestroika* might go much further and to retreat instead into a suspicious stance of disengagement that would never put *perestroika* to the test. Either approach would sacrifice the great opportunity before us.

Thus our mission must be to press the search for mutual advantage. ...

Let me sum it all up. We want *perestroika* to succeed at home and abroad because we believe it will bring about a less aggressive Soviet Union, restrained in the use of force, and less hostile to democracy. A *perestroika* that resulted simply in a more efficient and more capable Soviet state would, ineed, be a more formidable and dangerous competitor.

But I do not believe that *perestroika* can succeed without increasing measures of free markets, free speech and institutions, more accountable to the people - in short, without more freedom! And that means a more democratic society, more respectful of human rights and legal norms which could provide a lasting foundation for more constructive, less dangerous Soviet behavior abroad; a society that produces not subjects that are to be acted upon but citizens who participate in the policy process; and a society where citizens have a say in what their government does at home and abroad. ...That government is far more likely to establish as its measure of succes internal progress rather than external expansion. ...

Let me conclude this review of *perestroika* and Ameican foreign policy by reiterating my convictions that, indeed, we do have a historic opportunity to make lasting improvements in U.S-Soviet relations. It is an opportunity produced by actions on both sides. ...

And what could that aspiration, that shared optimism, really mean? Nothing less than an end to the dangerous East-West stalemate which has disfigured post-war international politics. It could mean a new U.S.-Soviet relationship, which replaces competition where possible with a creative and cooperative approach to international problems. A new relationship that would be sustained not by rhetoric or pious hope but by the reality of a Europe, free, whole, and at peace with itself. A new relationship where the reality of regional conflicts would be resolved at last so that the promise of development can be fulfilled. A new relationship that would produce a sustainable arms control process that provided more security through enhanced stability and greater openness at lower cost. And a new relationship, above all else, that would lead to the fulfillment of those human rights which are the birthright of all mankind.

Appendix 4
Quotes from the Sovietologists

France

Alain Besançon
Il me semble qu'on rend mieux compte des faits de ces cinq dernières années...en considérant que ce dirigeant communiste a été promu et a agi en vue de résoudre cette crise, d'empêcher cette décomposition, de sauver ce régime, quitte à l'adapter aux nouvelles conditions, sans le changer substantiellement. C'est dans cette assumption...que je me pose la question célèbre: Gorbatchev peut-il réussir?

Je suis loin d'en être certain. Je suis donc pessimiste de point de vue de Gorbatchev, et optimiste du mien, parce que je souhaite la fin de ce régime...

On devine ajourd'hui que l'action de Gorbatchev s'incrit dans un plan d'ensemble qui a été élaboré avant lui. ...

C'est probablement dans les milieux des K.G.B., professionellement mieux informés de l'état réel des choses, que naquit le grand dessein. Il fut mis en œuvre par Andropov et continué par Gorbatchev. ...

Il comportait deux volets, l'un de politique extérieure, l'autre de politique intérieure, conçus pour s'appuyer mutuellement.

En politique extérieure, les buts ne changent pas. Il s'agit de conserver les conquêtes du communisme, le domaine contigu acquis par Staline, le domaine lointain acquis sous ses successeurs; de désarmer et de dominer politiquement l'ensemble de l'Europe de l'Ouest; de forcer l'Occident à fournir en technologie et en crédits de quoi maintenir le système socialiste à un niveau de puissance satisfaisant. Cependant les moyens changent. Le connaissance plus raffiné que l'U.R.S.S. a des mécanismes politques et médiatiques occidentaux doit être mis a profit. ...D'abord il faut transformer l'image de l'U.R.S.S. ...Son chef (Andropov, Gorbatchev) sera donc présenté comme une personalité ouverte, réaliste, pragmatique, moderne, compétente, profondément humaine, mais avec une liberté de mouvement et un continuité de temps qui la placent naturellement audessus des hommes des États des démocraties.

Cela fait, les démocraties ne pourront plus repousser facilement des offensives de désarmement out des slogans comme la "maison commune européenne" (c'est-à-dire l'entrée en position dominante et parasitaire de l'U.R.S.S. dans la zone de prosperité européenne), ni s'opposer au démantélement du Cocom, ni refuser les crédits. ...

Sept ans sont passé, ou cinq, selon qu'on compte depuis l'accession au pouvoir d'Andropov ou de Gorbatchev, et nous pouvons déjà tirer un bilan. Il est fort inégal.

A l'extérieur, les résultats sont brillants, mais point décisifs. ...
Quant à l'intérieur, on peut parler d'un désastre. Comme le plan était connecté au programme extérieur, celui-ci est menacé de capoter avant d'avoir atteint ses résultats, ce qui aggraverait encore l'échec intérieur. ...
Le fait nouveau le plus menaçant est la montée irrésistible des mouvements nationaux. Le gorbatchévisme, vu depuis les républiques russes, a été interpretée comme une affaiblissement du pouvoir central et comme une baisse d'efficacité des moyens par lesquels elles étaient maintenues dans la soumission. Un pas de plus et elles prennent leur indépendance. De tous les effets de la nouvelle ligne postbrejnévienne, celui-ci était le moins prévu, et sans doute le plus dangereux.[1]
It seems to me that one better understands the events of the last five years...if one considers that this Communist leader was promoted and has acted with the aim of solving this crisis, of stopping this decline, of saving this regime, ended up by adapting it to new circumstances without making any substantial changes. It is from this assumption...that I ask myself the famous question: can Gorbachev succeed?
I am far from certain that he can. I am thus a pessimist from Gorbachev's point of view, and an optimist from mine, because I want this regime to end. We are today learning that Gorbachev's actions should be seen in terms of a larger plan that was drawn up before him. ...
It is probably within the ranks of the KGB, which was professionally better informed about the real state of things, that this plan was born. It was set in motion by Andropov and continued by Gorbachev. ...
It consisted of two parts, one in foreign policy, and the other in domestic policy, conceived to support each other mutually.
In foreign policy the goals do not change. It has to do with saving the conquests of Communism, the contiguous domain acquired by Stalin, the far-away domain acquired by his successors; of disarming and politically dominating all of Western Europe; of forcing the West to furnish in technology and in credits what it takes to maintain the socialist system on a sufficient level of power. Meanwhile, the means change. The very sophisticated knowledge that the U.S.S.R. has of Western political and media mechanisms have to be utilised. ...First, the image of the U.S.S.R. has to be transformed. ..Its leader (Andropov, Gorbachev) will thus be presented as an open, realist, pragmatic, modern, competent, profoundly human personality but with a freedom of movement and a continuity in time that naturally places him above the statesmen in the democracies.
Having accomplished this, the democracies can no longer easily reject the disarmament offensives or slogans like a "common European house" (that is to say, the entry of the U.S.S.R. into a dominant and parasitical position in the prosperous European zone), nor oppose the dismantlement of Cocom, nor refuse credits. ...
Seven years have passed, or five, depending on whether you count from the accession to power of Andropov or of Gorbachev, and we may already draw up a balance. It is very unequal.

---

[1] Alain Besançon (1990), 'Les Atouts de Gorbatchev: Une Évaluation', in *Après Gorbatchev*, Présenté par Jean-Marie Benoist and Patrick Wajsman (Paris: La Table Ronde, pp. 59-60. Notes omitted.

Seven years have passed, or five, depending on whether you count from the accession to power of Andropov or of Gorbachev, and we may already draw up a balance. It is very unequal.

In foreign policy, the results are brilliant, but far from decisive. ...

Considering the domestic side, one may speak of disaster. As the plan was connected to the foreign policy programme, the latter is at risk of failing before it has reached its results, in turn further aggravating the internal failure. ...

The new fact that is most threatening is the irrestible rise of nationalist movements. Gorbachevism, as seen from the Russian republics, has been interpreted as a weakening of central power and as a lowering of the efficacity of the means by which these republics were kept in submission. One more step and they will become independent. Of all the effects of the new post-Brzehnev line, this is without a doubt the most dangerous.

Pierre Hassner

Every government has a twin mission: relations with its own people and relations with other states. In the case of a totalitarian regime, particularly if it is communist, there is a structural conflict between the dynamics of the system and both the demands of civil society and those of the international order. Moreover, given that Gorbachev neither wants nor is able to impose impenetrable barriers between these two missions, the interior and the exterior of his regime are themselves constantly interacting, sometimes positively, sometimes negatively. The result is a genuinely triangular relationship between the Soviet government, Soviet domestic factors, and the external world.

Gorbachev strives simultaneously to control and manipulate this relationship and he succeeds in giving the impression of constantly holding the initiative in the face of divided or paralyzed adversaries. ...Thus, one might well ask: is Gorbachev truly looking for a real compromise with societies of the East and West? Does he acknowledge their aspirations in order to adjust to certain fixed realities? Or does he acknowledge them in order to conquer them and to reestablish control and the totalitarian initiative.

An answer seems nearly impossible to discern. ...

To date, real and irreversible changes in Soviet foreign policy are still too few and tentative to erase completely the impression that behind the changed outward appearances are traditional Soviet international policies and goals. Gorbachev has, however, broken with traditional positions in a number of important areas. ...If multiple causes exist, how should one choose between interpretations that emphasize Soviet economic problems and those that emphasize their role as alibis for Soviet political plans? Once again, the two are reconcilable if observers differentiate between long-term objectives and necessary short-term measures. From the Soviet point of view, current economic and military considerations seem to converge: the Soviets would prefer a return to détente (which would decelerate the U.S. defense effort and encourage East-West technology transfer) and an emphasis on the new civilian and military technologies.

Westerners should appreciate the primacy of Soviet economic difficulties while also understanding that the Soviet Union and particularly its current leader excel at taking advantage of the system's own weaknesses and at extending Soviet influence via measures to counter unfavorable trends'.[2]

Great Britain
—

Sweden

Kristian Gerner and Stefan Hedlund
We are approaching here the very keystone of political and social stability in Soviet society, as it functioned before Gorbachev. In sociological jargon it could be characterised as 'pluralistic ignorance'.[Note omitted.] While every single individual could see that his surrounding reality was very different from that which was depicted in the official propaganda, he had no way of knowing if this was a general phenomenon or if his particular case was simply an unfortunate exception. Far from permitting any communication on such topics, the system actually demanded from its citizens that they should openly and actively propagate the picture of Soviet society as it *should* be.

The outcome for the individual was that split perception of the world as two separate spheres — one private and one official — which has always been so characteristic of Soviet society. Anecdotal evidence provides by far the best evidence. ...

Of equal importance to the formation of expectations is the fact that while the individual Soviet citizen might have felt that the Party was to blame for the situation in the country, he had no way of knowing whether his was an isolated or a widely spread opinion. In addition to ignorance about the true state of the country, this observation underlines the absence of venues for political mobilisation, for articulating and aggregating demands in the way of a Western democracy. ...

It was in precisely this dimension that Gorbachev succeeded in finishing off the Soviet "project." Once open communication was allowed, the previous state of "pluralistic ignorance" was swept away overnight and the "official" world was utterly destroyed. With rallies in the street, with workers ousting Party cells from numerous industries, and with large sections of the media jumping onto the bandwagon, the landslide was inevitable.

The Soviet Union had been ripe to fall for a long time. What Gorbachev provided was the gust of wind that made it happen. In that process the ethnic variable was a

---

[2] Hassner: "Gorbachev and the West", (1988), *The Washington Quarterly*, Vol. 11, No. 4 (Autumn), pp. 95-96, 100-101.

crucial factor, determining the way in which the empire broke down. For all but the Russians — and a few "Soviet men" among the *nomenklatura* of other nationalities— the Soviet Union had ceased to be a point of reference or identification. ...

When we turn to look at events in the Baltic republics, we shall witness similar effects of ripening beneath the surface. We shall see how the Baltic peoples had retreated into various forms of soft Exits, expressing themselves with soft Voice, and how the habit of doing so had gradually caused them not to identify with the Soviet Union. What has needed for that transformation of mind to be manifested in concrete political action was simply a catalyst.[3]

The United States

Alexander Dallin
There is, I suggest, a cluster of interrelated developments that together, and in their interaction, formed the essential preconditions — necessary but not sufficient — for what occurred in the 1990s. In brief, they are: (1) the loosening of controls; (2) the spread of corruption; (3) the erosion of ideology; (4) the impact of social changes on values and social pathologies; (5) the growing impact of the external environment on S society and politics; and (6) the consequences of economic constraints. Against these background conditions, certain decisions of the G regime, in turn, appear decisive as catalysts for collapse.[9]

I have argued that none of these trends we have examined was the prime motor in this process. It is precisely the interaction among these variables that was critical. While we cannot 'replay' the events with one variable left out, some inferences as to the relative weights are plausibly strong. Thus, had the whole control structure not loosened up, much of the articulation of grievances could not have occurred, acquaintance with the outside world would have been far more modest, and the assertion of autonomy in various venues could not have been undertaken nor succeeded to the extent that it did. Similarly, the effect of the loosening up on the spread of corruption, the perception of stagnation, and contact with the West all facilitated the erosion of ideological commitments. So manifestly did social pathologies, the value shifts and the rising expectations among the new urban middle class erode the faith among among officials and non-officials alike.

True, the economic constraints alone should have been enough to engender doubts, comparisons, and grievances. However, the true economic facts were not widely known; indeed, some "derogatory" facts were scarcely even known, even in the highest leadership circles...We must then conclude that the cluster of trends we have focused on provided a set of necessary conditions for the changes that ensued.

The Gorbachev Factor
Taken together, the trends and developments discussed above suggest a number of

---

[3] Kristian Gerner and Stefan Hedlund: *The Baltic States and the End of the Soviet Empire*, (London/New York: Routledge, 1993), pp. 17-18.
[4] Dallin (1992): 'Causes of the Collapse of the USSR', *Post-Soviet Affairs*, Vol. 8, p. 282.

serious flaws and fragilities in the Soviet system. But there are no grounds for arguing that they doomed it. ...

...had Gorbachev and his associates *not* come to power, the Soviet Union would have hobbled along, and might have continued to muddle through without overt instability? That is the only possible conclusion. ...

There is room for counterfactual speculation, and I think the most responsible answer is that, while we cannot be sure, at least Moscow might have gained considerable time, might have avoided the destabilization and delegitimation that the Gorbachev years brought, and might have shaped the domestic and international environment very differently from what in fact occurred. ...

...the implication is that the Gorbachev years...are an essential part of the explanation of the collapse. They are not sufficient by themselves to explain it, but they are, ironically or tragically, a vital link in the chain of destabilization, delegitimation, and disintegration that led from the superpower status of the 1970s to the new, shrunken, confused, and impoverished Russian Federation of the 1990s. ...

...what was it about the Gorbachev policies...that contributed to the system's collapse? First and foremost, Gorbachev put an end to the claim that there was one single truth and therefore one single party that was its carrier. In association with this argument, he fostered *glasnost*, an end to censorship, an end to widespread political repression, and an end to the official monopoly on rewriting the past. In terms of sociopolitical impact, all this brought about a remarkable sense of having been lied to, of having been deprived of what the rest of the world had had access to, a "desacrilization"...and delegitimation of the authorities, a transformation of the Communist Party from the unchallenged clan of privilege to a hollow institution without a rational task other than self-preservation. This in turn opened the floodgates to massive and varied grassroots organization and articulation outside the party.

The other major arena in which the new policy of *glasnost* had an impact was the republics. From Estonia to Azerbaijan, *glasnost* mobilized opinion around issues of ethnic identity, beginning with language, school, or culture and ending with national-liberation fronts. ...Thus (to oversimplify a complicated process) *glasnost* made possible the political mobilization of doubting, contemptuous, and newly emboldened publics, and the invention of new organizations.[5]

---

[5] Dallin (1992): "Causes of the Collapse of the USSR", *Post-Soviet Affairs*, Vol. 8, No. 4, pp. 295-297.

Appendix 5
Official Foreign Policy Spokespersons Analysed

France

Président
François Mitterrand, Socialist (S) March 1985 — December 1991

Prime Minister
Laurent Fabius, S, March 1985 — March 1986
Jaques Chirac, Rassemblement pour la Republique (RPR; Gaullist) March 1986 - May 1988
Michel Rocard, S, May 1988 — May 1991
Edith Cresson, S, May 1991 — December 1991

Foreign Minister
Roland Dumas, S, March 1985 — March 1986
Jean-Bernard Raimond, civil servant (RPR), March 1986 — May 1988
Roland Dumas, S, May 1988 — December 1991

Great Britain

Prime Minster
Margaret Thatcher, Conservative (C), March 1985 — November 1990
John Major, C, November 1990 — December 1991

Foreign Secretary
Sir Geoffrey Howe, C, March 1985 — July 1989
John Major, C, July 1989 — October 1989
Douglas Hurd, C, October 1989 — December 1991

Sweden

Prime Minister
Olof Palme, Social Democrat (SD), March 1985 — February 1986
Ingvar Carlsson, SD, March 1986 — October 1991
Carl Bildt, Conservative (C), October 1991 — December 1991

Foreign Minister
Lennart Bodström, SD, March 1985 — December 1985
Sten Andersson, SD, December 1985 — October 1991
Margareta af Ugglas, C, October 1991 — December 1991

Under Secretary of State for Foreign Affairs
Pierre Schori, SD, March 1985 — October 1991
Lars-Erik Nilsson, civil servant, October 1991 — December 1991

United States

President
Ronald Reagan, Republican (R), March 1985 — January 1989
George Bush, R, January 1989 — December 1991

Secretary of State
George Shultz, R, March 1985 — January 1989
James Baker, R, January 1989 — December 1991

Under Secretary of State for Political Affairs
Michael Armacost, R, March 1985 — March 1989
Robert Michael Kimmett, March 1989 — August 1991
Arnold Kanter, August 1991 — December 1991

Bibliography

Agrell, W. (1986), *Bakom Ubåtskrisen (Behind the Submarine Crisis)*. Stockholm: Liber.

Ahlander, D.S. (1992), *Spelet om Baltikum (The Game for the Baltic Republics)*. Stockholm: Norstedts.

Albright, M. *Statement to the Senate Foreign Relations Committe, February 24, 1998*. Washington, DC: http://secretary.state.gov/www/statements/1998/989224.htm, 1998.

Allan, P. (1992), "The End of the Cold War: The End of International Relations Theory?", *The End of the Cold War: Evaluating Theories of International Relations*. Edited by in Allan, P. and Goldmann, K. Dordrecht/Boston, MA/London: Martinus Nijhoff Publishers, pp. 226-241.

Andrew, C. and O. Gordievskij (1990), *KGB Inifrån: Från Tjekan till Potsdam (KGB: The inside story of its foreign operations from Lenin to Gorbachev)*. Stockholm: Bonniers.

Åselius, G. (1994), *The 'Russian Menace' to Sweden: The Belief System of a Small Power Security Elite*. Stockholm: Almqvist & Wiksell International.

Beschloss, M.R. and Talbott, S. (1994), *At the Highest Levels: The Inside Story of the End of the Cold War*. London: Warner Books.

Beukel, E. (1989), *American Perceptions of the Soviet Union as a Nuclear Adversary*. London and New York: Pinter.

Bobrow, D. B. (1999), "Prospecting the Future", *International Studies Review*. Vol. 1, pp. 1-10.

Bonamour, J. (1982), "Soviet and East European Studies in France", *Soviet and East European Studies in the International Framework*. Edited by Buchholz, A. Berlin: Berlin Verlag, pp. 50-59.

Bullard, J. (1990), 'Perceptions of the Soviet Threat: Britain in the 1970s', *The Changing Western Analysis of the Soviet Threat*. Edited by Schweitzer, C.-C. New York: St. Martin's Press, pp. 136-150.

Bullock, A. and Stallybrass, O. (eds) (1977), *The Fontana Dictionary of Modern Thought*. London: Fontana/Collins.

Buzan, B. (1995), "The Level-of-Analysis Problem in International Relations Reconsidered", *International Relations Theory Today*. Edited by Booth, K. and Smith, S. Cambridge: Polity Press, pp. 198-216.

Choucri, N. (1978), "Introduction", in N. Choucri and T. Robinson (eds), *Forecasting in International Relations: Theory, Methods, Problems, Prospects*. San Francisco, CA, Freeman, pp. 3-22.

Choucri, N. and Robinson, T.W. (eds) (1978), *Forecasting in International Relations: Theory, Methods, Problems, Prospects*. San Francisco, CA: W.H. Freeman.

Clark, I. and Wheeler, N.J. (1989), *The British Origins of Nuclear Strategy*. Oxford: Clarendon Press.

Clarke, M. (1990), "British Perspectives on the Soviet Union", *Soviet-British Relations since the 1970s*. Edited by Pravda, A. and Duncan, P. J. Cambridge: Cambridge University Press, pp. 68-91.

Clarke, M. (1993), "British and French Nuclear Weapons after the Cold War", *Arms Control*. Vol. 14, pp. 116-145.

Cohen, S.F. (1985), *Rethinking the Soviet Experience: Politics and History Since 1917*. New York/Oxford: Oxford University Press.

Cox, M. (ed) (1998), *Rethinking the Soviet Collapse: Sovietology, the Death of Communism and the New Russia*. London/New York: Pinter.

Cox, M. (1998), "Whatever Happened to the USSR: Critical Reflections on Soviet Studies", *Rethinking the Soviet Collapse: Sovietology, the Death of Communism and the New Russia*. Edited by Cox, M. London/New York: Pinter, pp. 13-31.

Daniels, R.V. (1998), "Soviet Society and American Soviet Studies: a Study in Success", *Rethinking the Soviet Collapse*. Edited by Cox, M. London/New York: Pinter, pp. 115-134.

Destler, I.M. (1984), "Congress", *The Making of America's Soviet Policy*. Edited by Nye, J. S. New Haven, CT: Yale University Press, pp. 37-62.

Deudney, D. and Ikenberry, J. (1991), "Soviet Reform and the End of the Cold War: Explaining Large-Scale Historical Change", *Post-Communist Studies and Political Science: Methodology and Empirical Theory in Sovietology*. Edited by Fleron, F. and Hoffman, E. Boulder, CO/San Francisco, CA/Oxford, Westview, pp. 225-250.

Everts, P.P. (1992), "The Events in Eastern Europe and the Crisis in the Discipline of International Relations", *The End of the Cold War: Evaluating Theories of International Relations*. Edited by Allan, P. and Goldmann, K. Dordrecht/Boston, MA/London: Martinus Nijhoff Publishers, pp. 55-81.

Falkenrath, R.A (1995), *Shaping Europe's Military Order: The Origins and Consequences of the CFE Treaty*. CSIA Studies in International Security, no. 6. Cambridge, MA, MIT Press.

Founding Act on Mutual Relations, Cooperation and Security Between NATO and the Russian Federation. Brussels: http://www.nato.int/docu/basictxt/fndact-a.htm, 1997.

Freedman, L. (1986), *U.S. Intelligence and the Soviet Strategic Threat, 2nd ed.* Princeton, NJ: Princeton University Press.

Freeman, J.R. and Job, B.L. (1979), "Scientific Forecasts in International Relations: Problems of Definition and Epistemology", *International Studies Quarterly*. Vol. 23, pp. 113-143.

Friedman, T.L. (1998), "Gulf of Tonkin II", *The New York Times*. March 31.

Friend, J.W. (1989), *Seven Years in France: Francois Mitterrand and the Unintended Revolution*. Boulder/San Francisco/London: Westview.

Gaddis, J.L. (1982), *Strategies of Containment*. New York/Oxford: Oxford University Press.

Gaddis, J.L. (1992/93), "International Relations Theory and the End of the Cold War", *International Security*. Vol. 17, pp. 5-58.

Garthoff, R.L. (1994), *The Great Transition: American-Soviet Relations and the End of the Cold War*. Washington: Brookings.

Gerner, K. (1997), "Sovjetbildens struktur i Sverige efter 1941 (The Structure of Image of the Soviet Union in Sweden after 1941)", *Sovjetunionen och Norden (The Soviet Union and the Nordic Countries)*. Edited by Jungar, S. and Jensen, B. Helsinki, Finnish Historical Society, pp. 147-162.

Gilje, N. and Grimen, H. (1992), *Samhällsvetenskapernas förutsättningar (The Assumptions of the Social Sciences)*. Gothenburg, Daidalos.

Girard, M. (1994), "The Uncertainty of Influence: France", *Theory and Practice in Foreign Policy-Making: National Perspectives on Academics and Professionals in International Relations*. Edited by Girard, M., Eberwein. W.-D. and Webb, K. (eds), London/New York: Pinter, pp. 51-63.

Goldmann, K. (1992), "Bargaining, Power, Domestic Politics and Security Dilemmas", *The End of the Cold War: Evaluating Theories of International Relations*. Edited by Allan, P. and Goldmann, K. Dordrecht/Boston, MA/London: Martinus Nijhoff Publishers, pp. 82-103.

Gordon, P.H. (1993), *A Certain Idea of France: French Security Policy and the Gaullist Legacy*. Princeton: Princeton University Press.

Grunberg, I. and Risse-Kappen, T. (1992), "A Time of Reckoning? Theories of International Relations and the End of the Cold War", *The End of the Cold War: Evaluating Theories of International Relations*. Edited by Allan, P. and Goldmann, K. Dordrecht/Boston/London: Martinus Nijhoff, pp. 104-146.

Hallenberg, J. (1991), *The Image of the Soviet Union in U.S. Presidential Elections 1968-1988*. Report No. 1991:3. Department of Political Science, Stockholm: Stockholm University.

Haslam, J. (1996), "E.H. Carr and the Politics of Soviet Studies in Britain", *Reexamining the Soviet Experience: Essays in Honor of Alexander Dallin*. Edited by Holloway, D. and Naimark, N. Boulder, CO: Westview, pp. 7-24.

Hassner, P. (1988), "France and the Soviet Union", *Western Approaches to the Soviet Union*. Edited by Mandelbaum, M. New York: Council on Foreign Relations, pp. 25-52.

Hassner, P. (1990), "Perceptions of the Soviet threat in the 1950s and the 1980s: the case of France", *The Changing Western Analysis of the Soviet Threat*. Edited by Schweitzer, C.-C. New York, St. Martin's, pp. 169-189.

Hazareezingh, S. (1994), *Political Traditions in Modern France*. Oxford: Oxford University Press.

Heradstveit, D. (1979), *The Arab-Israeli Conflict: Psychological Obstacles to Peace*. Oslo, Universitetsforlaget.

Hermann, C.F. (1990), "Changing Course: When Governments Choose to Redirect Foreign Policy", *International Studies Quarterly*. Vol. 34, pp. 3-21.

Herrmann, R.K. (1994), "Policy-Relevant Theory and the Challenge of Diagnosis: The End of the Cold War as a Case Study", *Political Psychology*. Vol. 15, pp. 111-142.

Hill, R. (1998), "Social Science, "Slavistics" and Post-Soviet Studies," *Rethinking the Soviet Collapse: Sovietology, the Death of Communism and the New Russia*. Edited by Cox, M. London and New York: Pinter, pp. 202-218.

Hoffmann, S. (1968), *Gulliver's Troubles, Or The Setting of American Foreign Policy*. New York: McGraw-Hill.

Hollis, M. and Smith, S. (1990), *Explaining and Understanding International Relations*. Oxford: Clarendon Press.

Holloway, D. and Naimark, N. (1996), 'Introduction', *Reexamining the Soviet Experience: Essays in Honor of Alexander Dallin*. Edited by Holloway, D. and Naimark, N. Boulder, CO/Oxford, Westview, pp. 1-6.

Hough, J.F. (1997), *Democratization and Revolution in the USSR 1985-1991*. Washington, DC: Brookings.

Jervis, R. (1976), *Perception and Misperception in International Politics*. Princeton: Princeton University Press.

Jervis, R. (1978), "Cooperation Under the Security Dilemma", *World Politics*. Vol. 30, pp. 167-214.

Jervis, R. (1981), "Beliefs About Soviet Behavior", *Containment, Soviet Behavior and Grand Strategy*. Edited by Osgood, R. Institute of International Studies, Berkeley, University of California - Berkeley, pp. 56-59.

Jervis, R. (1991/92), "The Future of World Politics: Will It Resemble the Past?", *International Security*. Vol. 16, pp. 39-46.

Jönsson, C. (1990), *Communication in International Bargaining*, London: Pinter.

Kahn, E.J., Jr. (1976), *The China Hands: America's Foreign Service Officers and What Befell Them*. Harmondsworth/New York: Penguin Books.

Kegley C., W (1994), "How Did the Cold War Die: Principles for an Autopsy", *Mershon International Review*. Vol. 38, pp. 11-41.

Kegley, C.W. and Wittkopf, E.R. (1987), *American Foreign Policy: Pattern and Process*. New York: St. Martin's Press.

Keohane, R. (1984), *After Hegemony: Cooperation and Discord in the World Economy*. Princeton: Princeton University Press.

King, G., Keohane, R. and Verba, S. (1994), *Designing Social Inquiry: Scientific Inference in Qualitative Research*. Princeton, NJ: Princeton University Press.

Larson, D.W. (1985), *Origins of Containment: A Psychological Explanation*. Princeton, NJ: Princeton University Press.

Light, M. (1990), "Anglo-Soviet Relations: Political and Diplomatic", *Soviet-British Relations since the 1970s*. Edited by Pravda, A. and Duncan, P. J. S. Cambridge: Cambridge University Press, pp. 120-146.

Lustick, I.S. (1996), "History, Historiography and Political Science: Multiple Historical Records and the Problem of Selection Bias", *American Political Science Review*. Vol. 90, pp. 605-618.

McNeill, T. (1998), "Soviet Studies and the Collapse of the USSR: in Defence of Realism", *Rethinking the Soviet Collapse*. Edited by Cox, M. London/New York: Pinter, pp. 51-72.

Malia, M. (1993), "A Fatal Logic", *The National Interest*. No. 31, pp. 80-90.

Milburn, T.W. (1979), "Successful and unsuccessful forecasting in International Relations", *Forecasting In International Relations: Theory, Methods, Problems, Prospects*. Edited by Choucri, N. and Robinson, T. San Francisco, CA: Freeman, pp. 79-91.

Morgenthau, H.J. (1973), *Politics Among Nations: The Struggle for Power and Peace*. 5th ed. New York, Knopf.

Morrison, J.D. and Seton-Watson, G.H.N. (1982), "Soviet and East European Studies in Great Britain", *Soviet and East European Studies in the International Framework*. Edited by Buchholz, A. Berlin: Berlin Verlag, pp. 32-49.

Nye, J.S. (ed) (1984), *The Making of America's Soviet Policy*. New Haven, CT: Yale University Press.

Nygren, B. (1986), *Approaches to Soviet Foreign Policy in Sovietology*. Group for Research on Peace and Security Policy, Report No. 3, Department of Political Science: University of Stockholm.

Nygren, B. (1992), *American Sovietology and Knowledge Utilization in the Formulation of U.S. Soviet Policy*. Report No. 1992:2. Department of Political Science . Stockholm: Stockholm University.

Oberdorfer, D. (1992), *The Turn: From the Cold War to a New Era*. New York, Touchstone.

Portes, A. (1995), "On Grand Surprises and Modest Certainties: Comment on Kuran, Collins, and Tilly", "Symposium on Predictions in the Social Sciences", *American Journal of Sociology*. Vol. 100 (May), pp. 1620-1626.

Prados, J. (1982), *The Soviet Estimate*. New York, Dial Press.

Ray, J. L. (1995), "Promise or Peril? Neorealism, Neoliberalism and the Future of International Politics", *Controversies in International Relations*

Theory: Realism and the Neoliberal Challenge. Edited by Kegley, C. W. New York: St. Martin's, pp. 335-355.

Richardson, L. (1993), "British State Strategies After the Cold War", *After the Cold War: International Relations and State Strategies in Europe, 1989-1991.* Edited by Keohane, R., Nye, J. S. and Hoffmann, S. Cambridge, MA/London: Harvard University Press, pp. 148-169.

Richelson, J. (1987), *American Espionage and the Soviet Target.* New York: William Morrow.

Richelson J. (1995), *The U.S. Intelligence Community.* 3rd ed., Boulder, CO: Westview.

Riegert, K. (1991), *The Lebanon Crisis: the Influence of Foreign Policy Orientation*
in *International Reporting,* Licentiate dissertation, Department of Political Science. Stockholm: Stockholm University.

Riegert, K. (1998), *"Nationalising'"Foreign Conflict: Foreign Policy Orientation as a Factor in Reporting.* PhD thesis. Department of Political Science. Stockholm: Stockholm University.

Robertson, A. (1992), *National Prisms and Perceptions of Dissent.* PhD thesis. Department of Political Science, Stockholm: Stockholm University.

Rosenau, J. (1997), *Along the Domestic-Foreign Frontier: Exploring Governance in a Turbulent World.* Cambridge/New York/Melbourne: Cambridge University Press.

Rosenau, J.N. (1995), "Signals, Signposts and Symptoms: Interpreting Change and Anomalies in World Politics", *European Journal of International Relations.* Vol. 1, pp. 113-122.

Rosenau, J.N. and Sapin, B.M. (1994), "Theory and practice in foreign policy-making: academics and practioners — the American Experience", *Theory and Practice in Foreign Policy-Making: National Perspectives on Academics and Professionals in International Relations.* Edited by Girard, M., Eberwein, W-D. and Webb, K. London/New York: Pinter, pp. 126-135.

Rozman, G. (1992), *Japan's Response to the Gorbachev Era, 1985-1991. A Rising Superpower Views a Declining One.* Princeton: Princeton University Press.

Rutland, P. (1993), "Sovietology: Notes for a Post-Mortem", *The National Interest.* No. 31, pp. 109-122.

Rutland, P. (1998), "Who Got It Right and Who Got It Wrong? And Why?'" *Rethinking the Soviet Collapse: Sovietology, the Death of Communism and the New Russia.* Edited by Cox, M. London/New York: Pinter, pp. 13-31.

Shimko, K.L. (1991), *Images and Arms Control: Perceptions of the Soviet Union in the Reagan Administration.* Ann Arbor: University of Michigan Press.

Shlapentokh, V. (1998), "Soviet Society and American Sovietologists: a Study in Failure?", *Rethinking the Soviet Collapse*. Edited by Cox, M. pp. 95-114.

Shultz, G. (1993), *Turmoil and Triumph: My Years as Secretary of State*. New York: Charles Scribner's Sons.

Singer, D. (1961), "The Level-of-Analysis Problem in International Relations Reconsidered", *The International System: Theoretical Essays*. Edited by Knorr, K. and Verba, S. Princeton, NJ: Princeton University Press, pp. 72-92.

Snyder, J. (1984/85), "Richness, Rigor, and Relevance in the Study of Soviet Foreign Policy", *International Security*. Vol. 9, pp. 89-108.

"The Strange Death of Soviet Communism: An Autopsy (special issue)", (1993), *The National Interest*. No. 31, pp. 3-144.

Strayer, R. (1998), *Why Did the Soviet Union Collapse? Understanding Historical Change*. Armonk, NY/London: M. E. Sharpe.

Stutz, G. (1990), *Svenskar i den internationella förändringens tid* (*Swedes in the Times of International Change*). Report No. 155. Stockholm: National Board of Psychological Defense, 1990.

"Symposium on History and Theory" (1997), *International Security*. Vol. 22, pp. 5-85.

Tarschys, D. (1984), "Områdesstudier (Area Studies)", *Öststatsstudier - Teori och metod* (*Studies of Eastern Europe - Theory and Methods*). Edited by Arvidsson, C. Stockholm: Liber, pp. 16-18.

Vertzberger, Y.I. (1990), *The World In Their Minds: Information Processing, Cognition and Perception in Foreign Policy Decisionmaking*. Stanford, CA: Stanford University Press.

Waltz, K. (1959), *Man, the State, and War.* New York: Columbia University Press.

Waltz, K. (1979), *Theory of International Politics*. Reading, MA: Addison-Wesley.

Webb, K. (1994), "Academics and professionals in International Relations: A British perception", *Theory and Practice in Foreign Policy-Making: National Perspectives on Academics and Professionals in International Relations*. Edited by Girard, M., Eberwein, W.-D. and Webb, K. London /New York: Pinter, pp. 82-94.

Index